NUGGETS

OF GOLD

Providing You Encouragement

By

Nina McElwain

NUGGETS of GOLD: PROVIDING YOU ENCOURAGEMENT

ISBN: 978-1-7923-5550-9

Table of Contents

Foreword

NUGGETS of GOLD

Providing You Encouragement

Is your time limited today? Nuggets of Gold is your solution to give you the encouragement you need for the moment or for the day. Nina McElwain was widowed at age 63 and instead of retiring and setting herself on life's back burner...she did not "Retire" instead she "Refired."

Nina grabbed the nuggets of truths from her relationship with God and took them to foreign countries as a short-term missionary. WOW!

It is time for you to Solidify your faith.

It is time to Settle your heart that God wants to use you.

It is time to be Encouraged one nugget at a time.

Nina's passion is for you to allow her book to lead you to an intimate love that only a heavenly Father can give you.

Receive whole heartedly these Nuggets of Gold from Him and then hand them out to others.

Foreword by

Dr. Diane Gardner, D.D.

Amazon #1 Best-selling author of _Increase Your Capacity to Hear from God:_
Stop Walking in Presumption
Spiritual Life Coach and Trainer of new authors
Website: drdianeanswers.com

What Others Are Saying

I first met Nina McElwain in the 1980's while serving as a Pastoral Advisor to the Corona/Riverside chapter of Women Aglow where she was a local Executive Board member. She is a woman who has continually searched to increase her knowledge of God and her personal relationship with Him. She is a great teacher, mentor and encourager. As I read her book *Nuggets of Gold*, I was impressed by the simplistic manor that she wrote. Her style would encourage seasoned believers to search the deeper walk with God. While also teaching new believers, in a step by step way, to find the path in their newfound faith.

REVEREND VERNON BROWN, Pastor for 47 years—Retired.

I have known Nina for several years. I can honestly say that she is a woman of God who has a heart to help others. Her book is filled with encouraging words and powerful nuggets of truth backed by Scriptures. *Nuggets of Gold* will be a great inspiration to every reader.

DR. MARILYN NEUBAUER, author *My Three Miracles: The Journey*, marilynnuebauer.com.

This book is a must-read, you will not be able to put this book down. It is captivating from the first page to the last. Nina connected my real life issues to answers in Scripture. This facilitated my prayers to move forward when it seemed impossible to receive answers on my own.

JYOTHI PREM, H R Administrator, geoConvergence

About The Author

Rev. Nina McElwain is the author of *Nuggets of Gold*, an ordained minister, and missionary who has ministered both nationally and internationally. She is the Founder of Sweet Aroma Ministry. Nina is a sought-after Bible study teacher for over forty years. She mentors young mothers, leaders and marketplace small business owners. She is a former small business owner and learned to depend on God for the success and profitability of her business. She is a woman of wisdom.

Nina served for many years in various capacities with Aglow International especially as Southern California Area President. She is currently Vice President of Lotshaw Helping Hands for the underprivileged children.

Nina is a widow, mother of four daughters, grandmother of eleven and great grandmother of eighteen. She makes her home in Menifee,

California where she is known as a church ministry leader, mentor, life coach and respected intercessor.

To Contact Rev. Nina McElwain of Sweet Aroma Ministry

Intimacy1941@gmail.com

Acknowledgements

I've heard it said that it takes a village to raise a child. I am not sure about that but it did take one to get *Nuggets of Gold* to publication. It all started when I went to hear my friend, and now my coach, Dr. Diane Gardner speak at a women's meeting. She has known me for years. She encouraged me to write "the book in me." Thank you, Diane for not letting me give up. I prayed about it and joined her writing group. With their prayers and encouragement, I started on my journey.

Without the help of my granddaughter Harmony Vermilya and my spiritual daughter Jyothi Prem I could not have done this. These are two beautiful young women of God. Without whom you would not have this book in your hands today. They typed and reorganized many times while they encouraged me with their thoughts on whether it would minister to the young people as well as the more mature in the body of Christ.

To Marilyn, my friend in a rest home who when I would share a thought she'd say, "Oh, that needs to be in your book. We need these nuggets of gold in our daily walk. You inspire me."

My Aglow sisters, especially Linda Sherbon, my prayer partner, who interceded for me constantly through my journey. Thank you for all your prayers.

My family and friends, who listen to all my ideas and seemingly constant talk about the book, especially Deni for being so patient with me. Susan Titus Osborn, whose critique service was amazing as she edited my book. Last, but not least my closest friend, Holy Spirit, who inspired and pushed me forward when I came to a standstill, always with love, and guiding me on to finish my race.

My heart overflows with love and gratitude. Thank you all for being a part of my village.

Dedication

To Abba Daddy God who loves me unconditionally. Jesus, my Lord and Savior, who died and made it possible to spend an eternity in heaven with Him. Holy Spirit who teaches me and guides me every day and brings me comfort when I need it.

To my daughters, Bonny, Cari, Deni, and Shari; my eleven grandchildren; and eighteen great-grandchildren, you are the love of my life and I'm so thankful God chose me to be a part of your life!

Chapter 1

More Than A Feeling

Love suffers long and is kind; does not envy; love does not parade itself, is not puffed up; does not behave rudely, does not seek its own, is not provoked, thinks no evil; does not rejoice in iniquity, but rejoices in the truth; bears all things, believes all things, hopes all things, endures all things. Love never fails...

1 Corinthians 13:4-8

My heart for writing this book is to express how much our Abba, Daddy, God loves us, When we get a glimpse of how much He loves us, we can express love to Him on a new deeper level. It's not the love the world gives but God's agape love. Agape love is the deep love God feels for His people. This love is only from God, and we can only experience it unconditionally when it comes from God. This love shows care for others as Christ loved us. It brings true joy and peace that God gives us in storms, hurt, and pain.

1

Remember when you were in labor with the birth of your children? The pain is indescribable, yet, through it all you knew eventually it would be over. Soon you would be holding a miracle in your arms. As you look at this precious gift, the memory of the pain fades away. You feel such tremendous love as you look at the wonder of His creation. I think our Father felt wonder as He created us, and that is why he allowed His Son to go through such agony for us on the cross. He did this because He loves us so much and wants to have a personal relationship with us. When we walk in the love of the Father, we will know and understand true love. Our unconditional love and forgiveness of others is God's own forgiveness and love for us. The Father gave us much more than we deserved, and He now calls us to give others better than they deserve. This is what agape love looks like. It transforms relationships, and we can still love even when we're hurt or wronged.

All these are attributes of our Heavenly Father and should be ours also! There comes a time in our lives when we are searching for more. We want the truth but sometimes go down many rabbit trails before we find the answer. One such rabbit trail for me was in *spiritualism (My search for the truth.)* I read my daily horoscopes and read books on the spiritual world (dark false prophets), Then I tried Ouija boards, tea leaves, and tarot cards. I even went to see a psychic. One time she even described a beloved deceased family member who claimed to be an atheist.

She said that person was here today. She asked if I wanted to talk to him, but would God send someone who did not know Him? I thought, *I would rather talk to my Grandma who I was closer to.* So, I said "No, not today." That frightened me because I had never even mentioned that person to her.

Was she of God or not? I even took family members and friends with me to see her. I was evangelizing my loved ones in my search for truth. I'm so thankful for one of my Catholic friends. One day I was on the phone with her, excited to tell her about my last visit to a psychic. She said "Nina, you know that's not of God, right? It's a form of witchcraft." I told her no one had ever told me that before. She took me to Deuteronomy.

> "When you come into the land which the Lord your God is giving you, you shall not learn to follow the abominations of those nations. There shall not be found among you anyone who makes his son or his daughter pass through the fire, or one who practices witchcraft, or a soothsayer, or one who interprets omens, or a sorcerer, or one who conjures spells, or a medium, or a spiritist, or one who calls up the dead. For all who do these things are an abomination to the Lord, and because of these abominations, the Lord your God drives them out from before you. You shall be blameless before the Lord your God... The Lord your God has not appointed such for you." **Deuteronomy 18:9-14**

Once I heard what the Bible said, I made a choice to never go again but still I didn't know anything about repentance and deliverance. The first time I did a Bible study, I found several more

Scriptures that support this. Here are a couple more: Deuteronomy 17:2-3, 1 Samuel 15:23.

Shortly after that someone invited me to a charismatic praise and worship event. I loved it! From there I was introduced to Women's Aglow International. I became involved with this group. In one of the leadership training sessions they taught on repentance and deliverance.

I was one of the first ones at the altar to repent and get delivered. I was set free that day from many past things.

> *"Therefore, if the Son makes you free, you shall be free indeed." John 8:36*

John 8 :36 tells us those who He sets free are free indeed. We should never shy away from things in our past that we are ashamed of or feel guilty about. As long as it's in the dark Satan can and will have a hold on it to torment you. Once it's in the light the devil no longer has a hold on you! I have included a prayer below for you to become free.

Lord, I come to You today to repent of *serving false gods and taking others into sin with me.* I ask Your forgiveness and thank you for showing me my evil ways. Cleanse my heart and mind and create in me a new and pure heart while drawing me close to You. Thank You for showing me Your ways and truth and light to my sin. Satan no longer has a hold over me. I have been set free from his grip. Now I commit to fill my heart and mind with Your Word and worship You with my whole heart. In Jesus name, Amen.

> *If we confess our sins, He is faithful and just to forgive us **our** sins and to cleanse us from all unrighteousness.* 1John1:9

> *Create in me a clean heart, O God, and renew a steadfast spirit within me.* Psalm 51:10

Chapter 2

Nurturing Relationships

That they all may be one, as You, Father, are in Me, and I in You; that they also may be in Us, that the world may believe that You sent Me.
John 17:21

If someone were to ask me, "What is the most important thing in your life?" I would answer, "My Relationships." God created us to be relational. Many times in relationships we give more than what we get in return. There are so many types of relationships. First of course is our relationship with the Lord. After that, family and friends, business acquaintances, and so on. All of these are only as healthy as we make them. If we do not spend time to nurture them, they will wither and die. Relationships get better and better the more effort you put into them. Every step of commitment you make to a person, you will feel like you are investing in them. The more time and energy you invest in a relationship the closer you will be to that person.

When we spend time with the Lord we learn about agape love, faith, and wisdom. That is our covenant with God through the blood of Jesus. God's Word is a love letter to us. When we spend time with our grandparents and parents, we share our inheritance, bloodlines, and love to forgive even when we are wronged. Our elders can teach us respect for others. Siblings teach us to share and serve one another. Next to the Lord, we should spend the most time developing our relationship with our spouse. Here we give intimacy, passion, and forgiveness. We also learn how to dissolve conflicts, be submissive, and trust one another.

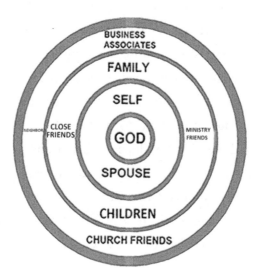

'For this reason, a man shall leave his father and mother and be joined to his wife, and the two shall become one flesh.' **Matthew 19:5**

With our children we learn patience. We understand the love of the Father for us on a deeper level. We learn how to become teachers and servants and how to see God's creation through the eyes of a child. We have a childlike faith and learn how to trust. The time we spend with our children is something they will always remember. They won't remember the money that we spent or the things we say, but what they will remember is the time we spent as a family.

Our children, grandchildren, nieces, and nephews are young for a short time. They are on loan to us from heaven. Our job is to teach them, love them, and nourish them. Some of the best memories my daughters and I have are when they were little, when we celebrated birthdays. I would sew them a little new dress and hang it on their bedroom door. When they woke up to this surprise, their eyes widened with such joy. There was so much happiness that came from sewing a new little dress, making their favorite dinner, and baking their favorite cake. It was far from perfect, but they loved every minute. These are the things they will always remember.

Train up a child in the way he should go, and when he is old he will not depart from it.
Proverbs 22:6

Our friends help broaden relationships. Some will be friends for a lifetime. Some friends will just be passing through our lives, but with each one we learn how to be a friend and how to choose friends. Some will help us grow, others will hurt us and teach us to pray for them, and some will show us areas we need to change in our own lives. Last, but not least, are the people we minister to and with. Sometimes we treat them better than our own families. Remember your family is your first ministry. Give them your best and not just the crumbs or leftovers.

In every relationship whether it be family, business, or ministry, there should be boundaries. We tend to think that saying "no" means that you are not putting others ahead of yourself. Not being available twenty-four hours a day seven days a week does not mean that you do not care for your friends or ministry partners. Do not give until you have nothing left and are burned out. When our relationship with the Lord is in order, everything else will usually fall into place. Some of this I learned the hard way. He does not ask us to be perfect but obedient.

Remember Obedience is better than Sacrifice.
Prayer You Can Pray:

Lord, I thank You for all you are doing in me! Continue to cleanse my heart. Holy Spirit guide me! Thank You, Lord. No matter how much beauty I see, it doesn't compare to all You have done for me, given me, and what I will see when I meet You face-to-face. I love the trees, the birds, the grass, the flowers, the sunset, and all else You created. I love You with an everlasting love. But it can't compare to the love You have for me! I am overwhelmed with it!

Thank You for the army You have put me into, and the family You have given to me.You are so awesome, Lord. I believe You have set the time for me. Forgive me for underestimating myself when I see powerful people, and I become afraid I will let people down because I am not like them. I know that those You have called, you prepare. Therefore, I put my trust in You!

I surrender my pride and false humility. I put myself totally into Your hands. Holy Spirit, I trust you to give me what, where, and when to say what will glorify my Father. Give me Compassion, hope, and peace to share You with them. Put a fire in me and them. Lord, I desire for visions and dreams, more and more. I desire to speak words to encourage, lift up, and edify the Body of Christ. Help me to show your unconditional love so they know what they have in You. Thank You for all the saved ones, Holy Spirit, as you continue to draw them to Jesus on the cross. Amen.

Chapter 3

Obedience and Trust the Holy Spirit

*"Does the Lord delight in burnt offerings and sacrifices
as much as in obeying the Lord?..."*
I Samuel 15:22 NIV

Riches: Richly, God gives to us. He meets all our needs according to His riches in glory. We should give love richly to God and to others.

A t: At all times an obedient heart always pleases our Lord. It teaches us to trust Him.

C hrist's: Christ loved you so much that He died for you. He told us to love one another as I have loved you.

E xpense: At the expense of Jesus's life on the cross, Our Father gave His Son for us to have a relationship in eternity.

Your word is a lamp to my feet and a light to my path. Psalm 119:105

Years ago, I was going through a trial. One day as I was talking to the Lord about it, He showed me Psalms 119:105, and it spoke to my heart. The Lord said, "I will show you how to go through trials, whether to go over it, under it, through it, or around it. Each trial will be overcome in a different way. "I saw a bridge, under the bridge there was a path on either side to walk around and a path under it. I was to trust Him as to which way I was to go. I just needed to follow Him. He has been showing me the way ever since, giving me peace, joy, and hope in every storm I go through. I just need to keep my eyes on Him. Isaiah 9 teaches us about a Wonderful Miracle from the Lord. Expect that wonder to happen as would a child. Remember the wonder He has already done. Be the wonder you were created to be! Your anointing is based on your availability and obedience. No anointing, no change! If there is an anointing on me where I am, then am I open to receive? Holy Spirit is our Guide, our Teacher, and more. He will lead us to the work we are called to do. He also supplies the anointing and power to do it. He works on us at our level, and that is what makes us unique. It is like a diamond prism with many facets. Think of it as a different sparkle with every turn. It is brilliant and beautiful. The more facets Holy Spirit makes in us, the more we shine to attract others to Him. The way to release and let that anointing flow in our lives is simple: obedience to Holy Spirit right now!

Chapter 4

The Necessity of Balance

Now it happened as they went that He entered a certain village; and a certain woman named Martha welcomed Him into her house. And she had a sister called Mary, who also sat at Jesus' feet and heard His word. But Martha was distracted with much serving, and she approached Him and said. "Lord, do You not care that my sister has left me to serve alone? Therefore, tell her to help me." And Jesus answered and said to her, "Martha, Martha, you are worried and troubled about many things. But one thing is needed, and Mary has chosen that good part, which will not be taken away from her."
Luke 10:38-42

Are you to be Martha today sharing, caring, loving, and going about the Father's business? Or are you to be a Mary today just sitting in His presence? Or maybe some of both each day. Be discerning to know what you are supposed to be doing. In Luke 10: 38-42, Jesus is asking His followers to discern when the time is best to act and when the time is best to be silent and listen.

We often look to see the pile of work ahead of us and become worried and distracted.

16

We may become frustrated. In those moments, when work seems overwhelming, that is the time to take a moment to sit and be in prayer. How long did it take you to reach where you are?

If you see someone who is not where you think they should be, what is your reaction? Was there ever been a time in your life like that? Each Christian has something to give. A humble contrite heart ensures open communication with God and others.

A: Active

C: Christians

T: Terrorizing

S: Satan

God declares it! Jesus performs it! The Holy Spirit reveals an action plan!

You can give without loving, but you cannot love without giving! Our greatest act of love to God is our *obedience*. Something I learned in 1988 is pride is not the same as self-esteem.

"God loves me" is self-esteem. Pride is trying to be something we are not. Food for thought: Crisis in Chinese means opportunity. The spirit of God works through me when I am humble.

I walk in faith when I rest in Christ. When I sit down and open my Bible (love letter), Jesus comes into my house, sits down, and fellowships with me. Holy Spirit teaches me about Jesus and Father. I must accept God's authority over my life to be of good soil. To be able to fulfill my calling on my life I must do the following:

1. Be obedient.
2. Be willing.
3. Have knowledge (be in the Word).

Having an understanding of God's Word and living in faith is how to fight the good fight!

Our faith does not grow any faster than our love and patience. Living works are actions to please God for other people. Dead works are done only for self. Steps to stop Satan:

1. Submit to God's gift over me.

2. Be subject to one another.

3. Be humble to the Word.

4. Cast all my cares on the Lord.

5. Be sober (serious) in spirit and attentive.

6. Be persistent and diligent.

Trust God to perform His promises.

Chapter 5

Persistence and Diligence

Give, and it will be given to you: good measure, pressed down, shaken together, and running over, will be put into your bosom. For with the same measure that you use, it will be measured back to you.
Luke 6:38

I was blessed that I was taught about Luke 6:38 very early in my Christian walk. If we are obedient to give, it is given back to us, pressed down, shaken together, and running over so that we are able to give again and give to many good works. We get to give! This is so exciting to me! We do not have to give, but we have the opportunity to give. This isn't just talking about tithing. It is about giving to ministries (with finances, time, and service) and helping to spread the Gospel and doing the work of the Lord. Although, when I first heard this, I thought it was talking about tithing and only this truth. It taught me to tithe.

"Will a man rob God? Yet you robbed me! But you say, 'In what way have we robbed You?" In tithes and offerings. You are cursed with a curse, for you have robbed Me, Even this whole nation. Bring all the tithes into the storehouse, that there may be food in My house. And try Me now in this," says the Lord of hosts, "If I will not open for you the windows of heaven and pour out for you such blessing that there will not be room enough to receive it. And I will rebuke the devourer for your sakes, so that he will not destroy the fruit of your ground, nor shall the vine fail to bear fruit for you in the field," says the Lord of hosts; Malachi 3:8-11

Finally, be strong in the Lord and in His mighty power. Ephesians 6:10 NIV

Each day I put my armor of God on. I start with my helmet of salvation. I am so thankful for my helmet. It helps me to protect my mind and to focus on my Savior. Then comes my breast plate of righteousness. Here I prepare my heart, asking the Lord to cleanse my heart then I gird myself with the belt of truth, knowing the Blood of Jesus is my strength, having shod my feet with the preparation of the Gospel of peace, taking back every inch the devil has taken from me. Next, I take up the shield of faith, knowing I can quench *all* the darts from the evil one. I take the Sword of the Spirit, which is the Word of God, praying for family and all saints in the body of Christ. Now that I'm dressed for today and covered in the blood of Jesus, I am an ambassador for Christ. I can speak boldly.

Chapter 6

Knowing Who I Am in Christ

Knowing this, that our old man was crucified with Him, that the body of sin might be done away with, that we should no longer be slaves of sin. Now if we died with Christ, we believe that we shall also live with Him. For the death that He died, He died to sin once for all; but the life that He lives, He lives to God. Likewise, you also, reckon yourselves to be dead indeed to sin, but alive to God in Christ Jesus our Lord.

Romans 6:6,8,10-11

Our goal is to become a reflection of Christ. How can we being sinful and flawed human beings ever portray our Father's flawless image? To simply put it, we need to follow Holy Spirit. As Christians if we are truly following His Word then we will reflect His character.

Holy Spirit shines through us as we allow God into our lives.

How Do I Become Intimate with Christ?

I know who I am by finding out what and who He says I am. We do this by focusing on Jesus by walking in light and not darkness. You are transformed into His likeness. You learn His love and holiness. God is most magnified in me when I am satisfied. Knowing who I am in Christ is a mind shift. He sees us as forgiven, redeemed the apple of His eye, His bride, unconditionally loved, and His chosen one. When we meditate on who we are in Christ, He dwells in us and shows us how He sees us. We see ourselves as unclean. God sees us as pure, clean, and forgiven as white as snow.

> *"Come now, and let us reason together," says the Lord, "Though your sins are like scarlet, they shall be as white as snow; Though they are red like crimson, They shall be as wool.'* Isaiah 1:18

The law and works do not produce miracles. Only faith in the Lord, with Holy Spirit, is helping us to build faith through teaching, leading, and guiding us. Then our faith grows. Trust the Lord, (lean on Him). Walk not by sight but by the Spirit of God. Hear the word, read the Word, and learn who we are in CHRIST.

24

Therefore, He who supplies the Spirit to you and works miracles among you, does He do it by the works of law, or by the hearing of faith?
Galatians 3:5

What Is Christ in Me?

- Power: Christ in me. Knowing whose I am.
    - End times: power and might.
    - Intimacy: Knowing who He is.

- Walk: Center my thoughts.
- Listen to *Him*: when was I last obedient?
- Follow Him
- Trust *Him*
- Agree with *Him*: He is always right.
- Obey *Him*: Better than sacrifice. Disobedience says "I know better than you" Obedience *must* be a lifestyle!
- Be in the Word daily: Stay in step with Him not ahead and not behind! Psalm 119:105 teaches us that listening and thinking about Him are *not* the same!
- Love *Him*.

- Forsake sin: "Cleanse my heart, oh God" You cannot walk in sin and Holiness at the same time!

- Repent: When God calls you home, what do you want people to say of you? You had an intimate walk with God? Or You did your own thing and it's hard to find anything good to say?

- Pray and talk with God. He is always listening.

Chapter 7

I Surrender All

The voice of my beloved! Behold, he comes leaping upon the mountains, skipping upon the hills. My beloved is like a gazelle or a young stag. Behold He stands behind our wall; he is looking through the windows, gazing through the lattice. My beloved spoke, and said to me: "Rise up, my love, my fair one, and come away. For lo, the winter is past, the rain is over and gone. The flowers appear on the earth; the time of singing has come, and the voice of the turtledove is heard in our land. The fig tree puts forth her green figs, and the vines with the tender grapes give a good smell. Rise up, my love, my fair one, and come away!" "Oh my dove, in the clefts of the rock, in the secret places of the cliff, let me see your face, let me hear your voice; for your voice is sweet, and your face is lovely.
Song of Solomon 2:8-14

Surrender means to yield ownership, to relinquish control over what we consider ours. This could be what we own, not only our time, it is *all* things. When we fully surrender to God, we understand what we "own" belongs to Him. God is the giver of all good things. By surrendering to God, we admit that He is in control of everything.

Have you ever read or heard the poem, "How Do I Love Thee?" It begins with, counting the ways. We

27

never totally comprehend how long, how deep, how high, and how wide His love is for us.

Today the Lord says, "Let me show you some of my ways I created you because I wanted to have a personal time with you. I created you to spend time talking with me and listening to each other. I wrote you a love letter, the Bible. I created the world, the thousands of different kinds of flowers, four different seasons, birds to sing for you, sun to warm you, the moon and stars, and rich soil to grow all your favorite fruits and vegetables. All of this I created and gave it technicolor for you to have beauty all around you. I give you life abundantly, joy unspeakable, family, loved ones in your life, friends to encourage you, pets to show you how to love unconditionally just as I do. All these things and so much more do I give you freely because I love you! Take time my beloved one to enjoy my gifts for you. See My love in them."

Chapter 8

A Prophetic Word

But those who wait on the Lord shall renew their strength; they shall mount up with wings like eagles, they shall run and not be weary, they shall walk and not faint.
Isaiah 40:31

At a meeting, a prophetess grabbed my hand and started running around a large room. The tables were full of women. She stopped and pulled out a chair for me, sat me down, and said, "Your ministry is to women." She prophesied that I would be busy running around ministering to them and would stop and rest but even then women would come sit at my feet, and I would minister to them. Then she grabbed my hand and said, "Run faster, faster, around the room!"

That has been exactly how my ministry is. It has been busy with much energy needed, which He has supplied. People have not always understood this and said slow down, but the Holy Spirit says, *"Come on, much has to be done before Jesus returns."* The prophetess also said I would speak before leaders, kings, and go to other *nations*.

I have been to other nations and taught, but I have not fulfilled all this prophecy. I knew at that time when she spoke this prophecy, it would be fulfilled over time. Many years later almost all of it has come to pass. *Many people hunger for the Word, risking their lives to be able to share what they learn.* He has taken me to nations where I have had to go underground to teach pastors and leaders. If the authorities had found my Bible I would have been arrested and put in prison. His grace has always covered me and protected me. What an exciting life when we live by His purpose.

I have been in countries where barbed wire has surrounded the airports and where international soldiers have stood on each street corner with rifles for protection. There have been witch doctors living on my street and chanting all night. I was mobbed by children begging for more gifts. I have been to places where they needed the presents, so they could sell them for food. There was gunfire going off all around us. I had peace because I knew I had been called there for that time and for that season. You know in your spirit, there is a peace that floods you, and no matter what happens it will be okay.

When I was in the church giving little dolls, and the children came to me and knocked me down the pastor removed his belt and started swinging it to keep me from being trampled. When you see small children being carried down dirt roads begging for medicine (aspirin) because of fever or children with orange hair and distended stomachs, or pregnant women with no food that are malnourished, working the mission field is all worth it. My heart bursts with love for them. I still pray for them at times as they come into my mind. I have seen babies left in orphanages deformed, unwanted, or under-nourished, with dirty faces and runny noses. They are crying with flies in their eyes and noses. Usually without enough staff to hold and care for them! My heart began to see a little of the love Jesus has for us all.

Chapter 9

Lonely Times

The Lord is near to those who have a broken heart, and
saves such as have a contrite spirit.
Psalm 34:18

God speaks to us by showing compassion. Through His compassion for us we are able to share with others. We may go through devastating times in our lives. Some people experience rejection. We are called to have compassion for relationships or families that are split. Healing time follows with intimacy with Him.

We should show more compassion for the elderly and lonely who are overlooked because they are alone or single. There are so many single-parented families and the elderly, who need love, support, and encouragement. Consider asking them to dinner, or your next friends gathering. Maybe you're a dad who could take a fatherless child to a game, or ask them to play basketball with you and your children. Or perhaps you're a mom, who could invite a child to bake or do a craft with your children. Maybe call, encourage, and pray with a single mom or dad. Consider calling a widow or widower. They have much wisdom to give, and there are so many ways to help those who are lonely. Teach your young to care for others of all ages. Get creative. The lonely will often isolate themselves and rarely know how or want to reach out and ask for help. You could be their hope just by reaching out.

I did not realize it, but I was being prepared for the next level of my walk. In February 2005, Clark, my husband had his third heart attack. It was early in the morning. He had gotten up and was having his coffee and reading the newspaper. I heard him come into the bathroom. He hit the shower door as he fell to the floor. I knew immediately what had happened. I jumped up and ran to him calling out to our granddaughter, who had spent the night to call 911. I called out to Jesus. I knew in my spirit he was going home. I held him in my arms. We talked of our love for each other, although he had a stroke and his speech was garbled, his eyes said what his voice could not.

I saw Jesus enter into the bathroom and lean down over Clark and put His mouth over Clark's nose and mouth and take his breath. Such peace and love filled me as I saw the Lord and Clark go to heaven. Many of my family and friends expected me to fall apart. But I just leaned into my Lord. God's grace, mercy, and love sustains me to this day. Do I miss Clark-- of course? You don't have an intimate relationship with the love of your life for over fifty years and not miss them when they are gone. But Jesus always takes me back to that day, the look on Clark's face, and the vision of Jesus and Clark going together, and I can't wish him back. I'm so thankful we had time to say our goodbye to each other.

A Father of the fatherless, a defender of widows, is God in His holy habitation.
Psalm 68:5

He has been my supplier of all my needs, protector, and defender every day.

Chapter 10

What Does It Mean, "Praying Without Ceasing?"

Rejoice always, pray without ceasing, in everything give thanks; for this is will of God in Christ Jesus for you.
1 Thessalonians 5:16-19

Do not quench the Spirit.

To "pray without ceasing" is a state of mind.

You have to *choose* to let every action and thought be a prayer. Let each action be a prayer to God whether it's stopping a child from squeezing toothpaste or pulling a cat's tail. It also may be cooking that favorite dinner or dessert your husband loves. That is praying without ceasing! If you have purpose in your heart, you are doing it to glorify God. You don't have to lay prostrate and pray in tongues to be praying without ceasing, although we need to set aside time to do that also. By consciously giving all that you do as a

35

prayer to the Lord, you are praying without ceasing! In other words, give Him your thoughts and actions every day.

I once sat with a dear friend who had a stroke. She was a woman with much Godly wisdom, but she was crying because she was in so much pain. She felt ashamed because she just wanted to die and felt so weak that she wasn't stronger in her faith. She felt she had let others and the Lord down. I shared with her that sometimes we try to be strong when the Lord is being strong for us. He is strong when we are weak.

Her fear was = False Evidence Appearing Real. This is a good acronym to remember. As we talked, God continued to show me it was not up to her to show others how strong she was but how loving God is. She was afraid of not being a good witness. She isn't a prideful woman, she is very humble. A loved one was watching her to see if she got well. She thought if she got well, then he would see about accepting her Jesus!

The Lord showed me in a way unknowingly, she was trying to play God. It wasn't up to her healing to make the loved one see Jesus. It was the loved one's choice to choose Jesus. The only thing He asked her to do was love Him! He takes care of the rest! We cannot work our way into heaven! It is about relationships with Jesus. That is the bottom line. Yes, as we accept Him, we do many good works, but my friend has always done that. It is out of love for Him we do them! He was pleased with her, even as she lays there, she constantly talks to Him with thanksgiving and praise.

Chapter 11

Entering His Courts with Praise!

Enter into His gates with thanksgiving, and into His courts with praise. Be thankful to Him, and bless His name. For the Lord is good; His mercy is everlasting, and His truth endures to all generations.

Psalm 100: 4-5

When I enter the courts of praise, I envision a small outer courtyard made of stone. Incense burns in a fire pit in the middle of the floor of flagstone. Sandstone walls open windows on each side look out at beautiful mountains, trees, and rivers. The roof is covered with fragrant flowering vines. Along one wall is a large table of stone. On the table is a beautiful ornate copper bowl of water. I wash my hands in the water. A vase of flowers and a candle are on the table. Praise music plays. I dance and praise His name. Continuing through this courtyard I step into a large bright golden-lit room. Sweet incense fills the place. I hear different instruments playing worship music while angels are singing and worshiping God!

Father and Son are talking about the love they have for me. Father invites me to sit upon His lap. He holds me close; I hear His heart beating. Jesus tells Father of my love for Him, and Father tells me He loves me just as I am. I cry for the pure joy of being in His presence! My heart fills with thanksgiving and praise for Father. Glorifying Father, Son, and Holy Spirit *are* looking on with pure joy. They work as a team, though they are three, they are One! The Father created it all, the Son died for it all, and Holy Spirit teaches and guides us all. This is the vision I get as I enter His courts. Holy Spirit will give you your own vision. Just ask Him!

Chapter 12

Gift of Prophesy

Pursue love, and desire spiritual gifts, but especially that you may prophesy. But he who prophesies speaks edification and exhortation and comfort to men.
I Corinthians 14:1,3

Promises are for everyone. You have to know they are for you, then believe it. When you speak into someone's life, you are sharing from Holy Spirit. They begin to see God's love through your eyes. Fear keeps us from using this gift. We don't have to earn it. The gift of prophecy is for *All* to be able to use. We cannot earn it. Our gifts are *nothing* if not given in love!

Giving a prophetic word should always exhort, comfort, or encourage. It should bring edification. Edification is exhortation that draws them closer to God. A word should comfort. That is speaking love and comfort to someone. A prophecy should be confirming what they already know. Don't use specifics, unless you are sure God gave you the specifics. Just encourage them, give them the goodness of God.

> *But the manifestation of the Spirit is given to each one for the profit of all!*
> 1 Corinthians 12:7

How do we hear from God? Through friends, a still small voice, insight, knowing, impressions, and circumstances. What is God showing you? Listen and see what is around you. Know His character: He uses pictures and creativity. He uses dreams, visions, colors and numbers. (Gold= glory, Silver-= refining, Blue=heavenly, Purple=royalty, Green= healing). There is a still small voice. Ask of Him. We can hear from God through smell which are fragrances.

Remember Prophetic tells the future. A Word of knowledge is for now. When you receive a word, there are three parts to it: Revelation, Interpretation and Application. Our responsibility is our response to Him. It is not always for right now, you may need to put the word on a shelf. I have had words given to me that I knew were not for right now. But were for later. It is important to judge your word. Does it bear witness in your spirit? It should draw you closer to God. If you

41

question it, set it aside, and take it to Holy Spirit. Ask Him to explain it to you. Sometimes we ask, "Why doesn't the prophecy come true?" Through intercession, it will help change and reveal our potential. We have a part to play in it. We could have misinterpreted it. You need to activate the prophecy. If you are the one giving the word, *Practice*! Ask Holy Spirit what He would say today. Ask Holy Spirit to show you. Going out among people, ask Holy Spirit. You do not always have to tell a person until you feel sure about it. Step out and take risks. It can sometimes be a Scripture that would speak into their life today.

Remember to always speak it in love.

Chapter 13

Changing into an Image of God

Show me Your ways, O Lord; teach me Your paths. Lead me in Your truth and teach me, For You are the God of my salvation; on You I wait all the day"
Psalm 25:4-5

Psalms 25 teaches us to wait all day. That is using wisdom. The meaning of this is the heart and mind are needed for right conduct in life. Wisdom is a practical applied lifestyle, not just knowing in your head but applying it to your lifestyle until it becomes part of you. Wisdom has us waiting- - waiting until you trust God at His Word. We should not only look to other books on the subject but focus on what the Bible says on the subject. The *Word*!

> But his delight is in the law of the Lord, and in His law he meditates day and night.
> Psalm 1:2

When we read Psalms 1:2, it shows us who is the source of wisdom. If we meditate on His Word, we are always learning, as long as we draw breath. Approaching how to obtain wisdom is by staying meek. He guides us. We ask Holy Spirit to be our teacher, guide, and comforter every day. Admitting I need to change. I will be more likely to stay humble, not falsely but truly humble.

All Scripture is God-breathed and is useful for teaching, rebuking, correcting and training in righteousness. **2 Timothy 3:16 NIV**

Lord search my heart, try me, keep my thoughts pure, show me my wicked ways as I follow you into eternity.

Yes, if you cry out for discernment, and lift up your voice for understanding, if you seek her as silver, and search for her as for hidden treasures; then you will understand the fear of the Lord, and find the knowledge of God. For the Lord gives wisdom; from His mouth come knowledge and understanding. Proverbs 2:3-6

This is how we obtain wisdom. We are transformed from caterpillar to butterfly. In Galatians we learn how we are crucified with Christ, our ego moves to the side and teaches us how we are crucified with Christ as He becomes centered in us.

Being confident of this very thing, that He who has begun a good work in you will complete it until the day of Jesus Christ. **Philippians 1:6**

Holy Spirit is our teacher. Not man, but Holy Spirit. Precept upon precept means leaving milk and going to meat. We do this by renewing the mind. Wisdom is given to all who ask for it earnestly. We can and do have a renewed mind to know the perfect will of God.

God *always* gives specific answers for specific needs at specific times! The Bible has many golden nuggets easily found. It is filled with wisdom and knowledge. You just have to dig in.

Read until God stops you!

Chapter 14

Repent and Release

The Lord God has given me the tongue of the learned, that I should know how to speak a word in season to him who is weary. He awakens me morning by morning; He awakens my ear to hear as the learned.
Isaiah 50:4

We need to repent for unfaithfulness. When I do not trust God to work in me and through me, I need to repent, or I can do what He tells me. God wanted to write a book through me. It's not my talent. It's His gift and talent He has put in me. I have creativity in floral arranging and entertaining and hosting. That is talent He gave me. I need to repent of unbelief because I didn't trust Him when the Bible says all things are possible to those who believe.

Forgiveness is like layers of an onion. Picture an onion blossom. You take one layer, but there are more layers left. Many times, we shed tears with each layer. Sometimes it's like that with forgiveness. You ask God to forgive you, or you forgive others with all of your heart, but later something comes up and you realize there is still some feelings like another layer that may bring tears like that onion. You repent and forgive again with all your heart for what God is showing you at this time. Other times once you forgive, you may never think of it again. You forgive to the best of your ability. Holy Spirit is our guide. As we grow, our ability to forgive on more levels also grows.

> *Create in me a clean heart, O God, and renew a steadfast spirit within me.* Psalm 51:10

Show me your ways. They are higher than my ways.

Holy Spirit says, "Let me be your guide, teacher, and comforter today!" Don't worry about all the lists that others think you should do each day. What is important is Holy Spirit will lead you and teach you what your Father wants you to learn and what is important is our relationship today! Trust in Him. Holy Spirit has stayed here on earth to be your friend, teacher, and mentor. He will lead you in *all* truth-- truth for you to walk in today, tomorrow, and every day.

*Over three hundred sixty-five times in the Bible
the Lord tells us not to be in fear for He will be
with us.* The Lord will take you where He wants
you to go. Follow *Him! You don't need to be
anxious if you prepare as He shows you. He will
bring all the power and anointing you will need.
Focus on Him, not on what to say or do. It's
about helping someone grow in Him. To know
Him better, to be set free in their lives so they
can help someone else grow in Him!*

A Morning prayer:

Dear Lord, good morning, Holy Spirit, guide me into
wisdom today! Lead me to who I am in Christ. Teach
me about agape love, take me deeper into my Lord.
Help me to magnify Him! I surrender all to you, Lord,
and have your will in my life. Thank you for showing
me when to go and when to wait. When I go, I want to
be soaked in agape love, sharing what You put into my
heart. To encourage, uplift and edify others.

Teach me Holy Spirit, to be a person who quickly
does as the Lord asks of me. Let me be a listener as
well as a speaker. Stir up gifts in me. I Pray in Jesus'
name. Amen.

Lord says, "Get prayed up to know who I am in you. Trust in me. Walk, talk, and listen to Me. I want to sow into you even in the little things. That is one of My ways of showing My love for you and others. Be thankful for what I have given you, pay attention to the things I take away from you. As I take, I give you more."

Chapter 15

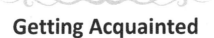

Getting Acquainted

Behold, children are heritage from the Lord, the fruit of the womb is a reward.
Like arrows in the hand of a warrior, so are the children of one's youth. Happy is
the man who has his quiver full of them; they shall not be
ashamed, but shall speak with their enemies in the gate.

Psalm 127:3-5

I was born in a small community in southwest Michigan. My family and I moved to Lake Elsinore, California in 1951. I am the oldest of ten children. Raised Catholic, I met my Jesus at the age of seven years old. I remember the day like it was yesterday. I recall vividly when I knelt and asked Him into my heart. His love enveloped me, and He has never left me since that moment. In the Catholic Church at age twelve, I was confirmed. The Catholic Bishop asked if I wanted to receive the Holy Spirit. I said," Yes" and the moment I said yes, my life changed. I began to sing in tongues. You might ask," Did I know what I was doing?" NO, because we had Latin masses, and I thought I was singing in Latin. I had not yet been taught about Holy Spirit and the gift of tongues. As I talked to the Lord, my heart would become so full of love I would start singing.

When I was fourteen at a Menifee Valley dance, I met a handsome, quiet, young man, Clark McElwain, who was seventeen. We dated two years, and at age sixteen, I married the love of my life. We had four beautiful daughters. We made our home in Menifee, California. Clark and I were married forty-seven years before he went home to be with the Lord. We have eleven grandchildren, and eighteen great grandchildren. It is true they are my heritage from the Lord as the Bible says in Psalms127:3-5.

In the seventies, I was involved in the Charismatic movement. I joined Women's Aglow International, a women's inter-denominational organization started in the Charismatic movement to help women grow in experience in their calling and giftings and bring unity to all. I taught Bible studies and held positions on the local and area board of Aglow, including the area president. Some of the best years of my spiritual growth I gained from this organization.

The calling on my life has always been to women. I am also called to bring unity. Looking back, I believe that was why Aglow was such a large part of my life in those days. I still attend their meetings as often as I can. I attended a wonderful spirit-filled church. I led the children's church, was head of the Altar Ministry and held many other leadership positions. It was such a wonderful time in my life. Part of the fruit of my training and calling was to answer God's calling to start my own ministry. In 1982, I founded Sweet Aroma Ministry, to teach others about the agape love God has for every race, color, and creed. He does not discriminate, and neither should we. He loves all His children.

And walk in love, as Christ also has loved us and given Himself for us, an offering and a sacrifice to God for a sweet-smelling aroma. Ephesians 5:2

I was ordained by Outreach Fellowship International, in February, 2004. I had home meetings, we studied the New Testament, and had healings weekly. I continue to teach Bible studies for women's groups and serve in the Body of Christ. It is my joy to go where God leads me. His voice will I follow.

He calls us to walk in love. Christ has also given Himself for us as an offering and sacrifice to God for a sweet-smelling aroma. He showed me a vision of a rainbow of flowers, flowing from a trumpet an angel was blowing from heaven. The Lord told me I was to be a sweet aroma to Him *first and then to the body of Christ.* I worship and give all my love to Him, then to my ministry to women. Showing unconditional love (His love) and teaching them of His love for them. They can also become a sweet-smelling aroma as they fall more in love with Him. Just as there are all varieties of flowers, His beloved are also each unique. Yet He loves them all the same. Whatever our need is, He will meet with love, and His love will heal us! God brings us into unity with Him and each other. All these are attributes of our Heavenly Father and should be ours also!

Chapter 16

Receiving Holy Spirit

*Nevertheless, I tell you the truth. It is to your advantage that I go away; for if I do
not go away, the Helper will not come to you; but if
I depart, I will send Him to you.*
John 16:7

When we ask Jesus into our hearts, Holy Spirit comes to reside in us, but Jesus told us after He left, He was sending a Helper to give us power to dwell in us and with us. Read John 14:16,17. He is the third person in The Trinity. His name is Holy Spirit. The Bible says we have not because we ask not. The infilling of Holy Spirit is a gift just like salvation is a gift. We invited Jesus in to be Lord of our lives and He came. We used our faith, we believed. We invite Holy Spirit in the same way, we use our faith to invite Him in and use our mouth to speak His utterances.

Imagine if you will, in heaven you have a room with your name on it. When you enter there are many beautiful wrapped gifts, all for you. The first gift you chose to open was the gift of salvation, another gift is the gift of tongues, gift of peace, etc. but until you open any gift, it's of no value to you.

This one gift has many other gifts attached. It *teaches* us how to walk in righteousness. It *guides* us into all truth and *comforts* us when we need to be comforted. This gift is a person, Holy Spirit. You can talk to Him, make Him a best friend. This gift next to salvation is the most important gift we receive. It gives us many more exciting benefits that you can and will use every day. Invite Holy Spirit into your life today. He is just waiting to be asked!

Remember He filled all! Believe, ask, and speak. Practice your new language often every day. You have control when to stop and start. Paul said that he speaks in tongues more than you all. If it worked for him, it will work for you. Below you will find a partial list of what these benefits are.

Holy Spirit Can Help You:

   1. Receive Power:

But you shall receive power when the Holy Spirit has come upon you; and you shall be witnesses to Me in Jerusalem, and in all Judea and Samaria, and to the end of the earth. Acts 1:8

2.   Pray a perfect Prayer:

For the Holy Spirit will teach you in that very hour what you ought to say. Luke 12:12

I indeed baptized you with water, but He will baptize you with the Holy Spirit. Mark 1:8

Man baptizes in water, Jesus baptizes in Holy Spirit, Holy Spirit baptizes in power.

3.   Receives Gift of God:

If you then, being evil, know how to give good gifts to your children, how much more will your heavenly Father give the Holy Spirit to those who ask Him! Luke 11:13

4.   Brings Us into One Accord:

When the Day of Pentecost had fully come, they were all with one accord in one place. And suddenly there came a sound from heaven, as of a rushing mighty wind, and it filled the whole house where they were sitting. Then there appeared to them divided tongues, as of fire, one sat upon each of them. Acts 2:1-3

5. Speak in Other Tongues:

And they were all filled with the Holy Spirit and began to speak with other tongues, as the Spirit gave them utterances. Acts 2:4

6. He is our Helper and Spirit of Truth:

And I will pray the Father, and He will give you another Helper, that He may abide with you forever- the Spirit of truth, whom the world cannot receive, because it neither sees Him nor knows Him; but you know Him, for He dwells with you and will be in you. John 14:16-17

7. He Makes Intercession for Us and Through Us:

Likewise, the Spirit also helps in our weaknesses. For we do not know what we should pray for as we ought, but the Spirit Himself makes intercession for us with groanings which cannot be uttered. Now He who searches the hearts know what the mind of the Spirit is, because He makes intercession for the saints according to the will of God. And we know that all things work together for good to those who love God, to those who are the called according to His purpose. Romans 8:26-28

8. Gives us prophetic Word:

   But he who prophesies speaks edification and exhortation and comfort to men. He who speaks in a tongue edifies himself, but he who prophesies edifies the church. 1 Corinthians 14:3-4

You build up your faith when you pray in your prayer language.

A few of the ways we can use our gift:

1. Pray in unknown tongues as He gives utterance. It builds up our faith.
2. Singing in the Spirit and in your native language.
3. Worship the Lord, then *listen* to what He is saying to you.

4. Dance in Spirit. Use flags, sign language. Be free in your worship.

Now that we have talked about reasons for wanting to have Holy Spirit in your life, are you ready to receive my Friend, Holy Spirit? The only prerequisite to being filled with Holy Spirit isbeing a born-again Christian. If you have not asked Jesus Christ to be your Lord and Savior, let's do that right now.

Pray with me:

"Jesus, I come to you now and ask You to forgive me of my sins and wash me in Your precious blood. I believe I'm made a new creation in You. Be Lord of my life as I surrender all to You. I thank You for making me a child of God. I love and praise your holy name. Amen."

Now you are a Child of God. You can ask Holy Spirit to come and fill you. Just believe He *wants* to fill you so when you ask, *trust* Him to give you your prayer language. He wants to teach you in all truth with revelation knowledge in the Word and comfort you with love of the Father. Because it glorifies God.

He wants to endue you with power to be an overcomer and guide you in your destiny.

> *And they were **all** filled with Holy Spirit and began to speak in other tongues, as the Spirit gave them utterance.* Acts 2:4

Let's pray:

"Lord Jesus, You as my Lord and Savior. I ask you to baptize me in the Holy Spirit. Thank You, that you hear my prayer, and you have answered it. I claim by faith the Baptism of the Holy Spirit right now. Thank You Jesus. Amen."

Now as an expression of your faith has answered your prayer, just open your mouth, and begin to praise God, but not in your own language. You are working together with Holy Spirit. You use vocal cords and Holy Spirit giving utterances. Remember it doesn't matter the words or sounds. That's Holy Spirit's part. Yours is obedience to use your vocal cords. Now practice often. In the shower, car, or wherever you feel comfortable at first. The more you use your language the easier it becomes.

Chapter 17

How is your walk?

I have always had a special relationship with my grandchildren. When Harmony and her family moved away, we kept in touch by phone. Especially in her teen years she would call in anxiety and tears. We would talk about her struggles, and then we would pray, sometimes for hours.

She has grown into a godly young woman. We were recently talking, and I asked her "What were some of the things I have shared with you that has affected your life?" She replied, "You always start by asking, "How is your walk with the Lord?" Here are some of the nuggets of gold we shared together. Use them as instructions to help guide you in your walk.

- Psalm 91: to dwell in His presence is an absolute must in my walk. I read my Bible every day.

- Trust Him: He never leaves me or forsakes me.

- How to come into His presence: Praise and worship Him in my private time.

- Pray until I find peace. Ask for prayer when anxiety attacks come.

- Listen and learn which is God's voice, Satan's voice, or my voice. Is it God's word or a lie from Satan, (Does it line up with The Word of God?) or my voice, do my thoughts line up with The Word of God? Are they condemning? Satan condemns, God will convict to bring us to repentance.

- Obedience: Obey His voice immediately. We don't grow in this area until we obey.

- Pray to make good choices: Ask God," What is best for me? "

- Remember We are overcomers: We can do all things through Christ.

- Don't hold offenses: Forgiveness keeps the heart pure.

- Forgiveness: Sometimes this comes in layers.

- Choose friends wisely: Where is their walk with God? Will they build me up or tear me down?

- How's my walk?: Take inventory on how I'm spending my time, am I making good choices?

- He loves me unconditionally: I am the apple of His eye.

- Be quick to repent: He's quick to forgive.

- He never leaves me nor forsakes me: He watches over me.

Beloved ask yourself today "How is my walk? What adjustments do I need to make? Then make them and walk in your freedom.

Chapter 18

China and Youth with a Mission (YWAM)

*Ask of Me, and I will give You the nations for Your inheritance,
and the ends of the earth our possession.*
Psalm 2:8

YWAM is a global movement of Christians from many cultures, age groups, Christian traditions, dedicated to serving Jesus throughout the world. Their goal is to know God and make Him known.

My first trip to China was with YWAM. One of our leaders took us on a sight seeing tour. In a boat we went down the Yaly River that separates China and North Korea. Going upriver we were in the North Korean side of the river. The land was totally bare. There were no trees, no grass, and very few buildings. It looked lifeless. We saw a women's prison, with no windows, just a tall gray building along the water's edge. There were, however North Korean soldiers who stood along the riverbanks with their rifles. There were bunkers made of brick or dirt. Some soldiers waved at us, but we could not stop the boat or we would have been shot.

At the head of the river was a huge dam that was owned and operated by the Chinese. It supplied electricity for most of North Korea. As we looked on the Chinese side of the river, we saw cities, grass, automobiles, people. Vibrant Life!

Every Sunday we went to the town square in the city where we were staying. Within ten minutes, more than twenty people gathered around us. Parents pushed their children up to us. They wanted us to speak English with them. We were there for hours.

We held English nights to speak to anyone who wanted to practice English at "Starbucks" the local coffee shop. We spent afternoons and evenings talking to them about America, or whatever they wanted to discuss. Our goal was to make friends and then we could share about Jesus with them.

When they found out I lived in California, they all thought I lived next to movie stars in Hollywood. We spent a good deal of time becoming friends with the people. But we also knew some of them were government agents. We were watched constantly by the secret police. We could only leave our house two or three at a time. They closed the home I was staying in not long after I left China.

All official churches are owned by the state. They are called The Three Self Church.

We attended their services. The government read all their sermons before they were preached and blacked out anything they didn't approve of. A small group from the church invited us to continue to worship and study the Word. One of our young Korean boys played the guitar. They ask him to teach some new songs to them. Then we broke up in small groups and taught them about Jesus and prayed for them. Of course, there were some in the group listening to be sure we didn't say something they disapproved of.

We taught Bible studies in different areas around the city we stayed in. I remember one lady gave me her business card, so proudly. She wanted me to keep in touch with her. She was a manager on a chicken ranch. She wanted to come to America because we had Social Security. She was so amazed you could retire and have some income.

I was there living and working at an orphanage in another city we ministered in. I was working with the most handicapped, so I was behind doors so children couldn't get out. This particular day the staff had the television on because there was a train of government leaders going from North Korea to South Korea. No one was getting off. Just going from north to south and back. They were so excited. There had not been such a train since the Korean War started. Some had family they had never seen. There are many Koreans in China. Can you imagine never knowing your family because the government closed the road to your loved ones?

In the airport when I first arrived, men walked up to me. I thought they were cab drivers wanting to get me to take their cab. When my guide came over and got me, it seems they were policemen trying to find out what I was doing in China. My guide explained I was a tourist.

We took an overnight train to Beijing. What an adventure that was. The girls had a sleeper with bunk beds to sleep in but no doors. We had an electric outlet so we could heat up noodles or food we had. You could only go to the restroom while the train was moving. It was a hole in the bathroom floor, going straight out onto the train tracks. In case you missed the hole there was a bucket of water provided to throw across the floor as you left the restroom. No toilet paper was provided so we took our own. Restroom doors are locked at every stop. You can only go while trains are moving.

We saw them building the birds nest for the Olympics. One year later I returned to China and saw it completed. We walked along the Great Wall of China. Although it runs all through China, and we walked it in different places. We went to Tiananmen Square. The smog was so bad in Beijing, the cab drivers told us that the government was allowing no cars on streets the last month before the Olympics.

We had the honor to teach a small group of underground church pastors. They were so eager to learn. They risked prison, torture, and their very lives to teach the whole truth. They invited us to an underground prayer meeting to pray over them. One pastor was North Korean. He planned to go back to North Korea to share Jesus with his people. The rest were Chinese pastors. We met in different places each visit for their safety.

One community where we stayed, we were praying for a small group, and I was asked to pray for a lady who wanted to receive Jesus. I later learned she had been a communist doctor. I met a woman who moved to a different city so the government wouldn't abort her baby (which they did even up to nine months) because she wasn't allowed to have a second child. This happened even though her husband worked for the government.

I read a book called, *Heavenly Man*. Authored by Brother Yun. It was a true story of one of China's underground church leaders and his horrifying persecutions. Would I have the faith and strength he had if I were in his shoes? I read this while in China. It shook me to my roots. At this time, I had been a Christian over thirty-five years, totally sold out to Jesus I thought. Would I have the faith and strength he had? I live in a nation I can openly talk about and read thousands of books about my Savior anytime I want. But he couldn't. What he did was make me take a long hard look at what I really believe and how far and how willing I am to go to share my faith (if indeed it was strong enough) with people. Will I put my life and more importantly my family's lives on the line?

I learned that if I have Jesus and don't share Him, I am like a parable. If you have truth (JESUS) and don't share it, you've buried your talents in the sand. God will never ask you to do something without a purpose and objectivity in mind. You don't get personal without saying "Yes." Then He shows you your purpose.

While we were there we ministered in a town in north-east China where we stayed awhile. There I stood with one foot through a fence. One foot on Russian and one foot on Chinese soil at the same time.

All the while I looked out, over the Yaly River, at North Korea. Wow! I really *felt* like an international world traveler! The group we ministered with invited me back to teach English, I returned one year later. This was to be my second and last trip to China.

Chapter 19

China and CRAM

"Then the righteous will answer Him, saying 'Lord, when did we see You hungry and feed You, or thirsty and give You drink? When did we see You a stranger and take You in, or naked and clothe You? Or when did we see You sick, or in prison, and come to You?' And the King will answer and say to them , '
Assuredly, I say to you, inasmuch as you did it to one of the
least of these My brethren, you did it to Me.'
Matthew 25:37-40

Christians Reaching Asians Ministry is based in America. It has missionaries from all over the world who go to China and Korea to minister love and the Gospel. In the mornings, the CRAM team and I worked with severely handicapped children. Most of the children couldn't walk. The instructor set the children on horses. They rode around the rink trying to put an embroidery hoop on a peg nailed on a post in the center of the rink. Their goal was to put the hoop on the peg. It was a joy to see their faces light up as they accomplished their task. They did something they never imagined they would be able to do!

The instructor placed each child's hand in a bucket of paint. Then he placed, the child'shand on the wall, to leave the painted image and wrote their name underneath. This made the children feel special. They would giggle and flail their arms. The children were bused from the orphanage school where most of them lived. Not all the children were orphans, but all were handicapped.

Some of our group taught the younger children at a school on the orphanage grounds. One of the young teachers and I took one young handicapped lad about eight years old, who lived with his mama in an extremely poor area of town, out to get a Korean pizza and ice cream. He was so excited. Instead of teacher, he called me pastor. Because this is what his teacher called me. He told his teacher he wanted to be a pastor like me when he grew up.

We returned him to his home in the pouring down rain by cab. His mother stood in the rain and thanked us over and over again for taking an interest in her son and feeding him dinner.

Afternoons I taught adult young people, professional men and women, doctors, beauticians, and people from all walks of life, fourth grade level English. One of my favorite students was a young man named John. He was about twenty-five years old who had acid thrown on him and set on fire by a family member! He was scarred over three quarters of his body. He wanted to learn English it was his second time taking the class. He failed the first time, but was willing to try again.

Another one of our students planned to marry, and she invited all the teachers. They were so honored and excited American teachers would come to their wedding. They were married in a Korean church, by a Chinese pastor. There are many Koreans in China. The reception was at a restaurant. The bride and groom had a head table on the stage. Fourth of July sparklers were at the end of each side of the stage. The sparklers went off like fireworks continually. The bride and groom came with a tray to each table with shot glasses for each person. The drinks were already on each table. There were bottles of wine or Coca-Cola. They poured our drinks and served us. They toasted us and thanked us for coming to celebrate with them.

It was raining when I left the reception. As I got out of the cab in my heels, I hurried around the back of the cab to get to the school. I slipped, fell, skinned my knee and twisted my ankle. I hobbled into the school building, and went up the stairs to the second floor to find someone to help me. I saw a fellow teacher and her friend who spoke no English but thank God she was a nurse. My friend interpreted for me. I had no clue how bad my injury was. I hobbled back down to the main floor and cleaned up my skinned knee, and the nurse got a cab and helped me back to my apartment.

I shared an apartment with a young Russian woman. Our place was on the fourth floor. We had no elevators. The Chinese nurse helped me up all four flights. As you know, ice is best for a swollen ankle, but in China ice is a rarity. We had none. So, the nurse walked to the nearest store and purchased an orange fifty-fifty ice cream bar and got a cold egg from the refrigerator to put on my ankle. She rubbed them up and down my ankle for about an hour. She used the fifty-fifty bar until it melted, then the cold egg. I was amazed how it took the swelling down.

The next day the teacher and nurse came to check on me and take me to the hospital. They had a two-wheeled bike waiting for me to wheel me to the car. At the hospital they took me directly by wheelchair to the second floor. The doctor looked at my injuries and he ordered an x-ray. I had a sprained ankle and a broken bone on the side of my right foot. He put a cast on my foot halfway to my knee. Although the cast was flimsy, my total cost was only $40.00. I was done in one hour. I was grateful God watched over me. I moved to the ground floor of another apartment complex with another Russian lady. I had no wheelchair or crutches yet so a slender, small framed young Chinese student put me on his back and carried me to my new apartment. I laid with my foot elevated for two weeks. It was almost time for me to come home. Fortunately, I saw the graduation exercises, although in a wheelchair.

My injuries caused me to leave over a week early. Yanji, a small airport, was my first airport on my journey home. I flew to Beijing with a cast, and with a small group from CRAM who were driving on to another city. Beijing is a huge beautiful international airport. My school companions set me on a luggage carrier full of luggage to escort me out of the terminal to a waiting car to drive us to the next terminal. A young man in our group got me a wheelchair and took me to the check-in desk. The check-in lady found me a bulk head seat so I would have more leg room. My stewardess found me a plastic crate and pillows to elevate it for the eighteen-hour flight home. My first port of entry in the U.S. was San Francisco. The authorities body-searched me and put her hand down into my cast. I returned to the plane and flew to LAX. My daughter met me and took me to her home to recuperate and to see an orthopedic doctor. They removed the cast and put on a boot.

I stay in contact with a few of the teachers. It was an experience I will never forget, the people I served with the beauty contrasted with the poverty I saw. I treasure the experiences and the interactions with the people of China. I even walked along the Great Wall of China. I would never have dreamt one day I would be a widow traveling all alone to a foreign country, having such an amazing time. What an *amazing* God I serve!

Chapter 20

Costa Rica

Is anyone among you sick? Let him call for the elders of the church, and let them pray over him, anointing him with oil in the name of the Lord. And the prayer of faith will save the sick, and the Lord will raise him up. And if he has committed sins, he will be forgiven
James 5:14-15

I lived in Costa Rica for a season with one of my daughters and son-in-law. They were living and working there. I had taken ISOM courses to teach. ISOM is an International School of Ministry which had the largest video Bible school in the world. I took the whole one-year program in Spanish and English with me in a notebook binder with DVD and curriculum tests. ISOM is Bible teachings taught by many different pastors. To train up and ordain new pastors and leaders domestic and international. My assignment was to find leaders and train some to become pastors.

I visited churches, met people and pastors. Much of my time was spent, getting to know the people in town and at the beaches. Their culture is more outdoors, most everything is done outside including church services, and dining.

I opened a prayer room to be open one afternoon a week at my daughter's home. Just like the ones I worked in at home. We invited people to come for prayer. Because we had talked about the healing room and people seemed to like the idea. We were bewildered no one came. Later I saw God had a different plan!

I noticed when we went to town to eat, people walked up to us and asked us to pray for them. So we asked if we could lay hands on them and pray for them at that moment instead of after we went home? They were hesitant at first but agreed. As they saw others prayed for and saw people being touched, they became more open to ask us to pray. I started to carry anointing oil with me even to the beach.

One restaurant owner who had a bad back asked me to pray for him. I anointed him and my daughter and I prayed for him and he was healed. He told others about it and others asked for prayer. God's plan was to take the healing room experience to them.

We need to make ourselves available to Holy Spirit's directions at all times. Our ways may be good, but His plan is great and gets powerful results.

Made in the USA
Middletown, DE
24 February 2021

PRAYING WITH JESUS AND MARY

PRAYING WITH JESUS AND MARY

OUR FATHER • HAIL MARY

Leonardo Boff

ORBIS BOOKS

Maryknoll, New York 10545

This book combines two works by Leonardo Boff: *O pai-nossa: a oração da libertação integral,* copyright © 1979 by Editora Vozes Ltda. Rua Freu Luís, 100, 25.600 Petrópolis RJ, Brazil, first published in English as *The Lord's Prayer: The Prayer of Integral Liberation,* copyright © 1983 by Orbis Books, Maryknoll, NY 10545; and *A Ave-Maria: O feminine e o Espírito Santo,* copyright © 1980 by Editora Vozes Ltda., © 2003 by Animus/Anima Produçoes.

English translation copyright © 1983, 2005 by Orbis Books

Published by Orbis Books, Maryknoll, NY 10545-0308.

Manufactured in the United States of America

Library of Congress Cataloging-in-Publication Data

Boff, Leonardo.
    Praying with Jesus and Mary : Our Father, hail Mary / Leonardo Boff.
      p. cm.
    Includes bibliographical references.
    ISBN 1-57075-575-2 (pbk.)
    1. Lord's prayer. 2. Ave Maria. I. Title.

BV230.B634 2005
226.9´606—dc22

                      2004061729

CONTENTS

Part II
THE HAIL MARY
The Feminine and the Holy Spirit

PART I

THE LORD'S PRAYER

The Prayer of Integral Liberation

Translated by Theodore Morrow

1

The Prayer of Integral Liberation

A spiritual teacher once said:
"If I have no love or I fail to act justly, then inevitably I sepa-
rate myself from you, O my God, and my worship is nothing but
idolatry.

"To believe in you, I must believe in love and believe in jus-
tice, and it is much more important to believe in these things
than to pronounce your name.

"Without love and justice it is impossible for anyone, at any
time, to be in contact with you.

"But those who take love and justice as their guide are on the
true path that leads to you."

The incarnation is more than just one of the central mysteries
of the Christian faith. It also opens the way to a new understanding of reality: the incarnation signifies the mutual presence of the
divine and the human, the compenetration of the historical and
the eternal. Each of these dimensions maintains its own identity,
and at the same time it enters into the composition of another, a
new, reality.

Jesus Christ, who was man and God at the same time, constituted the reality of a paradigmatic and supreme incarnation.
To understand this singular novelty, it is not enough to use the
categories of transcendence and immanence—the two key factors of Greek thought. These two categories capture the element
of *difference* between the two dimensions—the human is not divine and the divine is not human—but they do not succeed in

explaining their coexistence and joint inclusion in one and the same being.

We must have recourse to another category—that of transparency. This category undertakes to manifest the presence of transcendence within immanence, making each transparent to the other. It is in the human that the divine finds realization; the divine transfigures the human. What is most important is the fact that a new reality has appeared, a reality that is unified but in tension, because it is composed of two "others" of differing nature.[1]

THE LAW OF INCARNATION

Christianity can be understood as a prolongation of God's incarnation process. Just as the Son took everything upon himself in order to liberate everything, so the Christian faith seeks to become incarnate in everything in order to transfigure everything. It is in this sense that we say: everything belongs in some way to the kingdom of God, because everything is objectively connected with God and is called to belong to the reality of God's kingdom. Thus the Christian faith is not just interested in those realities described as spiritual and supernatural. It also places a value on the material and the historical. All of these pertain to one and the same schema of incarnation by which the divine penetrates the human and the human enters into the divine.

Against the background of this understanding, the Christian community commits itself to the *integral* liberation of human beings, not just of their spiritual dimension. Even their corporeality (and here we refer to the economic, social, political, and cultural infrastructure in their fullest sense) is "called" to absolute realization in God and to become a part of the kingdom of the Father. As a consequence, the Christian community, especially in recent years, has committed itself more and more to the liberation of the oppressed, to those condemned "to remain at the margin of life, experiencing hunger, chronic illnesses, illiteracy, poverty. . . ."

The church, as Pope Paul VI stated and as was reaffirmed at Puebla, "has the duty to proclaim the liberation of millions of human beings, among whom are many of the church's own children; the duty to help bring this liberation forth in the world, to bear witness to it and make sure it is total. None of this is alien to evangelization" (*Puebla* 26; *Evangelii Nuntiandi [EN]* 30).[2] The church involves itself in this temporal endeavor because it is aware that what is temporal is to be penetrated by grace and by the full reality of the kingdom of God. The temporal is to become transparent and sacramental. Well has the poet said: "O street cleaner, as you sweep the streets, you are sweeping the kingdom of heaven" (D. Marcos Barbosa).

NEITHER THEOLOGISM NOR SECULARISM

Two dangers have been called to our attention by Pope Paul VI in *Evangelii Nuntiandi* (1975) and by the bishops at Puebla (1979). The first is that of religious reductionism (theologism). It limits the activities of the Christian faith and the church to a strictly religious sphere—to worship, piety, and doctrine. Pope Paul VI clearly maintained that "the Church is not willing to restrict its mission only to the religious field and dissociate itself from man's temporal problems" (*EN* 34). The Puebla Conference states this even more bluntly: "Christianity is supposed to evangelize the whole of human life, including the political dimension. So the Church criticizes those who would restrict the scope of faith to personal or family life; who would exclude the professional, economic, social, and political orders as if sin, love, prayer, and pardon had no relevance in them" (*Puebla* 515).

What is emphasized here is the need to understand Christianity not as *an area* of reality (the religious field) but precisely as a process by which all of reality is incarnated in order to redeem it and make it a part of the kingdom of God. It is important for the Christian faith to be genuine and salvific. And it is salvific, and consequently genuine, when it is in the form of love. And the love that brings us to the threshold of salvation is not a theory, but a practice. Only faith that is compatible with the practice of love is worthy of the name. Its purpose is to integrate the Christian faith with the other realities of life.

The second danger is that of political reductionism (secularism). It restricts the relevance of the Christian faith and of the church to a strictly political area. This would be to reduce the church's mission "to the dimensions of a purely temporal project; its aims would be reduced to a man-centered goal; the salvation of which it is the messenger would be reduced to material well-being. Its activity, forgetful of all spiritual and religious preoccupation, would become initiatives of the political or social order" (EN 32; cf. Puebla 483).

The Christian faith has a dimension that is oriented toward society, but this dimension does not exhaust it. In its original meaning, its view is oriented to eternity, and from there it contemplates political activity and informs social action. From a point within history it proclaims and calls attention to a salvation that history itself cannot bring forth, a liberation so complete that it creates perfect freedom—and this has already begun here on earth.

These two reductionisms disrupt the transparency and unity of the incarnation process. The essential thing is to overcome this antithetical dualism and to establish a proper integration and an adequate way of relating human liberation to salvation in Jesus Christ (see EN 35; Puebla 485): "The Church strives always to insert the Christian struggle for liberation in the universal plan of salvation which it proclaims" (EN 38; cf. Puebla 483).[3]

The postulate of history and of the Christian faith is one of seeking a complete liberation, one that embraces every dimension of human life: physical and spiritual, personal and collective, historical and transcendent. No reductionism, whether it be spiritual or material in orientation, will do justice to the unity of humankind, to the unique design of the Creator, and to the central reality of Jesus' proclamation of the kingdom of God, which embraces creation as a whole.

THE LORD'S PRAYER IN ITS ARTICULATION

In the Lord's Prayer we encounter in a practical way the correct relationship between God and humankind, between heaven and earth, between the religious and the political, while maintaining unity throughout. The first part speaks on God's behalf: the Father, keeping his name holy, his kingdom, his holy will. The second part is concerned with human interests: our daily bread, forgiveness, ever-present temptation, ever-threatening evil.

The two parts constitute the one prayer of Jesus. God is not just interested in what belongs to him: his name, his kingdom, his divine will. He is also concerned about our affairs: bread, forgiveness, temptation, evil. Likewise we are not just concerned with what is vital to us: bread, forgiveness, temptation, evil. We are also open to the Father's concerns: sanctification of God's name, the coming of God's kingdom, the realization of God's will.

In the prayer of Jesus, God's concerns are not alien to those of human beings, and their concerns are not foreign to his. The impulse by which humankind is directed upward to heaven and supplicates God rebounds back to the earth and exerts its influence on earthly concerns. It is all one movement, enveloped in a profound unity. It is precisely this mutual involvement that generates the transparency to be found in the Lord's Prayer.

What God unifies—our preoccupation with him and our preoccupation with our own needs—let no one put asunder. God should never be betrayed for the sake of earthly needs; at the same time, it will never be legitimate to anathematize the limitations of our earthly existence because of the grandeur one finds in the reality of God. The two together constitute the material of prayer, supplication and praise. This is why we regard the Lord's Prayer as the prayer of integral liberation.

The reality encompassed in the Lord's Prayer is not a pretty picture but one of heavy conflict. Here the kingdom of God confronts the kingdom of Satan. The Father is near (he is our Father) but he is also remote (in heaven). Blasphemies are spoken in this world, which imposes on us the duty to sanctify God's name. The world is ruled by all sorts of evils that exacerbate our longing for the coming of God's kingdom, which is one of justice, love, and peace. The will of God is being violated, and we must give it concrete expression in our conduct. We pray for daily bread because there are many who do not have it. We ask that God forgive us our violations of fellowship, so that we can forgive those who have offended us. We pray for strength in temptations, because otherwise we would fail miserably. We cry out to be set free from evil, because otherwise we would turn our backs on the faith forever.

And in the midst of all this conflict the Lord's Prayer preserves an aura of joyful confidence and serene commitment, inasmuch as all of this is integrated into our encounter with the Father.

If we observe closely, we find that the Lord's Prayer deals with the major themes of the personal and social existence of all humankind in every era. There is no reference here to the church, not even a word about Jesus, his death, or his resurrection. God is at the center of the stage, where the other center—that of humanity and its needs—converges. Here we have what is essential. All the rest is corollary or commentary; it is appended to the essential. "Ask great things of God, and he will give you the small ones as well": this is a saying attributed to Jesus by a non-New Testament source, Clement of Alexandria (140–211 A.D.).[4] An important lesson has been preserved for us here: we must open our minds beyond our self-imposed horizons and widen our hearts beyond our self-imposed limits. Then we will find what is essential, so well translated by Jesus into the prayer that he taught us, the Lord's Prayer.

The *order* in which the petitions appear is not arbitrary. They begin with God and only then pass to us. It is in starting with God, from his vantage point, that we become concerned with our own needs. And in the midst of our sufferings we must be concerned with God. Suffering in heaven is connected with suffering on earth.

Any genuine liberation, from the Christian standpoint, starts with a deep encounter with God that moves us to committed action. It is here that we hear his voice as he tells us continually: Go! And, at the same time, any radical commitment to justice and love of others moves us back to God as the true Justice and supreme Love. Here also we hear his voice as he tells us: Come! Any liberation process that does not succeed in identifying the prime mover of every activity, which is God, does not achieve its purpose and does not reach completion. It is in the Lord's Prayer that we encounter this felicitous relationship. There are good reasons why the essence of Jesus' message—the Lord's Prayer—was not formulated as a doctrinal statement but as a prayer.

Our theological and spiritual meditation on the Lord's Prayer seeks to examine and integrate three levels of interpretation. The first level is that of the historical Jesus: What meaning did Jesus himself attribute to the words he spoke? What meaning does his prayer have? From earliest times the Lord's Prayer has been a kind of summary of the message of Jesus. In the form of a prayer it expresses his most radical and profound experience. At this first level we must take care to make use of the most certain findings of exegesis.

The second level of interpretation grows out of an examination of the theology of the apostolic church. The Lord's Prayer has been incorporated into the Gospels of Matthew and Luke in the context of a community prayer. Christians prayed the Lord's Prayer at all their meetings. They assigned a particular meaning to the words in relation to their own life context. It is reflected in the way they edited the gospels and in the theological accents that they imparted to the words of Jesus. Here we must seek to understand the Lord's Prayer in the light of the general theology of the New Testament.

Finally, we will seek to interpret the Lord's Prayer as we hear it in our own day. When we recite the Lord's Prayer today, we inevitably read into it the concerns of our own faith community. Today's Christian community seeks to live and reflect upon the Christian faith in its liberating dimension, in view of the enormous social inequities to which our brothers and sisters are subject. We experience the Lord's Prayer as the perfect prayer of integral liberation.

There are classical commentaries on the Lord's Prayer by the church fathers, such as those by Tertullian (c. 160–225), St. Cyprian (200–258), Origen (185–253), St. Cyril of Jerusalem (died 386), St. Gregory of Nyssa (died 394), St. Ambrose of Milan (339–397), Theodore of Mopsuestia (died 428), St. Augustine (354–430), and St. Francis of Assisi (1181–1226).[5] When we study them, we realize that their authors attach to their commentary on the Lord's Prayer a commentary on their own life, complete with the aspirations and anxieties typical of their times.

There is nothing more natural: to read means to *re*read. If we are to gain any meaning out of the past, we must energize it in terms of the present.

With an awareness of these processes, which are part of any learning experience, we accept the goal and the limitations of our own commentary, located as it is within this situation of our own, so characterized by oppression and by the longing for total liberation. Reciting the Lord's Prayer means evoking the words of his day and recalling the realities of our own. And, surprisingly, we discover ourselves to be the neighbors and contemporaries of Jesus Christ.

2

Praying the Lord's Prayer
with Real Meaning

Our neighborhood has a high concentration of migrants. They came from their own locality in search of a better life, or even for a way to make any kind of living. And they work, they work hard, when they can find employment. They work, but their hands are still empty. The difference is that they make more money for their employers here.

How do they survive? First, they spend as little as possible. They eat beans and, when available, rice, cereal, and eggs. Sometimes a little chicken; any other kind of meat almost never. Clothes and shoes are things they buy on rare occasions. Major purchases are seldom made, and payments are by installment. Even then, there is nothing. They have to work harder. And the whole family goes to work: father, mother, children. The young generation grows up hit or miss, with no care and no affection.

Living here is difficult. Real home life is almost nonexistent. Residents hole up where they can, in apartments and shacks. There are five persons to a room and two families to a shack. Living as they do, piled on top of each other, there is no place to throw their garbage. The water supply comes from the creek where the sewage goes. All the water is contaminated. Who could be healthy under such circumstances? They work hard, eat little, live like animals, and put up with all this filth. Who could stand it? They are subject to all the diseases of the poor: worms, malnutrition, dehydration, tuberculosis, bronchial pneumonia, meningitis. One disease is added to another and the net result is a short life span.

We are just an aggregation of scattered organisms; we are not a people. There is no social life for us. There is no help for our economic needs. There is no one to fight for our wages, control the escalating prices, or inspect the spoiled produce. This is reality for us: hard, ugly, and dreary.
—Report of the Santa Margarida basic ecclesial community,
on the outskirts of São Paulo,
published in SEDOC 11 (1978): 345–48

Prayer is not the first thing that a person does. Before praying, one experiences an existential shock. Only then does prayer pour forth, whether in the form of supplication, or of an act of thanksgiving, or of worship.[6]

It is no different with the prayer that Jesus taught us to pray, the Lord's Prayer. This prayer can be understood only from the context of Jesus' own profound experience, an experience translated into his words and his deeds. In fact, the Lord's Prayer—as Tertullian, a third-century commentator, wrote—is a summary of the whole gospel *(breviarium totius evangelii).*[7] What "existential shock" underlies the Lord's Prayer and the good news of Jesus?

THE WORLD'S OPEN VEINS: A GROANING CREATION (ROM. 8:22)

As we look around us we are struck by a blatant paradox: alongside the unquestionable goodness, beauty, and grace that are found everywhere, we stumble over the undeniable evil, brokenness, and perversity that corrupt humankind and its world. Suffering is a stumbling block to us. Reality is a tragic thing, bringing tears to our eyes. Humanity is aggressive; its fundamental law is: "my life or yours." Catastrophes, elemental convulsions, and disorders of cosmic dimensions are a threat to any equilibrium that might be achieved.

The world bleeds from every vein; the blood flows freely. "The whole created universe groans in all its parts as if in the pangs of childbirth," says St. Paul (Rom. 8:22). Creation is not its own master but has been made subject to diabolical forces. Not even in our wildest fantasies do we behold societies where there are no martyrologies, no massacres, no collective crimes. We cannot find creation beneath the rainbow of God's peace; idols rise up everywhere, demanding our worship and seeking to supplant the true and living God.

MISERABLE CREATURE THAT I AM, WHO IS THERE TO RESCUE ME . . . ? (ROM. 7:24)

The contradiction experienced at the human level is even more dreadful. The cry of Job ascends to heaven from one generation to the next, and every ear hears its cry. Everyone can understand how relationships with the world, with work, with other persons, with love, and with justice have come to be severed. This scission cuts across not only social structures but the human heart as well: "The good which I want to do, I fail to do; but what I do is the wrong which is against my will" (Rom. 7:20).

The urge to dominate is never satisfied, the instinct for destruction is never exhausted, and the number of sacrificial victims is never enough. Not even daily life can escape the shadows cast by the absurd, the enigmatic, and the cruelty of life. The final chapter to the history of pain has not been written.

Not even the Son of Man was spared "loud cries and tears" (Heb. 5:7), anguish (Luke 22:44), and learning "in the school of suffering" (Heb. 5:8). We hear the cry he raises to heaven, expressing his abandonment by God: "My God, my God, why hast thou forsaken me" (Mark 15:34). Paul's exclamatory question captures the heaviness of human tragedy: "Miserable creature that I am, who is there to rescue me . . . ?"

THE CREATED UNIVERSE: WAITING WITH EAGER EXPECTATION (ROM. 8:19)

In confronting this macabre situation there are three attitudes we can adopt: revolt, resignation, or hope against hope.

Revolt

There are those who revolt against the tragic condition of the world and raise their fists to heaven: God does not exist and has never existed! We have more questions to ask him than he has to ask us! The nerve endings of contemporary humanity are charged with accusations against God.[8] If there is a criminal—some say— who should be brought to the bar of justice, it is God. He is omnipotent, therefore he could save his children, and he does not. He delivers us up to torture and to violent death. He behaves like a criminal.

Others cry: I categorically refuse to accept a creation of God in which innocent creatures must suffer. He is a Moloch who thrives on tears, on mangled bodies, on executions by the sword. Such a God is unacceptable!

He is the father of nobody, said Marcion, a second-century heretic, in expressing his interpretation of God's lack of love and the impossibility of loving him as we view the tragedy of our world. Arnold Toynbee, the famous English historian of modern times, was tormented with "a sour note in the Lord's Prayer." He wrote: "God cannot be good and omnipotent at the same time. These are alternative conceptions of God's nature, and mutually exclusive. We have to choose between them."[9]

Reconciling the existence of God as love with the injustice found in the world has always been a challenge to reason since the times of Job. No matter how much such geniuses as St. Augustine or Leibnitz contrive arguments to exonerate God and explain suffering, the suffering still does not go away. Understanding suffering does not do away with it, just as listening to the recitation of recipes does nothing to dispel hunger.

We can understand Job's bluntness with all the "friends" who tried to explain the meaning of suffering: "You like fools are smearing truth with your falsehoods and stitching a patchwork of lies, one and all. Ah, if you would only be silent and let your silence be your wisdom! . . . But for my part I would speak with the Almighty and am ready to argue with God" (Job 13: 4–5, 3).

Resignation

Then there are those who give way to a *metaphysical* resignation: the ultimate principle of reality is good and evil in coexistence. It is God and the devil at the same time. We are subject to their caprices. The world and humankind are an arena where the contradiction inherent in the Supreme Reality is acted out.

There are those who allow for two principles eternally at war with each other: the principle of Good and the principle of Evil. The solution to the problem is not in overcoming evil but in striving to achieve a balance between good and evil, between integration and disintegration. Humankind must get used to living without hope.

There are others who submit to an *ethico-religious* resignation. In God there is no darkness, only light. Evil is done by human beings; they are not victims of fate or of an irresistible temptation, but agents of a freedom that can be frustrated by their own free will. The story of the fall of the human race (Gen. 3) seeks to emphasize this human responsibility. Human beings are so bogged down in their abuse of freedom that they become prisoners to it; they suffer from their historical inability to create a reasonable and comradely life standard. Persons must cultivate patience with themselves and recognize themselves as sinners.

Ecclesiasticus (Sirach) provides us with the prototype of the ascetical, resigned person. There are no illusions here concerning human life or the future of humankind.[10] He calls out to the reader of every age: "Hold fast to him, never desert him. . . . Bear every hardship that is sent you; be patient under humiliation, whatever the cost" (Sir. 2:3, 4). God will not remain remote and indifferent to the cries of the oppressed; he has decided to set them free (Exod. 3:8). The curses pronounced by the poor are heard by God (Sir. 4:6).

The New Testament portrays God in terms of his solidarity in suffering. The Messiah is the just sufferer, the incarnation of the Servant who "bore our sufferings," who was "tormented and humbled by suffering" (Isa. 53: 3–4 = Matt. 8:17). Because he himself "passed through the test of suffering, he is able to help"

(Heb. 2:18). This solidarity does not eliminate suffering, but creates fellowship among those who suffer, makes resignation bearable and protects against despair, through communion with the one who is greater and stronger who also suffered (Col. 1:24; Rom. 8:17; 1 Peter 4:13). But despite all this, the sores remain open and continue to bleed. Again we say: "Miserable creature that I am, who will rescue me?"

Hope against Hope

And then there are those who hope against hope. They are no less realistic than the others; for them also, the world is a vale of tears. They are always being harassed by personal and historical absurdities. Nonetheless, despite the record of suffering in history, they testify to a sense of triumph. In the climax of development and at the foundation of the world, it is not chaos that reigns but cosmos; not the dissociation of everything but its congregation in love. Creation is not evil because it is creation but because it has been sullied by the irresponsibility of human freedom. And they hope for the full revelation of light that will dispel all the darkness. In the language of the Scriptures they hear promises: "Swords will be beaten into mattocks and spears into pruning knives; nation shall not lift sword against nation" (Isa. 2:4; Mic. 4:3). "All the boots of trampling soldiers and the garments fouled with blood shall become a burning mass, fuel for fire" (Isa. 9:5), for "he shall judge the poor with justice and defend the humble in the land with equity" (Isa. 11:4), and there will be a reconciliation between humankind and nature and other life forces (Isa. 11:6–9). Finally "they shall never again feel hunger or thirst," or cosmic disturbances (Rev. 7:16), for God will be "a God-with-us, he will wipe every tear from our eyes, and there will be an end to death, and to mourning and crying and pain; for the old order will have passed away" (Rev. 21:3, 4). And then there will be a new heaven and a new earth (Rev. 21:1).

This is the language of utopia and of hope. The world's melancholy experience will always be in contradiction to this liberating vision. But the longing will never die; the fantasy is more real than are the brute facts. Thus there will always be spirits that are immunized against the virus of despair and impotence. The prophets of all ages become the cavalry of hope and rise above the horizon like stars of a better tomorrow.

The solution lies in the future; it is only in hope that we have been saved (Rom. 8:24). The evil times continue, and so does our shame. How long, O Lord?

FOR THOSE WHO DWELL IN THE DARKNESS OF DEATH THERE DAWNED A GREAT LIGHT (MATT. 4:16)

It is against this background that we are to understand the appearance of Jesus and the proclamation of his gospel: "The time has come; the kingdom of God is upon you; repent and believe this good news" (Mark 1:15). God has determined to intervene, to put an end to the diabolical situation, and to inaugurate a new order. He is not just proclaiming a future event. He speaks of the present: "Today, in your very hearing this text has come true" (Luke 4:21). The kingdom of God constitutes the central message of the historical Jesus. He never defined just exactly what this kingdom is. But it is not just a high-sounding word; it brings joy to all the people, it is already in our midst, and its total manifestation is imminent. It modifies the reality of this world, so that the blind see, the lame walk, the dead are raised, and sins are pardoned. The poor, the afflicted, and those who have been denied justice are the primary beneficiaries. The best thing we can do is change our lifestyle and adjust to the new situation. The kingdom does not come mechanically. This is not just some theory to explain the tragedies of the world but is a doing, a changing, a new praxis.

Thus the expression "kingdom of God" is a literary device—a synonym for the proper name of God, which the Jews, out of respect, did not dare to pronounce. In other words, "the Lord shall reign forever" (Exod. 15:18) is a way of saying that God appears as the only Lord of history, restores the order that has been violated, deposes the powerful who have lorded it over others, raises up the humble who have been humiliated, and does away with the last enemy, death (1 Cor. 15:26).

For God to free his creation in this way, human beings must participate, and not just as bystanders; otherwise the kingdom of

God would be unhuman and an imposition. As we well know, this world is not that kingdom; as God intervenes and we are converted and likewise act upon the world, it is transformed *in situ* into the kingdom of God. So then, it is both a bestowal and an assignment; a gift and a conquest; a present and a future; a celebration and a promise.[11] Hope is now renewed within tormented hearts: "The people that lived in darkness saw a great light" (Matt. 4:16), and that light is Jesus himself, the kingdom personified. Where he is, the kingdom also breaks in.

The plenary manifestation of the kingdom is very near. Jesus shares the conviction of his contemporaries that the total regeneration of everything is imminent. He is not concerned about the when or the how *(tempora et momenta)*, but is concerned rather with the "watching": we must pay attention because the kingdom will come like a thief.[12] And the kingdom of God is being built in opposition to the kingdom of this world. With Jesus the kingdom bursts forth, but the macabre situation of the world still continues. Thus the basic contradiction between the perversion of creation and the wholeness of the new heaven and new earth continues, at least for a brief time.

The apocalyptic of Jesus' day instilled a profound experience of this tension and sense of expectancy. If one does not understand this apocalyptic horizon, it is difficult to understand the historical Jesus, the abruptness of his proclamation, the hope that he aroused, the urgency of the times that it presupposes, and the radicality of the conversion needed as preparation for the supreme crisis.

Acceptance of this global, grass-roots restructuring of reality, such as is promised with the emergence of the kingdom of God, likewise requires faith. Jesus calls for this explicitly and on many occasions: believe this good news (Mark 1:15; Matt. 17:20). It is not at all obvious that *utopia* ("nowhere") is being transformed into *topia* ("somewhere")—that is, into a flowering reality. The Second Epistle of St. Peter reiterates for us the complaint of Jesus' hearers: "Our fathers have been laid to rest, but still everything continues as it always has been since the world began" (2 Peter 3:4). Is it fair to feed your hearers the promises of dreamers? Is it not more sensible and mature to accept reality with all its contradictions? And yet, there are those who go on hoping despite all the factual evidence. As Job said: "If he would slay me, I should not hesitate; I should still argue my case to his face" (Job 13:15). The heart cannot be cheated forever. Evidence that this is true is to be seen in the resurrection of Jesus: here we see the emergence of the first unmistakable sign of that new heaven and new earth, as the new Adam comes forth (1 Cor. 15:45). Here is perfect liberation!

INSTRUCTED BY JESUS AND BY THE SPIRIT, WE DARE TO SAY: "ABBA! FATHER!" (GAL. 4:6)

The existential shock, referred to above, constitutes the substratum of the Lord's Prayer, the prayer that Jesus taught the apostles. Here we find a crystallization of the very essence of Jesus' experience and the basic landmarks of his teachings. This experience is concentrated in the awareness that the final catastrophe is imminent;[13] the days of this evil world are numbered. But the message is not that of John the Baptist, one of judgment and punishment; it is the message of joy that comes from the final establishment of the kingdom.

In the interim we live in a time of transition; we find a brief waiting period between the termination of the old and the beginning of the new. It is a time of crisis, of temptations, of decisions. Everything is at stake. What can we cling to? How shall we properly prepare for it?

This is the historical context that provides the framework of the Lord's Prayer. Any reconstruction of the original meaning of Jesus' prayer must start with this emergency-type situation. Let us examine in greater detail the occasion on which it was uttered, its historicity, and its structure.[14]

The Lord's Prayer has been transmitted in two versions: a longer one in Matthew (6:9–13) and a shorter one in Luke (11:2–4). We reproduce the two texts here, in parallel:

Matthew	Luke
Our Father in heaven,	Father,[c]
thy name be hallowed;	thy name be hallowed;
thy kingdom come,	thy kingdom come.
thy will be done,	
on earth as in heaven.	

Give us today our daily bread.[a]	Give us each day our daily bread.[d]
Forgive us the wrong we have done,	And forgive us our sins,
as we have forgiven those who have wronged us.	for we too forgive all who have done us wrong.
And do not bring us to the test,	And do not bring us to the test.
but save us from the evil one.[b]	

[a] *or* our bread for the morrow   [c] *or* Our Father in heaven
[b] *or* from evil   [d] *or* our bread for the morrow

Why is it that during the years 75–85 A.D., the time when these two Gospels were put into their present form, the Lord's Prayer was transmitted in two versions? Did Jesus teach two versions on different occasions? The specialists tell us that what the evangelists have transmitted to us is the form found in their respective communities.[15]

Historically speaking, this is not—in its present form—a simple prayer of Jesus that we could retranslate from the original Greek text into the original Aramaic text—that is, into the exact words that Jesus spoke.[16] Rather, this is a prayer of Jesus that has been handed down and assimilated in various forms in the various Christian communities of early times, as the Didache also testifies.[17] The historical formula given by Jesus himself is not accessible to us. We know it only in these two versions.

Which one would be the earlier form, closer to the original? Luke gives a shorter form that contains everything that Matthew says in a more expanded form. According to the laws that govern the transmission of a liturgical text, the respected biblical scholar Joachim Jeremias says: "We know that when a shorter redaction is integrally contained in a longer one, the shorter one should be considered the original."[18] Thus Luke would be closer to the original.

The difference in context between Matthew and Luke helps us to understand the textual differences in the two versions. Both involve a context of prayer. Matthew 6:6–15, where the Lord's Prayer appears, is a catechesis on prayer, probably used with neophytes ("do not pray with the ostentation of the Pharisees, or the wordiness of the gentiles, and forgive if you wish to be forgiven"). We also find a catechesis in Luke 11:1–13, but written in another style. Whereas Matthew's Gospel is slanted to Jews who know how to pray and need only learn how to pray correctly, Luke's teaching is for gentiles who do not pray and must be initiated into a prayer life. Hence Matthew is more liturgical, with a tendency to expand, and Luke has a shorter version, with a tendency to concentrate on the essentials. In both cases we have a poetical format, with rhythm and rhyme: something to be read aloud by a group. Other differences will be discussed when we comment on the individual verses.

The roots of the Lord's Prayer are definitely to be found in Judaism, even though Jesus' prayer is very formal and concise, lacking the more rhetorical style found in the Shemoneh Esre (a prayer with "eighteen" benedictions, actually nineteen), the Qaddish (prayers recited at the end of celebrations), and the various types of rabbinical prayers.[19]

Luke's version gives us a glimpse of how the Lord's Prayer originated: "Once, in a certain place, Jesus was at prayer. When he ceased, one of his disciples said, 'Lord, teach us to pray, as John taught his disciples.' He answered, 'When you pray, say, Father . . .'" (Luke 11:1–2). The reference to John (the Baptist) hints at the historical background of the narration. The request, "teach us to pray," is equivalent to saying: "give us a summary of your teaching." We know that all religious groups in Jesus' day had their own form of prayer.[20] The prayer serves the function of a kind of creed that bestows unity and identity on the group. Thus the small group saying the prayer of Jesus felt itself a part of the total eschatological community created by Jesus.[21] Thus we may think of his prayer as summing up the quintessence of his purpose and mission. It makes reference to the Father—the intimately personal invocation of the historical Jesus—the coming of the kingdom, the divine providence that provides the essentials for biological life (bread) and for social life (forgiveness, healing of broken relationships), and the crisis of temptation.

Matthew's version gives a better definition of the significance of the Lord's Prayer as the form of prayer that Jesus stresses—distinguishing it from other prayer practices—by inserting it in a discourse on other practices of piety: giving alms (6:1–4) and fasting (6:16–18).

When we examine the structure of the Lord's Prayer, we immediately note two movements in opposite directions. One is upward, toward heaven: the Father, his holiness, his kingdom, his will; the other is earthward: bread, forgiveness, temptation, evil. Three optatives are directed heavenward; three petitions are made for the earth. Faith has two eyes: one that looks up to God and contemplates his light; another that is turned toward the earth and discerns the tragedy of darkness. On the one hand we sense the impulse of the inner person (spirit) straining upward (to God); on the other hand we experience the weight of the outer person (the flesh) that bends us downward (to the earth).

All of reality, in its greatness and in its obscurity, lies before God. In the Lord's Prayer both the infinite longing for heaven (Our Father in heaven) and its earthly roots (our daily bread) are offered to God on behalf of the world.

We know that in the primitive church the Lord's Prayer belonged to a "secret discipline"; it was only for those who had been initiated into the Christian mystery. It is in the light of this that we are to understand the introductory liturgical formulas, full of reverence and respect, that were used until quite recent times: "Admonished by your teachings and instructed by divine institution, we dare to say: our Father" (from the Roman Missal, prior to the reforms of Vatican II). The Lord's Prayer confronts us with the "secret" of Jesus communicated to the apostles. The prayer that our Lord taught us cannot be prayed in just any way and with just any attitude. It presupposes a perception of all this world's tragedy; as we suffer in the passion of history, it promises us liberation.

To pray the Lord's Prayer requires an act of faith, hope, and love. In order to pray it, as Tertullian noted, we must profess faith in God as Father despite his silence, his remoteness, and our overwhelming environment of suffering.[22] He is a kind Father. Looking about us at the world, we cannot confirm this, but we believe. It is also an act of hope: may your kingdom come, may your will be done forever! We firmly expect the Father to wipe away all tears and rework the structures of his creation. Then, and only then, will the shalom of God shine upon us. And it is an act of love. We do not just say Father, but *our* Father. Here we find all the warmth and intimacy of love; the word "Abba" that Jesus uses means something like "Dad," "Daddy," "dearest Father"!

Perhaps we may not have the courage to call God by such a familiar name. But the Spirit of Jesus, infused in our hearts, prays on our behalf: Abba, Father (Gal. 4:6; Rom. 8:15). For we recognize ourselves as sons and daughters in his Son because with Jesus we make up the eschatological fellowship and because the Spirit moves us so that we pray: Our Father!

3

Our Father in Heaven

Father,
descend from the heavens, forgive
the prayers that my ancestors taught me,
poor persons who are now at rest,
who could only wash and clean,
who could only be concerned, all day long,
with what they could wear,
who could only spend the nights in watching, painfully,
praying, asking you for things,
softly murmuring their complaints.

Descend from the heavens if you exist, descend,
for I am dying of hunger in this little corner,
not knowing why I had to be born,
looking upon my swollen hands,
having no work, having nothing;
come down a bit, and look at
this broken shoe,
this anguish, this empty stomach,
this city that has no bread for my mouth,
the fever that eats at my flesh,
thus to fall asleep,
under the rain, tortured by the cold, persecuted.

I tell you that I do not understand, Father,
come down, touch my soul,
look upon my heart,

I am not a robber or an assassin, I am a child,
and for that they give me blow after blow;
I tell you that I do not understand, Father;
come down, if you exist,
for I seek to be resigned to myself and cannot,
and I am filling up with anger
and preparing myself to do battle,
and crying out until my throat fills with blood,
for I cannot take it any longer, I have feelings
and I am a man.
Come down! What will you do with your creature, Father?
A mad animal who chews the paving stones of the street?

> —*"Oração de um desocupado"*
> *("Prayer of an Unemployed Man"),*
> *by Juan Gelman, Argentine poet*

In our initial comments on the Lord's Prayer, we attempted to recreate the existential atmosphere that gave birth to the prayer of Jesus. Underlying this is the impression created by the paradox of this world: God's good creation is dominated by the diabolical forces that torment our lives and threaten our hopes. The kingdom of God represents the reversal of this situation; out of the heart of darkness bursts a liberating ray of light. The kingdom is already at hand and is already happening in our midst! A great crisis is being prepared, a final decision is imminent. In the midst of this high pressure and the painful suffering of this world, Jesus teaches us to pray: Our Father in heaven.

As we look at the deformed and deviant course of this world, it is not in the least evident that God is a beloved Father (Abba). We need faith, hope, and love to overcome the temptation to skepticism and revolt, as we repeat with Jesus: Our Father. If he had not taught us this and asked us to pray it, then certainly we never would have dared to call out, with such confidence and intimacy, "Dear Father." We recite the Lord's Prayer and we live it each day, despite all the contradictions, because we are heirs of the inexhaustible source of hope in Jesus, which is opposed to all evidence to the contrary. Because of this hope and this confidence, the darkness is no less dark, but it is less absurd. The dangers have not been removed, but our courage has been strengthened.

We shall develop our reflections at two levels. First of all, we shall seek to enter into the thinking and experience of Jesus.[23] Secondly, we shall attempt to pray the Lord's Prayer in the context of the oppressive forces that weigh down upon contemporary humanity and make its life unhappy.

UNIVERSALITY OF THE EXPERIENCE OF GOD AS FATHER

The fatherhood of God—the central theme of the kingdom of God as taught by Jesus—has universal roots and reaches the most archaic levels of our internal archeology. Both the old and the new are present in Jesus. On the one hand he adopts what is universally human and brings it to its ultimate culmination. On the other hand he introduces an originality all his own. The utterance, "Dear Father," resonates with one of the most ancient archetypes of all human experience, and at the same time it reveals the unique and intimate relationship that Jesus enjoyed with God.

For the sake of clarity, we shall distinguish three modalities in the use of the expression "father" when applied to God: as designation, as declaration, and as invocation.[24]

A feature of the ABCs of any authentic religious experience is the unthematic perception of an offspring/parent relationship between humanity and divinity. Religious persons see themselves as the image and likeness of their God. They perceive of themselves as children, and they think of God as father or as mother.[25] Primitive peoples, such as the Pygmies, the Australian aborigines, and the Bantu, all the way to the most highly developed peoples of antiquity, such as the Egyptians, Assyrians, Greeks, Romans, and those of the Indus Valley, all designated God as father.[26] This expression is used to translate the idea of absolute dependence on God, and at the same time to denote an inviolable respect and unrestricted trust. Persons give thanks to divinity for their existence and relate to it as a child relates to mother or father, or as a young person relates to one who is older.

In more primitive times the expression "father" was less associated with generation and creation, which implies a material basis for the image and idea of the family. In a more primitive social organization based on groups of elders and groups of younger persons, the expression "father" is a translation of the authority, power, and wisdom of the elders. Thus we are dealing with a designation and title conveying honor.

"Father" then came to mean the creator and generator of everything; the Romans regarded Jupiter and other gods (Mars, Saturn) as *pater, parens, et genitor.*[27] Here divinity appears as universal lord and king. Homer, in his *Iliad*, speaks of the chief Greek divinity: "Zeus, father, you rule over gods and humans."[28] Aristotle, in his *Politics*, declares that the power of the father over his children is like that of a king.[29]

So then, the designation "father" must be understood in the light of these two activities: as generator-creator and as the highest authority and lord, not a sinister or frightening master but one who is approachable and full of kindness. Thus we are to understand the famous Sumerian hymn of Ur, dedicated to the moon god Nanna, which reads: "King, merciful father, in whose hand is the life of the whole earth," or the hymn to Marduk, which reads: "His wrath is like a tempest, and his serenity and kindness are like that of a merciful father."[30] Here we find the same divine qualities that were experienced by Israel: the God as father, possessing absolute authority and infinite mercy.

With reference to Israel and Israel's relation to God as father, there are some specific problems. The Old Testament is slow to represent God as father. There is a basic difficulty that justifies the rare occurrence—only fifteen times—of the name "father" applied to Yahweh.[31] Biblical authors were waging a constant war against the anthropology of the Middle East nations that held that human beings have their origin in a god (or the blood of a god) who was expelled from heaven and died; in other words, they maintained that humans are divine. Biblical faith would not accept this theistic anthropology: it is an indiscriminate mixture of God and humankind, divinizing what dare not be divinized (the creature) and profaning what dare not be profaned (God). This is why the sacred authors tended to avoid the use of a father-son relationship to express the way God relates to humans.[32] But, despite this, the figure of God as Father still emerges from the Old Testament background of Israel's experience of God.

The experiential basis for this is that of a God who takes his place at the side of the fathers of the nation to assist them in their journey (which is the significance of "Yahweh"). Thus he is represented as the "God of our fathers," of Abraham, Isaac, and Jacob. God makes a covenant with his people and gives them the Law as an expression of his covenant and way of holiness. He is a God—and this is unique in the comparative history of religions—who is represented by a name but not an image, with a connotation but with no denotation: "I am who I am." This is the true name of Yahweh, a name that makes no appeal to fantasy, to dream language, or to symbolism, thus nipping in the bud any attempt to establish anthropomorphism and idolatry. "If . . . they ask me your name, what shall I say? God answered: I AM who I am. Tell them that I AM has sent you to them" (Exod. 3:13–14). Thus we conclude that Yahweh was not initially experienced as Father.

By the same token, the experience of having been chosen as a people from among other peoples, whom Yahweh has liberated from Egypt and thus won for himself, allowed Israel to designate God as Father. This designation is allowed only by virtue of its creation as a people. In Exodus, God himself says: "Israel is my firstborn son" (Exod. 4:22). Israel recognizes that it owes its existence as a people to God: "Is he [Yahweh] not your father who formed you? Did he not make you and establish you?" (Deut. 32:6; see also Num. 11:12; Isa. 63:16, 64:8; Mal. 2:10).

This allusion to God as Father is expanded by the prophets. They developed a radical sense of ethics. If God is Father, we owe it to him to behave as submissive, obedient children. But this is not the end of it. God himself, speaking through the prophetic word, declares himself Father: "A son honors his father, and a slave goes in fear of his master. If I am a father, where is the honor due to me? And if I am a master, where is the fear due to me? So says the Lord of hosts" (Mal. 1:6).

The same criticism is found in Jeremiah: "Not so long since, you called me 'Father, dear friend of my youth'" (Jer. 3:4), and yet, God says, "You have played the harlot" (3:1).

Jeremiah depicts God's feelings:

> I said, How gladly would I treat you as a son,
>   giving you a pleasant land,
>   a patrimony fairer than that of any nation!
> I said, You shall call me Father
>   and never cease to follow me.
> But like a woman who is unfaithful to her lover,
> so you, Israel, were unfaithful to me.
>   This is the very word of the LORD [3:19–20].

As the prophets speak in the name of a repentant people, what emerges is an explicit declaration of God as a compassionate Father:

> Look down from heaven and behold
> from the heights where thou dwellest holy and glorious.
>   Where is thy zeal, thy valor,
>   thy burning and tender love?
> Stand not aloof; for thou art our father,
> though Abraham does not know us
>   nor Israel acknowledge us.
> Thou, LORD, art our father;
>   thy name is our Ransomer from of old
>   [Isa. 63:15–16; see also Isa. 64:8; Jer. 3:4].

It is Jeremiah who expresses in the name of God the promptness of his paternal pardon: "Is Ephraim still my dear son, a child in whom I delight? As often as I turn my back on him I still remember him; and so my heart yearns for him. I am filled with tenderness toward him. This is the very word of the Lord" (21:20). As may be seen, the paternal relationship of God is so tender and intimate that God emerges not only as father but also as mother (see Isa. 49:15, 66:13). We feel the same caring here as in the home of our parents: "When Israel was a boy, I loved him; I called my son out of Egypt" (Hos. 11:1).

Despite all these impressive passages, the name "father" applied to God is not a definitive one in the Old Testament.[33] It is one name among others, many of which occur more frequently and are of greater importance, such as Lord, King, Judge, Creator. The expression "father" usually occurs in conjunction with the sacred name Yahweh and other names for God. The relationship would seem to apply to the people as a whole and not to any one person in particular.

The invocation of God as "my Father" or "our Father" never occurs directly in any prayer in the Old Testament.[34] The language is always indirect, as though there were a promise that someday was to be fulfilled. "He shall cry to me, Thou art my Father, my God, and the rock of my salvation" (Ps. 89:26). It was for Jesus of Nazareth to introduce this innovation and thus to bring to its profoundest intimacy the religious relationship of the human person finding itself a child as it experiences God as Father.

ORIGINALITY OF JESUS' EXPERIENCE: ABBA

Calling God "Abba" ("dearest father, dad, papa") is one of the most salient characteristics of the historical Jesus. *Abba* belongs to the language of childhood and the home, a diminutive of endearment that was also used by adults for their own fathers and older persons for whom they wished to show respect.[35] It had never entered into anyone's head to use this familiar, commonplace expression to refer to God. That would be failing to show respect to Yahweh and would scandalize godly persons. And yet Jesus, in all his prayers that have come down to us, addressed God with the expression "Dearest Father" (*Abba*). We find this expression in the mouth of Jesus 170 times in the Gospels (4 times in Mark, 15 in Luke, 42 in Matthew, and 109 in John). And the Greek New Testament preserves the Aramaic expression *Abba*, thus retaining this remarkable example of Jesus' audacity (Rom. 8:15; Gal. 4:6).

"Abba" alludes to the secret of Jesus' intimate relationship with God and his mission in the name of God. "Jesus thus spoke with God as a small child speaks with its father—with simplicity, intimacy, confidence."[36]

Of course, Jesus also knew the other names of God found in the tradition of his people. His use of "Abba" in no way detracts from a respectful, serious attitude toward God, as may be seen in many of his parables where God is shown as King, Lord, Judge, and Vindicator. But all of these are subordinate to the great rainbow arc of God's incomparable goodness and tenderness as seen in "Dear Father." All the other titles are *common* nouns or names for God; Father is God's proper name. Jesus has received this revelation from God himself: "Everything has been entrusted to me by my Father; and no one knows . . . the Father but the Son and those to whom the Son may choose to reveal him" (Matt. 11:27).

The eschatological promise made by Yahweh to his people has at last been fulfilled, the promise that is implicit in the tetragram YHWH revealed to Moses: "But on that day my people shall know my name; they shall know that it is I who speak: here am I" (Isa. 52:6).[37] The name Yahweh means "I am here" (it is I who am with you). And what this actually means is now evident as Jesus calls upon God as "Dear Papa." Thus "Abba" signifies "God is in our midst; he comes near us with his mercy, kindness, and tenderness." We entrust ourselves to his care just as a small child confidently and serenely entrusts itself to its father or mother.

Jesus does not invoke God only as *my* dear Father, but also teaches us to invoke him as *our* heavenly Father, with the same confidence that he himself does. It is with this childlike approach that we open the gates of the kingdom of heaven: "Unless you turn around and become like children, you shall never enter the kingdom of Heaven" (Matt. 18:3). And this Father is not just Father of the faithful, as we read in Psalm 103:13 ("As a father has compassion on his children, so has the Lord compassion on all who fear him"), but he is the Father of everyone without discrimination: "He himself is kind to the ungrateful and the wicked" (Luke 6:35) and "causes his sun to rise on the bad as well as the good, and his rain to fall on the honest and the dishonest alike" (Matt. 5:45).

This closeness and intimacy with God that is implied in the expression "Abba" is identical with the "closeness" of the kingdom of God. Thus the name Father applied to God pertains to the content of Jesus' teachings as centralized in the theme of the kingdom.[38] This unrestricted trust in the Father's providence and total abandonment to the cause of the kingdom are not parallel subjects. On the contrary, the confidence that persons achieve by realizing they are in the hands of the Father frees them from the preoccupations of this world, so that they may aspire to the one thing necessary, which is the kingdom of God (Luke 12:29–31). The idea of a provident Father ("your heavenly Father knows that you need" [these things—i.e., food, drink, clothing, etc.]—Matt. 6:32) is incorporated into the more extensive theme of the kingdom of God, which is imminent and has already begun to emerge in the message, deeds, and person of Jesus: "Set your hearts on his kingdom, and these other things will be given you as well" (Luke 12:31). The benevolent goodness of God is now seen in its plenary form: it extends not only to creation ("Are not sparrows two a penny? Yet without your Father's leave not one of them can fall to the ground. As for you, even the hairs of your head have all been counted"—Matt. 10:29–30), but history has now in principle achieved its fulfillment: "Have no fear, little flock, for your Father has chosen to give you the Kingdom" (Luke 12:32).

GOD THE FATHER: NEAR AND YET FAR AWAY

When Christians, at Jesus' prompting, pray the Lord's Prayer, they are not thinking primarily of a creator of a fathomless mystery from which everything else emanates. This idea is not exactly absent, but it is not the catalyst for religious experience. The innovation is to be found in the recovery of what has been experienced by Jesus and transmitted to us through the apostles—namely, that God is here as a Father who cares for his children, that he has a heart that is sensitive to our problems, that his eye is always upon our sufferings, and that his ear is open to our cries. A person is not a digit or subparticle lost in the terrifying infinity of space, but is someone enveloped in the solicitous love of God. We know his name and keep it in our heart. We can trust ourselves to the care of this Father-God. We may abandon both life and death to him, because whatever is happening and will happen is for our good.

Drawing this close to the Father, we can feel that we are his sons and daughters. Here, being a son or daughter is not a causal category (a person biologically descendant from the Father), but mostly a category of personal relationship.[39] The son or daughter is so to the extent that they cultivate both intimacy and trust with respect to the Father. Paul says it very well:

> To prove that you are sons, God has sent into our hearts the Spirit of his Son, crying "Abba! Father!" You are therefore no longer a slave but a son, and if a son, then also by God's own act an heir [Gal. 4:6–7].

> The Spirit you have received is not a spirit of slavery leading you back into a life of fear, but a Spirit that makes us sons, enabling us to cry, "Abba! Father!" [Rom. 8:15].

Thus a new community is emerging here, one of brothers and sisters in the elder brother, Jesus; all of us are sons and daughters in the Son, and we are encouraged to call out with the same cry as the Son Jesus: Abba!

Having dealt with the vertical dimension of offspring to Father, we now pass to the horizontal dimension of fellowship: we pray together, *Our* Father. No one is an island. We are all involved in the messianic community of the Father's kingdom. The Father of Jesus Christ is not just the Father of *some* persons, but the Father of all, especially the lowly and the poor, in whom he is present (Matt. 25:34–45) and to whom he reveals himself (Matt. 11:25), to those who most frequently must call upon him for their daily bread.

IN HEAVEN

Matthew's version of the prayer is the one that we usually recite: Our Father (who art) in heaven. The phrase "in heaven" has various levels of meaning.[40] One level emphasizes the ubiquitous presence of the Father: he is not tied down to certain sacred places or to one people, one fraction of humankind. His presence is not concentrated in the Temple, or on Mount Zion, or on Sinai, or in the mountains, or in the desert. He is beyond all this, but he is there too, offering his paternal kindness to all.

We see at once that this emphasizes the uniqueness of the Father. He has no rivals, whether by way of fathers of the faith and of the nation, or earthly fathers. On the contrary, every family derives from him (Eph. 3:14–15). As his own Son Jesus has said: "You have one Father, and he is in heaven" (Matt. 23:9).

But there is another, more profound meaning, a theological interpretation: the expression "in heaven" is meant to highlight the remoteness of the Father. He is a Father who is near, by being compassionate and kind, but he is also a quite "other" Father. He is not to be confused with one's earthly father, for he is not a simple extension of the characteristics of one's biological father. He is by our side, and he is not indifferent to our lives or our pains, but he continues to be the totally Other. He "dwells" in heaven.

Heaven, in the oldest human cultures, is a symbol of transcendence, of the infinite that humankind cannot attain by its own efforts. Thus heaven becomes the archetypal symbol of God, the Most High, the God of glory and inaccessible light.

God is near, which is why he is Father, and he is so near that he is *our* Father. But this God is not a mannequin that we have erected as a disguise for the narcissism of our infantile desires for protection and consolation at any price. This God calls upon us to forget ourselves, our own desires and interests, ushering us into the kingdom of meanings that are beyond any earthly good or evil.

Access to the Father-God is not as easy as would seem at first glance. The path is rough and arduous, and requires courage to follow. As we have already said, it requires faith, hope, and love, the ability to bear with the contradictions of this world and, at the same time, to call out: Abba, Father. It calls us to the struggle of transforming this world from the kingdom of Satan to the kingdom of God, thus making the invocation "Our Father" more believable. Only a God who is so near and yet so far could help us find an earthly way of life that leads to heaven. Heaven, not earth, is our homeland.[41]

God, and not this world with its tyrannical structures and historical tragedies, constitutes "the hearth and homeland of human identity." Any "protection" or "care" that the idea of father can generate that is not directed toward this goal must be disqualified theologically in the name of the Father of our Lord Jesus Christ and of Jesus himself. The invocation "Our Father in heaven" basically implies a profound declaration of faith in the fact that God, the near and remote God, is the living and true God who, in defiance of all the mechanisms of death and destruction to which we are subject, is already building his kingdom—a kingdom of love, kindness, and fellowship—in our midst.

HOW SHALL WE PRAY THE LORD'S PRAYER IN A FATHERLESS WORLD?

We want to be aware of any fundamental obstacles that cause difficulty in praying the Lord's Prayer. There are four such obstacles: the seriousness of the crisis in the meaning of life, the emergence of a fatherless society, criticisms leveled at the father-figure and its function in religion by such thinkers as Freud and Nietzsche, and, finally, an awareness of the relativity of our own culture with respect to the father-figure. If we can overcome these obstacles, we shall have cleared a field of faith in which the recitation of the Lord's Prayer will recover its full liberative significance.

Some persons are so struck by the negative features of life that they have lost their hope and faith; they see no meaning in lifting their eyes to heaven and praying the Lord's Prayer. Such a recitation, for them, would not be authentic; in fact, it would be a lie. For them, God is not experienced as a Father. *Fata nos ducunt,* the ancients said: we are led by fate; blind, we are directed by unknown powers.

There are others who have joined in battle against the oppressions of this world and have succumbed to the feeling of impotence when confronted by the gravity of life's absurdities and the historical violence against human dignity and justice. They have lost their faith in the possibility of humankind's recovery and liberation. They say: we are forever condemned to devour one another, subject to the law of "might makes right." Yet they are always tormented by dreams of fellowship, freedom, and equality. Cynicism and despair kill faith. Resignation makes one speechless before God, so that one has only questions that could be asked of God, but no supplications, no invocations.

This is a terrible temptation, and it can come even to religious-minded persons. It can be overcome to the extent that a person succeeds in getting beyond the level of religious emotionalism to walk the path of faith. Religious emotionalism is built on just that: emotion; it comes from a desire for protection and a fear of punishment.[42] It is an age-old structure, tied to the rudiments of our emotional and social life. If God dwelt within this horizon, he would be assimilated only as a Father who protects or a Judge who punishes. God would be deprived of his divinity, to be instrumentalized in line with human needs.

The truth is that there are realities against which we cannot protect ourselves; we have to either resist them or put up with them. God does not pull us out of the perilous waves, but gives us courage. If God existed only to draw us out of the waves and not to give us courage in our crisis, then he would perish or be rejected when our hope died or our existential balance was lost.

We noted above that the Father of our Lord Jesus Christ is not a mere protector God. It is true that he comforts us and has compassion on his children. But he is in heaven, not on earth; this distance is always a fact. Thus he is only *our* Father to the extent that we accept him as the Father in heaven. That is, we have no other access to him except by faith as a decision freely made, establishing an independent filial relationship, not a dependent relationship. Faith prompts us to accept the goodness of God at the same time as we accept the evil in the world. Beyond earth, in heaven, there is meaning for everything, even for the contradiction that tears at our hearts here and now and fills our eyes with tears. God continues to be *our* Father despite the suffering we undergo. Our freely-made decision has already given us victory over the area of religious emotion and has inaugurated the kingdom of faith. Here is the true escape from the slavery of desire for protection into the freedom of living beyond it. It is the exodus from "woe unto you" to the joy of "blessed are you."

This faith is required of us in praying the Lord's Prayer. This faith was manifested by Jesus. He himself confided in God at the most despairing moment of his crucifixion; he was faithful to God despite contradiction, persecution, and condemnation.

We are, as some say, "on the road to a fatherless society."[43] Contemporary cultures are still patriarchal, but they are undergoing a profound crisis. Technological progress makes it impossible to maintain a paternal form of domination. The image of the working father has grown dim; his occupational activities are becoming increasingly less visible to his children. The distance between his residence and his place of work, the social division of labor, and the status of the wage earner have all destroyed his authority. He is reduced to a mere cog in the sophisticated machinery of society. The social order is no longer incarnated in a person—the father—as a symbol and guarantee of public order, but finds its incarnation in officials who perform their functions and then join the ranks with all the others. "Patriarchal society has been replaced by a fatherless society or by a peer society that performs anonymous duties and is directed by impersonal forces."[44] There is nothing deviant about this. It is the ripening of a social process that opens up a new phase in human evolution. Thus it consists in dismissing the father without bearing him any grudge.

In this situation, what does it mean to pray the Lord's Prayer? Does it not mean to perpetuate the parameters of a culture that is now obsolete? Although we are moving more and more into a society with increasingly impersonal, egalitarian ties (and this is what the world wants; it is not just something that we notice), we still cannot concede that the father-figure has been eliminated. We must search out the nuclear model of our patriarchal order, the anthropological principle of paternity. The historical social expression of paternity, as the axis around which a type of society is organized, may vary, but there is an anthropological constant of paternity that is not exhausted by the particular form of social concretization. This factor has an inalienable function, responsible for that first break in the intimacy between mother and child, the introduction of the child into the social milieu. The father-figure is not doomed to disappear, but will take on new roles compatible with a changed world. It continues to be internalized in the psyche of children, becoming a matrix by which they assimilate, reject, and come to terms with the world.[45]

Freud teaches that everyone forms the idea of God out of the image of their father; their relationship to God depends on the relationship they have had with their father. If the human father, as one of the active members of a changed society, has sufficient sincerity, fidelity, and responsibility to guarantee the protection that children need to provide a maturation of their ego, then he may again perform the function of a model—and free of any encumbrances from the patriarchal era. He may again exercise that function within the structuring that is inherent to the father-figure in human society. This anthropological base serves as a springboard for the child to develop its image of God as a fruition of adult faith, not as a sedative for the instinct of protection. He is a Father even in the darkness of internal night or the grief over nameless suffering.

These thoughts help us to understand and resolve another difficulty that is raised by those masters of suspicion, Nietzsche and Freud.[46] They have posed a number of criticisms of this religion of the Father, starting with a hermeneutic of evasions and conceal-ments that have to do with two profound impulses of human ex-istence: desire and fear. The desire for protection and the mecha-nisms for overcoming fear may create a language under which they may be hidden—that is, religion. According to these authors, religion has a significance as an escape for religious persons. They live within an illusion, thinking that they are dealing with God, his grace, his forgiveness, his protection, and his salvation, whereas in truth they are only taming and channeling their basic drives. The suspicion of the analyst (such as Freud or Nietzsche) must be able to detect this concealment, isolate those conscious, canon-ized meanings from the unconscious factors. Thus for Nietzsche religion, especially Christianity, has its origin in the resentment that the weak bear for the strong, born of impotence and frustra-tion, a kind of "Platonism for the poor." Values are inverted so that the weak become strong, the impotent become omnipotent, and God is crucified and defeated.[47]

For Freud, who takes the same line of interpretation, religion is a collective infantile neurosis, and God is "a projection that compensates for the feeling of infantile helplessness."[48] God the Father becomes a substitute for one's own father, a projection and, finally, an illusion by means of which one is sustained by a feeling of protection and comfort. Persons are set free when they renounce the principle of pleasure (desire) and adopt the principle of reality (*amor fati*, acceptance of fate).

Freud insists that everyone passes through the Oedipus com-plex. The problem is not that one enters it (everyone goes through it); the problem is how to get out of it in a way that retains one's humanity and integrates it into one's personal life plan. In its basic makeup, the Oedipus assumes a root-structure of desire in the form of megalomania and omnipotence. Desire has no limits. Thus the Oedipus, in fantasy, is transformed into the image of the ideal father, controller of all the values desired by the son. The son thus imitates his father and is fascinated by him. He wants to be like him. But how can he accomplish this?

There are various ways of getting out of the Oedipus. Repression, identification, and sublimation are unsuccessful approaches and are never totally achieved. One way to emerge from the Oedipus is by a demolition (dissolution or destruction) of the Oedipus. This is accomplished by recognizing that one's father is mortal and that he differs from his son. The son will never be the father. The father must be accepted as a father; this makes the son really a son. This is not a matter, then, of repressing our desires but only of unmasking them, of renouncing the omnipotence they possessed in childhood. The son thus interiorizes the father-figure without denying his own sonship; he himself becomes a father in his own right and achieves maturation as a human being. It is in this way that the Oedipus is once again incorporated, in its integrity, into the psyche.[49]

With the data that we have surveyed on the dialectical structure of the experience of God as near and remote Father, our Father and at the same time the Father who is in heaven, we are ready to respond to the criticisms of Freud and Nietzsche. We have to concede that there is a pathological form of living out this belief in God as Father that is an evasion of the suffering of this world and an insatiable search for consolation. In this case we have to accept the criticism of these two masters of suspicion; they exercise a purifying action on the true faith.

On the other hand, if we look carefully at the matter, we see that the faith required in praying the Lord's Prayer actually seeks to liberate us from the primeval drives of desire and fear that keep us in slavery, that impede us from saying, "Abba, Father" with freedom as adults, rather than with the immaturity of small children. St. Paul insists that we are no longer "during our minority slaves to the elemental spirits of the universe" (Gal. 4:3)—in other words, slaves to desire and fear—but adult offspring. The relationship that we have established with the Father-God does not grow out of an infantile, neurotic dependence but out of autonomy and a freely made decision.

In Jesus we see this Oedipal integrative attitude clearly shining forth. He does not live with a feeling of emasculation in the presence of his Father, nor is his feeling one of immobilizing dependence. On the contrary, he has his own mission, he sees himself as a son and recognizes the Father as his heavenly Father. He renounces the dream of infantile omnipotence, the urge to usurp the privileges of the Father, thus seeing himself and accepting himself as the Son.[50] On the one hand, he knows that he has received everything from the Father (John 17:7); on the other hand, he knows, through the relationship of intimacy and love that he has with the Father, that he is one with him (John 17:21). This free relationship of the Son-Jesus clears the way for the Father-God to have a relationship with other human beings. Jesus demonstrates a totally free and open relationship, one that loves to the point of sacrificing his life for others. The vertical dimension emerges as a source of power for the horizontal dimension. The liberation of human beings does not conflict with their relationship to God. Jesus demonstrates that he can have profound ties to God and yet be radically bound to men and women; in other words, liberation from human oppression does not necessarily imply liberation from the idea of God as Father.

Thus it becomes clear that Christianity does not have its origin in the resentment of the weak against the strong. It is not the religion of resignation and frustration but of dignity, the courage to keep up the two polarities that have to be maintained—of faithfulness to heaven and faithfulness to the earth, of hope against hope. At its origin, Christianity was a religion of slaves and marginals, but it did not confirm them in their slavery and marginality. It led them to freedom and to the stature of the dignity of a new person.

The fourth difficulty has to do with the historical consciousness of our culture centered on the father-figure and masculine orientations. Could it be that calling upon God as Father means paying tribute to a passing phenomenon? Could we not also call upon God as "our Mother in heaven"? The question is not without interest, although it is difficult. We do not want to involve ourselves here in the minute details of the subject to the extent we should like.[51] What we can say is that the Christian faith involved in praying to God as Father is not to be defined in sexual terms. Actually, it should express the conviction that what underlies all reality is a

Principle that need appeal to no other principle, an original source of everything, which itself has no source. We would go on to say that this Principle is not some bottomless pit, lost in a void, but that it is replete with love and communion. This Father has a Son, together with whom he has originated the Holy Spirit.

When the church fathers wrote their commentaries on the Lord's Prayer, they saw in its first line the presence of the Trinity. Basically, this was because it is the Spirit of the Son, Jesus, who causes us to cry out: Abba, Father! Furthermore, to say "Father" automatically invokes the reality of the Son. As St. Cyprian said in his commentary on the Lord's Prayer: "We say Father because we have been made sons," in the Son Jesus.[52] Tertullian further enlarges the circle to include Mother Church: "We also invoke the Son in the Father because the Father and I, he says, are one (John 10:30). But we must also not forget the church, our mother. To speak the name of the Father and the name of the Son is to proclaim the mother, without whom there would be neither Father nor Son."[53]

Thus when we say "Father," we confess the ultimate mystery that penetrates and sustains the universe of beings, a mystery of love and communion. This same reality expressed by a paternal symbol could also be expressed by a maternal symbol. The Old Testament even shows traces of a maternal aspect of God: "As a mother comforts her son, so will I myself comfort you" (Isa. 66:13; see also 49:15). Pope John Paul I said that God is Father and moreover Mother. This is not the place to go into the implications of this feminine terminology. Our culture, to the extent that it is being depatriarchalized, is also being set free from a masculinizing symbolism, opening the way to approaches to God by way of the feminine. The feminine and the maternal are also worthy symbols, and quite adequately express faith in the loving mystery that generates all things. Both expressions—father and mother—point to the same ultimate reality.

How shall we pray the Lord's Prayer today? With the same spirit in which Jesus addressed the Father and with the same courage that was exhibited by the first Christian martyrs when they prayed it. In the midst of these tortures they called upon the omnipotent God who was at the same time the merciful Father.

Jesus did not live an idyllic life. His existence was a heavy commitment, weighed down with conflicts that culminated in his crucifixion. In the midst of these excruciating experiences he prayed to his beloved Father.[54] In the end he did not ask to be spared the temptations or the cup of bitterness; he sought faithfulness to his Father's will. For him also, God was both near and far at the same time. The anguishing lament from the cross reveals the painful experience of Jesus confronted with the absence of the Father. But he also felt him near: "Father, into thy hands I commit my spirit" (Luke 23:46).

In praying the Lord's Prayer, the Christian's gaze should not be directed backward in search of an ancestral past, but forward, in the direction of the advent of that kingdom promised by the Father, which is above, in heaven. The forward look and the upward look depict the attitude of hope and of faith in the love that rejoices with God the Father who is near, while also loving the Father-God who is far away. This attitude is neither alienating nor dehumanizing. It puts us in our proper place of greatness as sons and daughters in the presence of a beloved Father.

4

Thy Name Be Hallowed

The first Franciscans arrived in Mexico in 1524. In the inner courtyard of the St. Francis Friary they took it upon themselves to enlighten some high-ranking Aztec officials. The friars condemned the ancient religious beliefs. Then an Aztec scholar stepped forward and, "with courtesy and urbanity," expressed his displeasure at seeing the ancient customs, so esteemed by his ancestors, attacked in this way. He said to the Christian missionaries:

> You have said that we do not know the Lord
> who is near at hand,
> the one from whom come the heavens and the earth.
>
> You say that our gods are not the true ones.
>
> This is what we say to you,
> because we are disturbed,
> because we are made uncomfortable.
>
> Our ancestors,
> who used to live upon the earth,
> were not accustomed to speak in this way.
>
> They gave us rules for our life,
> they believed that these were the true rules,
> they offered worship,
> they honored the gods.

*We know who it is
to whom we owe our lives,
to whom we owe our birth,
to whom we owe our conception,
to whom we owe our upbringing,
how we are to invoke the gods,
how we are to pray.*

*Hear this, O lords, do nothing to our people
that will bring them harm,
that will destroy them. . . .*

*Consider quietly and considerately, O lords,
what is really necessary.*

*We can have no tranquility with this way,
and certainly we do not believe this way,
we do not regard these teachings as true,
even if it means offending you.*

This is what we reply to your message, O lords!

—From "*Diálogos con los sabios indígenas,*"
in M.L. Portilla, El reverso de la conquista
(Mexico City, 1970), pp. 23–28.

If we are to understand well this supplication of the Lord's Prayer—thy name be hallowed—we need to recover the experience that underlies it. It is the experience already described in our reflections; we merely take it up here in greater detail.

CRY OF SUPPLICATION

The supplication finds its origin in a discovery and a desire. In this world, God the Father is neither objectively nor subjectively "hallowed" (sanctified) and glorified.[55] Circumstances objectively deny the honoring of God because of their profound internal distortions that disrupt comradely relations among persons and groups. Subjectively, men and women blaspheme the holy name of God by what they say and what they do.

First comes a cruel discovery: as has been pointed out, human society has been corrupted both in its structure and its functioning. There seems to be no corner of the world where sanity and symmetry can be found. Human conflicts and tensions do not foster growth toward justice for the great majority of humankind. Most persons have shown themselves antagonistic and destructive. They all live in a captivity that aggravates the anxiety to be free, for which they are always searching and are almost always frustrated. Objectively, we live in a situation of structural and institutionalized decadence.

Ours is more than an analytical discovery; there is also an ethical judgment. We confront the murky presence of evil, of offensiveness to God. This propagates sin, by which is meant a rupture of human beings and their sense of the transcendent, as well as a laceration of the social fabric. We can no longer look upon another's face and see a brother or sister.

Why has history come to this? The religious response, one of denunciation and accusation, may be stated thus: because the actors of history have refused to define themselves in terms of the Absolute; because the memory of God has slowly been lost; because idols of every sort have been fashioned to replace him; because the name of God is cursed. There are not a few persons who find in the misery of the world the grounds for cursing God, as did the biblical Job. Others will not tolerate God's silence in the face of injustices to the world's lowly. They intentionally reject him with the words: an impotent God cannot help us! How shall we sanctify his name?[56]

The discovery of this basic shortcoming gives rise to a desire that bursts forth in the form of a supplication: thy name be hallowed! This is the cry of Jesus' followers, addressed both to God and to their fellows. May God finally manifest his glory! May God the Father intervene, eschatologically, and put an end to what violates the divine order! May people live in such a way as to honor his name, and may they have the courage to transform the world until it is worthy of being his kingdom!

This is the experience underlying the supplication "thy name be hallowed," the experience that calls forth a cry of entreaty. To understand its content better, we shall need to clarify the two key terms: hallow (sanctify) and name.

THE SIGNIFICANCE OF
"HALLOWED" AND "NAME"

Biblically speaking, "hallow" or "sanctify" is a synonym of "praise, bless, glorify"; it means to "make holy."[57] Some synonyms of "holy" are "just (righteous), perfect, good, pure." All of this is true, but it does not capture the original meaning of "holy." Holiness constitutes the axial category between religion and the Scriptures and has two interrelated dimensions. The first of these defines "being" and the second "acting"; one relates to an ontological inquiry (What is God like? What is his nature?) and the other to an ethical inquiry (How does God act? What deeds does he perform?).

The word "holy" when applied to God expresses the peculiar mode of his being. Thus, to speak of a holy God is to speak of the totally Other, the Other Dimension. God is not an extension of our world; he is a completely other reality. He is understood as apart from our being and our acting. The Scriptures say on a number of occasions that his name—that is, his nature— is holy (Isa. 6:3; Ps. 99:3, 5, 9; Lev. 11:44, 19:2, 21:8; Prov. 9:10, 30:3; 1 Chron. 16:10). He dwells, quite simply, in light inaccessible (Exod. 15:11; 1 Sam. 2:2; 1 Tim. 6:16). This means that God totally eludes us; the term "holy" thus is a negative definition of God: he is the One who is on the other side, separate (which is the etymological meaning of *sanctus*: cut off, separate, apart).

The Lord's Prayer expresses this idea when it says: Our Father in heaven. Heaven, as we have noted, is a concrete expression of what is inaccessible to man, of the infinite. Saint John says: "Holy Father" (17:11). He is near (Father) and he is remote (holy) at the same time.

This peculiar mode of being of God, as someone completely differing from us, inhibits any sort of idolatry, because idolatry means worshipping some portion of the world as God. It also condemns any manipulation of God, on the part of religious powers or of political powers. The only attitude one can have in the presence of the Holy One is that of respect, veneration, and reverence; we are in the presence of the Ineffable, of a Word without synonyms, of a Light that casts no shadow, of a Profundity that has no measured depth.

Because of this diverse nature of God, the human reaction to the Holy One is twofold, a reaction that has been analyzed in detail by religious phenomenology scholars: flight and attraction.[58] A person is terrified before the Holy One because what is encountered is unknown and without dimensions; one wants to run and hide. This was Moses' experience with the burning bush. We hear God say: "Come no nearer . . . the place where you are walking is holy ground" (Exod. 3:5). "Moses covered his face, for he was afraid to gaze on God" (Exod. 3:6). But, at the same time, the Holy One fascinates and attracts; he is charged with meaning and full of light. Moses says to himself in front of the burning bush: "I must go across to see this wonderful sight" (Exod. 3:3).

This is the ontological meaning of holy. There is also an ethical meaning. It is derived from the ontological, because acting (ethics) is the result of being (ontology). This holy God, who is so distant, so "other," and so far beyond everything that we may think or imagine, is not an aseptic or neutral God. He has ears and he can say: "I have indeed seen the misery of my people . . . I have heard their outcry against their slave-masters. I have taken heed of their sufferings" (Exod. 3:7). He takes sides; he favors the weak and opposes the oppressors; he makes a firm decision: "I have resolved to bring you up out of your misery, into . . . a land flowing with milk and honey" (Exod. 3:17). The biblical God is the Father of our Lord Jesus Christ, and he is an ethical God: he loves justice and hates iniquity. Isaiah has well said of him: "By righteousness the holy God shows himself holy" (5:16). He is absolutely just, perfect, and good; only he is radically good (Matt. 19:17), pure, without spot or blemish, and unambiguous.

God, who is ontologically remote (holy), becomes ethically near (holy): he rescues the defenseless, avenges the oppressed, identifies with the poor. God himself bridges over the gulf interposed between his holy reality and our profane reality. He rises up from his inaccessible light and crosses over into our darkness. The incarnation of the eternal Son historicizes this tender sympathy of God with his creatures.

God has overcome the distance that (ontologically) separates him from human beings, and he wants them also to overcome this distance. He wants them to be holy, as he is holy (Luke 11:13, 20:22). "There must be no limit to your goodness, as your heavenly Father's goodness knows no bounds" (Matt. 5:48; see Luke 6:36). This affirmation brings with it a requirement that is of major anthropological significance: humankind's ultimate destiny is God. Only God is the concrete expression of utopia; in other words, human beings cannot be fully or rightly understood except on the horizon of utopia. They live in the world and with the world, but the world is not enough for them; they are historical beings, but their essential dynamism calls for a break with history and their realization in metahistory.

This understanding leaves far behind it any historical totalitarianisms, especially Marxism, which understands the human person as a factor in history, reducible to a complexus of social relationships.[59] The call to be perfect and holy as the Father is perfect and holy presupposes our irreducibility with reference to our infrastructure and our ability to extrapolate beyond the boundaries of historical positivism. In a word, our calling is to heaven, not to earth; it is to God, not to an earthly paradise. This does not mean that we are summoned to retire from historical tasks; on the contrary, we must elevate the earth and history, so that together they reach their supreme ideal in God.

Summing up the meaning of this call to be holy as God is holy, we may say: human beings are called to participate in God ontically (in terms of his nature) and to imitate God ethically (in terms of action). Human beings find their true humanity in a total extrapolation of themselves, and penetration into the dimension of God. It is in the "other," in the totally Other, that they find their own true selves. This is the ontological meaning of being holy as God is holy.

How is this accomplished? Again: being holy in the ethical sense, as God is holy, means being just, good, perfect, and pure, as God is. Anyone who walks this path is on the way to meet God. Anyone who is far from justice and goodness is also far from God, even if God's name is often on one's lips.

As may be seen, the term "holy" applied to God and to human beings both separates and unites, simultaneously. It separates, because holiness is an exclusive attribute of God, defining his proper being as distinguished from the being of the creature (world, persons, history); it unites because the holy Father becomes the ideal for human beings, the goal at which they arrive in achieving their full humanity. Between God and us there is not only a cleavage (in the ontological sense), but also communion. We are holy to the extent that we relate with the Holy One and maintain ties of communion with him. And the holy God wants to be sanctified in us: "I will show my glory in your midst" (Ezek. 28:22). The communion that takes place beyond these oppositions implies a mutual involvement of us in God and God in us, as is so excellently set forth in St. John's Gospel (10:27–29, 17:17–19). This is the universal law of salvation history, which reaches its peak in the incarnation.

We must now consider the meaning of "name."[60] Of the many possible meanings, within the context of the Lord's Prayer there is one that is most important: a name, in the Bible, designates a person, and defines his or her inner nature. To know someone's name is simply to know him or her.

God revealed his name to Moses—that is, he revealed his very self: the One who goes with the people and is always present (I am who I am—Exod. 3:14). With Isaiah in particular he reveals himself as holy—that is, as the One who transcends everything and at the same time commits himself to us (Isa. 6:3).

In Jesus, the definitive name of God is finally revealed: "O Righteous Father . . . I made thy name known to them" (John 17:25–26). Elsewhere he also speaks of God as "holy Father" (John 17:11). "Father" is the name of God. As the holy Father, God breaks through the confines of creation and yet dwells in the heavens; as the just Father, God has compassion on our lowliness and pitches his tent among us. In the language of Jesus: God is Abba, the kind, merciful Father.

LIBERATIVE SANCTIFICATION

Having pondered the meaning of the words "holy" and "name," we may now proceed to a better understanding of the supplication "thy name be hallowed (sanctified)." It means: may God be respected, venerated, and honored as he himself is, as the One who is holy, the impenetrable Mystery, fascinating and terrifying at the same time, as the One who is Yahweh (I-am-who-I-am), going with us and helping us, as the One who is Abba, a kind Father, both near and remote, totally beyond manipulation by human interests.

The least that we can do in God's presence is to recognize his otherness. He is not a human being, he does not move within the horizon of our thinking, feeling, and acting. He is the Other, and as such he is our origin and our future. If we do not recognize what he really is—someone different from ourselves—then we reduce him to a satellite of our own ego, an extension of our own desires, and this is a profound offense to him. It implies that we reject him, that we deprive him of the right to be himself (and concretely, every existent being is different), thus reducing him to a familiar, preconceived cliché.

We do not sanctify the name of God when we regard him as a "stopgap" for human weaknesses; in other words, if we call upon him and remember him only when we need help, when our infantile desires collapse around us. We then venerate God only as our own ego and put him at the service of our own interests. God is not recognized as the Other who has inestimable worth in himself, rather than by virtue of how he can help us. As long as we remain locked into a conception of God-who-helps and of religion as something good for human balance, we cannot break out of that vicious circle of our own egotism and meet with God. God is then found and venerated by us only in the extrapolation of our own vanity, in the fulfillment of desire, which, as Freud has shown, bears traits of childhood. We offend God not by denying him but by an egocentric supplication that implies that we do not recognize him as God, as someone different from ourselves and beyond the reach of our manipulations.

We do not sanctify God when our religious language (the language we use in our piety, liturgy, and theology) speaks of him as though he were an entity of this sublunar world: completely known, exhaustively defined, his will completely understood, as though we had had a personal interview with him. This reflects an irreverent attitude with a mere aura of religion; it leaves no margin for Mystery, for the Unknown, the Ineffable. It is one way of failing to sanctify God, a theological study and an understanding of the faith that domesticates revelation in the form of airtight dogmas, restricts the love of God to rules, limits the action of the Spirit to the church, and limits our encounter with the Father to outwardly recognizable religious practices.

We are not sanctifying the name of God when we erect church buildings, when we elaborate mystical treatises, or when we guarantee his official presence in society by means of religious symbols. His holy name is sanctified only to the extent that these expressions are related to a pure heart, a thirst for justice, and a reaching out for perfection. It is in these realities that God dwells; these are his true temple, where there are no idols. Origen said well, in commenting on this supplication of the Lord's Prayer: "They who do not strive to harmonize their conception of God with that which is just take the name of the Lord God in vain."[61] Thus ethics constitutes the most reliable criterion for discerning whether the God we claim to sanctify is true or false.

We sanctify the name of God when by our own life, by our own actions of solidarity, we help to build more pacific and more just human relationships, cutting off access to violence and one person's exploitation of another. God is always offended when violence is done to a human being, made in his image and likeness. And God is always sanctified when human dignity is restored to the dispossessed and the victims of violence.

Here we see emerging the challenge of a liberating sanctification in the effort to establish a world that objectively honors and venerates God by the high quality of life that it manages to create. For centuries, Christians did not consider this a central concern. Holiness was concentrated on the individual person, on complete mastery of one's passions, on purity of heart, on elevation of the spirit, on charity to one's neighbor, and on reverent submission to the ecclesiastical system with its hierarchies, canons, and time-honored paths to perfection. All of these have an inestimable and irreplaceable value; they constitute part of the ongoing task of personal sanctity and the creation of a new heart, in line with the "mind which was in Christ Jesus."[62]

But this preoccupation does not exhaust the challenge addressed to Christians; reality is more than a personal matter. It is also social. And the social aspect cannot be understood individualistically; it must be understood socially, as a woven fabric of relationships, powers, functions, and interests that are sometimes antagonistic, asymmetrical, and unjust, and sometimes symmetrical, participatory, and comradely. It is in the social dimension that God the Father is most offended at present. It is important that his holy name be sanctified in this area.

God is sanctified in the arena of history by someone who is ready to do battle alongside the oppressed in the quest for their freedom from bondage. The most holy name of the Father is sanctified by someone who seeks solidarity with subordinated classes, who enters into the social process with all its conflicts and helps to construct more egalitarian relationships within the social fabric. There is another asceticism besides that of the body. It is the asceticism of bearing with defamation, persecution, imprisonment, torture, and the degradation of hard labor. Above the ascetic tower the figures of the prophet and of the political activist who confront abusive power, who raise their voices in the name of conscience and the holiness of God and cry out: "It is not lawful for you!" (Mark 6:18). "You must not victimize one another" (Lev. 25:17). Today there are all too few Christians, especially in established church communities, who are experimenting with this new sanctification of the world.

Jesus was one who walked this path. He did not proclaim the kingdom just for life's emergencies, or just for the heart, but for the four corners of the earth and for all peoples. He envisioned not only a renewed humankind but also a new heaven and a new earth. It was no accident that the New Testament presents him as the Holy One of God (Luke 4:34; Mark 1:24; John 6:69). In other words, he is the one who purifies the world and puts it in the proper state to glorify God. He once more aligns the universe of things, persons, and history to the Holy One, so that they also become holy.[63]

When the world and humankind are sanctified, the glory of God bursts forth. In the Bible the words "glory" and "name" frequently occur in the same context: the name of God must be glorified (Ps. 86:9, 12; John 12:28). In other words, we must recognize that God is God; we must surrender to the holy Father as the Lord of history, whatever its contradictions! It is important that the world have an awareness of the true divine reality, that men and women have a religious discourse that evokes and communicates the real God, as the absolute Origin, Meaning, and Future of all things.

Sanctifying the name of the Father is the primordial task of the community of Jesus' followers—the church. The church celebrates his presence, his greatness, his victory! The church is thus itself the sacrament of the Father and of his glory in the world. To sanctify means to praise, to magnify, to glorify God despite whatever might seem to militate against it. In spite of everything, in spite of all the numerous tragedies and barbarities, history contains a sufficient manifestation of God to permit us to identify him and accept him. Tears cannot dissolve the smile, and bitterness cannot sour the joy of the heart. Here is the essential task of the Christian community: to speak of this, to reaffirm it, to celebrate it.

The supplication "thy name be hallowed" also contains an eschatological component. We discover in history that we can go beyond its possibilities and build a holy, perfect, righteous, pure world. What everyone most desires is justice, peace, and love, but they seem never to find permanent lodging in our world. Justice as a symmetry of *persons* (rather than just of social functions and social roles) is always off center. Peace as a balance between desire and its satisfaction, the absence of destructive antagonisms, and the enjoyment of freedom is always menaced. Love as self-donation to others and communion with them too easily succumbs to the mechanisms of habit, to the fetishism of rites, and the imposition of rules. We therefore supplicate God to do what history cannot: to sanctify all persons and all societies. God himself must sanctify his own name; we call upon him to manifest himself and to reveal his liberating omnipotence and dazzling glory. "It is not for your sake, you Israelites, that I am acting, but for the sake of my holy name, which you have profaned among the peoples where you have gone. I will hallow my great name, which has been profaned among the nations" (Ezek. 36:22–23).

This event will signify the eschatological conclusion of history. God will be God and we shall be his sons and daughters. Everyone will sing and glorify him and magnify him: How great is the holy God in our midst! (see Isa. 12:5–6). Then we will no longer say "thy name be hallowed" as a prayer for an unfulfilled hope—for his name will then always be holy.

5

Thy Kingdom Come

Experience has taught us that it is not necessary to say "Lord, Lord" in order to do good and to enter the kingdom. In our work in the factories and in the slums, we have found examples of persons who are totally disinterested and dedicated to others, and who do not say "Lord, Lord." These persons are prepared to sacrifice their jobs, their family, and even themselves for the good of all. The gospel is present in them, and the Spirit finds realization.

We have learned to judge these persons by what they are and do, and not by the institution to which they belong or by the doctrine they profess. We invite everyone to do the same, if they wish to understand what the prophet Amos meant when he denied the special election of Israel by Yahweh and taught the practice of justice as the only source of salvation.

It is thus that we understand our struggle and our faith. We believe that we are building up the kingdom. The "we" includes those of the worker ministry and all those who struggle with us. We do not separate things from persons. We do not feel that we are better. We work with all on a basis of equality.

All those who struggle for the building of the kingdom will live in it. There will be no privileges. Righteousness is based on works; those who pass judgment on the basis of dogmas condemn themselves. There will be no room for those who reject their equals in the name of a doctrine or those who think they are saved by what they have inherited.

They build houses and live in them, they plant and eat the fruit of their labor.

—Letter of the worker ministry,
Santa Margarida basic ecclesial community, São Paulo,
published in SEDOC 11 (1978): 362–63

With the supplication "thy kingdom come" we get into the very heart of the Lord's Prayer. At the same time, we are confronted with the ultimate intention of Jesus, because the proclamation of the kingdom of God constitutes the core of his message and the primary motive of his activities. In order to fully comprehend the meaning of this supplication—which burrows into the most profound depths of our anxiety and our hopes—we must begin at a distance and dig deeply. Only then will its radicality and novelty be appreciated.

THE NOBLEST AND DEEPEST PART
OF HUMAN NATURE

What distinguishes human beings from animals is not so much intelligence as imagination.[64] The life of an animal is confined to its immediate habitat; it simply mirrors the world around it. Only the human being interprets reality, adding something to it, symbolizing and fantasizing the facts of history and the world. Human beings are driven by desires that are not abated by any one concrete activity. They have a permanent openness, whether relating to the world, to others, or to themselves. They meet their match only when they turn to God as the Absolute, the Love, and the Meaning that fulfills every desire.

The human person is not so much a *being* as a *becoming*. This self-renewing potentiality means that any goal reached becomes a new beginning or, better, is then seen as only one element in a wider perspective. Present reality is merely an anticipation of something else to come. Only human beings dream in their sleeping and waking hours of new worlds where interpersonal relationships will be always more egalitarian—a new heaven and a new earth. Only the human person creates utopias. These utopias are not mere escape mechanisms by which the contradictions of the present are avoided. They are part of human life, because human beings continually project, plan the future, live on promises, and feed on hope. These are the utopias that keep the absurd from taking charge of history; they disarm built-in security systems and open up the present to a promising future.

Anthropologists say that we are inhabited by a "hope principle."[65] It takes the form of a tension, of an unending search for the new, of a world without frontiers, of a questioning of the de facto circumstances, of expectation, of tomorrow, of dreams of a better life, of a world where there is no pain or sorrow or weeping or death—because all this will have passed away (Rev. 21:4)— and of hopes for a new humanity. In this hope principle we find the deepest and most radical part of human nature, the part that never dies. It is only what is that dies; that which *is not yet* cannot die. Hope is for what has not yet been, but is present in desire and is anticipated by the longings of the heart.

All human cultures, from the most primitive to the most advanced, have their utopias. They constitute the womb of all hope. We know those of the Judeo-Christian tradition; they speak of the transfiguration of the present world in all its relationships. We read about the reconciliation of nature, when "the wolf shall live with the sheep . . . the lion shall eat straw like cattle, the infant shall play over the hole of the cobra, and . . . they shall not hurt or destroy in all my holy mountain" (Isa. 11:6–9). God will create a new heart and a new earth; "no longer need they teach one another to know the Lord; all of them, high and low alike, shall know me [God]" (Jer. 31:34); then "they shall never again feel hunger or thirst" and nature will no longer be malevolent (Rev. 7:16). The Messianic times are represented as days when all of these utopias finally come true. "When that day comes you will ask nothing of me" (John 16:23), because God will give an answer to all the endless inquiries of the heart.

These hopes become more fervent in direct proportion to the cruelty of this world's contradictions: "In their wickedness they are stifling the truth" (Rom. 1:18), "they have bartered away the true God for a false one. . . . They are filled with every kind of mischief, rapacity, and malice; they are one mass of envy, murder, rivalry, treachery, and malevolence . . . insolent, arrogant, and boastful" (Rom. 1:25, 29–30). The lowly are exploited, the weak brutalized, the honest ridiculed, and the historical structures of injustice and sin oppress everyone.

Objectively, this situation is in defiance of God's authority. Is he not the Lord of creation? How can there be so many dimensions that elude his power and are not subject to his order? Prophets have always appeared, not allowing hope to die: one day God is going to intervene and restore everything to its original goodness and raise everything to a fullness never dreamed of in the past. The Old Testament points to it again and again: "The Lord shall reign forever and ever!" (Exod. 15:18); "I am Yahweh, he who will be here" (Exod. 3:14); "And you shall know that I am Yahweh" (Isa. 49:23; Jer. 16:21; and 54 times in Ezekiel). These are promises that nurture hope while not fundamentally changing a situation of conflict. But the overall meaning is clear: God is not indifferent to the cry that rises to heaven. He is here and will make his reign manifest!

At one point in the Old Testament era it was thought that the lordship of God would become manifest in the lordship of the king of Israel (2 Sam. 7:12–16). The king would bring justice to the poor, restore the rights of widows, and defend the orphan, thus liberating the world from its unjust principles. But within a short time the corruption of power became evident in the very kings who were supposed to represent God with the title of "Son of God" (Ps. 2:7; 2 Sam. 7:14), until the ten tribes would ask the question: "What share have we in David?" (1 Kings 12:16). The kings were corrupted and took with them an entire people.

At another stage of Old Testament history it was thought that God would reconcile the world by means of a regulated temple worship, with its priestly orders, sacrifices, and prescriptions for holiness. God would reign from the temple, where his people would encounter him as though face to face (see Ezek. 40–43). But the prophets denounced any illusions of a worship that excluded conversion, fellowship, and mercy (Amos 5:21–24). The worship that God wants is justice and liberation of the oppressed (Isa. 1:17). The living God, more than being a God of worship, is an ethical God who despises iniquity and rejoices with the just.

Another group with a wide following in Jesus' time put its hope in a universal reconciliation in the apocalyptic sense. "Apocalyp-

tic" (Daniel and the Revelation of St. John are the two apocalyptic books in the Scriptures) refers to a doctrine of revelation.
The apocalyptics sought a secret wisdom, one that was accessible
only to the initiated, by which they interpreted the signs of the
times that anticipated a cosmic revolution, with the emergence of
a new heaven and a new earth. This event would come suddenly
and would invert every relationship: the unhappy would become
happy and the happy unhappy, the poor would become rich and
the rich poor, outcasts would be honored and the honored would
be despised. Along with this sudden transformation would come
the end of this world and the inauguration of a new heaven and
a new earth.

Whereas the apocalyptics expected the kingdom to come of its
own accord, the Zealots, another group of enthusiasts, felt that
they should accelerate it by the use of violence. Others, such as
the deeply pious Pharisees, thought that by strict observance of
the divine law they would accelerate the coming of this universal
transformation. They observed everything with a neurotic obses-
sion, to the point of oppressing the weak, seeking to be absolutely
faithful and thus to create the conditions for making the promises
come true.

But all this was in vain. The supplication that rose to God
was: Thy kingdom come! May the fullness of time come! With
full confidence the prophets proclaimed: The day of the Lord
comes! (Joel 3:11–15; Isa. 63:4; Mal. 4:1–5).

"HAPPY THE EYES THAT SEE WHAT YOU ARE SEEING!" (LUKE 10:23)

It is against this background of hope and anxiety that we hear
the voice of Jesus of Nazareth: "The time has come; the kingdom
of God is upon you; repent, and believe this good news" (Mark
1:15). This is no mere promise, as that of all the prophets before
him: the kingdom *will* come! Instead, he says: the kingdom is
already at hand.[66]

The unmistakable signs that the kingdom is already in effect are
that "the blind recover their sight, the lame walk, lepers are made
clean, the deaf hear, the dead are raised to life, and the poor are

hearing the good news" (Luke 7:22). Jesus accomplished all this and then sent word of it to John the Baptist (Luke 7:18–23). The prophet Isaiah predicted these signs (Isa. 61:1–2). Jesus comments upon them preemptorily: "Today in your very hearing this text has come true" (Luke 4:21).

The kingdom of God: this is the message of hope and joy proclaimed by Jesus. The word was not frequently used in the Old Testament (see Ps. 22:28, 45:7, 103:19, 145:11; 1 Chron. 29:11; Dan. 2:44, 4:34, 5:26) and yet it constitutes (as *malkuta* in Aramaic) the verbal matrix of Jesus' message. "Kingdom" does not refer here to a territory but to the divine power and authority that now is in this world, transforming the old into new, the unjust into just, and sickness into health.

Jesus now provides the elements for a definition of the content of the kingdom.[67] He uses parables that leave no doubt as to his meaning. The kingdom is something understood to a certain extent and yet at the same time hidden and desirable. It is like a treasure hidden in a field; whoever comes upon it sells everything in order to buy the field (Matt. 13:44). It is like a precious pearl whose acquisition involves sacrificing everything (Matt. 13:45). It is like a tiny seed that grows and becomes so large that birds build their nests in it (Matt. 13:31; Mark 4:26–32). It is a force that transforms everything (Matt. 13:33).

The figure of speech used most often is that of the house or city of God, where persons sit down to eat and drink (Luke 22:30; Matt. 8:11). The Lord invites guests to his table (Matt. 22:1–14). Some enter and others are ejected (Matt. 5:20, 7:21, 18:3, 19:17, 23, 25:21, 23). There are keys for entering (Matt. 16:19). Those who live there are "born to the kingdom" (Matt. 8:12). There are many dwelling places there (John 14:2). All are invited to this house and this table, even the servants, the crippled, and those who live on the margin of society (Matt. 22:1–10). They come from the East and the West and sit down at table (Matt. 8:11). The just shine as brightly as the sun in the kingdom of their Father (Matt. 13:43). From this and other imagery one may gather that we are confronted by an absolute, fulfilled meaning, and that creation and humankind have arrived at this point.

There are three main characteristics of the kingdom announced by Jesus that have to be kept in mind. First of all, it is universal.

It embraces everything; it brings liberation to such infrastructural dimensions as sickness, poverty, and death. It restructures interpersonal relationships characterized by the absence of hatred and a plenitude of fellowship. There is a new relationship with God, who is the Father of all his beloved children. The kingdom of God cannot be reduced to any dimension of this world, not even a religious dimension; Jesus regards as diabolical any temptation to reduce the kingdom to some particular segment of reality, whether political, religious, or miraculous (Matt. 4:1–11).

Secondly, the kingdom is structural: it not only embraces everything but it also signifies a total revolution of structure. It does not merely modify the outlines of reality but goes to the roots and brings total freedom.

Thirdly, it is definitive. Because it is of a universal and structural nature, it implies the end of the world. The kingdom defines God's ultimate and final will. This world in which we live and suffer is coming to an end; there will be a new heaven and a new earth where justice, peace, and concord among all God's sons and daughters will finally triumph in the Father's great house. We can understand Jesus' exclamation: "Happy the eyes that see what you are seeing!" (Luke 10:23).

The oldest of human hopes are beginning to be realized. Utopia ceases to be fantasy and future; it becomes radiant, concrete history. The kingdom is already in our midst (Luke 17:20–21) and is leavening all of reality in the direction of its fullness: "The eschatological (final, terminal) hour of God, the victory of God, the consummation of the world is near. Indeed it is very near."[68] The kingdom must be understood as a *process:* it is already emerging, it is becoming present in the very person of Jesus, in his words, in his liberating practices, and at the same time it is open to a tomorrow when its absolute fullness will finally arrive. One needs to be prepared. You do not enter it automatically. You have to repent. This is how we understand the requirements of conversion as stated by Jesus.

The kingdom of God is constructed in opposition to the kingdom of Satan and to the presently existing diabolical structures. Thus conflict is inevitable; a crisis cannot be avoided. We are urged to make a decision. The prime target is the poor. In them the new order becomes concrete, not because of their state of morality but merely because they are who they are—that is, the poor, victims of hunger, injustice, and oppression. Jesus with his kingdom wants to put an end to their degrading situation. The kingdom comes through the poor and in opposition to poverty, which will have no place in it.[69]

It is in this context that we are to understand the supplication "thy kingdom come." It complements the previous supplication: "thy name be hallowed." When God has brought into subjection all of the rebellious dimensions of creation, when he has brought everything to its happy conclusion, then the kingdom will be complete and his name will be blessed through the ages. All this is still in progress. The kingdom is a joyful state, celebrated in the present, but at the same time it is a promise that is to be realized in the future. It is a gift and a task. It is the goal of hope. Origen said it well: "The kingdom is in our midst. It is clear that when we pray 'thy kingdom come' we are praying that the kingdom of God is growing, that it is bearing fruit, and that it will reach full maturity."[70]

THE KINGDOM CONTINUES TO COME

The kingdom came in its fullest in the life and resurrection of Jesus. In him appeared the new humankind, holy relationships between persons and with the world, and a revelation of the destiny of matter, transfigured in his resurrected body. But the world still continues with its contradictions and violence. The devil still rules; he was able to eliminate Jesus and he continues to crucify the multitudes committed to building the kingdom of peace, fellowship, and justice. It is Jesus who has reminded us of the fact that the bearer of the absolute meaning of creation has been rejected.

God revealed the final end of his work: the goal is to be his kingdom. Here is an ultimate, transhistorical goal that God is achieving despite human rejections. It is like the seed of the parable: "A man . . . goes to bed at night and gets up in the morning, and the seed sprouts and grows—how, he does not know" (Mark 4:26–27). Even rejection, the cross, and sin are not insuperable obstacles to God. Even the enemies of the kingdom are at the service of the kingdom, just as those who killed Jesus were at the service of human redemption, engineered by God.

The rejection of Jesus Christ by those whose hearts are hardened demonstrates that there are "historical possibles." There are many roads that lead to the final goal, even though they contradict each other. History is not directed by fate, by a single type of behavior or a single type of development. It was Marx in his old age (1881) who recognized that one cannot make a theory concerning the laws of history, a theory of necessities, without first having a theory of the possibles that constitute the fields of practical possibilities for a given era of history—fields that do not admit of a single meaning but have a range of meanings and realizations.[71] Thus there is always a diversity of alternatives.

The cross of Christ is a demonstration of how persons, both individually and in groups, may be frustrated as they confront the ultimate meaning of creation. But God is powerful enough and merciful enough to transform this frustration into a possible path of realization. Creation in its totality is not derailed, because God will finally conquer and reign.

There is thus a guaranteed transhistorical end of things, and it is called the eschatological kingdom of God. But coexisting with this are the intrahistorical absurdities, the historical possibles that allow for denial, and the great rejection. But they will be unable to frustrate a happy outcome.

To believe in the kingdom of God is to believe in a final and happy meaning for history. It is to affirm that utopia is more real than the weight of facts. It is to locate the truth concerning the world and human beings not in the past or completely in the present, but in the future, when it will be revealed in its fullness. To pray "thy kingdom come" is to activate the most radical hopes of the heart, so that it will not succumb to the continual brutality of present absurdities that occur at the personal and social level.

How will the kingdom of God come? For the Christian faith there is an infallible criterion that signals the arrival of the kingdom: when the poor are evangelized—that is, when justice begins to reach the poor, the dispossessed, and the oppressed. Whenever bonds of fellowship, of harmony, of participation, and of respect for the inviolable dignity of every person are created, then the kingdom of God has begun to dawn. Whenever social structures have been imposed on society that hinder persons from exploiting others, that do away with the relationships of master and slave, that favor fair dealing, then the kingdom of God is beginning to burst forth like the dawn.

St. Augustine, in commenting on the Lord's Prayer, says with great wisdom: "Thus it is the grace of living the right way that you ask for when you pray: thy kingdom come!"[72] When persons live as they should in the world, the kingdom of God is anticipated, hastened, and made concrete within history. "Living the right way" calls for many renunciations, the commitment of one's own life, and even martyrdom. "The souls of the martyrs under the altar invoke God with loud cries," Tertullian tells us in his comments on this supplication of the Lord's Prayer: "How long, sovereign Lord, holy and true, must it be before thou wilt vindicate us and avenge our blood on the inhabitants of the earth?" (Rev. 6:10). He continues: "They will obtain justice at the end of the ages. Lord, hasten the coming of your kingdom!"[73]

We need to become worthy of this supplication, "thy kingdom come!" As we follow Jesus, we lend credibility to his unlimited hope at the same time that we make this concrete in the zigzag paths of our lives. St. Cyril of Jerusalem has given us good counsel: "They who keep themselves pure in their actions, thoughts, and words are able to pray: thy kingdom come!"[74]

The supplication "thy kingdom come" is a cry that springs from the most radical hope, a hope that we often see contradicted, but which we never give up despite everything, as we hope for the revelation of an absolute meaning that is to be realized by God in all of creation. Those who thus pray commit themselves confidently to him who has been shown to be stronger than the strong man (Mark 3:27) and who therefore has the power to convert the old into the new and to inaugurate a new heaven and a new earth, where the reconciliation of everyone with everyone and everything will be the rule of the day. We can already give thanks for this promise inasmuch as the supplication "thy kingdom come" is being heard and answered: "We give thee thanks, O Lord God, sovereign over all, who art and who wast, because thou hast taken thy great power into thy hands and entered thy reign" (Rev. 11:17).

6

Thy Will Be Done

. . . And the woman whom I had known for some years called me aside and said in a mysterious tone of voice: "Father, I am going to show you a secret. Come!"

We entered a room. In the bed was her son. He was a monster. He had an enormous head, like that of an adult. His little body was like that of a child. His eyes stared up at the ceiling. His tongue darted in and out like that of a snake.

"My God!" I exclaimed in a kind of groan.

"Father," she said, "I have looked after this child for eight years now. He knows only me. I love him very much. Almost no one knows about it."

She concluded: "God is good. God is our Father. . . ."

And she looked upward, serene: "Your will be done on earth as it is in heaven!"

This was all she said. And she said everything.

I left without saying a word. With my head bowed. The child frightened me. The mother caused me perplexity. There was only one thought in my mind: "Woman, what faith you have!" (Matt. 15:28).

In order to understand this third supplication of the Lord's Prayer—"thy will be done on earth as in heaven"—we have to return to the context of what we have said thus far.[75] Our gaze is lifted heavenward and our face is kept turned toward God. Amid the misery of this world and the negation of historical meaning, we dare to cry: Our Father. The world does not recognize God;

it blasphemes his holy name (his reality). It is with full enthusiasm that we pray: thy name be hallowed! The new heaven and the new earth have already begun to appear in the coming, the message, and the presence of Jesus. The kingdom is already in the process of realization; but the fullness, unhappily, is still delayed. It is with anxious expectation that we pray: thy kingdom come.

No matter how much we pray and commit ourselves to follow the steps of Jesus, we never actually see the approach of the kingdom. The antichrist continues his work and the devil still has his followers. We may be visited by a feeling of desolation: Why does God delay? What is his will, after all? And in this context we continue to pray: thy will be done on earth as in heaven! What does this petition mean? It is important to know the will of God, how our own will is coordinated with God's will and what value is to be found in historical patience.

WHAT IS THE WILL OF GOD?

This is one of the most basic questions confronting any religious-minded person. We want to do the will of God, but what is this will, concretely, for any given situation? Where do we find it?

Before looking for an answer, we need to take stock of the prior experience behind the supplication "thy will be done on earth as in heaven." Anyone who prays this presupposes that our present world is not doing the will of God and that humanity is rebelling against God's will. As we have seen, our human history resists being conformed to the will of God; justice seems to be silenced, the rich are getting richer at the expense of the poor, more and more reduced to a kind of "fuel" for the production processes of economic and social elites. Only the elite have a planned life; the great majority are not doing what they would like to do or what they are fitted for, but what has been determined for them by their social status.

There is a thunderously silent protest rising to heaven, provoked by all this suffering, humankind's oppression of humankind, the powerful on the backs of the weak. There is no fantasy capable of exorcising all the ghosts that have been turned loose in the minds of millions, worn out with their sobbing and drowned in their own tears. We have an almost insuperable difficulty accepting ourselves; the way that leads to "the other" is blocked with almost immovable obstacles. One who prays "thy will be done" must have overcome the temptation to despair that is implied in this situation.

We discover another kind of silent protest on the part of the person who refuses to do the will of God. There is a reluctance, a selfishness that insists on doing one's own will without asking whether or not it harmonizes with the will of God. It is not uncommon for the protest to be an open one, as the many despondent ones of history refuse to admit that there is a sovereign will to be found in the gloomy scenario of contradictions that history cannot conceal. To pray "thy will be done" implies the ability to get out of oneself, to believe in the power of God's love despite human ill will, and to have confidence that human malice can be overcome by divine mercy.

We have to listen to all the overtones that are present in this supplication of the Lord's Prayer. We shall not deal with all the main points of all the problems involved in doing the will of God. We wish to remain within the context of Jesus' prayer, the Lord's Prayer. What was the will of God for Jesus? The answer comes at three levels that need to be differentiated and emphasized.

For Jesus, the unmistakable will of God is to establish God's kingdom. Thus the proclamation of the kingdom constitutes the central theme of his preaching, as we have noted before. God wants to be Lord of his creation, and this happens to the extent that every disorderly element in creation is subjugated (sickness, unjust human relations, abuses of power, death—in a word, sin) and that all this is brought to its maturity. Then and only then will the kingdom have been established.

The liberation of creation and its maximum extension is God's immutable will. Jesus did not just proclaim this will of God; he transformed it into reality by the things he did. In this sense, the supplication "thy will be done" repeats and intensifies what precedes it—that is, "thy kingdom come." Luke, in his version of the Lord's Prayer, omits this supplication, possibly because it adds nothing to the preceding supplication. Furthermore, the original Greek of Matthew has: "May your will *come about* (*genetheto*)," an expression that is also applied to the kingdom.

In St. John's Gospel, Jesus says clearly: "It is meat and drink for me to do the will of him who sent me until I have finished his work" (John 4:34). In another passage he makes the statement: "My aim is not my own will, but the will of him who sent me" (John 5:30). And he clarifies this statement with another that adds an additional meaning to the word "kingdom": "It is his will that I should not lose even one of all that he has given me, but to raise them all up on the last day" (John 6:39).

To lose no one and to raise each one up to fullness of life—this is what is meant by the expression "kingdom of God." St. Paul uses another terminology to express the same idea of this kingdom that God wants to establish: "He has made known to us his hidden purpose—such was his will and pleasure determined beforehand in Christ—to be put into effect when the time was ripe; namely, that the universe, all in heaven and earth, might be brought into a unity in Christ" (Eph. 1:9–10). The kingdom (or will) of God is realized when everything reaches its full unity and perfection. Its mediation is effected in Jesus Christ, who has proclaimed and brought into being the will and kingdom of God.

This kingdom is being built in opposition to the kingdom of Satan, who represents opposition to the will of God. He is the prince of this world (John 12:31, 14:30, 16:11; Eph. 2:2)—that is, he also possesses power and maintains an organization. In his public life, Jesus confronted him with his words and deeds (Luke 12:20; Mark 3:22–26). He subjected Satan to a severe defeat when he died on the cross (John 12:31–32, 14:30, 16:11; 1 Cor. 2:8). But Satan continues as the great antagonist (2 Cor. 4:4; 2 Thess. 2:7). In the end, however, he will be decisively defeated (Rev. 20:10).

To pray, in this sense, that God's will be done is to call upon God himself to bring about his kingdom. He has already officially inaugurated this kingdom in history, through Jesus. From this standpoint, the kingdom does not depend upon human activity; it is the kingdom of *God*; God will realize his eternal plan (Eph. 1:4), which is to make creation the locus of his presence, his glory, and his love. To pray "thy will be done" is to ask that this take place quickly; to ask that God not delay in accomplishing what he himself has proposed to do!

We have considered the will of God as something that belongs to God—his kingdom and his designs. But this will of God, besides its objective aspect, also has its subjective side, in that it is to be accepted and realized by human beings. The kingdom (the objective will of God) consists basically of a gift and an offering. God is always the first to love (1 John 4:19).

The kingdom and everything that comes from God is structured as a proposal, not as an imposition; it is a gesture of invitation and not a preemptive command. This is because God is love (1 John 4:8) and the law of love is that of a free commitment, an uncoerced offering, and an acceptance made in freedom. We must become open to the gift of God. The Scriptures issue a call to this human process of conversion. It is necessary for the kingdom to come to our world, to become de facto history.[76] Thus Jesus, in his very first proclamation, announces that the coming of the kingdom is already in progress, and at the same time he makes the plea: Be converted and believe this good news (Mark 1:15).

The coming of the kingdom is not automatic, with no collaboration on the part of human beings. The kingdom is of God, but it has to be appropriated by us. God does not save the world and humanity by himself. He involves the human race in this messianic project in such a way that one person becomes a sacrament of salvation for another. And this cooperation is of such a decisive nature that our eternal salvation depends upon its fulfillment. Thus we are dealing with a course of action that is demanded by the supreme Judge, particularly for what relates to providing assistance, solidarity, and liberation for the oppressed: "Anything you did for one of my brothers here, however humble, you did for me . . . anything you did not do for one of these, however humble, you did not do for me" (Matt. 25:40, 45).

It is not enough to say "Lord, Lord" and thus decipher the mystery that Jesus has hidden under the seeming frailty of an unexpectedly unspectacular messianic mission; only those are truly saved "who do the will of my heavenly Father" (Matt. 7:21). What is this "will"? We do not have to go far or dig deeply to find out: it is to live out discipleship to Jesus, to have the same mind that he had (Phil. 2:2, 5), to be oriented by the spirit of the Beatitudes and the Sermon on the Mount (Matt. 5–7). This conversion constitutes a true rebirth, and "unless a man has been born over again, he cannot see the kingdom of God" (John 3:3).

God does not desire the death of sinners, but that they be converted and live (see Ezek. 18:23, 32, 33:11; 2 Peter 3:9). The "good, acceptable and perfect will of God" is that we not become "adapted to the pattern of this present world, but with minds remade and your whole nature transformed" (Rom. 12:2). Paul summed it all up: "This is the will of God, that you be holy" (1 Thess. 4:3). And we have the guarantee that "he who does the will of God stands forevermore" (1 John 2:17). We even have God's promise that he will not abandon anyone who seeks him and that we should not "live for the rest of the days on earth for the things that men desire, but for what God wills" (1 Peter 4:2). We pray that he make us "perfect in all goodness so as to do his will" (Heb. 13:21), because it is he, in the final analysis, who "is at work in you, inspiring both the will and the deed" (Phil. 2:13).

Thus, when we pray "thy will be done," we mean: your will be done *for us;* we may be faithful to the task you assign us and to the gift of your kingdom, seeking to live in accordance with the newness of the message, the attitudes, and the life of Jesus Christ. Whenever anyone does the will of God, it is not only for the person but also for the world that the kingdom of God comes.[77]

The will of God further involves a component of patience, of humble abandonment to the mystery of God, and even of resignation. We know what the will of God is: the realization of the kingdom on the part of God and on the part of humanity. But this knowledge does not give us an understanding of the postponement of the new heaven and the new earth. Why does God not accomplish his will speedily? Why does he not inspire men and women to decide more quickly to live according to the standards of the kingdom? History continues in its ponderous zigzag course, with its absurdities, its unjust, sinful mechanisms, and the constant questionings that our hearts send heavenward. This experience becomes even more disturbing when we note that often the best projects, the most highly motivated intentions, and the most holy causes are defeated. It is not uncommon for the righteous to become marginal to society, for the wise to be ridiculed, and for saints to be executed. We see the frivolous triumph, we see the biased and dishonest turn a profit, and we see mediocre persons command the destinies of entire nations.

In this context, praying "thy will be done" means abandoning oneself to the mysterious designs of God. Here is a resignation that does not mean choosing the easiest path or the one that is most reasonable: true wisdom is not measured by the criteria that we use with our limited powers of reasoning, but by the parameters of God's wisdom, which is as high above us as the heavens are above the earth. If we are to accept the mysterious path of God, even when we see and understand nothing about it, then we need to renounce ourselves and our own plans. This requires detachment from our own will, even when it has been honestly and genuinely oriented. The titanism of a will that will dare anything but that is not submitted to a greater will is not an expression of the most human part of human nature. True greatness of spirit is to recognize the limits of one's range of possibilities and the finiteness of one's forces; this human condition opens up the possibility of a humble decision for a more transcendent plan that involves each of us and all of creation.

To pray "thy will be done" is equivalent to saying: let what God wants be done! There is no element of complaint or despair in this, but a confident commitment, like that of a child snuggling into the arms of its mother. God is Father and Mother of infinite goodness. He has his eternal plan; we also have our plans. As children who have never quite understood everything that our father does nor the full import of his words, so also we, as we pursue our pilgrimage, do not comprehend all the dimensions of history, nor can we understand the total meaning of what is being realized. It is without bitterness that we recognize the finite nature of our own viewpoints and commit ourselves to him who is the beginning and the end, in whose hands rests our entire itinerary.

This abandonment finds corroboration in the ancient wisdom of our Western culture, in men such as Seneca, Epictetus, Socrates, Marcus Aurelius, and others.[78] Nor is it absent in the Old Testament (see 1 Sam. 3:18; Tobit 3:6; Ps. 135:6, 143:10; Wisd. 9:13–18; 1 Macc. 3:60; 2 Macc. 1:3–4). According to the author of the Epistle to the Hebrews, Jesus, when he came into the world, said: "Sacrifice and offering thou [God] didst not desire, but thou hast prepared a body for me. Whole-offerings and sin-offerings thou didst not delight in. Then I said: 'Here I am: as it is written of me in the scroll, I have come, O God, to do thy will' " (Heb. 10:5–7).

In the garden of Gethsemane, when Jesus saw that his violent death was inevitable, he became profoundly distressed. But his serene abandonment to the will of God prevailed: "Father, if it be thy will, take this cup away from me. Yet not my will but thine be done" (Luke 22:42). Here we see the profound and real humanity of Jesus. He, like us, is also a pilgrim and wanderer; he shares the anxieties of one who does not know everything immediately and is not aware of every step toward the will of God.

There is no doubt that Jesus knew the will of God; but because of his human condition he still had not been enthroned in the fullness of God's kingdom, where everything is transparent; thus he had to search concretely for the will of God in the here and now. What steps should he take? How could he best realize the known will of God? Jesus was confronted with his human limitations and with his own anxiety. He was subject to anger toward those who did not accept his message. He accepted this situation; he did not ask for the forces of heaven to come to his aid (see Matt. 26:53). Here the Epistle to the Hebrews sheds some light when it testifies to this acceptance of Jesus. We translate the passage directly from the Greek, in an attempt to capture the spirit of the original:

> Christ, during his mortal life, directed to him who had the power to set him free, even from death, the insistent supplication of his own pain and his own tears; he was heard precisely because he accepted the pain and the tears with docility. And so, though he was the Son, he understood from his own suffering that the destiny of humankind is reached only by acceptance [hypakoe]. Besides achieving this destiny to arrive at the fullness of his own being [teleiotheis], he became the basis for eternal salvation for all those who follow his path. Thus God has appointed him as our High Priest [Heb. 5:7–9].

It is no wonder, then, that Jesus' last word, according to St. Luke, was an exclamation of total abandonment: "Father, into thy hands I commit my spirit!" (Luke 23:46). Here is the expression of radical human freedom: to commit oneself to a greater being who commands the ultimate meaning of every quest and who knows the why of every failure. The expression that is a part of our daily language—"God willing"—has a profound theological root (see Rom. 1:10, 15:32; 1 Cor. 4:19, 16:7; Acts 18:21; James 4:15). It presupposes that the true center of the human person is not the "I" but the (divine) "thou." Human freedom will come to pass only if it is oriented toward this center; then the will of God is realized and the kingdom is at hand.[79]

ON EARTH AS IN HEAVEN

In the language of the Middle East and the Old Testament, the words "heaven and earth" are used to provide a spatial definition of the totality of God's creation (see Matt. 5:18, 24:35). Thus God is "Lord of heaven and earth" (Matt. 11:25) and the resurrected Christ received authority over heaven and earth (Matt. 28:18). To pray "thy will be done on earth as in heaven" means: to do the will of God everywhere and always. The kingdom of God is not and never will be a *specific geographical region* of creation; it is the *whole* of creation (heaven and earth) transfigured. The will of God encompasses the totality of his creation. For our part, our conversion, our sanctification (our own part in realizing the will of God), cannot be restricted to a particular dimension of human life, such as just to the heart or exclusively to the religious or ethical field; sanctification must occur in every sphere into which our existence extends.

Today we are especially sensitive to structural sin and social injustice; this is of essential importance in realizing holiness in social relationships, and in economic, political, and cultural mechanisms. There is no area of space that is to be closed off from the transformation intended by the kingdom of God; the leavening action of the new heaven and the new earth is to begin in everything. All of these requirements are bound up in the expression "on earth as in heaven"—in other words, doing the will of God in everything and in all dimensions.

On the other hand, the correlation, on earth *as* in heaven, allows us to enrich the above interpretation. In line with biblical thinking, God already reigns in heaven. That is where his throne is (see Isa. 66:1; Matt. 5:34–35; Ps. 103:19–21). All the inhabitants of heaven (angels and the righteous) do the will of God fully, as Psalm 103 says so explicitly. Earth is the place where the will of God is still opposed, where God exercises his historical magnanimity and patience (see Rom. 2:4). The supplication means: just as the will of God is already done in heaven, so let it also be done on earth as soon as possible. May the kingdom that is already victorious in heaven be also established on earth! Origen has an excellent comment on this petition: "If the will of God were done on earth as it is in heaven, earth would no longer be earth . . . we would then all be in heaven."[80]

Thus everything is to arrive at the point of full reconciliation: heaven is to come down to earth and earth is to be raised up to heaven. And then the end will come: God will be all and in all (1 Cor. 15:28). As long as this has not happened, then we must always and everywhere pray: "thy kingdom come; thy will be done on earth as in heaven!"

7

Give Us Today
Our Daily Bread

Early in the morning, as they do every day,
the young men are contesting with the dogs
over rights to the garbage can.

They mix and remix,
they take out what is edible from the garbage.

And they share this rotten refuse with the dogs.

In a dog-eat-dog world,
where there is no pity,
this is how God is left to answer
the prayer of the hungry ones:
give us today our daily bread!

Today—no, all week—
the bread on our table has not been the same.
It was bitter bread,
full of the curses of the poor
who had been begging God for it.

It regained its taste and goodness
only when it was shared with those starving creatures,
the boys and the dogs.

This petition—"give us today our daily bread"—marks a turning point in the Lord's Prayer. The first part was directed toward
heaven: the divine reality of God as Father, the transcendent one
(in heaven) and at the same time nearby (our Father) who must
always be sanctified, whose kingdom is to come and be made
history among us, thus achieving the ultimate will of God. The
tone is solemn and the phrases are cadenced. Now, in the second
part, our gaze is turned toward the earth and toward humankind and its needs: the bread necessary for life, forgiveness
for disruptions of fellowship, strength against temptation, and
deliverance from evil. The phrases are long, and their tone conveys the affliction that is so much a part of human life. In the
first part of the prayer, God's concerns are dealt with; in the second part, human concerns. Both belong in the prayer.

In the second part, we see no mysticizing or spiritualizing: here is
human life in its historical, infrastructural, biological, and social
concreteness, forever threatened. It is not concerned only with humanity; God is also involved. This makes it the stuff of prayer
and supplication. Thus there is no competition between the vertical concerns of God and the horizontal concerns of humanity.
Both meet under the rainbow of prayer. The unmistakable union
of material and spiritual, of human and divine, constitutes the
force emanating from the mystery of the incarnation. In the kingdom of God there is an interlocking of material and spiritual, of
human nature and cosmos, of creation and Creator. We should
not be surprised, then, if in the Lord's Prayer the two are brought
together; here the most sublime encounters that which is most
down-to-earth. That which is routine, obvious, and ordinary—
bread—has a standing both before God and before humanity.
The Lord's Prayer vigorously reaffirms this truth in defiance of
spiritualizers.[81]

BREAD: THE DIVINE DIMENSION OF MATTER

This petition centers on the word "bread." We need to deal
with this word, pure and simple, before dealing with the qualifi-
cations that go with it ("our" and "today" or "each day"). The
word "bread" has a highly significant content; we find here an

important aspect of anthropology—that is, the study of the human phenomenon. The meaning of bread goes beyond its physical and chemical composition. It is a symbol of all human food, the food that we cannot do without (Prov. 20:13, 30:8; Ps. 146:7; Lev. 26:5; Eccles. 9:7; Sir. 31:23–24). Bread is the "bread of life" (John 6:35).

Human life is indissolubly connected with a material infrastructure. No matter how high the spirit soars, no matter how deep our mystical probings, or how metaphysical our abstract thinking, the human being will always be dependent on a piece of bread, a cup of water—in short, on a handful of matter. The material infrastructure is so important that ultimately we find it the root and ground of everything we think about or plan or do. It is like the foundation of a building: it makes reference, ultimately, not only to the floors of the building and the furniture found in its rooms, but also the persons who live there. It is the condition that makes possible human existence and survival. It is thus like the human food that is symbolized by bread: life depends upon it, upon its opaque materiality, upon its material substance. Life is more than bread, but at any given moment it cannot get along without bread.

In theological terms, the human infrastructure is so important that God connects being saved and being lost with a just and comradely concern that we may or may not put into practice. Thus, in the final analysis, we are to be judged by the supreme Judge according to criteria found in the infrastructure: whether or not we have looked after the hungry, the naked, the thirsty, the prisoner. Our eternal destiny is thus ultimately involved with bread, with water, with clothing, and with solidarity with others (see Matt. 25:31–46).

Thus the stomach assumes an importance in line with that of the heart and the head. There is no prayer or spiritual activity that takes the place of bread, or of the frequently heavy labor required to earn it and to put it on the table of the hungry. Nor can pious speech quell the hunger of a starving person. God wants us to earn bread with our work, which involves time, sweat, tears, and some degree of remoteness from God, because we are so busy with earthly things instead of those of heaven. God wants us to be concerned not only with his affairs, his kingdom, his will, and his name, but also with human affairs, human needs, human hunger, the desperate need for protection and salvation. Human beings are not here on earth just for God, but also for themselves. God wants it that way. To pray to God means to include everything and offer it to the Father—both God's affairs and humanity's affairs.[82]

If we observe closely, we will see that a turning has been made in the Lord's Prayer. In the first three supplications (thy name be hallowed, thy kingdom come, thy will be done) we concern ourselves with God's affairs. In the next four petitions (concerning bread, forgiveness of transgressions, temptation, and deliverance from evil) it is God who is concerned with our affairs. These two dimensions must never be separated: the Lord has brought them together in his prayer. We should never feel ashamed of our needs. God cares about hunger; it is his intention to hear our pleas and to fill the hungry mouth. This provides a guarantee of life, the most precious gift that we have received from God.

Thus matter becomes the vehicle of a divine reality: it is sacramental; it becomes evident in proportion to our assurance that bread, according to the Scriptures, constitutes the historical symbol of the kingdom of God, represented as a great feast. It is the temporal sign of the eternal food that guarantees everlasting life. Bread conveys the promise of a fullness of life; even more, it makes present, right now, in the midst of this journey of hungry pilgrims, the bread that completely satisfies humankind's salvific hunger— that is, Jesus and his kingdom.

All this is contained in that monosyllabic, everyday, natural, simple word: bread.

THE SIGNIFICANCE OF "OUR": THE SECRET OF HAPPINESS

The need for bread is an individual matter, but the satisfaction of that need cannot be an individual effort; it must be that of a community. Thus we do not pray "my Father," but "our Father." There is here a profound meaning in Jesus' prayer. It is true that the Old Testament recognizes individual satisfaction: "Eat your food and enjoy it" (Eccles. 9:7); "share your bread with the hungry" (Isa. 58:7). But with Jesus we achieve a full awareness of human fellowship.[83] We have a Father who belongs to all of us, because he is *our* Father; we are all his offspring, and thus we are all brothers and sisters. Mere personal satisfaction of hunger without considering the others would be a breach of that fellowship. A person is not just interested in deadening hunger and surviving "somehow." Eating means more than a mere satisfaction of nutritional requirements; it is a communitarian act and a communion rite. Eating is not as enjoyable or fully human if done in sight of the misery of others, the Lazaruses at the foot of the table, waiting for the leftover crumbs. Daily bread provides a basic and necessary happiness for life. If there is to be any happiness, it must be communicated and shared. That is how it is with bread: it is *human* bread to the extent that it is shared and supports a bond of communion. Then happiness is found, and human hunger is satisfied.

Beneath the bread that we consume daily is hidden a whole network of anonymous relationships of which we need to remind ourselves. Before it reaches our table it receives the labor of many hands. The seed is planted in the ground; it has to be tended as it grows. Many hands harvest the grain or maneuver the powerful machinery. Many other hands store the grain and make the bread. Then there are the thousands of distribution points. In all this we find the greatness and the wretchedness of human nature. There can be relationships involving exploitation. Tears are shed over every loaf that we so calmly eat, but we also sense the fellowship and the sharing. Daily bread encompasses the entire human universe in its lights and shadows.

This bread that is jointly produced must be distributed and consumed in concert with others. Only then can we truthfully ask for *our* daily bread. God does not hear the prayer that asks only for *my* bread. A genuine relationship with God calls for maintaining a relationship with others. When we present God with our own needs, he wants us to include those of our brothers and sisters. Otherwise the bonds of fellowship are severed and we live only for ourselves. We all share the same basic necessity; collective satisfaction of that need makes us brothers and sisters.

When the bread that we eat is the result of exploitation, it is not a bread blessed by God. It may supply the chemical needs of nutrition but fail to nourish human life, which is human only when lived within the framework of justice and fraternity. Unjust bread is not really our bread; it is stolen; it belongs to someone else. The great medieval mystic, Meister Eckhart, well said: "They who do not give to another what belongs to the other are not eating their own bread, but are eating both their bread and the other's."[84]

The thousands of hungry persons in our cities and the millions of starving persons in our world question the quality of our bread: it is bitter because it contains too many children's tears; it is hard because its substance embraces the torture of so many empty stomachs. It does not deserve to be called *our* bread. If the bread is to be ours, then we must transform the world and deliver society from the mechanisms that permit wealth to be maintained at the expense of bread taken from the mouths of others.

Bread calls us to a collective conversion. This condition must be fulfilled if our prayer is not to be vain and pharisaical. The gospel forbids me to ask only for myself, disregarding the needs of others known by me. Only *our* bread is God's bread.

EACH DAY: BREAD NECESSARY FOR TIME
AND FOR ETERNITY

To the concept of "our" bread we add a very important qualifying phrase: "daily" or "each day" or "for the morrow." The Greek term used is *epiousios*.[85] The matter of its exact meaning is a problem for the experts, because this word, as Origen had already observed in his commentary on the Our Father,[86] has no parallel in any secular Greek text (except perhaps the Hawara papyrus of Upper Egypt, which dates from the fifth century A.D.)[87] and seems to have been coined by the evangelists. Thus our only recourse is philological analysis. There are three possibilities.

One interpretation derives *epiousios* from *epi* ("over, upon, through," etc.) - *einai* (from the verb "to be"). *Ousios* is an adjective; it would have the meaning: "bread for the day that is now, daily bread, the bread given day by day." The most ancient Latin translations (the *Itala*) understood it thus. One may also read it as: the bread "necessary for existence, indispensable for existence" *(epi ousia)*.

The bread that provides for our basic needs is each day's bread, as we commonly pray for it. In the Vulgate, St. Jerome translated the Matthean version of this petition *panis supersubstantialis* (which is a literal translation: *epi = super,* and *ousios = substantialis*), whereas for the Lukan version he translated it *panis quotidianus.*

The second interpretation understands *epiousios* as a derivative of *epi + ienai* ("to come" or "arrive"). The resultant meaning would be: "our bread for the morrow, for the day that is coming, our future bread." In his comments on the Gospel of Matthew, St. Jerome mentions that the Gospel of the Hebrews (an apocryphal Semitic writing) translates *epiousios* ("supersubstantial") with the Hebrew word *machar,* which means "tomorrow"—that is, the future.[88] The reading would then be: "give us today (or "each day") our bread for the morrow."

The third interpretation, which is the most recent, derives from the discovery that there are many compound words such as *epiousios* whose prefix has no specific meaning; it is an "empty" prefix.[89] Words of this kind are found in every language. In English, for example, we may speak of "loosening" a rope or shoestrings, or we may speak of "unloosening" them; both words are identical in meaning, even though the prefix "un" normally indicates a negation or opposite meaning to that of the root word. In French, there are words such as *partir* ("to depart") and *départ* ("departure"); *chercher* ("to investigate") and *recherche* ("investigation"). The prefix *de* of *départ* and the *re* of *recherche* add nothing to the root meanings of their respective words. In Greek there are thirteen compound adjectives formed with *ousios* (with the prefixes *an, en, omoi, hyper,* etc.), all of which have the substantive *ousia* as their root (meaning "substance" or "essence").

In the case with which we are concerned, in the combination *epi + ousios* the prefix *epi* is not to be translated *super*—as St. Jerome would have it—because *epi* conveys the idea of "concerning" or "belonging to." Thus *epiousios* would mean: "that which concerns the essence, the essential, the substantial." But this is already the common meaning of the word *ousios* without any prefix. At most, the prefix would have an intensive function, reinforcing the original meaning; but it adds nothing to the original meaning. There are various words in the Greek language with the prefix *epi* where it does not enrich the root (*epinephes* = "cloudy"; *epidorpios* = "relating to stew, stewed"; *epikephalios* = "relating to the head"). The word *epiousios* would seem to be of the same type. The prefix *epi* carries no special meaning. The phrase would thus mean: "essential bread, substantial bread, the bread necessary for life." But what is necessary for life belongs to our day-by-day experience, to each day. Thus the third interpretation approximates the first.

Which of these explanations is closest to the mark? Is it tomorrow's bread or is it today's? Both meanings are possible. To decide for one meaning or the other requires more than philological reasoning. Exegetes or theologians will decide upon the meaning that best corresponds to their conception of the historical Jesus and his message. Thus those who tend to interpret Jesus of Nazareth within an eschatological framework prefer the second meaning: give us today the bread of the future.[90] Others, who understand Jesus and his message from a noneschatological perspective (Jesus was not expecting an immediate end to history and the final coming of the kingdom), will interpret *epiousios* as bread for today (the bread that we need each day), the essential and substantial bread for our pilgrimage on earth (the first and third interpretations).

This problem of the Lord's Prayer is not solved just by recourse to historical criticism and its reference to the historical Jesus. The Lord's Prayer was the most important prayer of the Christian community at that time, for whom the *eschaton* was situated in an unknown future. It is in terms of the present situation, the temporal world, as history is being made day by day, that the Lord's Prayer is to be prayed today. The words take on a "church community" significance that may differ from that of its origin with the historical Jesus. In other words, to the primeval meaning that Jesus himself attached to it is added another, conferred upon it by the early community, already organized into churches, finally culminating in a meaning that we attribute to it today, in our own situation. All of these meanings can be true. The most ancient meaning need not be the only correct one; it is like a fountainhead that gives rise to other interpretations, all of which add meaning to a life of prayer.

Thus, in this intricate discussion of the original meaning of the expression *epiousios,* as to whether it means future bread, daily bread, or essential bread, we see three levels of meaning. Each of them presupposes the other and is interlocked with it. All of these interpretations are an echo of the same expression, "our bread for each day."

For my part, I feel that the meaning conveyed by the historical Jesus is that of future bread, tomorrow's bread. This choice is based on a conviction, which I cannot fully explain here, that the historical Jesus was motivated in the context of an apocalypti-coeschatological perspective.[91] He lived with the expectation that the kingdom of God was about to break forth, but without a clear-cut delineation of the "times and seasons" of its inauguration.

The hard core of his proclamation, the Sermon on the Mount, the radical nature of his demands—all lend a high probability to this interpretation. In line with such an interpretation, the gospels attest repeatedly that the kingdom of God is comparable to a feast. The true "substantial" bread will be served at the heavenly table. Our petition for food (bread) is related to this heavenly banquet. Thus we read in Luke 14:15, "Happy the man who shall sit at the feast in the kingdom of God." The same eschato-logical term is found in another text of Luke, 6:21: "How blessed are you who now go hungry; your hunger will be satisfied." On other occasions Jesus speaks of "eating and drinking at my table in the kingdom" (Luke 22:30), and he says that "many will come from East and West to feast with Abraham, Isaac, and Jacob in the kingdom of Heaven" (Matt. 8:11). The Apocalypse describes heaven as a place where the righteous will no longer be hungry (Rev. 7:16). This future bread in the eternal kingdom of the Father is the object of our petition, "give us this bread now." In other words, "May your kingdom come soon! Bring about your liber-ating intervention, Lord, as quickly as possible. Take us to the banquet where the real substantial food (bread) is served, the food that imparts eternal life."

The Old Testament provides some basis for this eschatological interpretation. Concerning the manna, it is stated in Exodus: "I will rain down bread from heaven for you. Each day . . . a day's supply" (Exod. 16:4). In Psalm 78:24, we find: "And he rained down upon them manna for them to eat and gave them the grain of heaven." Jesus himself refers to this text when he says: "It was not Moses who gave you the bread from heaven; my Father gives you the real bread from heaven" (John 6:32).

This interpretation—of giving us today the bread of tomorrow (the future)—seems to fit well into the framework of Jesus' eschatological mentality. But note carefully: the meaning of this future, eschatological bread in the kingdom of God is rooted in the materiality of a concrete, historical bread. Any real symbol (bread of heaven) has its basis in concrete reality (bread of earth). No real symbol exists in its own right; there is always some reference to the foundation on which it is constructed. In other words, to ask for the bread of heaven (future bread) we must at the same time ask for material bread for our bodies. Otherwise we could not understand what is meant by the really substantial bread of the kingdom of God. Deprive the symbol of its reality and it becomes nothing. Heavenly bread, deprived of earthly bread, is incomprehensible. Here we are not retracting anything that we stated above as to the down-to-earth reality of the bread that nourishes our lives, which allows us to be promised the bread that actually bestows eternal life in the kingdom of the Father.

In the noneschatological view of Jesus, the more reasonable interpretation of *epiousios* is bread for each day, "daily bread." This was the meaning arrived at by the Christian community that dwelt on the fringes of history and tried to live the ideal demanded by Jesus, of a serene abandonment to divine providence.[92] The Lord taught his disciples "not to be anxious about tomorrow" (Matt. 6:34), and not to be anxious about what to eat or what to wear (Matt. 6:25). In sending the disciples on a mission, he advised them not to take along any provisions: "no bread, no pack, no money in their belts" (Mark 6:8). The evangelical ideal consists in living a life of poverty, completely abandoned to the ministrations of divine providence. God would provide the basic necessities. It is a radical ideal. There have always been spirits, down through history, who took the words of the Lord seriously and lived this kind of life.

What is being asked for by this petition in the Lord's Prayer is the bread necessary for each day. Even the Old Testament taught: "Give me neither poverty nor wealth; provide me only with the food I need" (Prov. 30:8; see also Sir. 40:29). Thus one does not ask God for wealth or a comfortable life or for convenience; but neither does the Old Testament exalt poverty as the absence of what is necessary. It asks only for what is sufficient to keep the petitioner alive for today. The basic necessities are what this visualizes. Bread here stands simply for food, but always, in the Scriptures, this is related also to clothing (Deut. 10:18), to water (Deut. 9:9), to wine (Eccles. 9:7) and to oil (Ps. 104:15). Jesus rejects any sort of greed or unnecessary accumulation.

This daily bread, necessary to one's material life, serves as a basis for another meaning that would also have been in the thinking of the early Christian community. What is the bread needed for spiritual life and humankind's religious dimension? Jesus presents himself as "the bread of life" (John 6:35); "I am speaking of the bread . . . which a man may eat, and never die" (John 6:50); "he shall live forever" (6:51). The bread does not just refer to Jesus. In this daily bread there is also the echo of another bread eaten daily by the Christian community, the Eucharist: "The bread which I will give is my own flesh; I give it for the life of the world" (John 6:51); "whoever eats my flesh and drinks my blood possesses eternal life, and I will raise him up at the last day . . . whoever eats this bread shall live forever" (John 6:54, 58).

These varied meanings have a certain resonance, a vividness of meaning, for the faithful, when they pray: "Give us today our daily bread." Primarily it has to do with the material bread without which life cannot continue. This bread points to that bread in the kingdom of God where life will be eternal and happy. The bread of the kingdom has already been anticipated; it is Jesus himself in his life and message. Jesus finds continuity in history in the form of the eucharistic bread, which we have as the anticipatory firstfruits of the kingdom and of the salvation whose outlines have already been traced by Jesus himself. The historical Jesus, the early Christian community, and we ourselves in today's world, with all our material and spiritual needs, are to be found in this brief but weighty expression: our daily bread.

GIVE US TODAY—HUMAN WORK AND DIVINE PROVIDENCE

Scripture is full of passages expressing the conviction that it is God who gives bread or food. All nourishment is a divine gift. We should give thanks for it. The first of the table prayers recited by pious Jews begins: "Blessed are you, Lord our God, King of the universe, who feed the whole world by your goodness. By your grace, love, and mercy you give bread to every creature, for your mercy endures forever." Only a pagan or an atheist would not know how to give thanks for daily food. It is in this context that we must understand the petition: *give us* today our daily bread.

But what does it mean, concretely, to ask God for the bread we need? Is it not human labor that puts bread on the table? Jesus recognizes the importance of work. Paul tells us quite realistically: "The man who will not work shall not eat" (2 Thess. 3:10). But human labor is not all that goes into bread. We are dependent on so many predetermined circumstances, in the face of which everyone feels impotent and in the hands of divine providence. It is he who gives us good weather and rain; it is he who gives the strength by which we can do our work; it is he who causes the seed to grow. He is the Lord of creation, a creation that we may modify by our labor but which we cannot produce. In each piece of bread God's hand is more present than is the human hand. Thus believers are quite correct in directing their petition for bread to their Father in heaven.

Furthermore, this petition for bread has an eminently concrete meaning in our own day. There are millions who sort through garbage piles in search of bare necessities. Hundreds of thousands die every year for lack of sufficient bread. The specter of malnutrition and hunger becomes more and more a threat to the entire human race. To these millions of starving persons the plea for bread has a direct, immediate meaning. The words recall, to those whose hunger is satisfied, the admonition of God himself: "Share your food with the hungry" (Isa. 58:7). How bluntly it was put by St. Basil the Great (fourth century):

> The bread that is spoiling in your house belongs to the hungry. The shoes that are mildewing under your bed belong to those who have none. The clothes stored away in your trunk belong to those who are naked. The money that depreciates in your treasury belongs to the poor!

In St. Matthew's version of the prayer the petition is for our bread "today" *(semeron)*; in St. Luke's version it is bread for "each day" *(kat'emeran)*. Both meanings are valid.[93] The first version refers to the immediate sense of the petition: a request for the bread that is needed now, today. The second version refers to the continuing intention of discipleship: asking for the bread that is needed today and every day, thus commending oneself to divine providence.

THE HOLINESS OF BREAD

It is deeply imbedded in human consciousness that bread represents a holy reality. Bread is treated with respect and veneration. Only desacralized societies act otherwise, and it is because they have lost their basic point of reference as to what is holy and sublime for humankind and the world. Bread is holy because it is associated with the mystery of life, which is sacrosanct.

For the person of the Old Testament, bread was one of the primordial signs of the grace and love with which God sustained and surrounded his people. It was what God used to exorcise the demons of hunger and death. For the Christian believer, bread is even more holy because it symbolizes the final reunion of all the just at their banquet with God in the future kingdom. It is also a meaningful symbol of Jesus, the bread of life, who has redeemed us to eternal life. Daily bread is holy for still one other reason: it is the material that, when transubstantiated, constitutes the sacrament of the Eucharist, the bread of pilgrims. It nourishes their life, so that they may be resurrected and experience eternal happiness.

To the word "bread" the mysterious word *epiousios* ("supersubstantial, daily, necessary, future, essential") has been added—a word not found elsewhere in Greek literature. It seems to have been coined by the evangelists, as was recognized by Origen. It may possibly have been coined to express all the secret wealth that is hidden away in the simple reality of bread. The whole spectrum of varied meanings needs to reverberate in the soul of one who would understand this petition and include it in the daily recitation of the Lord's Prayer.

8

Forgive Us the Wrong
We Have Done

Lord,
as you look upon those who imprison us
and upon those who deliver us to the torture chamber;
when you consider the actions of our jailers
and the heavy sentences passed upon us by our judges;
when you pass judgment on the life of those who humiliate us
and the conscience of those who reject us,
forgive, O Lord, the evil that they may have done.

Remember, rather, that it was by this sacrifice
that we draw close to your crucified Son:
through torture,
    we obtain his wounds;
through jail terms,
    his freedom of spirit;
through punishment,
    the hope of his kingdom;
through humiliation,
    the joy of his sons.

Remember, O Lord,
that this suffering germinates, within us,
the crushed seed that sprouts,
the fruit of justice and of peace,
the flower of light and of love.

But remember especially, O Lord,
that we never want to be like them,
or do to our neighbors what they have done to us.
  —Brother Fernando, Brother Ivo, and Brother Betto,
  "Oração de um prisioneiro" ("Prayer of a Prisoner"),
  in O Canto na fogueira *("Song from the Execution Pyre"),*
  Petrópolis, 1977, p. 346

To be sure, we do not live by bread alone (Matt. 4:4), even though bread is needed. But apart from this minimum infrastructure (food) without which human beings cannot exist or survive, they find themselves caught up in a social fabric that is also an essential part of their very being. In this dimension, one not only lives, but also cohabits, "lives-with." It is here that the human being emerges as a person—that is, as someone capable of relating to others, of listening to or making a proposal, of giving a response to "the other," and of having a sense of responsibility.

To speak of a "person" is to speak of relationships, ties, and alliances that make persons responsible to others, fulfilling them, frustrating them, making them happy or unhappy. As a person, a man or a woman is a responsible being, which also means being responsible to God, either responding to his love or refusing it and withdrawing into a shell. Conscience is the place where one hears the call of "the other" and of God. Freedom brings a person to openness or closedness, to acceptance or refusal of responsibility.

THE EXPERIENCE OF OFFENSE AND INDEBTEDNESS

At the level of relationships, whether to God or to others, various attitudes take shape: love, friendship, sympathy, cooperation, indifference, withdrawal, humiliation, arrogance, exploitation. There is no neutrality here; taking a position is unavoidable: one is either for or against, at varying levels of commitment. The human ego always manifests itself in living with others and committing oneself to them.

Within all this interrelatedness one finds an experience of indebtedness to someone else, or even of reciprocal offenses committed. We feel indebted to others. We did not ask to be born. Once born, there were those who accepted us, fed us, and gave us the care that was indispensable to a healthy life, whereas so many others have been rejected and eliminated.

Religious persons experience something similar in relation to God: they are given existence, health, clothing, the roof over their heads, their intelligence, will to exist, friends, and many excellent things that are a part of life that could not be produced merely by human ingenuity. They experience them simply as a gift from the Father. We see ourselves as debtors; the emotion of thanksgiving arises quite naturally. This might be called an innocent debt, and in a sense it will never be paid. No matter how hard we might try, we shall never repay our debt to the author of life—whether our earthly parents or God.[94] There is a gospel passage that applies here: no matter how much we do to earn gratitude, we are servants and deserve no credit; we have only done our duty (Luke 17:10).

But there is another type of indebtedness that is not so "innocent," a debt of guilt. This is the debt resulting from offenses and sins, a debt that needs to be repaid. Our conscience perceives it as guilt in terms of a relationship that is damaging to human communication, to love, to human nature itself. This offense, or sin, in order to be experienced as such, presupposes a relationship with other persons and a communion with God. What should have been done was not done. Neighbors needed a word from me that would reassure them, and I denied it to them. The sight of them called out for mercy, but I was hardhearted and humiliated them. The poor tell me their troubles and stretch out their hand for help, but I pass by. The eyes of the children glitter with hunger, babies shiver feverishly in the arms of emaciated, undernourished mothers, and I turn away my face in order to keep my composure. On other occasions there has been blind hatred, the overt exploitation of the weak, of one's employees, of someone's ignorance, or physical elimination of troublemakers. Fellowship has been breached and humanity violated. There has been injustice and contempt. A brother or sister was offended. And God has been affected because what pleases him is mercy, love, justice, solidarity—and these have all been betrayed.

We are not giving full expression to this experience if we merely say that a law has been violated. The law commanded me to do to someone else what I should like to have done to me, and I did not do it! Vis-à-vis an abstract law, we do not really feel guilty, but mostly just regret. But what actually happened was a violation of a personal relationship. It was not just a law but a *person* whose dignity was wounded, whose needs were not met; a personal relationship was fractured—not to mention solidarity among all human beings and with God himself. This guilt is most sharply expressed when we feel the call of God and reject it; not a general call but a personal appeal, a vocation that requires commitment of our entire being. A call to fidelity, character development, and growth is not heeded; goods entrusted to our management are buried and yield no gain (see Matt. 25:14–30).

We experience a feeling of responsibility for the offense committed. It did not need to happen, but it did. We experience an indebtedness and the need to ask forgiveness. There is nothing psychopathic or obsessive about this (in such cases the guilt has no real object, and this is what makes it pathological); it is rather a healthy indicator of something that needs to be made right, that requires the restoration of a human relationship that has been violated.[95] Deeply rooted in every person is the awareness that not everything is right in his or her life: "All of us often go wrong" (James 3:2). To be sincere, we have to acknowledge to ourselves that we are sinners; "if we claim to be sinless, we are self-deceived and strangers to the truth" (1 John 1:8). And sin is revealed to the conscience as a debt that needs to be paid. Spontaneous supplication occurs frequently in the Scriptures: Lord, have mercy on us! "In the fullness of thy mercy blot out my misdeeds" (Ps. 51:1). Tormented in conscience, the psalmist cries out: "Look at my misery and my trouble, and forgive me every sin!" (Ps. 25:18). And Sirach suggests that the safest way to obtain forgiveness for our sins is to forgive those who have offended us: "Forgive your neighbor his wrongdoing; then, when you pray, your own sins will be forgiven" (Sir. 28:2). And Jesus says quite matter-of-factly: "Acquit, and you will be acquitted" (Luke 6:37).

Quite apart from this possibility of mutual forgiveness, we sense that we are always in debt. It is not just a matter of renouncing a sinful attitude or of making reparation for an offensive deed: sin has deeper roots and pervades our whole existence. We live in a sinful context; the very life-giving air that we breathe has been polluted, even though God's abiding grace and mercy are also present.[96] This is why we feel like the victims of the forces of evil that now and then lead us into sin and into breaking the ties of fellowship. It is not just a mistake to be corrected but a situation to be renewed; a new person must come to life. This is what is so profoundly liberating about the message of Jesus, who is the incarnation of the Father's mercy and forgiveness: "My son, your sins are forgiven!" (Mark 2:5). The good news of Jesus includes not only salvation and the genesis of a new heaven and a new earth inhabited by a renewed humankind, but also the radical and complete remission of all indebtedness and the final forgiveness of all sin.

FORGIVE US THE WRONG WE HAVE DONE

The observations made above were necessary in order for us to understand this fifth petition of the Lord's Prayer: "Forgive us the wrong we have done, as we have forgiven those who have wronged us." This petition expresses the cry, almost the lament, of hopelessly sinful humankind, a cry directed to the Father of infinite mercy.

The Matthean and Lukan versions do not completely agree. Matthew focuses on "wrongs" or "debts," an expression drawn from the business world (financial debts) but which with time had taken on a religious nuance, as a synonym for "offense." The word "offense" in turn emphasizes the personal nature of sin which, as we have seen, does not imply simply the violation of a standard but also the breaking of an interpersonal relationship that involves God, who is present in every person and in every human relationship. Luke's text runs: "And forgive us our sins, for we too forgive all who have done us wrong" (Luke 11:4). Luke translates "wrongs" or "debts" as "sins" to make it easier for his readership to understand, because they were Greeks, for whom "wrongs" or "debts" had none of the religious connotation that it did for Semites. Nevertheless, in the second part of the petition he uses the expression "who have done us wrong," where we would expect "sinners" or "those who sin against us." This reinforces the conviction that Matthew's version is more original than that of Luke.

We need to reflect on the good news of God's forgiveness, proclaimed and practiced by Jesus. This is the background against which this petition of the Lord's Prayer is uttered.

Jesus' proclamation does not just concentrate on the joyful news that the new heaven and the new earth are about to emerge, whereby total, global liberation is in process and is about to arrive in its fullness. What makes the good news "good" and "happy" is that its first hearers were the poor, the weak, those on the margins of society, and sinners. The Father to whom Jesus bore witness is a father of infinite goodness, who "is kind to the ungrateful and wicked" (Luke 6:35). He is the God of the lamb that strays (Luke 15:1–7), of the lost coin (Luke 15:8–10), and of the prodigal son (Luke 15:11–32). He is the God who rejoices more over one sinner who is converted than over ninety-nine righteous who have no need of conversion (Luke 15:7).

Jesus, who is the incarnation in this world of the Father's mercy, is himself merciful. He practices what he preaches to others: "Be compassionate, as your Father is compassionate" (Luke 6:36). This is why he visits the homes of sinners (Mark 2:15; Luke 19:1–9), to the point where he is regarded as a friend of sinners (Matt. 11:19). This is not a mere humanitarian gesture; it derives from his own experience of a merciful God. Jesus makes sinners feel that they are not automatically excluded from the Father's love, but that the Father loves them with infinite tenderness and that they may accordingly return to his favor. The Father will receive them with open arms and the kiss of pardon (Luke 15:20; 2 Sam. 14:33).

This gospel of mercy was a stumbling block to some religious persons of Jesus' day, and it continues to scandalize believers even now. Fervent Christians have worked hard to follow the Lord's ways, and so they imagine that because of this they are the only ones whom God loves. Such an attitude transforms them into Pharisees, who treat with harshness the weak and the errant. The principal parables of Jesus dealing with forgiveness and mercy are not directed to sinners but to the pious and those who criticize the prodigal liberality of Jesus and his Father. Jesus' proclamation and merciful practices—allowing himself to be anointed by a well-known prostitute (Luke 7:36–50)—generate criticism. Jesus defends his merciful approach very bluntly: it is not the healthy, but those who are sick, who needed a doctor (Mark 2:17); the Son of Man came to seek and to save what is lost (Luke 19:10); he is sent to the lost sheep of the house of Israel (Matt. 15:24). He speaks provocatively to the religious teachers of his day: the tax collectors and prostitutes (who recognize him) will go into the kingdom of heaven ahead of them (Matt. 21:31) because "you did not change your minds" (Matt. 21:32).

At that time there were three recognized categories of sinners: (1) the Jews who could approach God with repentance and hope; they could count on divine mercy; (2) gentile sinners who could come in repentance but without much hope of being heard; thus they were regarded as outside the reach of God's mercy; and (3) the Jews who became like gentiles; they could count neither on repentance nor on the hope of being heard. For all practical purposes, they were lost. This group included herdsmen, prostitutes, lepers, publicans (tax collectors), and the like.[97] And now these were the ones who were hearing the good news from Jesus: "I did not come to invite virtuous people, but sinners!" (Mark 2:17). To a paralytic belonging to this third group of sinners, Jesus spoke the liberating words: "My son, your sins are forgiven!" (Mark 2:5).

The gospel is understood as good news only if we understand this new idea that Jesus introduced. The God of Jesus is no longer the God of the Torah, the Law. He is the God of mercy, of unlimited goodness, and of patience for the weak who recognize that they are weak and start on the road back to God (Rom. 3:25–26). The parable of the prodigal son gives concrete expression to the God of Jesus Christ, who is full of mercy and overflowing love: "While he was still a long way off, his father saw him and his heart went out to him. He ran to meet him, flung his arms around him, and kissed him" (Luke 15:20). The heavenly Father is like this earthly father. And Jesus is the same in practice.

To justify his own attitude and that of God himself, Jesus supplies his critics with several parables.[98] That of the strayed sheep and the lost coin are addressed to the complaining doctors of the law and the Pharisees (Luke 15:2). That of the two debtors is for Simon the Pharisee (Luke 7:40). The dictum, "It is not the healthy that need a doctor, but the sick," is spoken against the religious specialists, who were the most pious of their day, the Pharisees (Mark 2:16). The parable of the Pharisee and the publican is likewise directed against the Pharisees (Luke 18:9), and so on. In each case, Jesus is seeking to defend the new idea that he has introduced: God is primarily the God of sinners, and the Messiah is he who liberates us from our debts and relieves us of the burden of a heavy conscience.

God's forgiveness knows no limits; it is unrestricted, as is seen in the parable of the servant with a heavy load of indebtedness who requested: "Be patient with me, and I will pay in full" (Matt. 18:26). And he was forgiven the entire debt because he asked, verse 32 tells us. At the same time, we have to understand the full meaning of mercy and forgiveness. They are not automatic or mechanical processes; they presuppose a relationship between the offended and the offender. A person has to seek forgiveness, turn to God and give an account of the embarrassing predicament. Those who regard themselves as righteous, with no sins and with no need for conversion, also see no real need for forgiveness. Unfortunately, they are laboring under false pretenses, not truly aware of the reality of the situation.

This is the illusion of the Pharisee in the parable (Luke 18:9–14) who judges himself to be holy when in fact he is quite hardhearted, "having overlooked the weightier demands of the Law: justice, mercy, and good faith" (Matt. 23:23). In other words, he is a sinner without realizing it. He thinks that he has no reason for requesting forgiveness. He does not ask for it, and therefore he does not receive it. God will forgive, and he is always ready to forgive, but the sinner has to be ready for forgiveness. Otherwise, forgiveness will not be real, and there is no healing of the impaired relationship between God and the sinner. God is merciful, but not overindulgent. When we acknowledge that we are sinners, like the tax collector (who was regarded as a sinner in his day), beat our breast, and say: "O God, have mercy on me, sinner that I am" (Luke 18:13), we may have the assurance of a full pardon and of the fact that the kingdom of God has already taken up residence in our heart.

This unrestricted forgiveness by the Father becomes historical fact when Jesus himself gives unlimited forgiveness to his executioners (Luke 23:34); he freely abandons himself into their hands (Matt. 26:52–54; John 18:8–11). He sees his life as being given to others and to sinners, so that all may be redeemed (Mark 10:45). He takes upon himself the predicament of the guilty and prays for God's forgiveness. And God hears and reconciles the world (1 Peter 1:18; Rom. 5:8–10; Acts 8:30–35; Heb. 9:15, 28; Rev. 5:9; 1 Cor. 6:20, 7:23). Residing in him is the full truth that love forgives all (1 Cor. 13:4–7).

Because all this is a reality, we can confidently ask God's forgiveness, as we do in the Lord's Prayer. Through Jesus we know that our petition is heard.

AS WE HAVE FORGIVEN THOSE
WHO HAVE WRONGED US

The second part of this petition seems to establish some conditions for divine forgiveness, for it says: "As we have forgiven . . ." (Matthew); "for we too forgive . . ." (Luke). Matthew underscores the correlation. At the end of the Lord's Prayer he adds the words: "For if you forgive others the wrong they have done, your heavenly Father will also forgive you; but if you do not forgive others, then the wrongs you have done will not be forgiven by your Father" (Matt. 6:14–15). Is this a kind of *do ut des* contract? Is it a kind of negotiation with God? The question, thus stated, seems to favor the development of a pharisaical attitude, as though God were requiring something in return. But such would be unworthy of the approach taught by Jesus, which is one of unlimited mercy, completely independent of any selfish considerations.

The parable of the heavily indebted servant (Matt. 18:23–35), who was totally forgiven because he requested it from his master, points us in the right direction. After being forgiven, he did not forgive his fellow servant who owed him a smaller amount. It was then that his master called him and said: "You scoundrel! I remitted the whole of your debt when you appealed to me; were you not bound to show your fellow servant the same pity as I

showed you?" (Matt. 18:32–33). The lesson is crystal clear: if
we ask for unrestricted pardon and receive it without reservation,
subject to no conditions, we shall also have to give unrestricted
pardon to someone who asks us for unlimited forgiveness. We
are to be merciful as the Father is merciful (Luke 6:36). We must
forgive seventy times seven times—that is, without limits (Matt.
18:22)—because this is how God forgives.

Thus there is no business deal here, and there are no strings attached; we are merely expected to maintain the same attitude toward God and toward our neighbor. This is the new element in
the experience of God that is communicated to us by Jesus Christ.
We cannot maintain two attitudes, one toward God and the other
toward our neighbor. Both are subject to a single motivation, that
of love. To love "the other" is to encounter God, and to love
God implies loving the neighbor, because "if he does not love his
brother whom he has seen, it cannot be that he loves God whom
he has not seen" (1 John 4:20). Worshiping God without being
reconciled with one's neighbor is idolatry (Matt. 5:23–24). The
basic commandment, of which Paul reminds us, is: "You must
forgive as the Lord forgave you" (Col. 3:13).

Now we can have a full understanding of Jesus' statement:
"Acquit, and you will be acquitted" (Luke 6:37); "whatever measure you deal out to others will be dealt back to you" (Matt. 7:2).
In other words: if we do not totally forgive our neighbor, then it
is a sign that we have not fully requested the Father's forgiveness
and we have thus made ourselves incapable of receiving the unrestricted forgiveness of God. If we have really had the radical
experience of forgiveness for our sins and our debts, if we truly
have felt the mercy of God at work in our sinful life, then we are
also impelled to forgive without limits, without reservations, and
with a carefree heart. The beatitude applies here: "How blessed
are those who show mercy; mercy will be shown to them" (Matt.
5:7). At the end of history and the end of life, only the works of
mercy will count; on these depend our salvation or our destruction (Matt. 25:31–46). We have no right to ask God's forgiveness if we do not want to forgive our neighbors.

Finally, as with the previous petition of the Lord's Prayer, we
see that this one also has a social dimension.[99] We see ourselves
as a community of sinners; we are indebted to God and indebted

to our fellow humans. The bread of our communal life is forgiveness and a reciprocal demonstration of mercy; if this is lacking, broken ties cannot be repaired. God's forgiveness reestablishes vertical communion with the Most High; forgiving those who have offended us reestablishes our horizontal communion. The reconciled world begins to flourish, the kingdom is inaugurated, and we begin to live under the rainbow of divine mercy. All this is bound up in the words we pray: "Forgive us the wrong we have done, as we have forgiven those who have wronged us."

9

And Do Not Bring Us
to the Test

A great spiritual teacher said to his disciple:
"You cannot trifle with the animal that lives within you without becoming completely an animal.

"You cannot play with lies without losing your grip on truth.

"You cannot play cruel games without bruising the tenderness of your spirit.

"If you want to keep your garden cleared, you cannot allow any room for weeds to grow."

The petitions of the Lord's Prayer grow in intensity until they culminate in this cry of anguish: "Do not bring us to the test!" This request to the Father presupposes a bitter awareness that human beings are fragile, subject to the temptation of betraying their hope, becoming unfaithful to God, actually succumbing to temptation, and consequently being lost. In order to grasp the fundamental meaning of this tormented cry of the soul, we need to become aware of the makeup of the human condition, this being the context into which temptation enters and a breakdown occurs.

THE HUMAN PERSON:
A BEING SUBJECT TO TEMPTATION

The basic orientation of human life incorporates two perspectives, one directed to the earth and the other directed to heaven.

Because we live on earth, we share in the earth's fate: frailty, vulnerability, every sort of limitation, and, finally, death. The Scriptures speak of our entire life on earth as life in the flesh; and "flesh-mindedness spells death" (Rom. 8:6).[100] This does not mean that earthly life has no dynamism or relevance; recent centuries have demonstrated the astonishing capacity of humankind to transform nature and society. Science and technology, despite their plundering of the ecosystems, have brought an easier life and a more habitable earth to a considerable percentage of humanity.

In the final analysis, however, we have to ask the question of the ancient wise man: "What reward has a man for all his labor, his scheming, and his toil here under the sun?" (Eccles. 2:22). All our undertakings and achievements are branded with the stigma of mortality, inasmuch as we cannot take charge of everything, we cannot do everything, we cannot become everything. In a word, even the greatest geniuses, the most radical revolutionaries, and the most dedicated protesters have to eat and drink, have to rest and spend time sleeping.

On the other hand, this same humankind that is so restricted lives among the stars, if one considers its desires and impulses. It is not content to resign itself to the pettiness of things; it breaks through all barriers and is always seeking to go beyond defined limits. This is not a question of the will; it is more an innate impulse that causes human beings to hunger for the infinite and thirst for the absolute until one may conclude with Sirach: "When a man has come to the end, he is still at the beginning, and when he has finished he will still be perplexed" (Sir. 18:7). The Scriptures speak of this mode of being as "life in the spirit."[101] The human being in its entirety feels an upward call, toward full freedom, toward final perfection, toward an ultimate resting place. "The spirit alone gives life" (John 6:63) and "spirit-mindedness is life and peace" (Rom. 8:6).

The combination of life in the flesh and life in the spirit comprises the objective structure of human nature. The two are out of balance and cause human life to be torn between them. The human person, ontologically speaking, is an unbalanced being; although confined to limits, we are of unlimited size; though anchored firmly in the ground, we reach up to the stars. What is there to integrate all this? How does this cacophony become a symphony?

Paul assures us, quite realistically: "That lower nature sets its desires against the spirit, while the spirit fights against it. They are in conflict with one another so that what you will to do you cannot do" (Gal. 5:17). And all this is found in the single reality we call "human."

These two existential states also constitute two approaches to life. Life is never a "given" or an accomplished fact; it has to be built and guided. Some can establish a lifestyle based on the dimension of the flesh; they are satisfied with what the world can offer, and they repress any suggestions prompted by the spirit. Paul warns us against this type of fundamental choice, because it does not lead to the kingdom of God (Gal. 5:21). This mind-set finds its concrete embodiment in such works as "fornication, impurity, and indecency; idolatry and sorcery; quarrels, a contentious temper, envy, fits of rage, selfish ambition, dissensions, party intrigues and jealousies; drinking bouts, orgies, and the like" (Gal. 5:19–20).

But we shall not content ourselves with generalities. Flesh-mindedness finds its historical expression in contemporary society, with its mechanisms that tend toward the accumulation of wealth in the hands of a few, to the detriment of the large majority, abandoned to poverty and hunger. The social system that predominates in our countries is profoundly inequitable, giving rise to institutionalized injustice and social sin, such as were prophetically denounced at the Puebla conference (*Puebla* 509 and 562). With its seductions and illusions imbedded in the minds of all, it constitutes a permanent collective temptation to selfishness, to insensitivity, and to the violation of fellowship. As a mind-set, it is opposed to life; its fruit is death.

It is also possible to orient life in the spirit dimension. Every manifestation of life (including those of the flesh) are seen as God sees them and from the standpoint of a destiny in which all humans participate more fully. This spirit-mindedness, mentioned in Galatians 5:25, finds its exterior expression in "love, joy, peace, patience, kindness, goodness, fidelity, gentleness, and self-control" (Gal. 5:22). Spirit-mindedness releases life, so that it may blossom. And the Scriptures give the promise: "Choose life, and then you will live" (Deut. 30:19).

Again, it is of importance to give these ideas a historical setting in our own time. All those who are presently committed to nurturing the relationships of production and community living in such a way as to promote community and participation at every level of life, for the largest possible number of persons, are in the process of realizing the designs of the spirit. It is only in such a society that real rather than illusory conditions exist for the emergence of the fruits of the spirit enumerated for us by Paul.

The crisis of the human condition resides in the fact that these two mind-sets are interwoven. The person who chooses spirit-mindedness must battle against the flesh-mindedness that writhes within: "In my inmost self I delight in the law of God, but I perceive that there is in my bodily members a different law fighting against spirit-mindedness and making me a prisoner to the sin-mindedness that is in my members. Miserable creature that I am, who is there to rescue me?" (Rom. 7:22–24).[102]

In order to receive affirmation and support, this spirit-mindedness must confront suffering and testing, both of which are implied in the very concept of faithfulness to this fundamental choice. These testings, despite their painful nature, are charged with meaning: they ratify, strengthen, and purify the fundamental choice. Judith, in her famous speech to the people before she assassinated Holophernes, made a statement that has become a kind of *locus classicus* for this subject: "We have every reason to give thanks to the Lord our God; he is putting us to the test as he did our ancestors. Remember how he dealt with Abraham and how he tested Isaac, and what happened to Jacob. . . . He is not subjecting us to the fiery ordeal by which he tested their loyalty, or taking vengeance on us; it is for discipline that the Lord scourges his worshipers" (Jud. 8:25–27).

Testing, as it is meant here, is the price we pay to be faithful to God. Its real function is not punishment but purification (1 Peter 1:6–7). It is even the subject of a supplication: "Test me, O Lord, and try me; put my heart and mind to the proof" (Ps. 26:2; see also Ps. 139:23). In other places, thanks is given to God for testing: "Bless our God, all nations . . . for thou . . . hast put us to the proof and hast refined us like silver" (Ps. 66:10; see also Isa. 48:10; Sir. 44:20). In the Epistle of James we are asked to regard these testings as "pure joy" (James 1:2). These things crop up in our lives to make the good even better.

All of these anthropological considerations were necessary to help us better understand temptations, which are the subject of this petition of the Lord's Prayer. We need to get beyond a mere moralizing of temptations (which is very superficial) and get into a more structural dimension, where we can see where they are rooted in our human nature. Without this perception we cannot hope to adequately grasp the temptations of Jesus nor the example they are supposed to set for our own life.

The human being, then, is structurally susceptible to temptation, subject both to the solicitations of the flesh and of the spirit. The human being is seen as a passionate being. This is not bad in itself; it only makes us more aware of the overflowing dynamism of our carnal-spiritual humanness. Evil, properly so-called, does not consist in having temptations but in yielding to them. We do not ask God to exempt us from temptation but to protect us when we confront it.

HUMAN NATURE: FRAILTY

The most unfortunate thing about human nature is that it has fallen, and continues to fall, into temptation. Testing, like any crisis (its original meaning being that of cleansing and purification), ceases to be an opportunity for growth and becomes an occasion for failure and denial. Sin denies the love of God, love of neighbor, and of the world, cutting tragically across all human history. And the more we become aware of the excesses of human sin, the more terrifying this tragedy is seen to be. Vatican II stated that "man finds that by himself he is incapable of battling the assaults of evil successfully, so everyone feels as though he is bound by chains" (*Gaudium et Spes* 13).

The great denial has its history and its victims: every person who has come into this world. As far as our salvation is concerned, we are born into a polluted atmosphere. We have been rendered anemic by the historical condition of personal and institutional sin, which increasingly incapacitates us for making our trials into stepping-stones and allows them to degenerate into temptations to unfaithfulness and the denial of our own being.

Righteousness, in its original meaning, signified the ability to integrate all the dynamisms of the flesh and of the spirit into a lifestyle centered upon God, whose offspring we are, on others as our brothers and sisters, and on the world in our capacity as free administrators of earthly goods. Sin has loosened our moorings, so that each impulse flies off in its own direction, disrupting the unity of our humanness.[103]

How is it that the human being can sin, can resist the truth, can become insensitive to community and to love? Could not God have made the human being differently? God is not completely exempt from the tragedy of sin, because, although he is not the author of sin, it occurs by his permission. Although he is omnipotent, he does not prevent sin from happening; he permits it. By faith we know that he permits it, because he knows how to bring a higher good out of evil. But we have not been granted the revelation of this higher good, no matter how much St. Augustine talks about his "blessed guilt"! We eagerly await the glorious revelation of his loving design (see Rom. 8:18). Theology, in its efforts to understand this, seeks to throw some light on this "mystery of iniquity."

In order for sin to exist, the possibility of sin must preexist. And this possibility is connected with the very mystery of creation itself.[104] To speak of creation is to speak of dependence. Every created being is dependent on God for its existence and sustenance; it is from God, is made by God, and exists for God. In comparison with the divine perfection, creation is imperfect. This imperfection is not something evil that we should protest or seek to eliminate. It is the very fact that the world is not God or an intrinsic emanation of God himself (that is, a divine person), that it is separate, different, limited, and dependent. Its ultimate reason for being does not reside in itself but requires Someone to give it meaning. This is an objective situation, an objective description of the structure of created beings.

In the case of human beings, there is an *awareness* of the perfection of God and of the imperfection of the creature. The supreme, infinite reality (God) is out of phase with a contingent, finite reality (the world with all its creatures), and the human spirit is caught between the two realms. Awareness of it takes the form of anxiety and suffering. This anxiety and this suffering cannot be healed by any medicine or therapy. They constitute the ontological structure of the human being and express its dignity as it relates to creation. Only humankind has been raised above other finite beings, and it alone establishes dialogue with the infinite. It alone stands between the finite and the infinite. The human person is not only of the world—although belonging to it—or only of God, even though said to be the image and likeness of God, and "suspended" between God and the world. This fact of belonging to two dimensions of reality causes suffering, for the two realities cut across a person's entire being: flesh (of the world) and spirit (of God), both perfect and imperfect.

This imperfection is quite innocent in itself, and need not cause any major problems. But it constitutes the possibility of testing, of temptation, and of sin. The human person, created and creative, finds this imperfection and finiteness hard to accept, and can very well have the desire to be like God (Gen. 3:5). And what is God like? He is the reality of infinite goodness and love that exists and subsists of itself; he has no need for someone or something else to authenticate his genuineness. God is the Truth, the Good, the Supreme. Human beings, on the other hand, see themselves as creatures permanently subordinated to God. They do not exist by and of themselves; their ultimate raison d'être is not in themselves but in God. Wanting to be like God means desiring the impossible: we can never be like God, because we shall always remain created beings.

Sin is the refusal to accept one's own limitations and the suffering of a spirit enclosed in flesh. This is why sin is always an act of violence against the meaning of creation, which has to be accepted as such. It is an attitude of arrogance (the *hybris* of the Greek tragedies) and is the very height of presumption. This is the true evil, the historical sin, the result of an abuse of freedom. This sin has been accumulating in all human societies and constitutes the sin of the world; it creates mechanisms that become internalized in persons, in lifestyles, becoming like a second nature within men and women.

Thus human society is "passionate" in the pejorative sense of the word; it tempts and solicits to evil. St. James has said it well: "God does not tempt anyone. Temptation arises when a man is enticed and lured away by his own lust" (James 1:13–14). In concrete terms, there exists in each one of us not only a call to altruism, to commitment, and to community, but also a penchant to egotism, to vengeance, and to the instincts of death. We feel righteous and sinful at the same time, both oppressed and liberated. Can we escape this tragic state? Paul asks the question: "Who is there to rescue me out of this body doomed to death?" (Rom. 7:24). And he answers with a sense of relief: "God alone, through Jesus Christ our Lord! Thanks be to God!" (Rom. 7:25). Let us consider how this has come about.

JESUS, HAVING BEEN TEMPTED, CAN HELP THOSE WHO ARE TEMPTED

The testimony of Scripture is explicit in affirming the fact of Jesus' temptation (Mark 1:13; Matt. 4:3, 26:41; Luke 22:28). "Because of his likeness to us he has been tempted in every way" (Heb. 4:15). For since he himself has passed through the test of suffering, he is able to help those who are meeting their test now" (Heb. 2:18). We need to be clear in our understanding of Jesus' temptation. It seems to have had a direct impact on the humanity of Jesus, and indirectly on his divinity, inasmuch as the humanity in him that was tempted was the humanity of God himself. The incarnate God was present in Jesus, and as such he was stripped of his divine attributes and identified with human limitations. This is an essential feature of the mystery of incarnation. The Son did not take upon himself an abstract nature, but the historical, concrete nature of Jesus of Nazareth.

Jesus of Nazareth in his humanity cannot be understood outside this historical framework. The humanity that he assumed was marked by the history of sin; not everything in that humanity was ordained by God's purposes. Paul emphasizes that "God sent his own Son in a form like that of our own sinful nature" (Rom. 8:3). John put it more simply: "the Word became flesh" (John 1:14)—that is, he entered into the darkness of our fallen and rebellious state.

Because he was true man, Jesus partook of the passionate state (in its positive sense) as we have defined it above. In this passionate state there is human flesh-mindedness and human spirit-mindedness. Because he was still a pilgrim and had not reached the eschatological stage, "he too [was] beset by weakness" (Heb. 5:2). Like all wayfarers, he lived in the penumbra of history; not everything was diaphanous and transparent to him; he had room to exercise faith and hope (Heb. 12:2–3). If he was to be made perfect, it had not yet been attained. He lived in an absolute submission to the Father and in total faithfulness to his will. Nevertheless, this will of the Father was to be revealed slowly, as it unfolded. He saw himself as the liberator sent by God, but not every step in the total process of liberation was completely diaphanous.

What steps did the Father want the Son to take? To the degree that Jesus was to perform his mission, he had to have the clear awareness that the kingdom was not to be established through the mediations of political or sacral power or by means of the charismatic and miraculous. The path that he was to take was that of the suffering servant, of the righteous one who abandons himself for the redemption of all sinners.

Jesus' temptations are not to be understood as solicitations to evil or to sin. Because he always lived with his life centered on the Father, this was not a historical possibility. His "temptations" consisted of a constantly faithful search for those concrete steps that would make the will of God a part of history. This meant that Jesus had to solve problems, to deal with deceptions on the part of the people, the Pharisees, and the apostles, and to confront the misunderstandings that culminated in his defamation and persecution.[105] In this sense, Jesus was tempted—put to the test—and he "offered up prayers and petitions with loud cries and tears" (Heb. 5:7). In the Garden of Gethsemane he prayed agonizingly and earnestly (Luke 22:44). The Epistle to the Hebrews makes a very realistic comment: "Son though he was, he learned obedience in the school of suffering" (Heb. 5:8). All obedience is onerous. Jesus was tested by this onus and he triumphed. He could thus serve as an example for those who follow him.

The gospels show a lifelong consistency in Jesus' confrontation with Satan, who is the embodiment of temptation and evil.[106] The Messiah defeated the devil point for point, bringing liberation to all of creation. Thus, immediately after his public appearance for baptism, he was led out into the enemy's camp—the desert—to be tempted there by the seducer (Mark 1:13; Matt. 4:3). The devil was driven off, but he was only marking time (Matt. 8:29), waiting for an opportune moment (Luke 4:13). Jesus gave him no rest and drove him out whenever he met him, whether in the sick or in the hardheartedness of the Pharisees. But he is the *inimicus hominis* who sows tares among the wheat (Matt. 13:25, 39) and enters the heart of Judas (Luke 22:3; John 13:2, 27). He tried to "sift" Simon Peter and the other apostles like wheat (Luke 22:31). Jesus himself asked his apostles to remain with him in his temptations (Luke 22:28). An attack was made during the agony in the Garden of Gethsemane, when Jesus warned his apostles: "Pray that you may be spared the hour of testing" (Luke 22:40). All of Satan's force was let loose at the cross, driving Jesus almost to desperation, so that he cried out: "My God, my God, why have you forsaken me?" (Mark 15:34). But Jesus defeated Satan by committing his spirit, not to the devil, but to the Father (Luke 23:46).

Temptations, then, were not some momentary happening in the life of Jesus but a dark shadow that followed him throughout his life history. The kingdom of God was being built in opposition to the kingdom of evil; evil does not remain idle but makes its iniquity known. Jesus triumphed over the whole history of sin, with its temptations, in his own flesh (Rom. 8:3), and not at some "safe," unreachable distance from the tentacles of tribulation. The greatness of Jesus was not to be found in the absence of temptations, but in his power to overcome all of them.

DELIVER US, LORD, FROM THE GREAT TEMPTATION!

Humanity, and every individual human being, has been exposed to temptation and seduction, and this has been true since the very beginning of human history (Gen. 3) and will be to its very end (Rev. 3:10). When we adhere to Christ and to the community of his followers, we are fortified against the assaults of the world's sin and are transferred to the kingdom of his beloved Son (Col. 1:13; see also Eph. 6:12; Gal. 1:4). Meanwhile, as life goes on, the battle continues and we should "leave no loophole for the devil" (Eph. 4:27).

But the moment will arrive for the great final confrontation—at the very end of the world.[107] This is the "ordeal that is to fall on the whole world" (Rev. 3:10). In the words of Jesus, "as lawlessness spreads, men's love for one another will grow cold" (Matt. 24:12). "Imposters will come claiming to be messiahs or prophets, and they will produce great signs and wonders" (Matt. 24:24; Mark 13:22) and will deceive many because they come with signs of Christ and of holy things. If God would not have compassion on the righteous, "no living thing would survive" (Matt. 24:22). The root of all temptation is that of unfaithfulness to Christ and his kingdom. The terrifying danger of defection and final apostasy runs rampant (2 Peter 2:9).

It is in this context that we hear the anxious prayer of the disciple: "And do not bring us to the test!" But this anxiety is swallowed up in the serenity of someone who has already called upon the Father for the coming of the kingdom and the consummation of his will. We have already known the victory of God through Jesus Christ. We hear his words: "Courage! The victory is mine" (John 16:33) and we know there will be an answer to his prayer: "I pray thee, not to take them out of the world, but to keep them from the evil one" (John 17:15). Despite everything, there is a need to be alert (Mark 13:23) and to ask for perseverance to the end, for only then will we be saved (Mark 13:13).

This petition has a universal eschatological dimension, but it also has an individual, personal dimension. When we die, we will pass through judgment; the most radical crisis of our existence will erupt, with the possibility of a complete purification for life in the kingdom of God. Here the most profound and ultimate decision comes into play, the fruit of all the decisions in our lives as human beings. Our hope may very well be endangered and our trusting commitment can grow weak. The specter of doubt and despair may take shape in our minds. The darkness of life's meaning may possibly bring clouds between us and the Father of infinite goodness, undermining the certainty of the kingdom and throwing doubt upon his will to save us. Then we shall need to make supplication, to cry out: "Do not bring us to the test!"

10

Save Us from the Evil One

The SS hanged two Jewish men and a youth in front of the whole camp. The men died quickly, but the death throes of the youth lasted for half an hour. "Where is God? Where is he?" someone asked behind me.

As the youth still hung in torment in the noose after a long time, I heard the man call again, "Where is God now?"

And I heard a voice in myself answer: "Where is he? He is here. He is hanging there on the gallows . . ."

—*Elie Wiesel in* Night

If the petition "and do not bring us to the test" contains an element of anxiety, the final petition of the Lord's Prayer culminates in a paroxysm, as we cry out to our Father: "but save us from the evil one!" There is now nothing left to ask; it has all been said. To be saved from evil and from the evil one means being ready to enjoy the freedom of the sons of God in the Father's kingdom. When evil has been conquered, the kingdom may come, and the new heavens and the new earth may be inaugurated, where God's name is hallowed and his will is fully done. But evil will have to be conquered, because it is still a persistent part of history and is continually threatening humanity, "like a roaring lion prowling around looking for someone to devour" (1 Peter 5:8).

EVIL AS SITUATION

It is important that we do not minimize our awareness of evil. It is not just some static in the airwaves, some detour of human activity that causes us to arrive late at the goal toward which we strive. It is much more; it is a dynamic thing, a direction taken by history, a design for our lives. Evil, in this sense, has the characteristics of a structure, and this structure organizes a system of transformations that confer unity, consistency, totality, and self-regulation to all the processes that are maintained within the confines of the system.[108]

This structure creates its own scenarios of sin and wickedness; the scenario is made up entirely of elements contained in a backdrop that characterizes a given moment in history. Evil deeds are expressions of predetermined structures and scenarios. We may appropriate these structures and scenarios, may internalize them in our lives, may make them actual life goals, and thus may move into iniquitous, sinful practices. For example, the Puebla conference denounced the capitalist system as a system of sin (no. 92). Due for the most part to this system, "sinful structures" have taken shape on the Latin American continent and give rise to "a grave structural conflict": the increasing wealth of a few running parallel to the growing poverty of the masses (no. 1209).

This system creates its conflict-ridden economic and political scenarios: political repression and labor-union repression, "national security" governments, social crises, and so forth. The political events appearing in the daily newspapers are embodiments of this backdrop. Concrete persons incorporate into their social life this system, which in essence is an exclusivist one, involving the accumulation of wealth and privileges in the hands of a few who bear little social responsibility and become the agents who maintain the system and participate in its injustice.[109] A whole cycle of evil is thus established.

Evil exists in history because there is temptation. And persons fall into temptation; they sin, they betray the promptings of conscience, they disobey the voice of God, which is usually articulated by the signs of the times.[110] This sin creates its own history and its own mechanisms of production. It achieves a relative autonomy; it exercises power over each one of us, to the point that we feel enslaved: "I am the purchased slave of sin. . . . The good which I want to do, I fail to do; but what I do is the wrong which is against my will. . . . I perceive that there is in my bodily members a different law . . . making me . . . a prisoner under the law that is in my members, the law of sin" (Rom. 7:14, 19, 23).

We live in the "sin situation" that St. John calls the sin of the world (John 1:29). It needs to be explained that "the sin of the world" does not mean that the world itself is sin. The world is primarily the good creation of God, for the sake of which the Father sent his beloved Son (John 1:9, 10, 3:16; 2 Cor. 5:19; 1 Tim. 1:15). Creation, however, has been polluted by humankind's historical wrongdoing. "Sin entered into the world" (Rom. 5:12) and, although not completely corrupting the world, it has left deep marks on it (James 1:27). Thus the world as we experience it at present is "enmity to God" (James 4:4), is the source of unhappiness (2 Cor. 7:10) and has not recognized Jesus Christ (John 1:10). Thus "the world" is not to be understood here in a metaphysical but in a historical sense; this world is the symbol of those who are capable of "stifling the truth in their wickedness" (Rom. 1:18), of "spilling the blood of the prophets since the foundation of the world" (Luke 11:50) and of giving support to every sort of hypocrisy and sin (Matt. 23:29–36).

The seriousness of sin lies in the fact that it constitutes a situation or structure. Every situation possesses its degree of independence and objectivity; sin is not just a personal matter, it has an important social and historical dimension. By a situation we mean "that combination of circumstances in which we find ourselves at a given moment; the situation completely envelops us, involves us, makes us a part of the world around us."[111] This situation was not humankind's original destiny, but it has become so. Its destiny was created by the sins of human beings across the whole sweep of history.

These sins did not die with the persons who committed them but have been perpetuated by actions that survived their perpetrators in the form of institutions, prejudices, moral and legal standards, and social customs. A large number of them represent a perpetuation of vices, racial and moral discrimination, injustice, against groups of persons and social classes; just because someone was born black or poor subjected him or her to a social stigma.

This historically created situation becomes a matter of destiny for those born into it: they become victims of the processes by which traditional norms are socialized and internalized—those norms that are so often the bearers of wrongdoing and sin. The person in question has already been categorized, quite apart from his or her own will in the matter or his or her own decisions.

Such persons participate in this process because of the sin of the world; to the extent that they appropriate and accept the situation, the sin of the world grows as their own personal sins are contributed to it. Thus on the one hand they are victims of the sin of the world (because already situated within it), while on the other hand they become agents to reproduce the sin of the world through their own personal sins (by helping to maintain and re-animate the situation).

There is a kind of sinister solidarity in the evil that rankles humankind throughout history (Rom. 5:12–14, 16). But we must not lose our perspective here: if there is considerable solidarity with the old Adam, there is much more with the new Adam, because "where sin was multiplied, grace immeasurably exceeded it" (Rom. 5:20), and "death established its reign . . . but life shall reign all the more" (Rom. 5:17). But there is no need to emphasize the power of evil; we know that it was so strong that it could do away with the Son of God when he appeared incarnate in human history (John 1:11). And it continues to do away with the other sons of God to this very day.[112]

EMBODIMENTS OF EVIL

Who is behind all this evil? Who really causes wrongdoing? The Scriptures are quite clear on this. There is a spiritual being who is by definition "the tempter" (Matt. 4:3), the "enemy" (Matt. 13:39; Luke 10:19), the great dragon (Rev. 12:9, 20:2), the serpent (2 Cor. 11:3), the one who was a murderer and liar from the beginning (John 8:44; 1 John 3:8), the evil one (Matt. 13:39; Luke 8:12; Acts 10:38), Satan (Mark 3:23, 26, 4:15; Luke 13:16), Beelzebub (Matt. 12:24, 27; Mark 3:22; Luke 11:15, 18, 19), the prince of this world (John 12:31; 2 Cor. 4:4; Eph. 2:2). Simply stated, he is the evil one, the author of lies, of hatred, of sickness, and of death (Mark 3:23–30; Luke 13:16; Acts 10:38; Heb. 2:14). Human beings who do not deal justly or love their brothers or sisters (1 John 3:10) are seen to be offspring of the devil, as was Cain (1 John 3:12) and Judas Iscariot (John 6:70, 13:2, 27). The tares of Jesus' parable are the children of the evil one, who are opposed to the children of the kingdom (Matt. 13:38)—who *are* the kingdom of God.

How are we to understand this malevolent spiritual being? Is this a being who was created good by God but who, while undergoing a period of testing, fell into rebellion against God, becoming the Evil One by antonomasia? Or is this a literary device, a metaphorical personification representing our experience of being held captive by a widespread evil historically generated by the apostasies of humankind itself? It is an important question in connection with this last petition of the Lord's Prayer. Is "evil" to be understood as the evil one or as "evil" in the abstract? Are we to be delivered from evil (sin, despair, sickness, death) or from the evil one (the devil, Satan)?

There is still some difference among biblical scholars on this point, because there is no satisfactory way of resolving the question on the basis of language analysis.[113] But the great majority understand "evil" as the evil one (Satan, the devil). This final petition intensifies the one immediately preceding it: "do not bring us to the test"—and *especially* (singling out the worst example)— "save us from the evil one."

The context of the Lord's Prayer, as we have mentioned several times already, is apocalyptic and eschatological. At the end of history there will be a great confrontation between Christ and the antichrist, between the children of the kingdom and the children of the evil one (Matt. 13:37–40). Christ and the antichrist will deploy all their forces. Human beings, historically weak and sinful, will run a most serious risk; they will be able to apostatize and fall into the snares of the devil. In this context, believers will pray from the depth of their being and with great anxiety: "Father, save me from the evil one, when he appears!" Paul well said: God the Father "has rescued us from the domain of darkness and brought us away into the kingdom of his dear Son" (Col. 1:13).

If the exegetes choose to interpret "evil" as "the evil one," this does not mean that the problem as to the existence of the evil one (Satan, the devil) has been theologically settled. It is not enough to establish that the evil one is clearly mentioned in the Scriptures. One has to inquire as to the theological content of this expression. Does it have to do with a spiritual being or with a literary embodiment of the prevalence of evil? On this point, more than a serious exegesis is required; there needs to be reflection at the epistemological and theological levels.

We know that the question of demons has been the subject of heated discussion among theologians.[114] Not a few theologians tend to grant only a symbolic existence to the demons. It is good for us to ponder the words of the respected Catholic exegete, Rudolph Schnackenburg:

> There is a new relevance to the question of whether it is necessary to understand Satan (having eliminated mythological and "humanized" conceptions of him) as a personal spiritual power or merely as the incarnation of evil, inasmuch as this evil is present in history and dominates it through human activities. Today we would not defend the first option with the same certainty as in the past. The demythologization debate counsels caution. The problem of how far one may and should interpret, in line with our present state of knowledge, the affirmations of the New Testament, being bound as they are to a worldview no longer held, is very difficult and cannot be answered by just one exegete. And this has relevance also to the discussion that has now been rekindled concerning angels and demons. The diversity of statements, the stylistic forms previously fashioned, the multiple sources of our ideas concerning Satan, the demons, and the "powers," all converge to indicate that in all this we are not dealing with modes of expression that should not be interpreted literally, as though they had no real substance.[115]

This position gives evidence of intellectual honesty in the face of investigations by exegetical science, and at the same time an awareness of the difficulty of resolving the problem by recourse to this science alone. We do not expect to decide the question here.[116] We only want to call attention to the fact that it is characteristic of religious thought the world over not to find the expression of evil in abstract principles but in living forces, whether benevolent or malevolent, which take on an objective metaphysical reality.[117] Evil has never been experienced in a vague, abstract form, nor have grace and goodness. We are always dealing with concrete situations, whether favorable or unfavorable, with the destructive or constructive historical forces of human relationships, of decent, comradely relationships, with ideologies of power and domination, or with those of cooperation and participation, with concrete bearers in the form of groups or of persons who embody these ideologies in their practical social life. Evil has a definite physiognomy, even though it may be concealed behind masks and disguises.

In the Old Testament, for example, there are incarnations of political powers that rise up against God and his holy people: Gog and Magog (Ezek. 38) or the "little horn" and the fourth beast of the Book of Daniel (7:7, 8), which probably represents the Syrian empire of Antiochus Epiphanes (175–164 B.C.) under whom the people of Israel were cruelly oppressed (Dan. 7:25). The apocalyptic environment has given us a "theology of the tyrant of the end times" as the last great adversary of God. The New Testament projects the figure of the antichrist (2 Thess. 2:1–12; Rev. 13:1–11; 1 John 2:18, 19, 4:3; 2 John 7). He experiences a *parousia* similar to that of Christ and is surrounded by a community of evildoers (2 Thess. 2:9–11; Rev. 13:8). Christ incarnates the mystery of piety (1 Tim. 3:16); the antichrist embodies the mystery of iniquity (2 Thess. 2:7).[118]

Religious metaphysics, with its tendency to concretization, hypostatizes these realities within a supernatural framework. This is its vocabulary and the grammar of the expression of its workings. Theological understanding, for its part, seeks to get beyond the pictures and, so far as possible, to identify the realities and the ideas pertaining to them. Although seeming to desacralize them, it seeks to understand them as intrahistorical realities, manifestations of human wickedness that become embodied in collective forces and representations, against whom mere individuals find it difficult to protect themselves. The evil one would then simply be the organization of injustice, or humankind's departure from its essential calling, the aberration that becomes historically stratified and is forever opposed to the spirit of God, of justice, of goodness—in a word, to the realities of the kingdom.

We may assume that psycho-social development does not move inexorably in the direction of a growth in truth, concord, community, and the participation of everyone in the whole of life, but toward the exasperation that comes from contradictions. In this type of representation, the end of the world will signify an immense process of catharsis, a purifying crisis, at the end of which God will triumph and will lead history on to a transhistorical stage. *Et tunc erit finis*—and then it will be over. That is, the end will then come, and with it a new beginning: there will be an end to this dialectical type of history, and a new phase of history will be inaugurated, a movement toward God for which human beings have anxiously hoped. The Christian faith expresses this truth in its symbolic vocabulary: "The Lord Jesus will destroy the lawless one with the breath of his mouth, and annihilate by the radiance of his coming" (2 Thess. 2:8).

JESUS AND THE VICTORY OVER EVIL

There is a profound and solid conviction in the New Testament to the effect that Jesus is the great deliverer from the power of Satan.[119] According to the mythology of that day, all diseases and infirmities are manifestations of the power of Satan. He holds humanity captive, so that it is subject to every sort of tribulation. But now one who is stronger has arisen to conquer the "strong man" (Mark 3:27).

Jesus accepts the religious metaphysics of the time. He understands Satan as a force in history (the *dynamis* of Luke 10:19) with an organization like that of an army of soldiers (Mark 5:9; Matt. 10:25). He himself is aware that the end of Satan's power is at hand: "If it is by the finger of God that I drive out the devils, then be sure the kingdom of God has already come upon you" (Luke 11:20).

The kingdom of God is being built in opposition to the kingdom of this world, and it inflicts damage on the evil one (Mark 1:23–25, 39, 4:39; Luke 13:16).[120] Each time demons are driven out, one more degree of victory over him has been achieved, in anticipation of his final destruction. This victorious power is conferred upon the disciples (Mark 6:7; Matt. 10:8; Luke 10:19). When the seventy-two disciples came back jubilant from their mission, saying: "In your name, Lord, even the devils submit to us," Jesus entered into their joy and said: "I watched how Satan fell, like lightning, out of the sky" (Luke 10:17–18). Jesus had a vision; in the annihilation of Satan's power he saw the state of paradise emerging, where humankind is to be reconciled with nature, for "nothing will ever harm you" (Luke 10:19).

As important as this perspective is in the gospels, we must not allow it to get out of focus. For Jesus, this focus is not so much the victory over the evil one as the proclamation of the good news of God's plan of salvation, especially for the defenseless, the poor, the lowly. It is the healings more than the victories over the diabolical dimension of life that manifest the presence of the kingdom, of the new order that God desires, and the inauguration of the new age. Thus the apostles are blessed in that they see what many prophets and kings desired to see and did not (Luke 10:23–24; Matt. 13:16–17).

As a consequence, Jesus' followers do not begin by requiring renunciation of the devil, as the Essenes of Qumran did, but what he asks of them is adherence to the kingdom. In his exhortations he does not warn them to beware of uncontrollable and diabolical forces, but to beware of the yearnings of their own hearts, for these are what corrupt a person's life (Mark 7:15). What keeps someone from entering the kingdom and experiencing the transcendent meaning of life is not so much the devil as wealth (Luke 6:24–25, 12:13, 21, 16:13), excessive worries (Matt. 6:19–34), a self-centered attitude (Mark 9:43–48), passing judgment on others (Matt. 7:1–5), lusting for power, honor, and glory (Mark 10:35–45), an exaggerated, sterile piety (Mark 11:15–19), gullibility (Mark 13:5–7), and the temptation to abuse the good faith of others (Mark 9:42; Matt. 18:6; Luke 17:1–3).[121]

The principal cause of the world's ills is to be found in our insensitivity, our lack of solidarity, and the failure to love. It is this that Jesus criticizes in the Pharisees (Matt. 23:23). These are the real demons that we must exorcise from our lives. When this is accomplished, the grace of God is seen to be victorious in the world. To follow Jesus, which is the central theme of the gospels, calls for creating this new mentality, a truly liberated attitude. "If God is on our side, who is against us?" (Rom. 8:31).

THE FINAL CRY OF THE HUMAN HEART:
SAVE US, FATHER!

The Greek term used in the Lord's Prayer for "save" is *rysai*. Its original sense differs from that of the Latin *liberare* or the English "liberate." The common meaning of "liberation" presupposes an experience of captivity, of being in chains and oppressed. This meaning could be verified here, inasmuch as the presence of sin and the evil one imposes slavery on human life. And God has been revealed as a liberator (Ps. 18:2, 40:17, 70:5, 144:2; Dan. 6:27). His liberating action has been conveyed in St. Jerome's Vulgate by the term *liberare* (about two hundred times).[122] For instance, a truthful witness *saves* lives (Prov. 14:25); the Israelites are *liberated* from Egyptian captivity (Exod. 3:8, 14:30, 18:10).

But the original meaning of the Greek *ruesthai* is that of snatching a person away from the brink of an abyss, protecting someone from the vicissitudes of a journey, protecting someone from the traps that lie in the path. As we read in the Psalms: "Keep me from the trap which they have set for me. . . . Let the wicked fall into their own nets, while I pass in safety" (Ps. 141:9–10); "let no flood carry me away, no abyss swallow me up" (Ps. 69:15); "he himself will snatch you away from fowler's snare or raging tempest" (Ps. 91:3).

The underlying experience is that of life as a pilgrimage, as a covenant with God to walk in his paths. Along this path we experience dangers of every kind; there are yawning abysses, there are traps laid by enemies, and we can be attacked. Within the framework of this figurative language, what does the evil one do? His task is to tempt us, to draw us away from the good path, to give us wrong directions. And what does God do? God protects us from the dangers, pulls us away from the ambushes, and shows us the right direction to travel. God said to Jacob: "I will be with you, and I will protect you wherever you go and will bring you back to this land; for I will not leave you until I have done all that I promised" (Gen. 28:15). In Isaiah, he says: "Thus says the Lord, your ransomer . . . I lead you in the way you must go" (Isa. 48:17). And the same prophet asks God in a rather complaining tone: "Thou, Lord, art our father . . . our Ransomer from of old. . . . Why, Lord, dost thou let us wander from thy ways?" (Isa. 63:16–17).

What are these ways or paths of God? They are the ways or paths that lead us toward justice, truth, and fellowship, overcoming the forces of selfishness and oppressive power. As may be seen from the above texts, "saving," "liberation," or "deliverance" is found in the context of a "pilgrimage," a "journey," and of the dangers that go with it, a trek that leads either toward the realization of human desires or toward their frustration.

Each generation has its own "evil one" against which it must particularly protect itself and because of which it must implore divine protection. This evil being embodies the widespread wickedness that permeates humanity. In our own time, the evil one who offends God and debases human persons appears in the form of a collective selfishness embodied in an elitist, exclusivist social system that has no solidarity with the great multitudes of the poor. He has a name; he is the Capitalism of private property and the Capitalism of the state. In the name of money, privileges, and the reinforcement of governmental structures he holds men and women in terror. Many of them are imprisoned, tortured, and killed. Two-thirds of the population are held prisoner under the yoke of a legion of demons: hunger, sickness, disintegration of the family, and a shortage of housing, schools, and hospitals. This evil one has his ways of tempting; he slyly creeps into our minds and makes the heart insensitive to those structural inequities that he has created.

In the context of apocalyptic eschatology the evil one directly named in this petition of the Lord's Prayer assumes that humanity is drawing close to its final destination. Emerging all along this final leg of the journey are the many obstacles, the many gaping abysses, and the danger of defection from the undertaking that is about to achieve its goal. In the midst of this distressing situation the believer and the believing community cry out: "Father, save us from the evil one and from all evil! As you have not allowed us to fall into temptation, now snatch us away from the maneuverings of the evil one!" But the danger does not beckon only at the end of history; it is part of the structuring of the present; it lurks in every corner and seeks to destroy us. And so we cry out to the Father: "Save us from evil! Protect us from moving away from the dimension of goodness. Father, do not let us forsake you!"

If we have prayed from the depths of our hearts, then our confidence can be restored, because it is Jesus who has given us his guarantee: "If you ask anything in my name, I will do it" (John 14:14); "courage! The victory is mine; I have conquered the world" (John 16:33); "stand upright and hold your heads high, because your liberation is near" (Luke 21:28).

11

Amen

Our Father in heaven
—and your name is holy—
why is your will not done
on earth as in heaven?

Why do you not give all of us
our daily bread?

Why do you not forgive our wrongs
that we might forget our complaints?
Why do we still yield to the temptation to hate?

Our Father, if you are in heaven,
why do you not save us from this evil
so that we may then say Amen?
> —Marialzira Perestrello, *prayer,*
> in Ruas Caladas *(Rio de Janeiro, 1978), p. 59*

The Lord's Prayer ends as it ought to end: with a resounding amen. The Hebrew word *amen* has its root in the verb *'mn*, which also forms a part of Hebrew words referring to faith, truth, assurance, firmness, and confidence. To have faith, biblically, means more than holding to certain truths; it also implies a serene trust in a mysterious, ultimate sense of reality. We can say to the world, to life, to everything that exists: amen, so be it! This is why the opposite of faith is fear, and the inability to entrust oneself confidently to a greater power. This greater power, whom we sense as being mysterious and ultimate, the meaning behind all meanings, is discerned as God, the Father of infinite goodness and love. Thus amen signifies: So be it! Yes, may it be so! The amen reinforces, confirms, and reaffirms a petition, a prayer, or an offering of praise (Rom. 1:25, 11:36; Gal. 1:5; Phil. 4:20; 1 Cor. 16:24).[123]

Being able to say amen implies being able to trust and be confident and certain that everything is in the hands of the Father; he has already conquered mistrust and fear, despite everything. The Lord's Prayer has encompassed the whole path of humanity in its drive toward heaven and its rootage in the earth. One finds in it the motif of light and the motif of darkness. And to all of it we say "Yes, so be it!" And we can say yes and amen to the threat of evil, to the promptings of temptation, to the insults we receive, and to the onerous quest for bread, only if we retain our certainty that God is our Father, that we are consecrated to his holy name, that we are confident that his kingdom will come, and that we are sure his will is to be done on earth as it is in heaven.

The Lord's Prayer begins with the confidence of those who lift their eyes heavenward, whence comes our deliverance. After passing through human oppressions, we end with the same confidence and pray amen. This confidence finds its starting point in Jesus himself, who is the one who taught us to pray the Lord's Prayer. He has taken upon himself all the contradictions of our dialectical existence and delivers us from them totally.

St. Paul communicates this with telling insight: "With him it was, and is, Yes" (2 Cor. 1:19). Everything that God has promised to us—and the Lord's Prayer sums up the promises of God, both for life eternal and for life here on earth—"is Yes in Jesus" (2 Cor. 1:20). St. John speaks of Jesus apodictically as "the Amen" (Rev. 3:14).[124]

If Jesus is the Amen that we add to our petitions, then we have the greatest certainty imaginable that God always hears us. Greater than the certainty of our needs is the certainty of our confidence in knowing that our Father looks after us. Amen.

Notes

1. A deeper and more detailed treatment of this subject can be found in Leonardo Boff, "O pensar sacramental, sua estrutura e articulação," *Revista Eclesiástica Brasileira (REB)* 35 (1975): 515–40.

2. For an English translation of the final document of Puebla, see *Puebla and Beyond*, ed. John Eagleson and Philip Scharper, trans. John Drury (Maryknoll, N.Y.: Orbis, 1979).

3. See Leonardo Boff and Clodovis Boff, *Salvation and Liberation: In Search of a Balance between Earth and Politics* (Maryknoll, N.Y.: Orbis Books, 1984).

4. See Joachim Jeremias, *O pai-nosso: A oração do Senhor* (São Paulo, 1976), p. 56; Eng., *The Lord's Prayer*, trans. John Reuman (Philadelphia: Fortress, 1964).

5. These have been translated into French from Greek and Latin by Adalbert Hamman, *Le Pater expliqué par les Pères* (Paris: Ed. Franciscaines, 1952).

6. For prayer in general, see the classic work of Friedrich Heiler, *Das Gebet: Eine religionsgeschichtliche und religionspsychologische Untersuchung*, 5th ed. (Munich-Basel, 1959); Eng., *Prayer: A Study of the History and Psychology of Religion*, trans. and ed. Samuel McComb with J. Edgar Park (New York: Oxford University Press, 1932, 1958). For Christian prayer, the best study available so far, see Adalbert Hamman, *La Prière*, 2 vols. (Paris: Desclée, 1963).

7. Tertullian, *De oratione*, P.L. 1, 1153. See H. van den Bussche, *Understanding the Lord's Prayer*, trans. Charles Schaldentrand (New York: Sheed & Ward, 1963), pp. 13–14.

8. See Charles Moeller, *L'homme moderne devant le salut* (Paris: Ed. Ouvrières, 1965); Eng., *Man and Salvation in Literature*, trans. Charles Quinn (Notre Dame, Ind.: University of Notre Dame Press, 1970); idem, "Aspectos do ateísmo na literatura moderna," in *Deus está morto?* (Petrópolis: Vozes, 1970), pp. 281–302; G. Greschake, "Leiden und Gottesfrage," *Geist und Leben* 50 (1979): 102–21, with many examples, esp. pp. 101–17.

9. In a discussion on the Lord's Prayer, in *Experiências* (Petrópolis: Vozes, 1970), pp. 192–94, Toynbee argues in this way: If God is omnipotent he can do everything. If he can do everything, why does he not eliminate evil? If he does not eliminate evil, he is either not omnipotent or he is not good. Goodness and omnipotence are mutually exclusive. If they could be joined, it would mean that God is God and also the devil (p. 193). We will see in due course how to overcome this false alternative: God is so omnipotent that he can tolerate evil without being defeated by it.

10. Stoicism was the school of philosophy and the way of wisdom that advocated fatalism vis-à-vis the world; it counseled adjustment to and insertion into the principle of reality and called for a certain titanism in the sense of bearing and suffering everything with serenity and magnanimity. This ideal even now attracts certain spirits, a Freud or a Toynbee among many others. It always remains an open question: Can a human being trust only in himself or herself and their own forces? Are there not demands made on human nature that, left to itself, normally bring it to disaster? Or is it not that the human being is called to yield to a Greater and repose in it? See the excellent reflections on this by Otto Kuss, "Zur Vorschungsglauben im Neuen Testament," in *Auslegung und Verkündigung*, vol. 2 (Regensburg, 1966), pp. 139–52, esp. pp. 139–46.

11. See Leonardo Boff, "Jesus' Historical Project," *Passion of Christ, Passion of the World* (Maryknoll, N.Y.: Orbis Books, 1987), pp. 10–24.

12. See F. J. Schierse, "Die Krise Jesu von Nazareth," in *Christentumals Krise*, by various authors (Würzburg, 1971), pp. 35–65, esp. pp. 38–41.

13. See the classic work on this interpretation, which provoked enormous discussion then and still does: J. Weiss, *Die Predigt Jesu vom Reiche Gottes* (1892), 2nd ed. (Göttingen, 1900); Albert Schweitzer, *Geschichte der Leben-Jesu-Forschung* (1906), 2 vols. (Hamburg, 1966), esp. vol. 2, pp. 402–51, 620–30; Eng., *The Quest of the Historical Jesus: A Critical Study of the Progress from Reimarus to Wrede*, trans. W. Montgomery (New York: Macmillan, 1961). In our interpretation of the Lord's Prayer, we hereafter take up the Catholic perspective of Otto Kuss and the Protestant one of Ernst Lohmeyer; see the following note.

14. The principal reference works that we will be using in our reflections are the following: Oscar Dibelius, *Das Vaterunser: Umrisse zueiner Geschichte das Gebets in der Alten und Mittleren Kirsche* (Giessen, 1903); Ernst Lohmeyer, *Das Vater-unser* (Zurich: Vanderhoeck & Ruprecht, 1952); Eng., *The Lord's Prayer*, trans. John Bowden (London: Collins, 1965); Joachim Jeremias, *Abba: Studien zur neutestamentlichen Theologie und Zeitgeschichte* (Göttingen: Vanderhoeck & Ruprecht, 1966),

esp. pp. 15–57 (*The Prayers of Jesus* includes chaps. 1, 2, and 4 of *Abba: Studien* [Philadelphia: Fortress, 1978]; see also Part 3, "The Lord's Prayer in the Light of Recent Research"); Otto Kuss, "Das Vater-unser," in *Auslegung und Verkündigung*, vol. 3 (Regensburg, 1966), pp. 277–333; A. Hamman, "La prière du Seigneur," *La Prière*, vol. 1 (Tournai: Desclée, 1959), pp. 94–134; W. Marchel, *Abba, Père: La prière du Christ et des chrétiens* (Rome, 1963); H. van den Bussche, *Le notre Père* (Brussels, 1960); Eng., *Understanding the Lord's Prayer*, trans. Charles Schaldenbrand (New York: Sheed & Ward, 1963); T. Soiron, *Die Bergpredigt Jesu* (Fribourg, 1941), pp. 314–70; L. Sabourin, *Il vangelo di Matteo: Teologia e Esegesi* (Rome, 1976), pp. 425–57.

15. Kuss, "Das Vater-unser," pp. 279–80; Lohmeyer, *The Lord's Prayer*, pp. 15–20 and passim.

16. See the retranslation made by Jeremias, *The Prayers of Jesus*, p. 94.

17. The *Didache*, 8, 2, calls for the recitation of the Lord's Prayer three times a day. The *Didache* is dated between A.D. 50 and 70; see J. P. Audet, *La Didachè: Instructions des Apôtres*, Etudes Biblique (Paris: Gabalda 1958); Eng., *The Didache*, trans. James A. Kleist, in Ancient Christian Writers, no. 6 (Westminster, Md.: Newman, 1948).

18. Jeremias, *The Prayers of Jesus*, p. 89.

19. See the parallels drawn by Hamman, *La Prière*, vol. 1, pp. 98–99. The Shemoneh Esre was for the Jews prayer par excellence; many of the eighteen benedictions are from the first half of the first century, the rest may go back to earlier times. A final form was made of them in the 90s under Gamaliel II: Paul Billerbeck and Herman Strack, *Kommentar zum Neuen Testament aus Talmud und Midrash* (Munich: Beck, 1922–1961), IV, pp. 208–49, cf. I, p. 407. The Qaddish is dated in the 600s, C.E.

20. Jeremias, *The Prayers of Jesus*, pp. 89–91.

21. See Lohmeyer, *The Lord's Prayer*, p. 13; Kuss, "Das Vater-unser," p. 280.

22. Tertullian, *De oratione*, P.L. 1, 1153.

23. See Jeremias, *Abba*, pp. 15–66; idem, *The Prayers of Jesus*, pp. 29–65; idem, *Neutestamentliche Theologie: Die Verkündigung Jesu* (Gütersloh: Mohn, 1971); Eng., *New Testament Theology: The Proclamation of Jesus*, trans. John Bowden (New York: Scribner's, 1971), pp. 61–67; Lohmeyer, *The Lord's Prayer*, pp. 314–18; W. Marchel, *Dieu-Père dans le Nouveau Testament* (Paris: Cerf, 1966); idem, *Abba, Père*, pp. 101–77; A. Merad, A. Abecassis, and D. Perezil, *N'avons-nous pas le même Père?* (Le Chalet, 1972), pp. 111–29; F. J. Schierse, "O pai de Jesus," *Mysterium Salutis* II/I (Petrópolis: Vozes, 1972), pp. 84–85.

24. See Paul Ricoeur, "Fatherhood: From Fantasy to Symbol," trans. Robert Sweeney, *The Conflict of Interpretations: Essays in Hermeneutics,* ed. Don Ihde (Evanston, Ill.: Northwestern University Press, 1974), pp. 468–97, esp. pp. 487–88; Marchel, *Dieu-Père,* pp. 33–34.

25. See Gregory of Nyssa (died 394), *De Dominica oratione,* P.G. 44, 1136–1148, trans. Hamman, *Le Pater expliqué,* p. 114: "It is clear that no levelheaded person would use the name of father unless he or she recognized some likeness to him."

26. See the wealth of examples in the classic works: Heiler, *Prayer,* pp. 74–103; Gerardus van der Leeuw, *Phänomenologie der Religion* (Tübingen, 1933); Eng., *Religion in Essence and Manifestation: A Study in Phenomenology,* 2 vols., trans. and ed. J. E. Turner (New York: Harper Torchbook, 1963; reprint, Gloucester, Mass.: Peter Smith, 1967), vol. I, pp. 177–80; H. Tellenbach, ed., *Das Vaterbild in Mythos und Geschichte* (Stuttgart-Berlin: Kohlhammer, 1976).

27. Hamman, *La prière,* vol. 1, p. 82.

28. *Iliad,* iv, 235, v, 33, xii, 631; cf. *Odyssey,* xiii, 128, xx, 112.

29. Aristotle, *Politics,* I, 12.

30. Jeremias, *Abba,* p. 15; idem, *Abba, Jésus et son Père* (Paris: Seuil, 1972), p. 9.

31. Certainly the following passages: Deut. 32:6; 2 Sam. 7:14, 1 Chron. 17:13, 22:10, 28:6; Ps. 68:8, 89:27; Isa. 63:16 (twice), 64:7; Jer. 3:4, 19, 31; Micah 1:6, 2:10. God compared with an earthly father: Deut. 1:31, 9:5; Ps. 103:13; Prov. 3:12. The idea of God as Father is preserved in many personal names in Israel; e.g., Abi-ram (My Father is lofty), Abi-ezer (My Father is help), Abi-yah (My Father is Yahweh), Abi-tub (My Father is goodness); see Albert Gelin, *Les idées maîtresses de l'Ancien Testament* (Paris: Cerf, 1950); Eng., *Key Concepts of the Old Testament,* trans. George Lamb (New York: Sheed & Ward, 1955), p. 33.

32. See C. Vriezen, *Theologie des Alten Testaments in Grundrissen* (Neukirchen, n.d.), pp. 118–22.

33. Cf. this other text, Isa. 64:8: "But now, Lord, thou art our father, we are the clay, thou the potter, and all of us are thy handiwork."

34. Origen in his *De oratione* (P.G. 11, 485–549) recognizes this: "In the Old Testament there exists no prayer invoking God in the name of Father"; cf. Hamman, *Le Pater expliqué,* p. 50: "Now God is invoked in this sense by reason of that complete confidence that the Savior has transmitted to us." Jeremias has found confirmation of the fact that in the Old Testament and in later Palestinian Judaism there is no personal invocation, "My Father": *Abba: Studien,* pp. 19–33, *Abba, Jésus et son Père,* p. 26.

35. See the documentation in Jeremias, *Abba: Studien,* pp. 62–63; idem, *New Testament Theology,* p. 66; idem, *The Prayers of Jesus,* pp. 97–98.

36. Jeremias, *The Prayers of Jesus,* p. 97.

37. For the exegesis of these passages, see Lohmeyer, *The Lord's Prayer,* pp. 38–44.

38. See Ricoeur, *Conflict of Interpretations,* p. 490: "It is on the basis of this category that we must interpret the category of fatherhood. Eschatological royalty and fatherhood remain inseparable, right into the Lord's Prayer; this begins with the invocation of the Father and is continued by the 'petitions' concerning name, kingdom, and will, which are understandable only in the perspective of an eschatological fulfillment. Fatherhood is thus placed in the realm of hope. The Father of the invocation is the same as the God of the preaching of the kingdom, which one enters only if one is like a child."

39. Leonardo Boff, "Filhos no Filho," *A graça libertadora no mundo* (Petrópolis: Vozes, 1976), pp. 220–30; Eng., *Liberating Grace,* trans. John Drury (Maryknoll, N.Y.: Orbis Books, 1979), pp. 184–92.

40. See Lohmeyer, *The Lord's Prayer,* pp. 57–62.

41. St. Gregory of Nyssa in his commentary on the Lord's Prayer (P.G. 44, 1136–1148) (translation by Hamman, *Le Pater expliqué,* pp. 116–17) has good comments on heaven as fatherland. St. Ambrose, commenting on the Lord's Prayer (P.L. 16, 450–454), says in regard to heaven, "Heaven is where there is no fatal wounding"—*uni nullum mortis est vulnus.*

42. See the lucid study of Ricoeur, "Religion, Atheism, Faith," in, *Conflict of Interpretations,* pp. 440–67; and also Louis Evely, *We Dare to Say Our Father* (New York: Herder & Herder, 1965; Doubleday, 1975), pp. 22–43.

43. The famous work of A. Mitscherlich treats of this, *Auf dem Weg zur vaterlosen Gesellschaft* (Munich, 1963); a presentation and critique of this book has been done by M. Juritsch, *Sociología da paternidade* (Petrópolis: Vozes, 1970), pp. 134–41. We highly recommend this book on the anthropology of paternity in an interdisciplinary dialogue.

44. Juritsch, *Sociología,* p. 137.

45. See the important work of C. G. Jung, *Die Bedeutung des Vaters für Schicksal des Einzelnen* (Zurich, 1949).

46. Rubem Alves, *O enigma da religião* (Petrópolis: Vozes, 1976); the whole first part is dedicated to a discussion of critiques of Freud, Marx, Nietzsche, and others.

47. See Friedrich Nietzsche, *Beyond Good and Evil: A Philosophy for the Future,* translated by Walter Kaufmann (New York: Random

House, 1966); and *On the Genealogy of Morals*, translated by Walter Kaufmann (New York: Random House, 1967).

48. See the work of J. M. Pohier, *Au nom du Père* (Paris, 1972), where he discusses the principal themes of Christian faith within the framework of the questions raised by Freud.

49. See the judicious statements of Ricoeur, *Conflict of Interpretations*, pp. 470–73.

50. See the reflections of C. Surian, *Elementi per una teologia del desiderio e la spiritualità di San Francesco d'Assisi* (Rome, 1973), pp. 113–15.

51. See the exposition in Leonardo Boff, *The Maternal Face of God* (San Francisco: Harper & Row, 1987).

52. See St. Cyprian, *De oratione*, P.L. 4, 521–38, in the translation by Hamman, *Le Pater expliqué*, p. 27.

53. Tertullian, P.L. 1, 1153–1165; translation by Hamman, *Le Pater expliqué*, pp. 16–17.

54. See the collection of these expressions in Hamman, *La Prière*, vol. 1, pp. 172–83.

55. Origen, in his commentary on the Lord's Prayer, observes that this supplication presupposes that the name of the Father has not yet been sanctified; *De oratione*, P.G. 11, 489–549; translation by Hamman, *Le Pater expliqué*, p. 58.

56. St. Francis warned his confreres not to count up or recount the miseries of this world so as not to question God or blaspheme his name.

57. See Santo de Fraine, in *Dicionário Enciclopédico da Bíblia* (Petrópolis: Vozes, 1971), pp. 1389–93; one of the more detailed studies, by Otto Procksch and Karl George Kuhn, can be found in *Theologisches Wörterbuch zum Neuen Testament*, ed. Gerhard Kittel (Stuttgart: Kohlhammer, 1957), vol. 1, pp. 87–116; Eng., *Theological Dictionary of the New Testament*, ed. Gerhard Kittel, trans. and ed. Geoffrey W. Bromiley (Grand Rapids, Mich.: Eerdmans, 1964), vol. 1, pp. 88–115.

58. The classic work is that of Rudolf Otto, *The Idea of the Holy: An Inquiry into the Non-Rational Factor in the Idea of the Divine and Its Relation to the Rational* (1931), trans. John H. Harvey, 2nd ed. (New York: Oxford University Press, 1950).

59. This is the famous sixth thesis of Marx against Feuerbach.

60. See A. M. Besnard, *Le mystère du nom* (Paris, 1962); van den Bussche, *Understanding the Lord's Prayer*, pp. 65–75; J. Dupont in *Dictionnaire de la Bible*, Supp., vol. 6, "*nom*," pp. 514–41.

61. Origen, *De oratione*, P.G. 11, 489–549, translation by Hamman, *Le Pater expliqué*, p. 59.

62. See the beautiful text of 1 Cor. 6:9–11, where it says that we have been dedicated to God and justified through the name of the Lord Jesus and the Spirit of our God.

63. For the Bible everything is in relation to the Holy One (God) and becomes holy through participation: the nation, the temple, sacred objects (holy things), the land, persons, etc. This holiness is never considered in itself outside this bond with God, the unique font of all holiness: *tu solus sanctus!*

64. See the reflections of Alves, *O enigma da religião*.

65. See the reflections and bibliography in Leonardo Boff, *A ressurreição de Cristo, a nossa ressurreição na morte* (Petrópolis: Vozes, 1976) and *Vida para além da morte: O presente—seu futuro, sua festa, sua contestação* (Petrópolis: Vozes, 1978), pp. 17–26.

66. W. Knörzer, *Reich Gottes, Traum, Hoffnung, Wirklichkeit* (Stuttgart, 1970); Walter Nigg, *Das ewige Reich: Geschichte einer Hoffnung* (Munich-Hamburg, 1967), which traces the history of the idea of the kingdom of God along the trajectory of the centuries.

67. See Lohmeyer, *The Lord's Prayer*, pp. 95–100; Jeremias, *New Testament Theology*, pp. 108–21.

68. Jeremias, *New Testament Theology*, p. 102.

69. See Jean Dupont, *Les béatitudes*, II, *La bonne nouvelle* (Bruges: Abbey of Saint André, 1958; Paris, 1969); E. Semain, "Manifesto de libertação: O discurso-programa de Nazaré (Luke 4:16–21)," *REB* 34 (1974): 261–81, esp. 279–80.

70. Origen, *De oratione*, P.G. 11, 489–549; translation in Hamman, *Le Pater expliqué*, p. 61.

71. See the letter of Marx, Feb. 16, 1881, to Vera Zassoulitch, cited by M. Godelier, "Marxisme, anthropologie, et religion," *Epistémologie et marxisme* (Paris, 1972), pp. 223–24.

72. St. Augustine, *Sermo 56*, 4–14, P.L. 39, 379–386; translation in Hamman, *Le Pater expliqué*, p. 139.

73. Tertullian, *De oratione*, P.L. 1, 1153–1165; translation in Hamman, *Le Pater expliqué*, p. 20.

74. Cyril of Jerusalem, *Catequeses mistagogicas*, P.G. 33, 1117–24; translation in Hamman, *Le Pater expliqué*, p. 107.

75. See Raymond E. Brown, "The Pater Noster as an Eschatological Prayer." *Theological Studies* 22 (1961): 175–208.

76. See Leonardo Boff, *Passion of Christ, Passion of the World*, pp. 18–19.

77. This is the interpretation preferred by the fathers of the church in their explanations of the Lord's Prayer. See Hamman, *Le Pater expliqué*.

78. See statements of these authors in Lohmeyer, *The Lord's Prayer*, p. 116, and Heiler, *Prayer*, pp. 89–93.

79. Tertullian, in his commentary (P.L. 1, 1153–65), says, "In this petition we warn ourselves to have patience"; Cyprian declares, "It is not that God should do what we want, but that we should do what God wants" (*De oratione dominica*, P.L. 4, 521–38); see Hamman, *Le Pater expliqué*, pp. 19 and 33.

80. Origen, *De oratione*, P.G. 11, 489–549, translation in Hamman, *Le Pater expliqué*, p. 68.

81. The commentaries of the church fathers prefer the spiritual interpretation of this petition, with the exception of Theodore of Mopsuestia. The bread refers immediately to Jesus Christ and the Eucharist; for this see Hamman, *Le Pater expliqué*. As for later commentaries, see the collection of texts where the spiritual interpretation predominates: K. Becker and M. Peter, *Das heilige Vater-unser: Ein Werkbuch* (Freiburg: Herder, 1951), pp. 224–50.

82. See the reflections of Gerhart Ebeling, *Vom Gebet: Predigten über das Unser-Vater* (Tübingen: Mohn, 1963); Eng., *On Prayer: The Lord's Prayer in Today's World*, trans. James W. Leiten (Philadelphia: Fortress, n.d.).

83. See the pertinent reflections of Karl Barth, *Das Vater-unser* (Zurich, 1965), pp. 76–79.

84. *Magistri Echardi Tractatus super oratione dominica*, in *Werke* V/1–2, ed. E. Seeberg, pp. 103–28; this citation, p. 120.

85. On this word (*epiousios*) there are innumerable studies. We cite only the more recent: F. M. Braun, "Le pain don't nous avons besoin (Mt 6;1, Lc 11,3)," *Nouvelle Revue Théologique* 110 (1978): 559–68; W. Rordorf, "Le 'pain quotidien' (Math 6, 11) dans l'histoire de l'exégèse," *Didaskalia* (Journal of the Faculty of Theology of Lisbon) 6 (1976): 221–25.

86. Origen, *De oratione* 27, 7, P.G. 11, 509c.

87. See F. Preisigke, *Sammelbuch griechischer Urkunden aus Aegypten* (Strasburg, 1915), I, 5224. This papyrus has vanished; its editor, Sayce, as Raymond E. Brown informs us ("The Pater Noster as an Eschatological Prayer," *Theological Studies* 22 [1961]: 175–208; here p. 195, note 86), was not particularly meticulous. In this papyrus the word *epious* appears, probably as an abbreviation of *epiousion*, in the context of a list of distributions, signifying "what is necessary for one day," "wages of one day," "a day's rations."

88. St. Jerome, *Comm. in Matthvi, 11*, P.L. 36, 43. Decidedly against this view is the study of P. Grelot, "La quatrième demande du Pater et son arrière-plan sémitique," *New Testament Studies* 25 (1979): 299–314.

89. H. Bourgoin, "Epioúsios expliqué par la notion de préfixe," *Biblica* 60 (1979): 91–96.

90. Classic works go back to this interpretation, in accord with Jeremias, *The Prayers of Jesus,* pp. 100–102, and Lohmeyer, *The Lord's Prayer,* pp. 134–59, as also Brown, "The Pater Noster," *Theological Studies* 22, note 7.

91. See Leonardo Boff, *Jesus Cristo Libertador,* 7th ed. (Petrópolis: Vozes, 1979); Eng., *Jesus Christ Liberator: A Critical Christology for Our Time,* trans. Patrick Hughes (Maryknoll, N.Y.: Orbis, 1978); and *Passion of Christ, Passion of the World.*

92. This point is well explored in Romano Guardini's commentary on the Lord's Prayer, *Das Gebet des Herrn* (Mainz: Grünewald, 1934); Eng., *The Lord's Prayer,* trans. Isabel McHugh (New York: Pantheon, 1958), pp. 17–25, 69–78; and that by Grelot in the article cited in note 88.

93. Van den Bussche, *Understanding the Lord's Prayer,* pp. 116–17.

94. See the excellent reflections of Origen in regard to this point, *De oratione,* P.G. 11, 489–549, in the translation by Hamman, *Le Pater expliqué,* pp. 81–84.

95. See A. Moser, "Pecado, culpa e psicanálise," *REB* 35 (1975): 5–36.

96. Clodovis Boff, "Pecado social," *REB* 37 (1977): 675–701.

97. See L. Goppelt, *Teología do Novo Testamento* (São Leopoldo-Petrópolis, 1976), p. 154.

98. A detailed analysis of the parables of mercy and pardon will be found in Joachim Jeremias, *Die Gleichnisse Jesu* (Munich-Hamburg, 1966), pp. 84–99; Eng., *The Parables of Jesus,* trans. S. H. Hooke (New York: Scribner's, 1963), pp. 124–46.

99. See Lohmeyer, *The Lord's Prayer,* pp. 186–90.

100. Enrique Dussel, *El humanismo semita* (Buenos Aires, 1969); H. W. Wolff, *Antropología do Antigo Testamento* (São Paulo, 1977), I, 2; Leonardo Boff, "Aprendendo a ser: Momentos da antropología cristã," *Grande Sinal* 32 (1978): 323–34.

101. See Ignace de la Potterie and Stanislas Lyonnet, *La vie selon l'esprit: Condition du chrétien* (Paris: Cerf, 1965); Eng., *The Christian Lives by the Spirit* (Staten Island: Society of St. Paul, 1971), pp. 156–193.

102. J. B. Libânio, *Pecado e opção fundamental* (Petrópolis: Vozes, 1975), pp. 42–87.

103. For this whole problematic, see Leonardo Boff, "O pecado original: Discussão antiga e moderna e pistas de equacionamento," *Grande Sinal* 29 (1975): 109–33, and A. Villalmonte, *El Pecado Original* (Salamanca, 1978).

104. See J. Kamp, *Souffrance de Dieu, vie du monde* (Paris: Casterman, 1971), pp. 47–92; Leonardo Boff, *Teología do cativeiro e da libertação* (Lisbon: Multinova, 1976), pp. 113–34.

105. See Edward Schillebeeckx, "Jesus e o fracasso na vida humana," *Concilium* 113 (1976): 88–99.

106. Van den Bussche, *Understanding the Lord's Prayer*, p. 134; Lohmeyer, *The Lord's Prayer*, pp. 195–208.

107. The original sense of the petition was situated within an apocalyptico-eschatological horizon; see Brown, "The Pater Noster as an Eschatological Prayer," *Theological Studies* 22 (1961): 204–8; a very lucid study is that of K. Kuhn, "Jesus in Gethsemani," *Evangelische Theologie* 12 (1952): 260–85.

108. See Jean Piaget, *Le Structuralisme* (Paris: Presses Universitaires de France, 1968), pp. 5–16; Eng., *Structuralism*, trans. Cheminah Maschler (New York: Basic Books, 1970; Harper Torchbooks, 1971).

109. See E. Támez, S. Trinidad, et al., *Capitalismo: violencia y antivida*, 2 vols. (San José, Costa Rica: DEI, 1978).

110. See Clodovis Boff, *Os sinais dos tempos: Pautas de leitura* (São Paulo, 1979), which is a very important work on this theme.

111. Piet Schoonenberg, "O pecado do mundo," *Mysterium Salutis* II/3 (Petrópolis: Vozes, 1972), p. 306.

112. Boff, "O pecado original," pp. 109–33.

113. See Sabourin, *Il vangelo di Matteo*, pp. 448–50; J. Schmid, *Das Evangelium nach Mattäus*, Regensburger Neues Testament, vol. 1 (Regensberg, 1965), pp. 133–35; Lohmeyer, *The Lord's Prayer*, pp. 209–17. In Greek, the phrase is *apo tou ponerou*; the noun *(ponerou)* is in the genitive case; we do not know morphologically whether the nominative is neuter *(poneron)* or masculine *(poneros)*. In the first case it would signify iniquity or evil; in the second, the evil one. Probably the masculine *(poneros)* is intended, because of the definite article *(tou)* that precedes it. The neuter normally appears without the article. Luke omits this petition; it is in Matthew's version. The Greek fathers, sensitive to the nuances of their language, interpret this in the sense of the evil one (masculine). The Latin fathers, on the contrary—because in Latin the article does not exist—take it in the sense of iniquity, evil (neuter)—*libera nos a malo*.

114. On this question, see the two basic positions: Christian Duquoc, "Satan—symbole ou réalité," *Lumière et Vie* 78 (1966): 99–105; Herbert Haag, *El diablo, un fantasma* (Barcelona: Herder, 1973); and Joseph Ratzinger, "Abschied vom Teufel?" in *Dogma und Verkündigung* (Munich, 1973), pp. 225–34.

115. Rudolf Schnackenburg, "Der Sinn der Versuchung Jesu bei den Synoptikern," in *Schriften zum Neuen Testament* (Munich, 1971), p. 127.

116. See the fundamental work of Herbert Haag in collaboration with other exegetes and theologians, *El diablo: Su existencia como problema* (Barcelona: Herder, 1978).

117. See Van der Leeuw, *Religion in Essence and Manifestation,* vol. 1, chaps. 15, 16, and 19.

118. See J. Ernst, *Die eschatologischen Gegenspieler in den Schriften des Neuen Testaments* (Regensburg, 1967), pp. 221–40.

119. A systematic and rigorously exegetical treatment of this can be found in Haag, "Jesús y la realidad del mal," *El diablo: Su existencia,* pp. 199–246.

120. Jeremias, "Overcoming the Rule of Satan," in *New Testament Theology,* pp. 85–96.

121. See Haag, *El diablo: Su existencia,* p. 244.

122. See *Reallexikon für Antike und Christentum,* vol. 8 (1972), p. 303, "*Freiheit.*"

123. See F. Reiniker, "Amen," in *Lexikon zur Bibel* (1960), pp. 67–68.

124. For an exegesis of these passages, see H. Schlier, "Amen," in *Theologisches Wörterbuch,* vol. 1, pp. 339–43; Eng., *Theological Dictionary,* vol. 1, pp. 335–38.

PART II

THE HAIL MARY

The Feminine and the Holy Spirit

Translated by Phillip Berryman

1

Mary, the Feminine, and the Holy Spirit

Hail Mary,
full of grace,
the Lord is with thee.
Blessed art thou among women
and blessed is the fruit of thy womb, Jesus.

Holy Mary,
Mother of God,
pray for us sinners
now and at the hour of our death.
Amen.

Our culture thirsts for emancipation and hungers for liberation. A religious interpretation of this hunger and thirst sees in them the in-breaking of the Holy Spirit. Where the Spirit is present, there is freedom (cf. 2 Cor. 3:17).

For centuries women—and the feminine—have been relegated to subordinate status in the way humanity is understood and society is organized. Without conscious integration of the feminine we are all left poorer. Today we understand the urgency of women's liberation, of removing the prejudices hindering the emergence of the riches that only women can bring to human endeavors. There is something of the sacred and the messianic in the process of human liberation, a process whereby more space is opened so that each may reveal the fruitfulness proper to being a man or woman, with great respect and appreciation for the

identity of each sex. Liberation does not mean historic vindica-
tion or competition between the sexes. It means that action that
liberates the freedom of both men and women, overcoming
mechanisms of domination and fostering pathways from woman's
heart to man's, and from man's heart to woman's. We all thereby
grow toward the reign of a more fruitful freedom.

THE FEMININE: PATH TO GOD AND GOD'S PATH

The word of revelation makes us discover in woman an image
and likeness of God (Gen. 1:27). In history she reveals and embodies values, dimensions of the human, and promises that give us
some idea of what the mystery of God is. Without that word we
would know less of God. She is a route to God in a way that is
proper to her and irreplaceable. Whenever women are marginal-
ized in the church, our experience of God is diminished; we are
impoverished and we are closed to a radical sacrament of God; at
the same time, we suppress within ourselves a depth that exists and
acts within each human being, the feminine dimension that is not
restricted to women but constitutes a part of every human being
in differing intensities and embodiments, as is proper to each sex.
    Woman and the feminine are ways in which God seeks en-
counter with human beings. God has a motherly as well as a fa-
therly face. God's revelation and liberating deeds are marked by
feminine, virginal, spousal, and maternal traces. The fullness of
humanization is found in the awareness of being completely enveloped in God's motherly and infinite womb. Only then do we
have the certainty of being fully accepted.
    Christian faith presents Mary as the great icon revealing God's
feminine countenance. God's will of self-surrender is realized in
Mary in a fullness that can grow no further. The Holy Spirit indeed came over her (Luke 1:35); he envisioned her as his temple
and his tabernacle among human beings. Every woman is Eve,
that is, mother of life. In Mary, however, what was conceived
was divinized life. Hence her maternal fruitfulness is also divine,
for she became pregnant through the Holy Spirit (Matt. 1:18);
what would be born of her could only be Son of God and Holy
with the holiness of the Holy Spirit (Luke 1:35).

All this is Mary's reality. At the same time, it is promise for all women. She signifies a supreme archetype, the end point of everything feminine. Hence the marvels worked in her by Mystery far surpass Mary's biographical meaning; they extend to all of the human reality in its feminine dimension. And because the feminine does not pertain solely to women but is proper to the human condition, that meaning also concerns men.

THE HAIL MARY: THE CHURCH'S COLLECTIVE MEMORY

The Hail Mary, a prayer that along with the Our Father is so deeply a part of the daily piety of Christians from the first stammerings of infants, encompasses all the riches of the mystery of God in Mary. It is like a gold mine; the more you dig, the more nuggets you find. The phrases are simple, but they conceal the gift of God. Throughout history, God's gift has never involved the tortuous paths and thickets of many words. God prefers doing to speaking. Religious people and prophets have come along later and tried to say with human words that which cannot be verbally expressed. With many words also come sophistication, subtlety, and often enough confusion.

In a few brief phrases, the Hail Mary crystallizes the collective memory of Christians. When we recite it we bring to the surface, to the level of praise and petition, that which otherwise occurs only on the level of mystery.

Our effort at exegesis, theology, and piety consists of returning to Christians that which is their age-old legacy. Our purpose is to gather, deepen, and systematize what is implicit and latent in the words of the Hail Mary in order to make the meaning more explicit and so enhance the sweetness of this beautiful prayer.

2

When It Makes Sense
to Pray the Hail Mary

Deep, boundless Mystery
permeates and lights up all
his kind and ineffable countenance.
What way leads to him?

We are always in it:
we are never beyond the glow of its radiance.
We never journey to him.
His Light opens us to the light.

Father is his name: Mystery,
luminous sun of light and heat.
Two emissaries from the ethereal:
the Spirit and the holy Jesus.

Jesus is the Light that guides us,
Heat is the Holy Spirit.
Heat and Light are the way
leading back to the bosom of the Father.

Through them we glimpse the face of God,
the Father of Goodness.
One made Mary his home,
the other made his flesh in Jesus.

True prayer presupposes living faith. More than an adherence to religious truths, faith entails a way of being, a way of conducting one's life, of interpreting it and living it in the light of the mystery of God, especially as that mystery has been revealed in the life of Jesus Christ. The person of faith affirms that the center of our heart is not in our own heart but outside it, in God, for "God is greater than our hearts" (1 John 3:20). This "out-centering" is the essence of faith. And, as is evident, faith touches on all the dimensions of human life, even the most secular. Everything can be illuminated by the light of God: all human activity in the economic and social realms, in the spheres of family life and intellectual life, in the world of relationships. Nothing escapes God. God permeates everything, underlies everything, and draws everything to himself. In God, people of faith live their lives, bear their tribulations, delight in their fleeting joys, and accept the enigma of death.

Prayer translates the supreme expression of living faith. Through prayer a person, as it were, leaves the universe of all things behind and seeks a relationship with the Divine. Here we have the manifestation of true human transcendence. Only human beings can place themselves in an "ex-static" position. Only human beings can contemplate God face-to-face, cry out to him "my God" and so surpass all limits imposed by creation and history. In this stance they find their highest dignity. Praying is an act of courage. It entails an expansion of spirit and the bravery to venture beyond the boundless times and open spaces of the universe, all of which fade before the greatness of God and before the impulse of the heart that says not *"sum"* (I am), but *"sursum"* (up)!

That is why those who are truly prayerful people are deeply humane and extremely humble. Prayer raises them above all great things, which shrink before the greatness of God. Yet the greatness of God is not annihilating; it confers a sense of dignity on the dust that, while knowing it is dust, at the same time knows that it exists in a unique relationship with God, that it is indwelt by the Infinite.

Because of the decentering that prayer entails, it has a deeply healing aspect. Whenever the self breaks out of the closed circle in which it finds itself and establishes a relationship, it becomes more human. Communicating with the Divine, it too becomes in some fashion divine.

THE TWO POLES OF CHRISTIAN PRAYER

There are two poles of access to the holy and ineffable mystery, originless origin of all that exists and can exist, he whom we call Father: the Son and the Holy Spirit. Whatever we can know about God the Father who "dwells in unapproachable light" (1 Tim. 6:16) and whom "no one has ever seen" (1 John 4:12), we know through the revelation of the Son and the Holy Spirit.

Both have an extra-trinitarian mission directed toward the divinization of the human being. The Son was incarnated in Jesus of Nazareth, thereby "Christifying" everything that he touched, conferring on every creature a sonship and fraternal character. We are conceived by the Father as children in his beloved, unbegotten, and gentle Son. In his way of being, in his words, in his liberating deeds, Jesus has revealed to us the hidden face of the Father of infinite kindness (cf. Luke 6:35). Because he could rightly say "The Father and I are one" (John 10:30), he could also say "Whoever has seen me has seen the Father" (John 14:9). Everything must go through him, because "all things came into being through him" (John 1:3), and "in him all things hold together" (Col. 1:17), and he is simply "all and in all" (Col. 3:11). He is the way and the necessary mediator to the heart of the mystery of God (John 14:6; 1 Tim 2:5). The masculine has been supremely embodied in Jesus; it is fully realized only if it is assumed by God. That is what happens in Jesus Christ: his humanity in masculine form is the humanity of the very Son of God incarnate.

This is one pole of Christian prayer. It can never cease to be Christocentric; were it to do so, it would lose access to the ultimate meaning of everything, which is the Father.

The other pole of Christian prayer is given to us by the Holy Spirit, who has also been sent to divinize creation and "pneumatify"* human beings with his grace. He came over Mary (Luke 1:35), making her his temple of the Spirit, an eschatological and

---

*Translator's note: Boff uses the neologism *pneumatizar* and cognates from Greek *pneuma*, "spirit," to parallel on the side of the Holy Spirit the incarnation of the Word. This translation accordingly uses the admittedly infelicitous "pneumatic" and "pneumatify" in quotes throughout the book to convey the meaning intended by Boff.

definitive sanctuary, in such a real and radical manner that she is uniquely united to him.[1] The Spirit prolongs the mystery of the incarnation of the Son, taking what is of Jesus and in him and making it fully known (John 16:14). Hence the Spirit is the Son's witness (Paraclete: John 14:16; 16:7), his permanent memorial in the world (John 14:26), in a word, the Spirit of truth (John 14:17; 16:13). Through the Spirit the feminine reaches its complete fulfillment. Acting really and intimately in Mary, the Spirit has made her mother of God. She is united to the Holy Spirit, and the one who is born of her is Holy, the Son of God (Luke 1:35). Thus Mary's feminine form becomes part of the very mystery of God. As the masculine in Jesus is divinized by the Son, so the feminine in Mary is divinized by the Holy Spirit. Hence the Mariological principle is not something marginal in the history of God's revelation; it completes the Christological principle. Together Jesus and Mary reveal the mysterious face of the Father and lift human beings—who are ever simultaneously masculine and feminine in proper portions—to their true destiny in God.

We can now understand why all the prayers of the church end with the ritual formula: *to* the Father, *through* the Son, *in* the Holy Spirit.

When we pray the Hail Mary, faith articulates the aspect of this truth that relates to the Holy Spirit through whom we have access to the Father. In the person, life, and work of Mary the Spirit has intensified his presence. In her and through her a message is communicated and we touch something ultimate. Saint Bernard rightly said that in the angel's greeting hidden mysteries are contained: *arcana mysteria reservans.*[2] Our reflection will attempt to draw out these hidden mysteries. Let us briefly look at three decisive points: Mary as the place of God's revelation, as the place of the revelation of woman, and as the place of the revelation of the female in its eschatological form.

MARY, PLACE OF GOD'S REVELATION

In Mary we contemplate and marvel at a series of divine interventions that place her at the center of God's self-communicating will. First, she is preserved from all sin; she has never belonged to the fallen order of creation. From all eternity Mary has been thought and willed by God to be the perfect vessel of the Holy Spirit. Hence she is eternally the Immaculate Conception. When the fullness of time arrives, when the Father determines to send his Son and the Holy Spirit, he wills Mary's birth. Completely open, she is the living temple of God, prepared to receive the visit from on high. The Spirit is sent to her. The new being, the *novissimus Adam* (1 Cor. 15:45), begins to grow within her, and she will be found to be with child by the Holy Spirit (Matt. 1:18). The Spirit has established a permanent dwelling and will remain in humankind forever, radiating out from Mary to the church and from the church to all humanity. While respecting her perpetual virginity, the Spirit makes her also mother of God. The fruit of Mary is the eternal Son of God who assumes flesh, generated by Mary, thereby becoming brother to every human creature. Mary and Jesus are completely at the service of the Father's design. Both of them liberate humanity and refashion the original orientation of creation toward its happy and transcendent end.

At every decisive moment, at the beginning, in the middle, and at the end of her son's life, Mary was always alongside him, always in solidarity with human beings, especially the oppressed in whose name she had the valor to plead for God's avenging arm (cf. Luke 1:46–55). Like Jesus she was assumed into heaven, where she continues to intercede for and await the arrival of her children. Throughout the history of the church Mary has always occupied a central place; the faithful experience in her an ultimate instance of life, grace, and acceptance. Her appearances demonstrate her motherly concern for the salvation of her children, particularly the most abandoned.

Mary obviously constitutes a privileged means of the self-communication of God's mystery. The divine story of God's sympathy for human beings is incomplete without the peerless figure of Mary.

MARY, PLACE WHERE WOMAN IS REVEALED

That God has performed his saving action in a woman is not insignificant. She has a dignity equal to that of man; without her, something would be missing from the history of all human beings, for we would be deprived of the collaboration and presence of woman, who comprises half of humankind. Mary's behavior in response to God's initiative was not passive. She acted within her own specificity as woman. Indeed, here Mary gains universal significance. She is not alone in salvation history. With her is all of female humanity. Under the power of the Spirit, Mary extends all the grandeur, depth, capacity for listening and acceptance, commitment, and self-giving that women throughout history have embodied. Just as any star needs its aura to shine, so Mary needs to be placed within the multitude of women throughout history to manifest her true greatness.

What woman means in the design of the Eternal must be sought in the life and work of Mary. She is the *ecce mulier*, the supreme archetype for all other women. She evokes and fosters all the positive qualities that exist potentially in the depth of each woman.

Paul VI's apostolic exhortation, *Marialis Cultus* (1974) clearly states that Mary

can be considered a mirror of the expectations of the men and women of our time. Thus, the modern woman, anxious to participate with decision-making power in the affairs of the community, will contemplate with intimate joy Mary who, taken into dialogue with God, gives her active and responsible consent, not to the solution of a contingent problem, but to that "event of world importance," as the Incarnation of the Word has been rightly called.

The modern woman will appreciate that Mary's choice of the state of virginity, which in God's plan prepared her for the mystery of the Incarnation, was not a rejection of any of the values of the married state but a courageous choice which she made in order to consecrate herself totally to the love of God. The modern woman will note with pleasant surprise that Mary of Nazareth, while completely devoted to the will of God, was far from being a timidly submissive woman or one whose piety was repellent to others; on the contrary, she was a woman who did not hesitate to proclaim that God vindicates the humble and the oppressed, and removes the powerful people of this world from their privileged positions (cf. Luke 1:51–53). The modern woman will recognize in Mary, who "stands out among the poor and humble of the Lord," a woman of strength, who experienced poverty and suffering, flight and exile (cf. Matt. 2:13–23). These are situations that cannot escape the attention of those who wish to support, with the Gospel spirit, the liberating energies of man and of society. And Mary will appear not as a Mother exclusively concerned with her own divine Son, but rather as a woman whose action helped to strengthen the apostolic community's faith in Christ (cf. Jn. 2:1–12), and whose maternal role was extended and became universal on Calvary.[3]

These are some examples that make manifest the virtues of Mary the woman and that give bodily form to the best qualities of any woman. Woman finds in Mary, as in a mirror, the vocation to which she has been called by God. As woman is revealed to herself, God's self-revelation is made to humankind in a human countenance.

MARY, PLACE WHERE THE FEMININE IS REVEALED

The feminine is not solely of women; it constitutes an essential aspect of every human being. Each human person is at once male and female;[4] woman embodies the female more intensely, which is why she is woman rather than man, but she always has the male dimension in her being. Man expresses the male in his being and hence is man rather than woman, but within himself he always has the female dimension. The feminine has been manifested in history in very diverse ways. Hence, no conceptual definition does justice to the riches of the feminine, nor can its meaning be considered invariably set. It is an inexhaustible fountain of the human mystery, open to new expressions, flowing from a source whose origins are lost within God's own mystery.

The feminine has to do with tenderness, *finesse,* vitality, depth, interiority, feeling, receptivity, self-giving, care, and acceptance, all of which are expressed in the human existence of both man and woman. These qualities are grounded in God, who has also manifested female dimensions in salvation history. The sacred texts present God as a mother who consoles (Isa. 66:13), who always remembers the child of her womb (Isa. 49:15; Ps. 25:6; Ps. 116:5) and who lifts it up tenderly to her face (Hos. 11:3), and who, at the end of history, like a great and kind mother, will wipe away the tears from our eyes (Rev. 21:4). God is not only Father of infinite kindness but also Mother of limitless tenderness. And the salvation that has been enacted in history shows the tender and welcoming trace of God the Mother. Mary was the privileged instrument of this. In her, the radical and universal feminine found its supreme embodiment. The feminine was penetrated by the Holy Spirit at the time of the annunciation (Luke 1:35; Matt. 1:18) and thus lifted up to God.[5] We can now know what the final destiny of the feminine is: to be the place of revelation of the feminine face of God. The feminine is also called to its highest realization in God through a particular association with the Person of the Holy Spirit.

Mary has already embodied in history the eschatology of the feminine; each woman in her own measure will share with Mary in finding complete fulfillment in the Reign of God by means of a unique insertion into the mystery of God through the third Person of the Blessed Trinity.

When we pray to Mary, we cannot forget the depth of this mystery that she incarnates, or the significance that she has for the feminine dimension of all human beings—not only women but also men.

HOW WE WILL PROCEED

As we ponder the Hail Mary, we want to have all these levels of meaning in mind. Although they are contained in the text, they may not be immediately evident. The task of our reflection is to draw out the wealth hidden under the frail veils of the words. Only then does letter become spirit; and the spirit always gives life.

Our method will be as follows. We will begin with the text, identifying its plain meaning. Then we will try to penetrate into deeper levels of meaning, recognizing that the text itself represents one moment among others in the manifestation of an underlying anthropological reality. Finally, we will try to uncover the theological and Marian meaning of each portion of the Hail Mary. This final step will involve dealing not only with the human being, Mary, but also with God, who is revealed through Mary.

As is evident, we will not cling to a meaning set in the past when the angelic greeting was pronounced; we will strive to grasp what is permanently valid in the Marian prayer and we will try to state it for the present, for the time in which the Lord has destined us to live and pray the Hail Mary. Hence, our single task of interpretation will encompass past and present, the manifest and the hidden. Working in this manner is doing theology. It goes beyond merely seeking knowledge to nourishing piety and deepening what is ours in faith.

HOW THE HAIL MARY CAME ABOUT

Before moving into our analysis, we should sketch out the history of how the Hail Mary came about.[6] It is comprised of three parts. The first part comes from the greeting of the angel Gabriel: "Hail Mary, full of grace the Lord is with thee" (cf. Luke 1:28). The second part is taken from Elizabeth's praise of Mary: "Blessed art thou among women and blessed is the fruit of thy womb" (cf. Luke 1:42). The third part is an invocation formulated by the church, and its origins are much later: "Holy Mary, Mother of God, pray for us sinners, now and at the hour of our death. Amen." It took a thousand years, from the sixth to the sixteenth century, for the Hail Mary to become fixed in its present form. Like almost all the great popular prayers of the church, this prayer has a history full of zigzags and its exact origins are not known. It is like devotion to Mary: initially it seems to have had the insignificance of a tiny rivulet, and then slowly it built until it became a torrent, like the Amazon, a powerful expression of the magnificent meaning of faith.

The practice of connecting the angel's greeting with Elizabeth's praise is attested to in a sixth-century baptismal liturgy of the Syrian church; the words of the liturgy are attributed to Severus of Antioch (d. 438). We know that the Eastern churches began very early to venerate the Virgin Mary. We can find evidence of this in the Syriac liturgy of Saint James, the Egyptian liturgy of St. Mark, and the Ethiopian liturgy of the Twelve Apostles. On an ostrakon (potsherd) found in Egypt at Luxor and dating from the seventh century, the following prayer appears: "Hail Mary, full of grace, the Lord is with you, blessed are you among all women, and blessed the fruit of your womb, because you conceived the Christ, the Son of God, the Redeemer of our souls."[7] In the church of Sancta Maria Antigua in Rome there is a fragmentary inscription, dating from the year 650, of the first two parts of the Hail Mary in green letters. We know that a little earlier, in the time of Pope Saint Gregory the Great (590–604) these two parts of the Hail Mary had already been combined to form the offertory antiphon for the fourth Sunday of Advent. From that point, the prayer grew in importance and was increasingly commented on in sermons, such as those of St. John Damascene (d. 749) and St. Bernard of Clairvaux (d. 1153).

From the liturgy, the Hail Mary moved into popular piety. Legends about the special power of intercession linked to the recitation of countless Hail Marys began to spread. The Hail Mary appeared on stamps, bells, glasses, candelabra, and furniture. The first two parts of the Hail Mary, as far as "blessed is the fruit of thy womb," began to be recited as an ejaculatory prayer. At the end of the eleventh century, the German countess Ada is said to have prayed it sixty times a day. In 1140 the holy monk Albert said 150 Hail Marys a day, as the 150 psalms were prayed. Penances began to be associated with the prayer as a way of venerating the Virgin. Blessed Ida of Louvain (d. 1310) genuflected eleven hundred times a day as she prayed corresponding Hail Marys. Likewise, the blessed Mary Magdalene Martinengo, an eighteenth-century Capuchin, prayed the Hail Mary a hundred times while prostrating herself the same number of times, and she urged novices to do the same.

Taking a step beyond popular piety, synods of bishops began to make the praying of the Hail Mary obligatory. In the synod of 1198 Bishop Odo of Paris made the Hail Mary as obligatory as the Our Father and the Creed. The synods of Trier, Germany (1227), Coventry, England (1237), and Valencia, Spain (1255) did the same. The religious rules formulated in the thirteenth century by the Cistercians, the Camaldolese, and other groups made recitation of the Hail Mary obligatory. In 1266 the Dominicans ordered that lay brothers pray the Hail Mary in their divine office.

The addition of "Jesus" to "Blessed is the fruit of thy womb" is attributed to Pope Urban IV (1261–1264). The formulas varied. Some were short and others longer, as this one from the sixteenth century: "Jesus Christ, amen, who is God glorious and blessed through the ages."

The third part, the church's "Holy Mary, mother of God, pray for us . . ." initially appeared under various formulas. A thirteenth-century Carthusian breviary simply read, "Holy Mary, pray for us." Another one in the fourteenth century added, "Pray for us sinners." Finally St. Bernardine of Siena, in a sermon commenting on the Hail Mary, said, "I cannot refrain from adding: 'Holy Mary, pray for us sinners.'" The phrase then spread among the people and in 1551 the Council of Narbonne made it official.

The final addition, "now and at the hour of our death," can be found in a Carthusian breviary dating from 1350. It was adopted by the Trinitarians and the Camaldolese, and by 1525 it was found in catechisms.

The formula that we have today was set by Pius V on the occasion of the liturgical reform in 1568. He ordered the silent recitation of the Our Father and Hail Mary before the canonical hours. The practice remained in place until 1955 when Pius XII undertook the liturgical reform that did away with this obligation.

The Hail Mary is still associated with the Angelus, a custom maintained in many countries and in rural towns in Brazil. Three times a day, in the morning, at noon, and at around 6 PM, the bell is rung and the Hail Mary is said three times. Little is known for sure about the origins of the Angelus. First came the evening Angelus, to which we have references dating from the thirteenth century. In 1318 Pope John XXII gave final approval to the custom of granting indulgences for recitation of the prayer. The morning Angelus came next; it is mentioned in the chronicles of Parma in 1318. The noontime Angelus came later. It was introduced through the custom of ringing the bells on Fridays in memory of the Lord's passion. By the fifteenth century they were rung every day. Uniformity was established in the seventeenth century with the ringing of the Angelus bells three times a day. The original purpose of the Angelus had been to pray for peace, especially in view of the threat from the Turks who loomed over European Christendom for centuries. It was customary to cast bells with inscriptions like *O rex gloriae, veni cum pace* (O King of glory, come with peace!).

Recitation of the Hail Mary found its best context in the rosary,[8] which is composed of 150 Hail Marys, broken up into groups of ten by the Our Father and Glory Be to the Father, with the announcement of a mystery of our redemption and liberation before each decade. Normally only a third of the rosary, i.e., fifty Hail Marys, five Our Fathers, and five Glorias, is recited. Each third is devoted to meditation on a set of mysteries—the joyful mysteries (part 1), the sorrowful mysteries (part 2), and the glorious mysteries (part 3)—in the lives of Jesus and Mary. (In 2002 Pope John Paul II added the luminous mysteries.)

The rosary of Hail Marys derives from the rosary of Our Fathers, which was probably introduced by Saint Benedict. Monks who were not very literate, who were unable to recite the 150 psalms in Latin, prayed 150 Our Fathers instead. To facilitate counting, they used beads strung together on a string. In the tenth and eleventh centuries the faithful used to have rosaries of Our Fathers in their hands. It was in around 1150 that rosaries of Hail Marys began to appear, and they then became very popular. According to legend, Saint Dominic had a vision of the Virgin, who asked him to spread the practice of saying the rosary. The Dominicans became the main promoters of this devotion, especially in the fifteenth century with Alan de la Roche, who created confraternities of the blessed rosary throughout Europe. On October 7, 1571, the Ottoman fleet was defeated by the Christians. Pope Pius V credited this victory to recitation of the rosary. Subsequent popes such as Leo XIII, Pius X, and Pius XI greatly encouraged the devotion, which was more and more confirmed by apparitions of the Virgin at Lourdes and Fatima, where she was seen with a rosary hanging from her hands.

The structure of the Hail Mary illustrates the essence of true Christian prayer. The first impulse goes out to heaven in a hymn of praise: it sings God's deeds in Mary. Although the words speak of Mary, the focus is on God, author of the wonders worked in her who is blessed among women. The posture is selfless and other-directed, as is all true praise and thanksgiving.

The last part of the prayer takes into account the human tragedy, where there is sin and death. We ask for help, aware of our weaknesses and inability to save ourselves. The tone is not one of bitterness or resentment, because we view our fallen state in the light of God and Mary. Having previously been able to praise and give thanks, we can ask for help with confidence. How can the God who acted so effectively in Mary not have mercy on his sinful children condemned to death? That is why we conclude with a firm and consoling "Amen."

3

Hail Mary: Rejoice, Beloved of God!

Creatures, condemned to grow old,
Were rejuvenated through Mary.
                    —*Jacob of Sarugh, Syrian bishop (421–451)*

Before considering the content of the angel's greeting—"Hail Mary"—it is important that we clarify our methodology. We can interpret the texts of the Christian scriptures in one of two ways. The first involves looking at the passages in terms of exegesis and form criticism; the second involves examining them with a view to discerning their theological and spiritual content. The exegetical-critical reading focuses on the literal meaning of the words employed by the sacred authors. The terms are understood as expressing the meaning that they had in the culture at the time when the books in question were written. Thus, for example, the angel Gabriel's greeting to the Virgin Mary—"Hail"—is simply the traditional morning greeting used by Greeks. There is nothing special about it; the messenger from heaven uses a form of greeting that would have been employed by any Greek-speaking citizen.

This method has been fruitful and has revealed to us the human face of the Word of God. Still, it represents a secular approach; it has no religious or theological character. The same method can be applied to any text, ancient or modern, whether penned by Greek historians or medieval philosophers or modern writers. When it is applied to the sacred texts, they are approached simply as texts and not as sacred. This kind of reading does not reveal the divine face of the Word of God.[1] Even a person with no faith could interpret the scriptures in a similar manner.

The theological-spiritual reading of the biblical texts, on the other hand, presupposes faith, by which we know that the scriptures are sacred because they contain God's revelation and communicate to us God's final design for human beings, history, and the world. The words are at the service of content that is broader than that set by the surrounding culture. Beyond the literal meaning of the text (which is always important to grasp) there is a theological meaning. Thus the angel's greeting—"Hail"—has a more profound meaning than that denoted by words spoken by one citizen in greeting another. The Virgin Mary is certainly a citizen, but at the same time she is that unique individual on whom God's merciful gaze has rested to make her his mother. In her, the final destiny of the feminine is fulfilled: being able to fully welcome the Divine by placing oneself completely at the service of the Holy Spirit's self-communication. History encounters in Mary an unsurpassable culmination. The angel's "hail" is not just any greeting. The literal meaning here takes on unimaginable resonances that must be heard by the believer. The exegetical-critical interpretation is enriched by the theological-spiritual interpretation.

This is not about posing a false alternative: either one or the other. One must be combined with the other. The literal meaning opens the door to a theological meaning that translates the newness of God's breaking into our history. This is the method that we will try to apply to the text of the Hail Mary.

HAIL! REJOICE!

The Greek term for "hail" used by Luke (1:28) is *chaire*.[2] As we have already said, it is the Greek greeting (cf. Mark 15:18; Matt. 27:29; John 19:3) corresponding to the *salamalek* of Arabs today or to the *shalom lak* of the Hebrews, and it may be translated as "Hail, peace be with you!"[3] There is a connotation of joy in the word *chaire*, because in Greek "joy" is *chára*, which has the same root as *cháris*, "grace." Many exegetes regard the "hail" spoken by the angel to Mary as a simple greeting, albeit obviously very deferential,[4] given the exceptional character of the circumstances. Others[5] think that it is not properly a greeting, but an imperative, an invitation to joy. The correct translation would then be: "Rejoice, Mary!" This meaning derives from the context of the entire pericope of the annunciation (Luke 1:26–28), which is based on three Old Testament prophecies: Zephaniah 3:14–17, Joel 2:21–27, and Zechariah 9:9.[6] The angel's announcement echoes these three ancient prophecies, the content of which is: "Rejoice, daughter of Zion (Israel) because Yahweh, your king, Yahweh, your God, is in your midst!" The prophecies proclaim messianic joy, and all three use the expression *chaire,* which St. Jerome rendered into Latin as *ave.*

The angel's "hail" or *ave* seems to be a tiny, insignificant word, but actually it conceals the supreme manifestation of joy. Humankind had long been awaiting the revelation that would fully embody the feminine in God. Now, like a flower fully opening to the sun, appears Mary, the new Eve, inhabited by the life whose source and plenitude is found in the Spirit.

For centuries, all humankind had yearned for its liberator; all hearts had secretly been longing for him who would finally bring peace to this world; the age-old dreams, the deepest hopes of generations, were set on this. And now the Messiah comes forth definitively. Joy is uncontained and overflowing. God's messenger invites Mary to be associated with this unique event that will change the world forever. Instead of simply saying "Hail," we ought to proclaim: "Be glad! Rejoice!"

All true joy is rooted in reasons for joy; no one is joyful out of stupidity. Mary is invited to rejoice for two reasons. First, because she has "found favor with God" (Luke 1:30); the angel reveals that she is "full of grace" (Luke 1:28). The Holy Spirit will come upon her and "overshadow" her (Luke 1:35). Mary is to become the living temple of the Spirit, who will be present within her in a personal way. In her, the Spirit will act so completely that he will elevate her maternal capacity to the point that she is truly God's mother.[7] Second, because "the Lord is with" her (Luke 1:28), the child to be conceived by the Spirit in Mary is to be the Son of God, Jesus Christ (Luke 1:35). Within Mary there will begin to grow the fruit of the Holy Spirit (she will be "found to be with child from the Holy Spirit": Matt. 1:18) who is God with us, the incarnate Word.

Hence, there are plenty of reasons why messianic joy is over-flowing, for in Mary two divine Persons make themselves present: the Holy Spirit and the unbegotten Son.

This astounding reality was predicted in the prophecies of Zephaniah, Joel, and Zechariah. The daughter of Zion of whom the ancient texts spoke is really Mary. In her are embodied the hopes not only of all Israel (represented by the daughter of Zion), but of all expectant humankind (Israel representing all nations). Yahweh, who according to the prophecies would come to reside in the midst of Zion as king (Zeph. 3:15; Zech. 9:9) or a savior (Zeph. 3:17; Zech. 9:9), is in fact called Holy Spirit and eternal Son. History thus reaches its fullness. Mary becomes pregnant with God, carrying within herself the divine Persons of the Trinity; all heaven has descended to earth. Mary is the place where everything comes together. At the moment of the annunciation, the entire history of humankind converges at a decisive point in Mary. Everything depends on her *fiat*, her acceptance of the service that she provides God in his will to incarnation and to loving kindness toward human beings in their pursuit of redemption. How can one not rejoice before God's saving deed, which is so astonishing?

The entire immensity of the ocean is hidden in this drop of water, the whole mystery revealed in this tiny word: Hail!

MARY: GOD'S BELOVED

In today's world, names are generally arbitrary; their etymological meaning has little or nothing to do with the people who bear them. That was not the case in antiquity, however. Names had a mystique.[8] They were thought to endow people with the qualities signified, or they were expressions of the person's destiny, his or her mission in this world. Hence, choosing a child's name entailed very careful and thoughtful family discussions. Sometimes a name was chosen by God and revealed by a heavenly messenger. That is how the gospels paint the scenes of the choosing of the names of John the Baptist (Luke 1:13, 60) and Jesus (Matt. 1:25; Luke 1:35; 2:21). We have no way of knowing whether this was true of Mary's name. However, the most widely accepted etymological meaning of the name is wonderfully appropriate to the role the person of Mary in salvation history.[9] Indeed it seems that the name itself bears the promise of everything that Mary would exemplify historically: being God's beloved par excellence. That is the meaning that many scholars give to the name "Mary"—*Maryám* or *Miryám*.[10]

The name "Mary" is composed of two roots, one Egyptian and the other Hebrew. *Myr* in Egyptian means beloved, and *yam* in Hebrew is one of the abbreviations of Yahweh *(ya* or *yam)*. Mary or Miryám thus means Yahweh's loved one, God's beloved. There is a historical basis for the likelihood of this philological derivation. The first known use of the name Mary is in the book of Exodus, where we find a Mary, the sister of Moses and Aaron, who were Egyptians (Exod. 15:20). Moses and Aaron are also Egyptian names. We know nothing of what the name Aaron means. As the biblical account says (Exod. 2:10), Moses means "drawn from the waters," the name that the daughter of Pharaoh gave him because she had saved him from the waters of the Nile. His sister was named Mary, which was certainly also an Egyptian name. We know that the Egyptians often combined names: they often began with *myr* or *meri* (loved one) and added the name of some god (Ra, Amon, etc.). It is likely that the Jews, following this custom, gave the name Mary to the sister of the two great figures of liberation from Egypt, taking care to add an ending referring to the Hebrew divinity, who was Yahweh *(Yam, Ya)*. Thus, to repeat, Mary means Yahweh's beloved.

The ancient Latin adage *Nomen est omen*—that is, "the name is the true sign of the thing"—is valid for Mary. In other words, Mary's proper name is an indication of Mary's unique destiny to be eternally God's beloved,[11] the one chosen to be the vessel of the Holy Spirit and the eternal Son, conceived in her womb. This privilege is not intended to diminish other women in history. God the Father wishes to show in Mary, within history, that which he has prepared for all women who share in Mary's likeness. The feminine of creation is raised to the dimension of God; God himself shows through Mary and in Mary, the beloved, his feminine, virginal, and maternal face.

There are many other considerably less convincing etymologies,[12] most of them deriving from Marian piety and devotion. We will take note of only a few.

An etymology with some probability was claimed on the basis of the discoveries of Ras Shamra, in Syria, in 1929–1932. When the ancient city of Ugarit was excavated there, a large number of potsherds with cuneiform inscriptions were found. Some of these inscriptions contained the word *myrm,* often used to designate a mountain known today as Jebel al Aqra, which rises to more than 5,000 feet above sea level. Transcribing the Ugaritic word *myrm,* which means "height" or "the high, sublime, exalted (feminine)" into Hebrew could give *maryám,* because the consonants are exactly the same. In Hebrew, height is translated as *marôm.* This word connotes importance and solemnity; God dwells on high (Isa. 33:5), is "God on high," (Mic. 6:6), and dwells on the holy height of Zion (cf. Jer. 31:12; Ps. 101:19). By the very nature of Hebrew, *maryám* can be derived from *marôm.* Moreover, the Hebrews could have had contact with the inhabitants of Ugarit because their decline in the thirteenth and twelfth centuries BCE occurred roughly at the same time as the Israelite exodus from Egypt.

If this interpretation is accepted as plausible, Mary would then mean "the sublime, the exalted, the high one" in the likeness of the holy and imposing mountain of Ugarit. Such a meaning would perfectly translate the function that Mary actually performs in the history of God's revelation and our salvation.[13]

Other interpretations of the meaning of Mary's name derive from the way the word *Miryám* or *Maryám* can be divided. In Hebrew, *mar* means bitter; *mir* means illuminating; *yam* is the word for sea. The combination *mar-yam* means sea of bitterness. In this interpretation, the name Mary would point to the co-redeeming aspect of Mary, which is an important aspect of Catholic piety; she shares in the passion of Jesus, and she is rightly venerated as the *Mater dolorosa,* the mother whose heart is pierced with seven swords. If the *mir* derivation is accepted, Miryám would then mean the illuminating one, the one who makes God's design visible. The *am* would be simply a grammatical inflection.

Others derive the meaning of the name from *mary,* which means "fat." For Semites, a fat woman symbolized beauty. So Mary would simply be "the beautiful one." An effort has been made to deduce Mary from *mery,* which means "rebellion." Mary would then be the prophetic woman of the Magnificat who proclaims the divine rebellion, reversing social roles: overturning the powerful and exalting the humble, filling the hungry with good things and sending the rich away empty-handed (Luke 1: 52–53).

Finally, there have been those who have derived the meaning of Mary from *mar* or *mary*, which means Lord, and in Syriac means lady, as St. Jerome notes. Mary would thus be our "lady par excellence," that woman in whom the divine design for the feminine is most fully realized.

These latter etymological explanations have all been abandoned because they do not make enough sense philologically. Only the first two derivations, with their Egyptian or Ugaritic roots, have remained factually plausible. Still, the various explanations have served piety, which seeks to discern a secret meaning in the name of that person who occupies such a decisive place in our journey to God.

4

Full of Grace, the Contemplated One: Mary's True Name

We find it horrifying to say
that this feminine figure
destined one day
to crush the serpent's head
should be defeated by the serpent
and that, Mother of God,
she could ever have been
daughter of the devil.
                —Denis, monk (d. 1471)

The terms examined thus far—"Hail" and "Mary," "rejoice," and "beloved of God"—open up a perspective that helps us understand the most important word of the entire angelic message. That decisive, prophetic word, a term charged with promises and mysteries, is *kecharitoméne*,[1] "full of grace" (Luke 1:28). To gain a deeper understanding of this expression—*kecharitoméne* (which St. Jerome translates as *gratia plena*, "full of grace")—we need to make one observation of a philological and exegetical nature and another of a theological nature. We begin with the theological one.

MARY ASSOCIATED WITH THE HOLY SPIRIT

Theology and piety have generally associated Mary strongly with Jesus. Both are united in the same destiny and in the same saving function. There are good biblical and theological reasons for this, for why Mary is venerated as co-redemptrix, mediatrix of all graces, universal queen. The primary reason for her surpassing dignity lies in the fact that she is mother of the Messiah, mother of God. This Christocentrism in Mariology is enriched by another fundamental pole of the Christian mystery: the presence and mission of the Holy Spirit. We have already noted that the Absolute Mystery (Father) is revealed in two ways, or salvation-history sendings: that of the eternal Son and that of the Holy Spirit. They communicate to us what is knowable and lovable of the Father. At the same time, the Son and the Holy Spirit constitute the route by which we return to the mysterious and welcoming bosom of the Father or Mother of infinite tenderness. We must not lose sight of this underlying perspective when we contemplate the mystery of Mary. In her, both the Son and the Holy Spirit are manifested with a unique intensity. Tradition has almost exclusively emphasized the Christological dimension in Mary, but today it is becoming increasingly important to consider the pneumatological perspective.[2]

The basic text is found in Luke 1:35: "The Holy Spirit will come upon you, and the power of the Most High will overshadow you." Most interpreters read this text Christologically: the conception of Jesus is due not to a man but to the Holy Spirit; Mary's immediate and direct relationship with the Holy Spirit, clearly expressed in this sentence, usually goes unnoticed. Here, however, we will focus on the pneumatological dimension because this is where the secret and ultimate meaning of the expression "full of grace" lies. The Holy Spirit is sent expressly over Mary: "The Holy Spirit will come upon you" (Luke 1:35). It is the first time in all of scripture that the Spirit is said to descend directly over a woman. The Old Testament is familiar with the anointing of the Spirit in the womb of one's mother: thus with Samson (Judg. 13:5), Jeremiah (Jer. 1:5), or the Servant (Isa. 49:1). The New Testament says of John the Baptist: "Even before his birth he will be filled with the Holy Spirit" (Luke 1:15); St. Matthew relates Jesus directly with the Holy Spirit: "The child conceived in her is of the Holy Spirit" (Matt. 1:20). What is new in the Lukan text[3] is the fact that the Holy Spirit rests not on Jesus in Mary's womb but directly over Mary. And it is over her that the

Holy Spirit is sent by the Father and by the Son. Vatican II says correctly that Mary is "as though fashioned by the Holy Spirit and formed as a new creature" (*Lumen Gentium* 56). In order to be able to bear the newest Adam (cf. 1 Cor. 15:45), Jesus Christ, Mary was the newest Eve. In order to be able to bear the Son of God, she was made divine.* The Lukan text is explicit: "Therefore the child to be born will be holy; he will be called Son of God" (Luke 1:35). Only God can generate God. Mary is raised to this divine height by the Holy Spirit who has come to dwell in her.[4]

The text of St. Luke continues: "The power of the Most High will overshadow you" (Luke 1:35). This phrase reminds us immediately of Exodus 40:34–35: "Then the cloud covered the tent of meeting, and the glory of the Lord filled the tabernacle. Moses was not able to enter the tent of meeting because the cloud settled upon it, and the glory of the Lord filled the tabernacle." The cloud represents the mysterious presence of God in the midst of the people. Covering with his shadow (of the cloud) means making himself intensely present. In the case of Mary, the angel comes and says that she is the true temple, filled with God's presence.[5] She is made a sanctuary, a living Holy of Holies. Vatican II says accurately that she is the "tabernacle of the Holy Spirit" (*Lumen Gentium* 53). The daughter of Zion, the dwelling of God of which the ancient prophecies spoke so much (cf. Zeph. 3:14–17), is Mary.[6] From all eternity she was contemplated to be the temple of the Holy Spirit. In her the Spirit was "pneumatified," that is, assumed human form; like the Son, who pitched his tent among us in the figure of Jesus of Nazareth (John 1:14), the Spirit pitched his tent *(shekinah)* among us in the person of Mary.

Two divine missions take place in Mary: that of the Holy Spirit who descends on her and that of the Son who begins to exist as an incarnate being in her womb. At a moment in history, at the annunciation, Mary suddenly becomes the center of God's design and the unsurpassed apex of human ascent toward di-

---

*Editor's note: we do not defend the theological hypothesis (it is not official church doctrine) that there is an ontological relationship between the divine Person of the Holy Spirit and Mary so that she really becomes (without euphemism and metaphor) the temple of the Spirit.

vinization. Through Mary the feminine celebrates for the first time an espousal with the divine, thereby reaching its absolute fulfillment. God's mystery reveals feminine traces, and the feminine finds that it is indwelt by God, by the Holy Spirit.

FULL OF GRACE: THE ONE CONTEMPLATED

Now we are able to understand the angel's greeting to Mary: "Greetings, favored one! The Lord is with you" (Luke 1:28). We note that the angel Gabriel does not use the name "Mary"; he replaces the name "Mary" with the true name that she has in God's design: that of being the one contemplated from all eternity to become the temple of the Holy Spirit. The Greek term is *kecharitoméne,* which properly translated means: "the one favored, privileged, contemplated, she who has been made the object of God's love."[7] Saint Jerome's translation in the Vulgate, "full of grace" *(gratia plena)* is correct but insufficient; it misses the deepest meaning of the mystery of Mary. The expression "full of grace" draws our attention to Mary's interior plenitude of grace; we contemplate the unprecedented event of Mary being inhabited by the Holy Spirit. We emphasize the effect of this and we exalt Mary's greatness. Such a perspective is correct, but it is not what is most fundamental.

What is most fundamental is the initiative of the Holy Spirit, who in his utterly free and overflowing love goes out from himself to meet Mary and descends upon her (Luke 1:35). Mary thus becomes the object of the Holy Spirit's love. She becomes his sanctuary. From all eternity she has been chosen and privileged to be able to receive within herself the Holy Spirit's full self-communication. God has ever thought of her and cherished her as the chalice completely open to receive the divine outpouring, the third Person of the Blessed Trinity. Mary's stance is that of one who waits, readies herself, and receives the divine inbreaking. Because the Spirit has come upon her, she is full of grace. The fullness of grace is the consequence of the presence of the Holy Spirit. In scripture, the Holy Spirit and grace are interchangeable realities (cf. Acts 6:8 and 10:38). Hence, "full of grace" and "full of the Holy Spirit" are equivalent expressions.

The Greek term *kecharitoméne* fully expresses what it means to be contemplated and made the object of the love of the Holy Spirit. The verb is *charitóo,* which means to infuse divine grace, to furnish with divine favors. At its root is the word *cháris,* which means grace, love, goodness, beauty, kindness, attractiveness, favor, charm. *Kecharitoméne* is the passive perfect of *charitóo.* The perfect form of the verb expresses a permanent state resulting from an action that has already taken place. The passive indicates that Mary has been the object of the Spirit's action; she has received the communication of the Holy Spirit and from now on is habitually and permanently possessed by the Spirit.[8] African translations (prior to Saint Jerome) were right in rendering *kecharitoméne* as "favored." [9]

We prefer the word "contemplated" for a very specific reason. On the basis of the biblical texts, church tradition sees Mary as the temple of the Holy Spirit.[10] Etymologically speaking, the word "contemplate" comes from "temple" *(con-template).* Accordingly Mary was "contemplated" by the Holy Spirit to be his temple. This is Mary's true name. As Gideon received from the angel of Yahweh a new name, "valiant hero," as Simon was given the name Peter to indicate his calling as foundation of the church, so Mary receives from the angel the revelation of her proper name[11] which defines her eternal vocation: *the one contemplated* to be the temple of the Holy Spirit. The Spirit has loved her first; the Spirit dwells in her as in his temple. Only now can we venerate her as the one full of grace, filled with the Holy Spirit. Here, then, is the meaning of the annunciation: "Rejoice, for you have been contemplated to be the temple of the Holy Spirit!" Nothing more need be said. Everything is summed up in this: the one "contemplated." Mary is made the personification of the Holy Spirit.[12]

THE LORD IS WITH YOU

These words spoken by the angel reinforce what has just been said. In the Old Testament, God's active and effective presence is often expressed by the Holy Spirit (cf. Hag. 2:4–5).[13] The expression "the Lord be with you" (cf. Gen. 21:22; 26:3, 24,

28; 31:3; Exod. 3:12; 18:19; Deut. 20:1; 31:8, 23; Josh. 1:5, 9; 3:7; Judg. 6:12; Ruth 2:4) is generally spoken in a context of covenant.[14] Through the covenant with the people, God wants to establish a permanent presence and offer the guarantee of being always with them. The words signify something very special; they are an expression of predilection and protection. At the annunciation, the angel's use of "Lord" is not intended to signify the moment of Jesus' conception.[15] "Lord" *(Adonai)* stands for the name of God (*Yahweh,* translated by the Septuagint as *Kyrios* and by the Vulgate as *Dominus*), which, out of respect, the Jews rarely pronounced. The literal sense is therefore "God be with you." Through the words the angel will soon speak, however, we know that in this context God has a proper name: Holy Spirit (Luke 1:35).

The Spirit has established a permanent covenant with Mary.[16] That is why she is also called the living and true "ark of the covenant."[17] In Mary, the Spirit finds a permanent and unconditional dwelling. She is not like the prophets who are possessed by the Spirit at particular times in order to carry out particular missions. Now the Spirit has a place of constant and continuous presence and activity: together with the Son he divinizes creation; from Mary he will radiate out to the whole church and to all of history. There is now a center where he is all in all: the life of the Blessed Virgin Mary. The angel has a powerful reason for the invitation to rejoice: the Spirit dwells definitively with us through his temple, which is Mary.

5

Blessed Art Thou among Women

I see you lovingly expressed in a thousand images, O Mary,
Yet none of them can describe you as my soul sees you.
—Novalis, nineteenth-century German poet

Mary, carrying the incarnate Son in her womb and with the
Holy Spirit dwelling within her, hurries to visit her cousin Elizabeth, who has scarcely heard Mary's greeting when the child in
her womb trembles. Almost instantly, filled with the Holy Spirit
and recognizing the Spirit in Mary, she cries out: "Blessed are
you among women, and blessed is the fruit of your womb!"
(Luke 1:42). This greeting correctly grasps the truth of Mary;
truly living temple of the Holy Spirit and bearer of the incarnate
Word, she is blessed among all women. Only the Spirit reveals
the mysteries of the Spirit. That is what we see in Elizabeth's
praise of Mary. Let us delve more deeply—both exegetically[1]
and systematically—into this praise.

MOST BLESSED OF WOMEN

To "bless" (in Hebrew *barak,* in Greek *eulogein,* and in Latin
benedicere) is one of the terms most often repeated in the scriptures.[2] Fundamentally it means to give thanks, to praise with
words, to acclaim, congratulate, celebrate. "Blessed" *(barukáh,*
baruk) here means: you are the object of congratulations, of
praise; you are the reason for giving thanks to God because you

were contemplated *(kecharitoméne)* to become the living temple of the Holy Spirit and to become mother of the Messiah. Israel effusively congratulates itself with Mary for having been chosen to perform this salvific service for the Spirit and the Word.

It is important, however, to understand clearly the meaning of the past participle (blessed) of the verb "to bless." Here we have something similar to the expression "favored," full of grace, contemplated *(kecharitoméne)*. It is not so much a matter of re-garding Mary in herself *as* blessed, but of recognizing the action of the Holy Spirit that makes her blessed. God's infinite incarna-tional love rests upon her; he has contemplated her to be "the place" of the total self-giving of the Holy Spirit; blessings and graces and favors have been heaped upon Mary by the Holy Spirit. Hence she is blessed among all women. The presence of the Holy Spirit in her becomes the object of Elizabeth's exalta-tion and praise. The term "blessed" is connected to the term "contemplated": one reinforces the other. The phrase "blessed among women" translates a Semitic phrase expressing the superla-tive: "the most blessed of women"; "so blessed that the blessing elevates her to a different level among women."[3] These expres-sions from the gospel of St. Luke reflect the great veneration that the early church devoted to Mary. All her excellence comes from two things: that she is temple of the Spirit and that she is mother of God. The "pneumatification" of the Holy Spirit and the in-carnation of the Son, the two fundamental pillars of the Chris-tian mystery, shape Mary's life and being.

INTENSIFICATION OF THE FEMININE

It is not enough to proclaim in faith that Mary, as a result of her involvement with the Holy Spirit and with the incarnate Son, is placed in a unique situation in the history of humankind. The words of Elizabeth, "exclaimed with a loud cry" (Luke 1:42), must be placed in the context of a more structured discourse so that the reasons for Mary's greatness can be seen in a proper light. That is the role of theological reflection.

In order for Mary to be the living temple of the Holy Spirit and the mother of God in the flesh, there must be in feminine human nature a predisposition to this, placed there by God's creative act.[4] God shaped female human nature with this sublime end in mind. That nature finds its full perfection and absolute fulfillment only when this potential to receive the Holy Spirit within oneself incarnationally and allow oneself to be "mother of God" actually takes place. Hence, the path of human history in its feminine determination must be contemplated in the light of its end as embodied historically in the Virgin Mary. All the lines of the journey converge on this end, and from this end they derive their meaning.

Moreover, to be able to be temple of the Holy Spirit, woman must have been created by God to have a deep affinity with the Holy Spirit. More than any other creature and more than the male, she is image and likeness of the Holy Spirit. Thus, in being sent to and descending upon Mary (Luke 1:35) the Spirit finds a living vessel, prepared and fitting. He comes to what is his and to that which from all time has been thought, loved, and created for this singular moment in history: the encounter of the feminine with God and of God with the feminine.

It should be kept in mind that when we speak of the feminine we are not speaking of something exclusive to woman.[5] The feminine is a human reality and hence is shared by all male and female human beings; each in his or her own fashion shares in the feminine and bears the feminine principle within. However, it is best made explicit and embodied in woman; that is why woman is woman and not man. Still, we also find the feminine in man, just as we find the masculine in woman. The creative tension of the coexistence of masculine and feminine constitutes the essential reality of every human being.

Let us briefly reflect on the feminine dimension present in every human being. The feminine, in man and especially in woman, is associated with everything having to do with life, its gestation, protection, and nourishing; everything related to creativity, intuition, and depth; whatever has to do with intimacy, interiority, and mystery; whatever involves feeling, receptivity, and care; whatever relates to tenderness, kindness, and acceptance. All of these things imbue the concrete reality of every human being and they take on a special intensity in woman. Throughout history there have been different cultural embodiments of these qualities, indeed to such an extent that for centuries a true "gynoc-racy" (a system in which woman has social power in a matriarchal system) was the norm. Pathological expressions have also existed.

As woman, Mary takes her place within this current of feminine life. She is a humble, poor, and anonymous villager, but in her is located the focal point of convergence for vital feminine impulses. Woman reveals the intensity of her feminine riches in four principal areas: as mother, wife, sister, and friend.

As *mother* she is linked to the mystery of life. The mother is the first continent that the child discovers; it is through the figure of the mother that the little child first becomes psychologically oriented to life in terms of good and evil, acceptance and rejection. Being a mother involves more than giving birth biologically; maternal power pervades the warp and woof of woman's life. It is the dimension of welcome, care, and safety.[6] Every woman is a mother, even if she has no children, because wherever she is, it is she who creates and generates a space without which life feels threatened and meaningless.

As *wife,* woman first emerges as bride, promise of life, source whose gathered waters have not yet found their outlet. After maternal intimacy, spousal intimacy is the most fulfilling human experience. The wife-bride is near and distant at the same time. She is near through love, through trusting communication, through the fascination she holds for the lover. She is distant because she remains a promise, an offering not yet fully realized and accepted; everything in the wife-bride is ready to blossom and bear fruit. This is the setting in which the value of virginity shines. In terms of the soul's structure, virginity represents the archetype of the whole, closed in on itself, yet open to the fruitful. When the spouse-bride becomes her husband's wife, it is a celebration of love and mutual surrender and joy on all levels of human existence. The fullness that flourishes is exceeded only by God. All plenitude that is not God is less than that between husband and wife. Without woman, man is truly alone (Gen. 2:22); the only living creature that can be a genuine match for him is woman.

As *sister,* woman appears as man's first companion in a place where proximity overcomes distance; she is support for the male self as it slowly gains independence from its maternal connection. She helps her brother to internalize the mother figure and to develop his feminine dimension by moderating the exaggeration of the masculine principle.

As *friend* she is confidant, a fellow traveler in solidarity on the same road. Man comes to see woman as friend, evoking and shedding light on the feminine dimension; she is Beatrice guiding Dante in the discovery of new paths, which may lead to hell, purgatory, or heaven itself.

Mary fully lived out each of these areas. She was mother of Jesus, wife of Joseph, sister of all believers, and friend of Elizabeth and Zechariah. She lived the full wealth of the dimension of the feminine in a thoroughly natural way and, because she was who she was, in a radically profound way.

The New Testament refers to Mary not only as mother, wife, sister, and friend but also in symbolic terms having to do with economic and political realities. She is God's servant (Luke 1:38) who places herself at the service of the Lord's design; she is a prophetess who raises her voice and begs for the justice of the Reign on behalf of the humiliated against their oppressors (Luke 1:51–53).

Summing up, we can say that Mary is blessed among all women because in her life has been revealed the supreme vocation to which woman is called in relation to men and to God. First, she reveals a radical dimension of the human, the feminine, and thus she becomes the exemplar not only of women but of all human beings. Second, as woman, she reveals a new facet of God, insofar as woman too is made in the image and likeness of God (Gen. 1:27). Mary reveals the feminine, maternal, spousal, virginal, and welcoming depth at the heart of God. Third, this depth is made manifest historically through the Person of the Holy Spirit who overshadows Mary and sets in motion the eschatological realization of the feminine in God. The Holy Spirit appears as the divine Person who is intimately related to the feminine. In biblical tradition the proper Hebrew term for Spirit—*Ruah*—is feminine. The Spirit's functions are feminine: the Spirit is the creative and life-giving principle (Gen. 1:2), the Spirit of life. In the New Testament the Spirit is seen in the motherly function of consoling (John 14:18) those made orphans. The Spirit as a solicitous mother helps the children understand and delve more deeply into the lessons of the master, Jesus (John 14:26). Like any mother, the Spirit teaches us the prayer that invokes God as Father (Rom. 8:15); and it is through the Spirit, as through a mother, that we make our pleas (Rom. 8:26). Finally, Revelation assures us that it is the Spirit and the Bride who will call for God to finally break into his Reign at the consummation of the ages, saying: "Come!" (Rev. 22:17).[7]

This Spirit did not remain concealed in unapproachable mystery and anonymity but was embodied in the Blessed Virgin Mary. Hence she will always be proclaimed as "Blessed among women!"

6

Blessed Is the Fruit of Thy Womb, Jesus

Oh Virgin Mother: may your Son grant us
that in imitation of your most holy life
we may conceive the Lord Jesus
in our innermost soul,
and once conceived
may we never lose him.
                    —*Erasmus of Rotterdam*

It is evident that, with the Holy Spirit dwelling within her, Mary is by the work and grace of the Mystery raised to God's level. She is sanctified with the holiness of the Holy Spirit to the highest degree. Hence, the sacred text rightly says that the child to be born of her "will be called holy, the Son of God" (Luke 1:35). As we have already noted, Mary becomes blessed among women because only she was contemplated to be the living temple of the Spirit. The child who is to be born of her must also be blessed. That is what Elizabeth, inspired by the Sprit, proclaims: "Blessed is the fruit of your womb" (Luke 1:42).[1] Tradition has spelled this out by adding the name "Jesus."

BLESSED JESUS: EVER BEARER OF THE SPIRIT

From Mary we go to Jesus. Both are ever bearers of the Holy Spirit.[2] The ancient prophecies had revealed that in the fullness of time, at the coming of the Messiah, the Spirit would be poured

172

out over all the earth: "I will pour my Spirit over all the earth" (cf. Joel 2:28); "A new heart I will give you, and a new spirit I will put within you" (Ezek. 36:25–27). The Messiah will be characterized by the permanent presence of the Spirit: "The spirit of the LORD shall rest on him, the spirit of wisdom and understanding, the spirit of counsel and might, the spirit of knowledge and the fear of the LORD" (Isa. 11:1–2). Even as suffering Servant of Yahweh, he will not cease having the Spirit: "I have put my spirit upon him" (Isa. 42:1).

Indeed, Jesus is entirely work of the Spirit, because he has been conceived "by the Holy Spirit" (Matt. 1:18, 20; Luke 1:35) and because he is born of Mary, who is filled with the Spirit. At his baptism there emerges publicly into history what was hidden in Jesus as the full presence of the Spirit (Mark 1:10), who has existed in him from the beginning. In Jesus' first public appearance, when he inaugurates his mission and begins preaching his message at the synagogue in Nazareth, a text from Isaiah is cited: "The Spirit of the Lord is upon me, because he has anointed me to bring good news to the poor" (Luke 4:17–19 = Isa. 61:1ff). Full of the Spirit, Jesus commits himself to preaching the Reign and embodying it in his liberating actions: "But if it is by the Spirit of God that I cast out demons, then the kingdom of God has come to you" (Matt. 12:28). He himself is surprised when he heals an old woman hemorrhaging blood, for he realizes that a powerful force is going forth from him (Luke 8:43). What prophets and wonder-workers possessed fleetingly, Jesus has in a permanent and ultimate way. The fullness of time has come when new life begins with a new human being, the woman Mary and the man Jesus. The resurrection reveals all the transparency of the Spirit in Jesus. His body is transfigured into a "spiritual body" (fully penetrated by the Spirit: 1 Cor. 15:45). Paul says clearly that the inauguration of the new being through the resurrection is the work of the Spirit: "He who raised Christ from the dead will give life to your mortal bodies also through his Spirit that dwells in you" (Rom. 8:11). That is why Jesus in the gospel of John warns that "no one can enter the kingdom of God without being born of water and the Spirit" (John 3.5). It is the Spirit who gives life to everything and inaugurates the new heavens and the new earth, the new Adam and the new Eve.

Hidden in the little word "blessed" are all the riches of Jesus entirely possessed by the Spirit in union with his own mother. Jesus is made blessed by the Spirit. That is why he can be greeted with the words, "Blessed is he who comes in the name of the Lord."

JESUS: LIBERATING GOD

Only with Mary and Jesus do given names coincide exactly with the real and historic significance of the persons. Hence, the name of Jesus must be seen as given from on high (Luke 1:31; Matt 1:21). It encompasses the entire mystery and mission of the Son of God incarnate.

Jesus was a common name among Jews from about the second century BCE.[3] In Hebrew there are two versions of the name Jesus, one complete and the other abbreviated. The complete form is *Yehôschuah,* a compound word made up of the abbreviation *Yah* (Yahweh, which fundamentally means the God who accompanies the people), and *yoh,* from the verb *yaschah,* which means to liberate, rescue, aid, save, and attain victory. The meaning is: Yahweh is liberation, salvation, aid. The simplified form is *Yeschuah* (in Greek *Iesous* and in Latin *Jesus*). It avoids the hard-to-pronounce consecutive sounds ô-û (of *Yehôschuah*), while keeping the same meaning. Thus Jesus means liberating God, saving God. True liberation and salvation are ultimately the work of Mary's son. Hence the very name of Jesus represents the primordial mission of the eternal Son incarnate in the world of our oppression. He willed to rescue us from the iniquitous situation in which we find ourselves, a condition that is humiliating for human beings and offensive to God. He became incarnate not to legitimate this situation but to protest against it, to free us from all bonds and to liberate us for the fullness of divinization in the Son and in the Holy Spirit to which all are called, in the footsteps of Jesus himself and Mary.

In the light of this etymology we can understand the importance given by St. Paul to the name of Jesus: "God also highly exalted him and gave him the name that is above every name, so that at the name of Jesus every knee should bend, in heaven and on earth and under the earth" (Phil. 2:9–10). The name Jesus contains a prediction: it signifies the complete victory of God and human beings over all enemies. Jesus is indeed the Lord (Phil. 2:11), and "of his kingdom there will be no end" (Luke 1:33). As St. Matthew says in explaining the name of Jesus, "he will save his people from their sins" (Matt 1:21).

The entrance antiphon of the Mass of Holy Thursday beautifully describes the real meaning of the name of Jesus: *in que es salus, vita et resurrectio nostra, per quem salvati et liberati sumus:* "in whom is our salvation, our life and our resurrection; through him we are saved and made free."

Thus concludes the first part of the Hail Mary. It begins with the name of Mary and ends with the name of Jesus. Male and female rightly come together, because both attain the supreme goal of creation. Being wholly impelled toward God, both are henceforth and for all ages inseparably united to the mystery of God the Son and God the Holy Spirit. In them there has occurred the full self-communication of the Son (Jesus) and of the Holy Spirit (Mary). This is why we encounter in them an ultimate instance of salvation and grace. With Mary and Jesus we find ourselves before the very mystery of God. When such an event blossoms in our history, then everything has reached its consummation. We need only rejoice and, filled with jubilation, say with the angel: "Hail, rejoice, contemplated one!"

Holy Mary: The Holiness
of the Holy Spirit in History

As someone standing under a waterfall
becomes wet from head to toe,
so the Virgin Mother of God
was entirely anointed
by the holiness of the Holy Spirit
who descended upon her.
From that moment she accepted
the Word of God, living
in the perfumed chamber
of her virginal womb.

—*Theodorus of Ancyra (d. 446),*
Hom. in S. Deiparam et Simeonem, 5: *P.G. 77, 1400*

We now consider how Mary is taken into the mystery of the
Holy Spirit and the eternal Son. At a certain moment in the history of God's self-communication, Mary becomes the convergence point: the Spirit dwells in her definitively, and the unbegotten Son begins to form in her womb. The wedding of male
and female, of the human with God, begins finally and forever.
Believers marvel, and they proclaim: Holy Mary!

Just what does this greeting mean? What does Mary's holiness
mean? What is its relevance for the mystery of the human being,
at once male and female?

HOLY: ANOTHER NAME FOR GOD

In the scriptures, "holy" is not just one of God's many attributes; it is another name for God.[1] Its etymology is suggestive: *santo* ("holy") comes from *sanctus,* the past participle of the verb *sancire,* which means "to be separated, to be distinct." Holy God means: the Other, the one who transcends humankind and the world (Hos. 11:9). Everything comes from God, but creation is not an extension of him. He dwells in light inaccessible (Exod. 15:11; 1 Tim. 6:16). Only he is Holy *(fanum* in Latin); all other beings stand before the Holy *(pro-fanum).* Thus understood, the Holy is inaccessible to human beings because it defines the essence of God (Isa. 6:3). Holiness clearly entails more than a moral quality, a perfection and purity that one may or may not have. Rather, it is the very definition of God as Mystery, as Otherness, as the other side of what we see and experience empirically.

Faced with the other—and especially the Other—the only worthy human stance is respect and reverence. Ignoring the other or reducing it to a mere extension of ourselves means desecration and violence. When Moses saw the burning bush he sought to approach it, but as he drew near to it he heard a voice saying, "Come no closer! Remove the sandals from your feet, for the place on which you are standing is holy ground" (Exod. 3:5). Even today, removing one's shoes is a sign of respect. The sacred text goes on to say, "Moses hid his face, for he was afraid to look at God" (Exod. 3:6). Looking involves a certain violation; lowering one's eyes expresses respect and deference. Such an attitude is required by the reality of the Holy. In standing before God, the divine reality, we feel the *tremendum,* the fear charged with veneration that simply overcomes us and almost annihilates our own reality. We then experience God as truly Other, different from what we can say, think, or even imagine. But this Other is not sinister; it is loving and attractive *(fascinosum);* it is Father and Mother of infinite goodness and kindness.

Hence, the fact that the Holy God is not the world and humankind and is separate from them does not mean that he is distant or beyond them. He is essentially present to all beings, and is especially sensitive to the cry of those who are wronged and the little ones (Exod. 3:7–9). He bridges the essential distance

with his love, a love that brings near, shows solidarity, and identifies with. When the Holy, God, communicates and shares his
own holiness, we then speak of holy things, holy persons, sacred
history—all permeated by the reality of God and made divine
and holy. We will consider three kinds of participatory holiness
in greater detail.

1. Someone is holy when the Holy, God, has so entered into
that person that God himself is present and enters into our history. When something like this occurs we must speak of the incarnation of God himself. Thus it is said that Jesus, the only-
begotten Son made flesh, is the "Holy One" par excellence (Mark
1:24; Rev. 3:7) or the adjective "holy" is applied to him (Luke
1:35; Acts 3:14; 4:27, 30; Heb. 7:26). Holy Jesus is worthy of
adoration and the complete surrender of human beings. Before
him we are before the Ultimate, the Supreme, the Holy. He is
holy because the essence of God is in him.

2. Someone is holy when, while remaining only a creature, he
or she receives a divine mission and goes on to act in God's
name, carrying out a divine function without being God. Such a
creature is also called holy. Hence the entire people of Israel, instrument of God's revelation, is called holy (Deut. 7:6; 14:2;
28:9); the prophets and apostles are holy because they are missionaries of God (Luke 1:70; Acts 3:21; Eph. 3:5; 2 Pet. 1:21);
women are also called holy (1 Pet. 3:5; cf. Matt. 27:55). St. John
the Baptist is called holy (Mark 6:20); the church is holy insofar
as it is sign and instrument, that is, a sacrament of God in the
world; the New Testament speaks of all Christians who, taken
up into Christ's mission, are saints (Acts 9:13; Rom. 1:7; 1 Cor.
1:2; Eph. 1:1; Col. 1:2; Heb. 3:1; Rev. 5:8). It is not only persons
who are holy; things too can be assumed into a divine function,
such as the temple (1 Kgs. 9:3), the altar (Exod. 29:37), sacrifice
(Exod. 28:38), Jerusalem (Isa. 52:1), Zion (Isa. 27:13), ministers
of worship (Exod. 29:1–35; Num. 8:5–22)—all these are likewise called holy. The things themselves are profane, but because
they enter into a relationship with the Holy, God, they serve the
Holy and share in this holiness.

3. Someone is holy when he or she directs and shapes his or her
life in imitation of the Holy, God. This was ordered in the Old
Testament: "You shall be holy, because I am holy" (Lev. 11:45;

19:2; 20:26). In the New Testament Jesus urges: "Be perfect . . . as your heavenly Father is perfect" (Matt. 5:48). St. Paul tells us: "This is the will of God, your sanctification" (1 Thess. 4:3). Sanctification means the action by which we become similar to God.

Jesus Christ, God's Holy One in our midst, is our model (1 Pet. 1:15); he is simply without sin (1 John 3:5). Being holy in this ethical sense entails being true, being just (Rev. 15:3), being full of mercy and love to the point of being able to bear everything, like God who bears everything and loves even the ungrateful and evil (Luke 6:35). Holiness includes the perfection of all virtues. Being perfect means doing well everything that is done, whether heroic acts or the routine everyday actions of life. Holiness as perfection includes an element of purity, which means integrity, absence of any stain, shadow, or imperfection. St. Paul reminds us: "God did not call us to impurity but in holiness" (1 Thess. 4:7). In other words, we are called to be perfect, to be radically human.

MARY, GOD'S HOLY ONE: THE HOLY SPIRIT IS "PNEUMATIFIED"

The foregoing remarks help us understand something of the wealth hidden in the tiny exclamation: *Holy* Mary. Mary is holy in the three senses explained above.

The Holiness of the Holy Spirit Is Personalized in Mary

First, Mary bears within herself a substantial holiness, that of the Holy Spirit. She not only has holiness; she is holy. The fundamental reason for this is that the Holy Spirit has been "pneumatified" in her: "The Holy Spirit will come upon you, and the power of the Most High will overshadow you" (Luke 1:35). We have already meditated on this unique salvation-history event: like the unbegotten Son, the Holy Spirit also seems to have a proper mission and a full personalization.[2] Mary emerges as the temple prepared, the receptive and living ark in which the Holy Spirit dwells definitively. She is rightly called the one contemplated, that is, the one full of grace (Luke 1:28). She is holy, not primarily for having achieved eminent personal perfection but for having been assumed by the Holy Spirit: that is our theological hypothesis.

From scripture and our theological tradition we know that the sanctification of human beings and creation is the work of the Holy Spirit, who represents holiness personified.[3] By indwelling in the life of human beings, the Spirit brings about the proliferation of saints and prophets. In the formal language of theology, he is the *causa quasi formalis* of the life of grace poured out into our lives. Consequently, the fruits of the Spirit are the fruits of holiness: "love, joy, peace, patience, kindness, generosity, faithfulness, gentleness, and self-control" (Gal. 5:22). All that is meant by holiness is personalized in Mary by reason of the Holy Spirit who dwells in her.

In this sense of essential holiness, Mary belongs to God's own history. The focus is not on her, but on the Holy Spirit. It is the Spirit who gives himself entirely to a historical person and is thus inserted into our journey toward eschatological plenitude in God. It is the Holy Spirit who "in some fashion" attains self-realization in a dimension other than intratrinitarian (the union of the Father and the Son) by assuming as his own the human nature of Mary, thereby divinizing the feminine of this nature which is shared also with men. Mary is holy, we insist, through the very holiness of the Holy Spirit. This is not a matter of merit, but of a pure and sparkling free gift. The Spirit chooses Mary so that he may shine within the creature and sanctify all things. Mary is generated as the place where this mystery happens with all intensity and for the first time in a "pneumatifying" way.

Mary emerges as holy for yet another reason: she is the mother of God. We will delve deeper into the meaning of this in the next chapter. Here we need only emphasize that by the fact that she is really the mother of Jesus, God incarnate, something of Mary is also assumed by the only-begotten Son of the Father. Mary provided Jesus with his full humanity. And from the first moment of his conception, this Jesus belongs to the eternal Son who thus comes to live in our midst. Therefore, something of Mary's being is in God and is divinized and made holy, that is, made part of divine reality.

Having grasped this dimension of Mary's substantial holiness[4] by reason of the Holy Spirit and of the eternal Word in her, we must then say: Mary's holiness is not a reflected holiness of the source-holiness who would be Jesus. Mary does not embody the mystery of the moon *(mysterium lunae)* receiving its light from the mystery of the sun *(mysterium solis)*. Her holiness is proper to her, because it is the holiness of the Holy Spirit. The new Eve together with the new Adam translate for us the Holy of Holies, which is the mystery of the Father. The feminine with the masculine, each in its own way, become bearers of the divine holiness through the Holy Spirit who is "pneumatified," and through the only-begotten Son who is incarnated.

Mary, Sacrament of God's Holiness

We mentioned above a second meaning of "holy," now not in the order of being, but in the order of doing and function, of lending oneself to be an instrument of God's saving work. In this sense too we can say that Mary was eminently holy.[5]

Every woman is made in the image and likeness of God (Gen. 1:27); through her are revealed facets of the mystery of God that would otherwise remain forever hidden from us. Thanks to Mary's involvement with the mystery of the Holy Spirit and the Son, she is the image and likeness of God in a singular manner. God's self-communication and all salvation history have maternal and feminine dimensions. In Mary they are intensified. She becomes the instrument of the co-redemption of humankind along with her Son Jesus; the graces of the Holy Spirit pass through her; her assumption into heaven shows what God has planned for all human beings and anticipates the divinization to which the feminine is called by the Father's eternal design. Through Mary, God wanted to make evident the overcoming of the old Eve and the full realization of woman's vocation as the new Eve. All this makes Mary supremely holy, for she is placed at the service of God's holy plan.

Holy Mary: Pilgrimage of Faith

The third meaning of holiness is ethical: the human effort toward God's perfection. What matters here is each person's work to craft his or her own life. In this sense we can say that Mary was holy without equal, as litanies to Our Lady have ever sung out over the centuries.

First, Mary stands out as a woman of faith: "blessed is she who believed" (Luke 1:45). Faith consists of an attitude of radical surrender to God and to his design, even when one has questions. Before conceiving Jesus in her womb, Mary believed in her heart.[6] She said "yes" to the message from on high. In Hebrew, saying "yes" means believing. To live in faith means to live in pilgrimage, in darkness, and often in perplexity. Thus, when she finds Jesus missing, Mary returns from the pilgrimage to the temple in Jerusalem. Puzzled, she asks, "Child, why have you treated us like this? Look, your father and I have been searching for you in great anxiety" (Luke 2:48).

Certainly she is equally perplexed at the wedding feast of Cana when Jesus says to her: "Woman, what concern is that to you and to me?" (John 2:3–4). Jesus practically dismisses his mother. On another occasion Mary is on the fringes of the crowd. She approaches and wants to talk with her son. Jesus reacts surprisingly: "Who is my mother, and who are my brothers?" Then pointing to his disciples, he says, "Here are my mother and my brothers! For whoever does the will of my Father in heaven is my brother and sister and mother" (Matt 12:48–50). Jesus emphasizes the fact that ties of faith are more important than ties of blood. But what appears to be blame turns into praise, because indeed Mary is the one who most believed, and thus she becomes doubly mother of Jesus. Faith coexists with the darkness of life, with not being able to understand everything. Hence the evangelist Luke comments on the attitude of Joseph and Mary: "But they did not understand what he said to them. . . . His mother treasured all these things in her heart. And Jesus increased in wisdom and in years, and in divine and human favor" (Luke 2:50–51). "All these things" were the object of faith and meditation. Vatican II rightly says that Mary "advanced in her pilgrimage of faith" (*Lumen Gentium* 58).

Seeing Mary as a woman of faith enables us to gain a better understanding of her immaculate conception. Because she belongs to the Holy Spirit, she is not part of the sin of the world. From all eternity she was contemplated and willed to be the temple of the Spirit and the mother of God. In view of this divine

function, she was preserved from sin when she entered our contaminated history; that is why she is the immaculate conception.
However, this situation of the fullness of grace (Holy Spirit) does
not transfer her to the Reign of God; she lives in the flesh and
within human situations marked by the taint of sin. Her greatness lies not in being exempt from the contradictions of life, but
in being able to confront them, bear them, and grow with them.
Hence Mary's life should not be imagined as a romantic idyll.
Pope Paul VI's words on devotion to the Virgin Mary point out
that Mary was "a woman of strength, who experienced poverty
and suffering, flight and exile (Matt. 2:13–23)."[7]

We must overcome the cultural fixations that have tended to
paint Our Lady with the symbols of family, of home and hearth,
of the privacy of husband and children. What is important is not
the ever changing social and cultural references, but the spirit
with which Mary lived out her concrete reality:[8] her total and
responsive attachment to God's will (cf. Luke 1:38). That will
was revealed to her by God's word and incorporated into her life
through works of charity and service that went beyond her family circle, so that, in the words of Pope Paul VI, we see her "not
as a Mother exclusively concerned with her own divine Son, but
rather as a woman whose action helped to strengthen the apostolic community's faith in Christ (cf. John 2:1–12), and whose
maternal role was extended and became universal on Calvary."[9]

As mother and spouse and subsequently as widow, Mary lived
the small and difficult virtues that characterize family life and
the ills inherent in our life in the flesh. In all of this she was not
at all alienated or removed from what was happening in the history of her people. On the contrary, her canticle, the Magnificat, reveals a remarkable capacity for ethical indignation and a
willingness to protest against the injustices of society. As Pope
Paul VI says, "she was a woman who did not hesitate to proclaim that God vindicates the humble and the oppressed, and
removes the powerful people of this world from their privileged
positions (cf. Lk. 1:51–53)."[10] Mary "stands out among the
poor and humble of the Lord," (*Lumen Gentium* 55) who await
their liberation.

Mary is holy by a holiness won in suffering, so much so that
the evangelist Luke says, "a sword will pierce your own soul

too" (Luke 2:35). Thus she can be a guiding star in our journey toward perfection.

This perfection of Mary, although realized without great visible projects or impressive historical achievements, demands great human effort. It requires complete integrity at every moment, an intense presence of mind and heart in every action. As God is all and totally in each thing, the holy is likewise all and totally in each deed done. Being holy thus means a way of being rather than the doing of grand things. Being holy implies a process of radical humanization; the more human someone becomes, the more the divine flourishes in him or her, to complete divinization, as in Mary, full of the grace of the Holy Spirit.

ANTHROPOLOGICAL RELEVANCE: THE FEMININE UNITED TO THE HOLY SPIRIT

The espousal of Mary with the Holy Spirit by which the Virgin is made the Holy Mother of God is not a private event that concerns only Mary. It concerns all human beings, particularly in terms of the feminine that is embodied in all, but primordially in women. The feminine is the path of perfection and the site where the Holy Spirit brings the divine Holiness into history. Mary's holiness, assumed by the Spirit, is different from the holiness of Jesus; while both are expressions of the holiness of the mystery of God, they are embodied differently. All that is virginal and material, all that is intuitive, profound, and fine, all that is intimate, welcoming, and receiving, all that concretely expresses nearness, communion, and participation—all these human realities that are found in everything but most intensely in woman are embodied in Mary and assumed by the Holy Spirit. The feminine culminates in the Holiness that is the Holy Spirit. This radically human dimension thus finds its true and full destiny. It begins to be part of God's own history, through Mary, God's Holy One.

8

Mother of God:
The Spirit and the Feminine

*The mother conceives. As mother she is different from the
woman who is not yet a mother.*
*Nine months in a row she bears in her body the consequence of
one night. Something is growing.*
*Something is growing in her body, and from her body it will
never disappear. For she is a mother.*
*And she remains mother, even if the child or all her children
die. For she bears the child beneath her heart. Later, when
the child grows, she will continue to bear it in her heart.*
And from her heart it will never disappear.
Not even when the child has died.
The man is unaware of all this. He knows nothing about this.
*He does not know the difference between the before and after
of love. Only the woman knows and can speak and attest.*
—Abyssinian Text

The observations we have made on Mary's holiness pave the
way for us to understand the supreme privilege of her divine
motherhood. Let us repeat the main connections: first, the Virgin was visited by the Holy Spirit in a manner so personal and so
deep that it signified a real elevation to the height of the divine;
by reason of this self-communication of the third Person of the
Blessed Trinity, Mary was made holy by the holiness of the Holy
Spirit, thus becoming his living temple; then, while keeping her

virginity, she conceived Jesus Christ by work of that same Holy Spirit; she bore and gave birth to the eternal incarnate Son; the divine bears the divine; hence the fruit of her womb is holy and the Son of God (cf. Luke 1:35). Mary thereby becomes mother of God.[1]

WHAT OUR FAITH TEACHES
ON THE DIVINE MOTHERHOOD

We want to deepen our understanding of this truth of our faith without losing sight of the two poles that help us understand the mystery of Mary: the Holy Spirit and the unbegotten Son of the Father. We seek to comprehend more fully the meaning of the tradition that has defined once and for all, and in a manner obligatory for all, the truth that Mary is the *Theotókos* ("Mother of God," in Greek) or the *Dei Genetrix* or *Deipara* (Progenitor of God, in Latin). It is important that we grasp the content of what our faith teaches on Mary's divine motherhood so that we can then move forward to enrich our understanding.

We know that the New Testament does not contain the expression "mother of God," but simply refers to Mary as the "mother of Jesus."[2] However, the expression "mother of God" was already in circulation throughout Christendom in the third century, and was made canonical at the ecumenical council of Ephesus (431 C.E.) in a Christological context. The disputes about the real divinity of Jesus that took place during the entire fourth century also fostered the development of the concept of the divine maternity of Mary. Nestorius (patriarch of Constantinople starting in 428 C.E.) taught that there was no substantial, indivisible, and clear bond between the eternal Son and the historic Jesus. He asserted that, although there was indeed a deep connection—even greater than that between God and the soul of a just person— this connection was something less than total, so that it could not be said that one and the same Jesus was simultaneously God and man. God and the man Jesus were separate and discrete entities. By reason of this doctrine, Nestorius concluded that Our Lady could not be called mother of God, but only mother of Christ *(Christotókos)*.

Believers in Constantinople revolted against their patriarch, arguing that if Christ was not truly God, if the man Jesus was not united hypostatically to the eternal Son of the Father, then we cannot say that our humanity (which also belongs to Jesus) has been touched by God; hence we are not redeemed in our own flesh. Since this is not the case, we must strongly affirm that Jesus really is the incarnation of the Son of God; the human-God union is so strong that one and the same Jesus Christ emerges clearly, indivisibly, and immutably as true human and true God. Thus, Mary who bore him is mother of God without metaphor or euphemism. Denying Mary's divine motherhood means denying the real incarnation of God.

The meaning of the dogma of the divine maternity is as follows: Mary is mother of God because she bore God made human. She gave birth not only to the flesh of God but to God in the flesh; she did not give birth to a man who was subsequently assumed by God, but she conceived someone who from the very first moment belonged to God. The person whose human reality was conceived *in* the womb and *from* the womb of the Virgin Mary is really and truly the second Person of the Blessed Trinity, the Son of the eternal Father.[3] By reason of the divinity of Jesus, Mary's motherhood, by which Jesus was humanly generated, is also divine. Christ confers divinity on the maternity of the Virgin. That is what faith has always professed: Mary is mother of God.

THE DIVINE MOTHERHOOD OF THE HOLY SPIRIT

It can easily be seen that Mary's divine motherhood is a consequence of the affirmation that Jesus, Mary's son, is God. However, we can ponder this truth from another pole, that of the Holy Spirit, under whose action Mary goes from being virgin to being mother. We have already set forth our observations along these lines and hence need not repeat them. What remains is to draw out the consequences of this truth to arrive at a deeper understanding of Mary's divine maternity.

Based on Luke 1:35 ("the Holy Spirit will come upon you . . .") and Matthew 1:18 ("she was found to be with child of the Holy Spirit"), we affirmed a unique self-communication of the Spirit to Mary, as concrete and real as that of the eternal Son to Jesus of Nazareth. The Spirit was "pneumatified" in Mary.[4] If this is plausible, then we must say that in the person of Mary the various functions linked to the reality of woman begin to be divine. Consequently, virginity is divine, maternity is divine, conception is divine, giving birth is divine—all by virtue of the divinization that comes through the self-communication of the Holy Spirit. Mary is accordingly mother of God on two grounds: first, because she was assumed by the Holy Spirit who divinized her motherhood, and second, because she bore the eternal Son, who also divinized the maternity of his mother Mary.

In a word, Mary is mother of God not only because her son Jesus is God but also because Mary, in her maternal capacity, was assumed by God the Holy Spirit, who made her maternity a divine maternity. That motherhood is more than the living, human, free, and holy means for the incarnation of the Son; it is indeed more than a unique instrument for the mystery of redemption in Jesus Christ. Mary's own motherhood, assumed by the Holy Spirit, is in this sense itself an event of salvation and divinization.

Theological tradition has seen Mary's maternity almost solely in an instrumental perspective relating to the incarnation of the Son;[5] exegesis of the texts on the annunciation has concentrated on Christ;[6] this has hindered seeing Mary's unique relationship with the Holy Spirit. The sacred text, "The Holy Spirit will come *upon you*, and the power of the Most High will overshadow *you*" (Luke 1:35) relates Mary directly to God the Holy Spirit.[7] At this moment Mary is the center; the text does not speak simply of a supernatural conception, but it speaks about the one conceiving, Mary. Mary emerges as the object of the action of the Holy Spirit who *comes over* her and transforms her into a living temple, makes her the one contemplated to be the dwelling place of the Spirit, the ark of the covenant where God himself resides (Exod. 40:35). Consequently, we must understand in an ontological sense Elizabeth's praise: "Blessed are you among women" (Luke 1:42) and even more the words of the angel: "Greetings, favored one" (Luke 1:28). The Pneumatological pole enriches the Christological pole, enabling us to arrive at a deeper understanding of Mary's divine maternity.

What is appropriate for a mother whose son is God? That she likewise be at the divine level. *That is why* the one born of her can only be Son of God (Luke 1:35). Mary's maternity is divine in its source and in itself, not only in its consequence, because of her son who is God.

THE DIVINE VIRGINITY OF MARY

The first characteristic of Mary's motherhood is that it is a *virginal* motherhood.[8] Mary lived a perpetual virginity; at the same time she was mother, without thereby sacrificing her virginity. Theological reflection is needed to shed light on this paradox.

First, we accept in faith that Mary's virginity has a biological dimension; the New Testament texts presuppose acceptance of this fact in the early Christian community and take it as a starting point for reflection. The concrete and historical virginity of Mary constitutes the foundation for all the additional meanings that are given to Mary's virginity, even when they go beyond its biological meaning.

At the same time, while affirming the biological character of Mary's virginity, we reject the curiosity-driven representations that would violate the spirit of delicacy required in this area. We must preserve the character of mystery shrouding Mary's virginity. Just as we cannot conceive of the concrete way in which Mary's body and soul were transfigured upon her assumption into heaven, so also the *how* of the virgin birth totally eludes us. What faith maintains resides in this: Mary had a mysterious relationship with the Spirit that made her virginity fruitful; virginity was maintained within maternity; maternity encompassed within itself virginity without destroying it.

What is the deeper meaning of Mary's virginity, the significance of this historic and saving fact? Christian reflection has shed light on different aspects of its meaning. Let us look at some of these aspects.

Mary's physical virginity externalizes what takes place in her from the first moment of her existence: she is completely and entirely free from original sin. Mary is virgin in her spirit and in the totality of her life; in her there is nothing of the split that so afflicts and dramatizes our existence. She belongs to the initial design of the Mystery that sought to divinize the feminine through its assumption by the Holy Spirit. Mary's entire integrity before God is tangibly embodied in virginity. In her, physical virginity symbolizes a much more real and dense internal reality than an empirical reality. The fathers of the church rightly said that Mary first conceived in her mind and heart and only later in her body.

Virginity also expresses the radical quality of Mary's surrender to God. Her virginity is a living testimony to the fact that God is absolutely central to her existence. Virginity here entails no disrespect for human love or marriage; they are also forms of love of God. But Mary's virginity reveals a uniquely radical quality, such a concentration on God that every other form of love will always be a love based on love of God, a love in God.

We have already proposed the hypothesis that Mary has been assumed by the Holy Spirit in order to divinize the feminine and reveal God's maternal face. Nothing is more appropriate for such a salvation-history event than that Mary should be virgin, totally set aside and preserved to be the living temple of the Spirit.

Finally, Mary is mother of the incarnate Son of God. By the fruitful power of the Spirit, her womb hosts God himself. Her whole life will be a service to this Son; to help him to grow, to accompany him on his redeeming mission, and together with him to reveal to all human beings the countenance of the Father of infinite goodness.

In order to be complete, Mary's virginity clearly could not remain enclosed within itself; it had to be open to motherhood. Woman is always *parens vitae*, as St. Eugenia, virgin and martyr, said.[9] Woman is always "mother of life," even if she is a virgin. The great ancient writer Prudentius (d. 405) rightly referred to virginity as "mother chastity,"[10] and Pope Saint Leo the Great (d. 461) spoke of "motherly virginity."[11] Virginity and motherhood do not exclude one another but demand one another, for motherhood is more than a sporadic function of woman; it defines a basic structuring of her being. Woman is always mother, even when she does not conceive any child, because it is proper to her to be begetter of life, protector of life, intimately connected to the mystery of life.

MARY'S DIVINE MOTHERHOOD

Mary was mother in the full and direct meaning of the word. This means that everything that happens in motherhood took place in her. First there is the biological dimension: conception, gestation, nourishment of the embryo, and giving birth, phenomena that have their own rhythm independent of the laws of consciousness. Then there is the specifically human dimension. Motherhood is a free option. It implies an attitude of acceptance and love, a secret and deep relationship with the child of one's womb. The human sciences reveal to us through the collective unconscious the complex relationship established between mother and child, a relationship that will shape in the child the basic patterns that will accompany it throughout life. In the case of Jesus, who is the fruit of the Spirit acting upon Mary, we can see signs of Mary's having shaped the human reality of Jesus in his genetics and his biological inheritance as well as in his psychological personality. Mary provided God all the humanity that was hypostatically assumed; something of Mary, generated by Mary, belonging to Mary's life, begins to be of God. Something of the feminine is accordingly divinized and made eternal.

Being a mother is not an event that takes place at a particular time; it constitutes a mode of being that covers all one's existence. Participating in the child's growth and education, his or her choice of a direction in life, the historical destiny that the child will assume—these are all part of motherhood. A true mother keeps bearing her child until death. So it was with Mary.

Mary's divine motherhood is built and sustained on this human reality. We have already observed that two poles are operative: the pole of the Spirit who makes her maternity fruitful, and that of Christ who, as son, begins to form in her womb. The human nature that she has conceived is assumed hypostatically by the eternal Son. Mary shares, albeit indirectly, in the hypostatic union, because a relationship that begins in her—the fact that she is mother of Jesus—enters directly into the mystery of the incarnation; she is co-assumed.

A unique relationship is established between the Holy Spirit and Mary. The Spirit is Spirit of life par excellence (Ezek. 37; 1 Cor. 15:45; 2 Cor, 2:6, 17); the new heaven, the new earth, and the new human being are the Spirit's creations; the resurrection of Jesus is his work (Rom 8:11), and living according to the Spirit gives us access to the new creation (2 Cor. 5:17; Gal. 6:15; Eph. 2:15; 4:24). The era of the Spirit with life in the Spirit and according to the Spirit is inaugurated with Mary at the moment of the annunciation (Luke 1:35) when he, as divine Person, comes over her. As we have said countless times, we find ourselves facing here a unique and new salvation-history event, namely that of the incarnation of the eternal Son. This is the simplest and most coherent interpretation of the pericope of Luke 1:35 ("The Holy Spirit will come upon you, and the power of the Most High will overshadow you; *therefore* the child to be born will be holy; he will be called Son of God"). The conjunction "therefore" *(dià kai)* is extremely important, even decisive, for understanding the real and true meaning of the coming of the Spirit over Mary, raising her to his divine level. The Lukan text clearly says that the divine sonship of Jesus is a result of the Spirit's coming over Mary, bearer of Jesus. All possible kinds of exegesis have been tried to explain the causal connection between the function of the Holy Spirit and Jesus' sonship.[12] *In what sense can it be said that Jesus is Holy and Son of God because he was born miraculously and "spiritually" from a virgin made fruitful by the Holy Spirit?* That is the question that must be answered. A Christocentric exegesis that sees in the Lukan texts only the relationship to Jesus and not to the Spirit cannot convincingly address the issue of the conjunction "therefore." It is not enough to appeal to the pre-existence of the Son and say: he is Holy and God's Son because that is how he is within the Trinity. Where is the meaning of the conjunction?

Father S. Lyonnet has taken a step forward by deepening the theology of the *shekinah* (holy tent) evoked in the expression "shall overshadow you" *(episkiázein)*. The divine presence in Mary would make her the "temple of God himself, the only place on earth where God was to live. . . ."[13] Hence, "the Son to be born must be Son of God . . . not only a divine being but God."[14] Yet Lyonnet concentrates once more on Christ. Mary is like an empty temple: its inhabitant is the eternal Son, it is God. Lyonnet does not see that God himself assumes the living temple that is Mary. He does not delve deeper into the relationship between the Spirit and Mary, but considers only the relationship that goes from the Spirit to the Son.

L. Legrand[15] tries another route to show the relationship existing between Jesus' divine sonship and his supernatural mode of generation. With a number of other exegetes, he claims that Luke 1:35 is partially dependent on Romans 1:3–4, which contains the early formulation of faith of the Christian church: the Son, who was "descended from David according to the flesh and was declared to be Son of God with power according to the spirit of holiness by resurrection from the dead." By that expression Paul did not mean that Jesus became Son of God only through the resurrection; in the biblical sense, what the statement means is that what was hidden has been shown in power and glory. That is just what Luke 1:35 states, which is that already in his conception Jesus is what the action of the Spirit is going to manifest on the day of resurrection: Son of God, filled with divine glory and enlivened by the power of the Spirit of holiness. The evangelist John says it in his way: "that which is of the earth is earthly" (John 3:31) and "that which is born of the Spirit is spirit" (John 3:6). Jesus is not of the earth; he is "spirit" in the biblical meaning of the term, that is, he belongs to the order of the renewed world of the Spirit (John 6:53–63); he has been born of the Spirit, and hence is Holy One and Son of God. Thus "his flesh, tabernacle of God, is indwelt by wisdom, by the power and glory of the Father."[16]

Again the accent falls totally on Jesus, and Mary remains a mere external instrument for the great work of the Father in the Son through the Spirit.

Manteau-Bonamy[17] takes a significant step forward. He decisively recognizes that the text of Luke 1:35 allows for the admission of a *proper* (not simply appropriated) mission of the Holy Spirit, a visible self-communication related to Mary.[18] But according to this author, the Holy Spirit does not assume the Virgin's flesh as the Son has assumed the flesh of Jesus. The Spirit "assumes the Virgin's maternal potency so that she will be capable of conceiving. . . . It is the fruitfulness of the Virgin that becomes sensitive to the presence in her of the Holy Spirit."[19] Manteau-Bonamy brings Mary closer to the Holy Spirit than any previous writer, to the point of affirming a true assumption of something of Mary by the Spirit. However, we must bear in mind that this French theologian has not delved deeply into what motherhood means in woman. Since every woman has a maternal structure, motherhood is not simply a function; it is an overall reality that encompasses all of woman's identity.[20] If the Spirit assumes maternity, this means that, in terms of a more complete anthropology, he assumes the woman Mary, as we have been claiming through all our meditations here.

Mary was predestined from all eternity to be the vessel of the Spirit so that through her and in her would begin the renewed creation, a reality that is ever new and has never been contaminated: Mary and Jesus. She was "conceived" to be the temple of the Spirit and on that basis to become mother of the Son, Jesus. She was created in the Spirit and hence she has an eternal connaturality with him. As a text from the old liturgical office of the Immaculate Conception says, *Elegit eam Deus et praeelegit eam et creavit eam in Spiritu Sancto.*[21] God chose her and pre-elected her and created her in the Holy Spirit. Mary is thus placed within the very mystery of God; her motherhood is divine through its eternal origin in God's design, not just on the level of temporal history; it is divine through the divinity of the Holy Spirit.

THE HOLY SPIRIT, DIVINE MOTHER OF THE MAN JESUS?

If we say that Mary has been assumed by the Spirit and that the Spirit must have taken historical form in her, can we then say that the Holy Spirit is the divine mother of the man Jesus? We believe that this is the conclusion that follows logically.

First, the Spirit has a feminine connotation, as we have already noted. Biblically, it is the Spirit who is responsible for life; he is source and origin of all life, especially new and divine life (cf. 1 Thess. 4:8; 2 Cor. 6:16; 1 Cor. 15:44–50; Rom. 8:11, 29; Col. 1:18; Heb. 1.6; Rev. 12:5). It is therefore fitting that the full manifestation of the divine life in our history should be initiated by the Spirit. By the Holy Spirit we have the new Eve (Mary) and the new Adam (Jesus Christ). Through him, as divine Mother, is begotten the man Jesus, manifestation in the flesh of the eternal Son himself.

Some ancient texts refer to the Spirit in this manner. Origen says, "In the gospel to the Hebrews, the Savior himself said about the Transfiguration on Tabor: 'Suddenly, *my Mother, the Holy Spirit* seized me by one of my hairs and led me over the great mountain of Tabor.'"[22] In another commentary on the gospel of St. John, Origen cites this same text again.[23] St. Jerome, who is ever so critical, cites the text of the apocryphal gospel to the Hebrews in his commentary on the baptism of Jesus in the Jordan:[24] "And it happened that when the Lord came out of the water, the source of all, the Holy Spirit descended and rested on him and said to him: 'My Son, among all the prophets I was awaiting you, I was waiting for you to come to rest upon you. You are indeed my repose, you are my only-begotten Son who reigns eternally.'"[25] It is curious to note that neither Origen nor Jerome criticizes this text. They would certainly have done so had they seen it as not being compatible with the faith. The text says that the Spirit is the divine Mother of Jesus. It is a temporal maternity, affecting the humanity of Jesus, because in its eternal dimension the sonship of Jesus derives not from the Spirit but solely from the Father. Because the man Jesus was born from the divine Mother, the Holy Spirit, he is presented as full of the Spirit from the outset. The perfect work of creation is of the Spirit: Mary and Jesus.

THE UNIVERSAL MOTHERHOOD
OF MARY AND OF THE SPIRIT

The Spirit has generated the new Adam; it is he who through the ages generates new human beings and implants in the mortality of each life that comes into this world the seeds of resurrection. What point would there have been in the Spirit having come over Mary and having made her fruitful had he not come to each one of us, causing us to beget within ourselves the eternal Son of God and our brother Jesus Christ? Once begun in Mary, the process continues throughout history. That is why

Mary is the first among many brothers and sisters; we will follow her, in our own way and in the manner that is appropriate for us. Mary is the first member of the community that bears the Spirit, which is the church. The Spirit began by intensifying his action in a specific being in history, Mary, so as to spread from there to all human beings who are also willing to say *fiat*—let it be done! There is a reason why some theologians claim that there is an intimate and ontological relationship of the Spirit with the church, constituted as a *mystica persona*, a mystic person with the Spirit. The incorporation of the church with the Person of the Holy Spirit is understood as a derivation and extension of what took place between Mary and the Spirit.

The Spirit thus enjoys a maternal function in relation to the new and redeemed life that was visibly inaugurated in history with the salvation-history sending of the Spirit and the Son. In begetting the Son Jesus, the Spirit continues to beget sons and daughters in the Son; the new creation emerges from his breathing out as on the first day of creation when it was he who breathed upon the waters and made creation bloom in its morning order and harmony.

Ontologically united to the Spirit, Mary becomes the great and generous universal mother of all living things, truly the new Eve. The feminine principle in men and women has been most highly honored, indeed, even divinized, as bearer of God and living temple of God himself. Human maternity reflects divine maternity; it is a real parable of the mystery of God in God's feminine and motherly face.

9

Pray for Us Sinners
Now and at the Hour of Our Death

Among the evils in which I am involved, Lady,
for your name, I anxiously cry out
and I resolve to entrust myself to your arms
with wounded soul and broken body.

For wherever I open my eyes
the seductive image of sin
seizes with dusty tentacles
my poor contaminated heart.

Well do I know that I do not deserve your graces.
But I would not come to you if you were not
that kind Mother that I know.

Open, break open the protective barriers.
I come dead from the evils that I suffer,
safe shelter of sinful souls.
                    —Brother Roberto B. Lopes,
                       Jardim Fechado *(1952)*

The Hail Mary is a set of praises to the blessed Virgin and
Mother, culminating in a great petition: "pray for us sinners."
What should children do before such a kind and blessed mother
if not beg and implore for the highest thing that we can desire,
namely salvation? It is the happy outgrowth of the authentic

stance of a Christian after having contemplated the depth and breadth of the mystery enveloping Mary, temple of the Spirit and mother of Jesus.

What is the meaning of the prayer of petition? Doesn't God already know everything? Is Mary by chance ignorant of the needs of her children? So why implore and ask? Let us delve into the theological meaning of these matters.[1]

INTERCESSION AS A HUMAN PHENOMENON

Many Christians can no longer discern any meaning in prayers of petition. They say: nothing in personal and social history escapes God's design. In the Old Testament, Isaiah said, "I am the Lord, and there is no other. I form light and create darkness, I make weal and create woe; I, the Lord, do all these things" (Isa. 45:6–7). Speaking of prayer, Jesus himself says, "Your father knows what you need before you ask him" (Matt. 6:8). These statements notwithstanding, we must say that it does make sense to ask and pray, as we do in the Hail Mary, in the Our Father, and in the common practice of piety. Ultimately, we must conclude as Tertullian (d. 220) did in his wonderful treatise *De oratione* (on prayer): "Why discuss the problem of prayer any more? For us this is enough: the Lord also prayed."

We should start from the everyday evidence of our human experience. We always have needs that for some reason we are unable to satisfy. We may ask someone to lend us a bit of oil, to stand in for us on some job, to bring us a couple of pounds of beans from the market, to pay for our bus fare. At other times we ask for help with some inner problem, for advice or direction; we ask for understanding and forgiveness; we ask for a favor, for a person to put in a good word for us with someone else. Life is full of such situations. It is interwoven with these relations of solidarity and mutual help. We experience what Dom Helder Camara expressed so wonderfully: "No one is too rich to receive; no one is too poor to give." We find ourselves connected to one another by human needs, requests for help, and service in solidarity.

If one human being depends on another, how much more do we not all depend on God? It is no wonder that this same type of relationship of request-service is transferred to the creature-Creator relationship.

The Old Testament is full of prayers of supplication, expressed often with great intensity in terms of sighing, weeping, crying, pouring out one's heart, one's soul, and one's complaints to God. One example will suffice: "We cried to the Lord, the God of our ancestors; the Lord heard our voice and saw our affliction, our toil, and our oppression" (Deut. 26:7). One who cries to God places in him all his or her trust and expects to be heard. And God is so all-powerful that he can intervene in history, move heaven and earth for his children and his generous design.

Jesus preaches a God who is Father of infinite goodness and kindness.[2] He is not a sinister, far-off God; he is close and attentive to the least movement of the heart of his children. And Jesus teaches us to address him in a human way, calling him "Daddy," and feeling his loving closeness. This is the light in which his words that sound so absolute must be understood: "Ask, and it will be given you; search, and you will find; knock, and the door will be opened for you" (Matt. 7:7). Jesus urges a trust so all-powerful that it can move mountains, that is, achieve the impossible, because God makes the impossible possible: "So I tell you, whatever you ask for in prayer, believe that you have received it, and it will be yours" (Mark 11:23–24). In the gospel of John Jesus himself shows the omnipotence of prayer: "I will do whatever you ask in my name" (John 14:13–14). Jesus' insistence is so great that he proposes the following comparison: "If you then, who are evil, know how to give good gifts to your children, how much more will your Father in heaven give good things to those who ask him!" (Matt. 7:11). The two parables of the friend who in the middle of the night comes begging from the other friend who has already gone to bed (Luke 11:5–8) and of the widow who pleads with the judge for justice by pestering him to his limit (Luke 18:1–8) seek to show that our perseverance should be unlimited: "And will not God grant justice to his chosen ones who cry to him day and night? Will he delay long in helping them?" (Luke 18:7).

God may delay; our patience may even reach the end of what we can bear. Yet even that is not reason enough to stop asking and to stop praying. This is why Jesus tells us that we must ask, "even if God makes us wait." The crucial thing in our prayers is not many words and shouting (cf. Matt. 6:7), for that is typical of pagans, but unshakable perseverance and stubborn persistence (Luke 11:5–8; 18:1–8; Matt. 7:7–8).

Jesus himself prayed to his Father in sweat and tears on the Mount of Olives: "Father, do not let me die now" (cf. Mark 14:36). The author of the epistle to the Hebrews even notes that Jesus "offered up prayers and supplications, with loud cries and tears, to the one who was able to save him from death" (Heb. 5:7). Hence Jesus takes his place in the huge torrent of petitioners throughout the religious history of humankind.

INTERCESSION AS THEOLOGICAL REALITY

If God knows everything and knows our needs long before we ask him for help, why is he so insistent that we pray? Are his omniscience and omnipotence not enough? In order to understand the legitimacy of prayer of petition, we need to make the following three observations.

First, we must have an adequate *image of God*. He is indeed holy, that is, transcendent, and an abyss of mystery: that defines God's essence. However, this transcendence and holiness is not empty; it is not a nameless and sinister mystery. In God we are dealing with dialogue and infinite communication. Despite God's infinite distance, he allows himself to be reached. He is especially accessible to the humble and those who suffer. We can cry out to him: Father! And we have the assurance that he hears us, for in the depths of our heart we can hear his Word saying to us: "You are my beloved child! I have loved you with an eternal love!" An intimate exchange between two lives and two depths is therefore established: God and human being. Two freedoms and two loves connect, making possible praise, gratitude, and also supplications and prayers. Without such an image of God we would not understand that prayer—particularly the prayer of petition—is dialogue. We would stand mute before the abyss of silence, rooted in our own despondency.

Second, we need to understand that God has always wanted to *associate* us with his history of salvation. The unfolding of the ages and the psychosocial development that began at the stage of anthropogenesis were not simply the work of God's love projected outward, creating time and myriads of beings in it. He wanted to associate human beings with his creative action; he created us as creators; he created our ability to civilize nature, and he sustains this powerful energy and incorporates it into the design for his Reign. Thus, everything is not predetermined and established before we have spoken our prayer. Our entreaty enters into the shaping of that work which is both God's (at his transcendent level) and ours (at the immanent level). God and human beings are not concurrent causes on the same level. They come together on the basis of their own reality to produce history, which is thus always human-divine, temporal and eternal. We must not imagine eternity as an indefinitely extended time or as a state of unending immobility. Following the formulation of the French Catholic philosopher Gabriel Marcel, Schillebeeckx says that eternity

> may be regarded as the *meaning in depth* of our temporal decision or our prayer of petition. In this way, it is possible to see that my prayer is in reality a genuine initiative on the part of a free creature of God, directed towards the divine and all-embracing Being, whom I, at the moment of my prayer, address as "Thou." What is more, it is also possible to see that this Being has not arranged and decided everything before I come into contact with him, but that he does this in an actual eternal now that brings the moment of my prayer to his immediate attention and creatively controls it. The more intimately we are united to him, the bolder and the more efficacious our initiative in prayer will be. This intimate surrender to God has the effect of bringing our will into harmony with God's loving being. As a consequence of this, anything that the Christian who is intimate with God asks will always be granted to him.[3]

We have the experience, so often verified, that God really hears our prayers. Even when we feel the silence of God, we are aware that his design has been achieved through routes other than those of our prayers, and so we have the promise that he always hears us and that our petition does not remain outside the mystery of his love. The very fact of entreaty, of our tears and sighs, frees us and opens us to the Mystery that surpasses our grasp but enwraps us in his generous design.

Finally, we must grasp the profound *solidarity* that links all human beings. As a human being, each person constitutes something truly irreducible placed immediately before God. But no person is ever alone, an island unto oneself. Being a person means being a being-in-relationship, immersed in the reality of one another. Ultimately, we are a single humanity before God; we are his family, bound together in a single origin, in a single journey, and in a common end for all. The more we enter into one another, the more faithful we will be to the calls of life to justice, to brother- and sisterhood, to mutual acceptance. We build our identity not by defining ourselves over against others but by opening up and standing in solidarity, if possible even to the point of identifying with the anguish and hopes of each traveling companion. Everything good that we do—every gesture of love, every idea that builds—does not remain forever enclosed in the realm of our tiny universe but resounds across vast distances and affects all of humanity, elevating it and consolidating it in its journey toward God.

MARY, INTERCESSORY OMNIPOTENCE

In light of these observations, it becomes easier for us to understand the final petition of the Hail Mary: pray for us sinners. If we can all intercede for one another before God, how much more can Mary, spiritual mother of all human beings, intercede for us?[4] It was by her *fiat* that the Spirit could be accepted within our humanity, divinizing our feminine dimension and making it fruitful; it was by her *yes* that the eternal Son could begin to grow within her virginal womb. At all key moments of our liberation, Mary was present: in the beginning with the coming of the Holy Spirit and the eternal Son, throughout the earthly pilgrimage of her son Jesus, who worked salvation in the power of the Holy Spirit, at the foot of the cross, in the resurrection, in the ascension of Jesus, and at Pentecost when the Spirit who makes his dwelling in her begins to *visibly* dwell in the community of the followers of her son Jesus.

Mary exercises a universal intercession simply by being intimately united to the Holy Spirit. She is both road to and point of arrival at God, because the Spirit dwells in her as in his living tabernacle. In her own human reality as woman she unites us to God. In Mary, through the effect of her assumption by the Holy Spirit, we find a final instance of consolation and salvation. Her intercession has God's efficacy. Together with Christ she is the absolute mediatrix. The unfathomable mystery of the Father is mediated to us through Jesus and Mary who serve as vessels of the Son and the Holy Spirit, respectively. Through them we see God in his most intimate and loving mystery; through them we go to the very heart of the Father.

Through Mary, divine salvation has feminine, virginal, maternal, and wifely dimensions. The feminine becomes the fitting place for complete and full encounter with God, because, through the Spirit, God becomes Virgin, Spouse, and Mother. Mary, all pure and sinless, transfigured by the shadow of the Spirit, full of grace and "contemplated," glorified in heaven, makes ultimate and complete intercession. She shares in the very nature of her children; through the Spirit, who dwells in her, she has us plead the true petitions that she makes her own. Mary does not assist in the working of divine power (which would be a crude anthropomorphism), acting in response to the vagaries of human prayers and dealing with them in sequential order. The divine power is incorporated into Mary through the Spirit who dwells in her and through her divine motherhood of Jesus. In her praying for us, it is God himself who is praying; in the hearing of our prayers, it is God in Mary who kindly turns toward his children.

MARY, REFUGE OF SINNERS

Those who pray acknowledge that they are sinners. "Sinner" means one who in the use of his or her freedom has consciously taken a false step on the way to God. Sin constitutes opting for a negative stance toward God. Ethically and religiously, it consists of a deafness to God's voice; it is a deviation from the route pointed out by conscience; it is a turning away from God's call to relate justly to the other, to see the other as brother/sister, to accept responsibility for the things of the world, and to be open like a child to the Father.

Sin always consists of violence against the thrust of creation. That is why it entails dehumanization and ultimately the loss of absolute human fulfillment in God.

It is in this fallen situation of having been rebellious children that we turn to the bountiful Mother and say: pray for us. And there we discover Mary as the *refugium peccatorum*, the safe refuge of sinners and mother of all mercies. There is no one like a mother to forgive her children and lead them back to the right path. Because Mary is truly woman and mother and because the Spirit of all graces and of all new life took human form in her, we can very humanly speak of the forgiveness and conversion that flow from her and reach into the depths of the heart, the place where our eternal destiny is determined. Just as Jesus announced a Father who goes looking for the lost sheep and waits for the prodigal son, so Mary is especially the mother of her children who have been led astray.

NOW AND AT THE HOUR OF OUR DEATH

"We all sin a great deal in many things" (Jas. 3:2), the scriptures tell us. Sin accompanies us like a black cloud at all times, even at the hour of death. In this situation, we need Mary's intercession more than ever. From the glory in which she dwells, she accompanies every child like a mother. Her kind gaze proves stronger than the impulse of sin. That is why piety rightly venerates her as co-redemptrix and universal queen. There really are no obstacles hindering her welcoming gesture. Even though the serpent has been definitively crushed (Gen. 3:15), we can still feel its poison seeping through all the fibers of our personal and social life. That is why it is important that we entreat Mary to complete her victory in us from generation to generation, now, at each moment, and especially at the supreme moment of life, at the hour of death.

We need not consider death the *terribilium terribilissimum,* the most terrible of frightful moments. Since Jesus has died on the cross and risen from the dead, since Mary has shared in the destiny of every human being and then been assumed into glory in heaven, death has lost its drama and has been changed into the antechamber of life. Indeed, at death each person is afforded a unique opportunity: he or she can make his or her ultimate and definitive synthesis of life; he or she can encompass everything in an act of love that surrenders to the Supreme Mystery and defines his or her eternal path toward God.

At the moment of our death we will be alone before God: descending into the hell of ourselves, we will make a decision, we will say that word that will define us eternally. We pray that Mary and Jesus may be present with us at that moment. They will go with us, Mary as Mother and Jesus as Brother, even to the boundaries of our hell. So we will have nothing to fear. What is there to fear when we know that we are held in our mother's arms? Who could feel threatened when protected by such a brother?

That is why we joyfully acclaim Mary as *vita, dulcedo, et spes nostra, salve*—our life, our sweetness, and our hope. The prayer of St. Bernard expresses well the serene trust of the church and of everyone devoted to the Virgin Mary: "Remember, oh most gracious Virgin Mary, that never was it known that anyone who fled to thy protection, implored thy help, or sought thy intercession was left unaided."

10

Amen

Hail Mary
Pregnant with the aspirations of our poor
The Lord is with you
Blessed are you among the oppressed
Blessed are the fruits of liberation of your womb.

Holy Mary, Latin American mother,
Pray for us that we may confess in the Spirit of God
Now that our people are taking on the struggle for justice
And in the hour of achieving it in freedom
For a time of peace,
Amen.

—*Frei Betto*

Like all Christian prayers, the Hail Mary ends with an Amen. The Amen expresses our full adherence to Mary. It is the repose of mind and heart. Everything—including the greatness of grace and the depth of sin—is part of a transcendent design. Being able to say "Amen" means recognizing the sovereign lordship of God. Everything he does is done well, despite our weariness on the twisting roads and our limited comprehension. The Amen is connected to faith. Its philological roots in Hebrew indicate that having faith entails trusting surrender to a supreme, accepting, and fulfilling Meaning beyond our own desires.

We see this Meaning embodied in the person of Mary. Before we say our own "Amen," it is God who has said "Amen" to

Mary. He has said "Yes" and "Amen" to the feminine, assuming it as his and making it part of his history of self-surrender in revelation and love. He has said "Yes" and "Amen" to woman, his image and likeness, making her his tabernacle, his wife, his mother, a moment of his own "fulfillment."

God's full Amen to Mary took place at her assumption into heaven in body and soul. Mary is fully enthroned in the mystery of the Blessed Trinity. There her assumption by the Holy Spirit reaches culmination, divinizing the feminine in woman and man to the maximum.

And we, like God, repeat the Amen. We accept in gratitude what faith reveals to us through Mary. We are all called, each in his or her own measure and way, to be temples of God, dwelling places of the Spirit, to be transfigured into celestial glory. This promise is now embodied in the person of Mary by the work and grace of the Mystery. Hence we say "Amen."

Sin dulls the brightness of these truths; it causes us to stumble and lose our way. We pray to the Virgin to bring us back to the right path and to be our advocate against the forces of the evil one. Despite our hesitancy, despite our falls, beyond all weakness, we repeat "Amen." This kind of faith is not an evasion; it is not a substitute for the courage to be and to embrace the misery of existence. On the contrary, it is the foundation that supports our courage to be able to say "Amen" and that confirms our hope beyond any failure.

Our Amen does not spring easily to our lips. It is the end of a trajectory of faith that has crossed the night of the senses and of the spirit. Mary also had to say this Amen when she was journeying among us in the darkness of faith, unable to understand so many things that she kept in her heart (Luke 2:51). Now she says eternally, "Amen, Amen."

Our earthly Amen at the end of the Hail Mary is united to God's Amen and echoes the Amen of our great and kind Mother in heaven. Amen.

Notes

2. When It Makes Sense to Pray the Hail Mary

1. For deeper consideration of this question, see Leonardo Boff, *O rostro materno de Deus* (Petropolis, 1978), pp. 92–107 (English translation, *The Maternal Face of God* [San Francisco, 1987]).

2. *De diversis Serm. I* 52, 2; P.L. 183, 675.

3. Cf. Pope Paul VI, *Marialis Cultus*, Apostolic Exhortation for the Right Ordering and Development of Devotion to the Blessed Virgin Mary (1974). English text available at http://www.newadvent.org/docs/pa06mc.htm

4. For this entire issue: Leonardo Boff, "Masculino e feminino: o que é?" Fragmentos de uma ontologia, *Vozes* 68 (1974) 677–90; see also E. Sullerot, ed., *Le fait féminin* (Paris: Fayard, 1978).

5. Cf. E. Doyle, "God and the Feminine," *The Clergy Review* 56 (1971) 866–77; Andrew M. Greeley, *The Mary Myth: On the Femininity of God* (New York, 1977); J. E. Burns, *God as Woman, Woman as God* (New York Toronto, 1976).

6. The information has been gathered from the following sources: U. Berlière, "Angélique (Salutation)," in *Dictionnaire de Théologie Catholique* I (1905), 1273–77; H. Thurston, *Dictionnaire de Spiritualité Ascetique et Mystique* I (1935), 1161–65; M. Roschini, "L'Ave Maria: note storiche," *Marianum* 5 (1943) 177–85; I. Cecchetti "Ave-Maria," in *Enciclopedia Cattolica* I (1949), pp. 512–16; J. A. Jungmann, "Ave-Maria," in *Lexikon für Theologie und Kirche* I (1957), 1141; L. Angel, "El ave maria a través de los tiempos," in *Cultura Biblica* no. 31 (46) and no. 32 (1947).

7. The text is cited by Thurston in *Dictionnaire de Spiritualité*, 1162. Recent excavations have discovered the inscription *Xê Maria*, "Hail Mary," in the ruins of the church-synagogue of Nazareth, built over the house of Joseph and Mary by the second and third centuries, thereby

indicating very early devotion to the mother of God: B. A. Bagatti, *A Igreja da circuncisão* (Petropolis, 1975), p. 140.

8. Cf. F. M. William, *Storia del rosario* (Rome: Orbis Catholicus, 1951); L. Andrianopoli, "Il rosario," in *Enciclopedia mariana Theotokos* (Genoa-Milan, 1959), pp. 434–42; W. Krifel, *Der Rosenkranz, Ursprung und Ausbreitung* (Wallsdorf, 1949); E. Schillebeeckx, *Mary Mother of the Redemption* (New York, 1964), pp. 164–71; A. Klein, "A oração do rosario," in the collection *O culto a Maria hoje* (São Paulo: Paulinas, 1980), pp. 266–73.

3. Hail Mary: Rejoice, Beloved of God!

1. For this whole question, see Clodovis Boff, *Sinas dos tempos. Pautas de leitura* (São Paulo, 1979), pp. 11–12; C. Mesters, *Por trás das palavras* (Petropolis, 1975), pp. 20–26, 223–31.

2. See the specific literature on *chaire-ave*: S. Lyonnet, "Chaire kecharitomne," *Biblica* 20 (1939) 131–41; idem, "Le récit de l'Annonciation et la Maternité divine de la Sainte Vierge," *L'Ami du Clergé* 66 (1956) 33–46, esp. 39–41; R. Laurentin, *Structure et théologie de Luc I-II* (Paris, 1957), pp. 64–68; J. P. Audet, "L'announce à Marie," *Revue Biblique* 63 (1956) 346–74, esp. 357–58; P. Benoît, "L'annonciation," in *Exegèse et Théologie* II (Paris, 1968), pp. 197–215; A. Strobel, "Der Gruss an Maria (Lk 1.28): Eine philologische Betrachtung zu seinem Sinngehalt," *Zeitschrift zur neutestamentlichen Wissenschaft* 53 (1962) 86–110. See also the commentaries by: H. Schürman, *Das Lukasevangelium*, Herders theologischer Kommentar zum Neuen Testament (Friburg, 1969), pp. 43–44; J. Ernst, *Das Evangelium nach Lukas*, Regensburger Neues Testament (Regensburg, 1977), pp. 68–69; Howard I. Marshall, *The Gospel of Luke*, The New International Greek Testament Commentary (Exeter, 1978).

3. The Latin *ave* seems to have been borrowed from the Carthaginian *hawa*, which means "live!" from the verb *hawah* "to live" or also "to desire." The Romans also used *ave* as a greeting. In old Latin, *avere* (defective verb only used in the imperative: *ave, aveto*) meant to prosper, have good health, enjoy good health. Hence, it could mean to enjoy or be happy, which fits quite well with the modern meaning given to *chaire*, "to rejoice." The common Latin greeting is *salve*, which comes from the verb *salvere (salvus esse)*, meaning to have good health, to feel good; the meaning would be: have good health; be well. For more on this, see Ernout, *Dictionnaire étymologique de la langue latine*, and also the *Thesaurus linguae latinae*, vol. 2, entries "ave," "aveo."

4. From the rabbinic traditions we know that "one should never greet a woman" (Qid 70a); on this see also Ernst, *Das Evangelium nach Lukas,* p. 68.

5. Notably Lyonnet, Laurentin, and Audet.

6. Here is the text of the prophets: Zephaniah 3:14–17: "Sing aloud, O daughter Zion; shout, O Israel! Rejoice and exult with all your heart, O daughter Jerusalem! The Lord has taken away the judgments against you, he has turned away your enemies. The king of Israel, the Lord, is in your midst; you shall fear disaster no more. On that day it shall be said to Jerusalem: Do not fear, O Zion; do not let your hands grow weak. The Lord, your God, is in your midst, a warrior who gives victory"; Joel 2:21–27: "Do not fear, O soil; be glad *(chaire)* and rejoice, for the Lord has done great things! [words of Mary's Magnificat] . . . O children of Zion, be glad *(chairete)* and rejoice in the Lord your God; . . . You shall know that I am in the midst of Israel, and that I, the Lord, am your God and there is no other"; Zechariah 9:9: "Rejoice greatly *(chaire),* O daughter Zion! Lo, your king comes to you; triumphant and victorious is he." The text of the annunciation to the Virgin Mary is grounded in such prophecies. In New Testament times, a frequently used literary genre would tell of an event in the present (the fact of the annunciation of the angel Gabriel to Mary) in the light of an ancient event, using the same terms to underline the correspondence of the facts, thus better showing God's design in which there are anticipations, preparations, and finally full realization in history.

7. Cf. H.-M. Manteau-Bonamy, *La Sainte Vierge et le Saint-Esprit* (Paris, 1971); L. Boff, *O rostro materno de Deus* (Petropolis, 1978), pp. 158–67 (English translation, *The Maternal Face of God* [San Francisco, 1987]).

8. Cf. A. F. Key, "The Giving of Proper Names in the O.T.," *Journal of Biblical Literature* 83 (1964) 55–59; J. Heller, "Namengebung und Namendeutung. Grundzüge der alttestamentlichen Onomatologie," *Evangelische Theologie* 27 (1967) 255–66.

9. See the best bibliography: E. Vogt, "O nome de Maria á luz de recentes descobertas arqueológicas," *Revista Eclesiástica Brasileira* 1 (1941) 473–81; M.-J. Lagrange, *Evangile selon Saint Luc* (Paris, 1918), pp. 27–28 (the most detailed of all); G. Roschini, *La vita di Maria* (Rome, 1947), pp. 55–60; J. J. Stamm, "Hebräische Frauennamen," in *Festschrift Baumgartner* (Leiden, 1967), pp. 301–39.

10. The difference between *Maryám* and *Miryám* is merely phonetic and is found in other names like Samson or Simson, Balaam or Bileam, Magdala or Migdal. Mary is a Greek adaptation of the Hebrew word *Maryám.*

11. See Roschini's beautiful poetic observations in *La vita di Maria*, pp. 59–60.

12. O. Bardenhewer, *Der Name Maria. Geschichte der Deutung desselben* (Freiburg, 1895) lists around sixty different interpretations of the name Mary.

13. This interpretation is ardently defended by the Brazilian Ernesto Vogt in "O nome de Maria à luz de recentes descobertas arqueológicas," p. 480: "Grammatically speaking, no other derivation is even remotely as natural as this one, and none gives a meaning as excellently in harmony with the laws of the formation of proper names. If this interpretation is rejected, there remains no other that is solidly probable." The former derivation from Egyptian origins has been presented with detailed argumentation by F. Zorell, "Maria soror Moisis et Maria Mater Dei," *Verbum Domini* 6 (1926) 257–63.

4. Full of Grace, the Contemplated One: Mary's True Name

1. See the primary bibliography on Luke 1:28: R. Laurentin, *Structure et théologie de Luc I–II* (Paris, 1957), pp. 34–35, 47, 148; S. Lyonnet, "Chaire, kecharitoméne," *Biblica* 20 (1939) 131–41; idem, "Le récit de l'Annonciation et la Maternité Divine de la Sainte Vierge," *L'Ami du Clergé* 66 (1956) 33–46; J. Fantini, "Kecharitoméne (Lc 1.28) Interpretación filológica," in *Salamanticenses* I (1954), pp. 760–763; M. De Tuya, "Valoración exegético-teológica del Ave gratia plena (Lc 1.28)," *La Ciencia Tomista* 83 (1956) 3–27; J.-P. Audet, "L'Annonce à Marie," *Revue Biblique* 58 (1956) 346–74; M. Cambe "La charis chez Saint Luc. Remarques sur quelques textes, notamment le kecharitoméne," *Revue Biblique* 70 (1963) 193–207; F. Bourassa "Kecharitoméne (Lc 1.28)," *Sciences Ecclésiatiques* 9 (1957) 313–16; E. R. Cole, "What did St. Luke mean by kecharitoméne?" *American Ecclesiastical Review* 139 (1958) 228–39; A. Strobel, "Der Gruss an Maria. (Lk 1.28). Eine philologische Betrachtung zu seinem Sinngehalt," *Zeitschrift zur neutestamentlichen Wissenschaft* 53 (1962) 86–110; see also the recent commentaries: H. Schürmann, *Das Lukasevangelium*, Herders theologischer Kommentar zum Neuen Testament III/I (Herder, 1969), pp. 44–45; I. Howard Marshall, *The Gospel of Luke* (Exeter, 1978); R. Brown et al., *Mary in the New Testament* (Philadelphia, 1978) pp. 111–34.

2. In this regard, see L. Boff, *O rostro materno de Deus* (Petropolis, 1978), pp. 106–17 (English translation, *The Maternal Face of God* [San Francisco, 1987]), with the extensive bibliography cited there; see also J.-M. Salgado, "Pneumatologie et mariologie: bilan actuel et orientations possibles," *Divinitas* 15 (1971) 421–28; J. Richard, "Conçu du

Saint-Espirt, né de la Vierge Marie," *Eglise et Théologie* 10 (1979) 291–321; the best collection of studies is still *Le Saint-Esprit et Marie*, 3 vols., *Bulletin de la Societé Française d'Etudes Mariales* for 1968, 1969, 1970.

3. Cf. X. Pikaza, "El Espíritu Santo y María en la obra de San Lucas," *Ephemerides Mariologicae* 28 (1978) 151–68.

4. For detailed argumentation, see Boff, *O rostro materno de Deus*, pp. 106–17.

5. S. Lyonnet strongly advocates this position in "Le récit de l'Annonciation," esp. pp. 44–46; see also Laurentin, *Structure*, pp. 148–61; Richard, "Conçu du Saint-Esprit," pp. 315–16.

6. L. Deiss, *Marie, Fille de Zion* (Paris, 1958), pp. 83–89; Laurentin, *Structure*, pp. 64–68, 148–61.

7. Cf. Cambe, "La charis chez Saint Luc," p. 203: "object of grace (or favor)"; Laurentin, *Structure*, p. 148: "you who are and remain furnished with grace"; Audet, "L'annonce à Marie," p. 360 suggests calling her "privileged."

8. Cf. Fantini, "Kecharitoméne," p. 762: "in possession of divine grace personally"; Fr. Zorell, *Novi Testamenti Lexicon Graecum*, translates it as "Dei benevolum amorem experta."

9. The Codex Palatinus(e) of the African tradition contains the following translation: *abe (ave) gratificata;* likewise in the q codex; cf. J. Leal, "El Saludo del Angel a la Virgen (Lc 1.28)," *Cultura Biblica* 11 (1954) 293–301, here 296.

10. For this, see H. M. Manteau-Bonamy, *La Sainte Vierge et le Saint-Esprit* (Paris, 1971) and M. G. Bonado, "El Espíritu Santo y Maria en el Vaticano II," *Ephemerides Mariologicae* 28 (1978) 201–03.

11. J.-P. Audet in "L'annonce à Marie" has traced the parallel between the announcement of the angel to Gideon and the angel's announcement to Mary: pp. 358–60.

12. See similar formulations: Lyonnet, "Le Recit de l'Annonciation," p. 41: "Mary is like this divine favor personified"; Cambe, "La charis," p. 205: "the personal and personified expression of divine favor." Revelation (21:2–3) also presents us with a woman as "temple (*skené* = tent) of God among human beings."

13. W. C. Van Unnik, "Dominus vobiscum: The Background of the Liturgical Formula," in *New Testament Essays* (Manchester 1959), pp. 270–305.

14. See H. Schürmann, *Das Lukasevangelium*, p. 45, for a careful treatment of all the passages; see also P. Holzmeister, "Dominus tecum," in "Exégesis lingüistica del Avemaria," *Cultura Bíblica* 11 (1954) 302–19, here 309–10.

15. Marshall, *The Gospel of Luke,* p. 65.

16. This claim is defended by G. Voss, *Die Christologie der lukanisch-en Schriften in Grundzügen* (Paris-Bruges, 1965), p. 65.

17. With regard to the entire question of the analogy between the ark of the Lord and Mary, mother of the Lord, see the detailed exegesis of the passages, especially of 2 Samuel 6:9–11 with Luke 1:43, 56, in R. Laurentin, *Breve Tratado de Teologia Mariana* (Petropolis, 1965), p. 33, n. 10, or idem, *Structure,* pp. 43–116.

5. Blessed Art Thou among Women

1. For exegesis of the texts, see H. Schürmann, *Das Lukasevangelium,* Herders theologischer Kommentar zum Neuen Testament III/I (Herder, 1969), pp. 67–69; I. Howard Marshall, *The Gospel of Luke* (Exeter, 1978), p. 81; R. Laurentin, *Structure et théologique de Luc I-II* (Paris, 1957), pp. 81–82; R. Brown et al., *Mary in the New Testament* (Philadelphia, 1978), pp. 134–37.

2. D. G. Jaeso, "Exégesis linguística del avemaria," *Cultura Bíblica* 11 (1954) 310–12.

3. M. J. Lagrange, *Evangile de Saint Luc* (Paris, 1918), p. 43.

4. The most complete theological argumentation is found in L. Boff, *O rostro materno de Deus* (Petropolis, 1978) [English translation, *The Maternal Face of God* (San Francisco, 1987)], with bibliography cited there.

5. Cf. L. Boff, "O feminino no conflito das interpretações," in *O rostro materno de Deus,* pp. 37–117, 215–59, with the vast bibliography cited there.

6. Cf. F. Z. J. Buytendijk, *La femme. Ses modes d'être, de paraître et d'exister* (Desclée de Brouwer, 1967); P. Evodkimov, *La femme et la salut du monde* (Paris, 1958); A. Manaranche, *O Espirito e a Mulher* (São Paulo, Loyola, 1976), esp. 52–62.

7. We recall the important study by A. Lemmonneyer, "Le rôle maternal du Saint-Esprit dans notre vie surnaturalle," *Vie Spirituelle* (1921) 241–51; S. Verges, *Imagen del Espíritu de Jesus* (Salamanca, 1977), pp. 289–325.

6. Blessed Is the Fruit of Thy Womb, Jesus

1. For the exegesis of this passage, see I. Howard Marshall, *The Gospel of Luke* (Exeter, 1978), pp. 80–81; H. Schürmann, *Das Luka evangelium,* Herders theologischer Kommentar zum Neuen Testament III/I (Herder, 1969), pp. 68–69; R. Laurentin, *Structure et théologie de*

Luc I–II (Paris, 1957), pp. 81–83; D. G. Maeso, "Exégesis linguística del avemaria," *Cultura Biblica* 11 (1954) 312–14. The expression blessed is the "fruit of your womb" is traditional in the Bible (cf. Gen. 30:2; Deut. 28:4; Jer. 1:5). We find the same phrase that the angel Gabriel says to Mary in the book of Judith 13:18 with a small modification in the name: "Blessed are you, daughter, by the Most High God, above all the women on earth; and blessed be the Lord God." For a good explanation of these parallels, see R. Laurentin, *Breve Tratado de Teologia Mariana* (Petropolis, 1965), pp. 23–35, here p. 33; R. Brown et al., *Mary in the New Testament* (Philadelphia, 1978), pp. 134–37.

2. Cf. the term *Esprit* in the *Dictionnaire Biblique* of G. Kittel (Geneva, 1971); Y. Congar, *Je crois en l'Esprit Saint*, vol. 1 (Paris, 1979); L. Boff, *Die Kirche als Sacrament in Horizont der Welterfahrung* (Paderborn, 1972), pp. 361–75.

3. Cf. J. Jeremias, *New Testament Theology: The Proclamation of Jesus* (Philadelphia, 1971); Maeso, "Exégesis, linguística," pp. 313–14.

7. Holy Mary: The Holiness of the Holy Spirit

1. On this issue, see H. Gross, "Santidade," in *Dicionário dos conceitos teológicos fundamentais* (São Paulo: Loyola, 1974); P. van Imschoot, "La sainteté de Dieu dans l'Ancien Testament," *Vie Spirituelle* 309 (1946) 30–44; E. Pax, "Heilig," in *Bibeltheologisches Wörterbuch* (J. B. Bauer, Herder 1959), pp. 398–403.

2. We again insist that in making this claim we are not teaching an official doctrine of the magisterium, but presenting a theological reflection that we regard as well founded and capable of inspiring a new Marian piety: see H. Muhlen, "A temporalização do Espirito Santo," in *Mysterium Salutis* (Vozes, 1974), pp. 21–23.

3. The best text on this point is "Esprit," in Gerhard Kittel et al., *Dictionnaire biblique* (Geneva, 1971); B. Froguet, *De l'Habitation du Saint-Esprit dans les âmes des justes* (Lethielleux, 1937); Y. Congar, *Je crois en l'Esprit Saint* (Paris: Cerf, 1979).

4. Cf. A. Bover, *Soteriologia mariana* (Madrid, 1946), pp. 345–53: Mary's substantial or quasi-substantial holiness.

5. Cf. R. Laurentin, "Santità di Maria?" in *Enciclopedia cattolica*, vol. 10 (Vatican, 1953), pp. 1874–77; for the historical aspect: G. Joussard, "Le problème de la sainteté de Marie depuis les origines de la patristique jusqu'au Concile d'Ephèse," *Bulletin de la Société Français d'Etudes Mariales* 5 (1947) 13–28; C. Journet, "Sainteté de Marie et sainteté de l'Eglise," *Bulletin de la Société Français d'Etudes Mariales*

10 (1952) entire issue; see the collection of essays in *O culto a Maria hoje* (São Paulo, 1980), esp. 29–50.

6. It is a very common expression among the fathers of the church, such as Saint Augustine, *"Fide plena, et Christum prius mente quam ventre concipiens . . ."* Sermo 215, n. 4: P.L. 38, 1074, or St. Leo the Great, Pope, "Prius mente quam corpore . . ." *Sermo* 1 in Nativitate: P.L. 54, 191.

7. Pope Paul VI, *Marialis Cultus,* Apostolic Exhortation for the Right Ordering and Development of Devotion to the Blessed Virgin Mary (1974), no. 37. English text available at http://www.newadvent.org/docs/pa06mc.htm

8. Ibid., no. 35.

9. Ibid., no. 37.

10. Ibid.

8. Mother of God: The Spirit and the Feminine

1. For pursuing the issue more deeply and for a primary bibliography, see L. Boff, *O rostro materno de Deus* (Petropolis, 1979) pp. 165–77 (English translation, *The Maternal Face of God* [San Francisco, 1978]); cf. also R. Laurentin, "Bulletin sur Marie, Mère du Seigneur," in *Revue des sciences philosophiques et théologiques* 60 (1976) 309–45; 451–500; H. U. von Balthasar et al., *O culto a Maria hoje* (São Paulo: Paulinas, 1980), pp. 132–46.

2. For a view from an ecumenical standpoint, see R. Brown et al., *Mary in the New Testament* (Philadelphia: Fortress Press, 1978).

3. The human (generation, giving birth, etc.) and divine (relationship with the Father and the Son) implications are developed by R. Laurentin, *Breve Tratado de Teologia Mariana* (Petropolis, 1965), pp. 130–41.

4. Theophanus of Nicea (a fourteenth-century Orthodox theologian) says that "from her very beginning Mary was united to the Spirit, author of life; everything she tasted in life was shared with the Spirit, for her share in the Spirit became a participation in being." Strotmann, a scholar on the matter, says: "For Theophanus the Holy Spirit was everything in the Virgin's life and when the archangel Gabriel came to bring her the message of salvation, he found there the Spirit who had sent him from heaven, previously dwelling in the Virgin as in the heavens; in her the Lord, descending over her, found an incorruptible and unstained land, while the whole earth was corrupt before him"— T. Strotmann, "Le Saint-Esprit et la Theotokos dans la Tradition Orientale," *Bulletin de la Société Français d'Etudes Mariales* 25 (1968) 77–91, here p. 85, The text of Theophanus of Nicea is found in *Sermo in S. Deiparam 30* (Ed. Jugie, Lateranum I), pp. 178–80.

5. Cf. E. Schillebeeckx, *Maria, Mãe da Redenção* (Petropolis, 1968), pp. 73–78 (English translation, *Mary, Mother of the Redemption* [New York, 1964]); Laurentin, *Breve tratado de Teologia Mariana,* pp. 125–26.

6. S. Lyonnet, "L'annonciation et la mariologie biblique, ce que l'exégese conclut du récit lucanien de l'annonciation concernant la mariologie," in *Maria in Sacra Scriptura,* vol. 6 (Rome, 1967), pp. 59–60. The author notes that "St. Luke's entire account of the childhood of the holy Virgin is always considered in terms of Christ the Savior. Jesus is unquestionably the central person in chapters 1–2 of Luke on whom everything else converges . . . With regard to Mary, she herself is always ordered to Jesus; not only her maternity, properly understood, but also the virginal conception *ex Spiritu sancto;* and it is so because Jesus will be conceived of a virgin mother in whom the Holy Spirit will be present in a unique manner; and also the child will therefore be called Son of God. How this should be interpreted matters little, the bond of causality is underlined" (pp. 60–61). However, it is this "unique manner" of the presence of the Spirit in Mary that should be reflected upon and not simply subsumed into a Christological perspective.

7. Cf. A. Feuillet, "L'Esprit Saint et la Mère du Christ," *Bulletin de la Société Français d'Etudes Mariales* 25 (1968) 39–64.

8. For an overview of this issue, see E. Vallauri, "A exegese moderna diante da virginidade de Maria," *Revista Eclesiastica Brasileira* 34 (1974) 375–99; M. O'Carroll, "The Virginal Conception: Some Recent Problems," *Marianum* 37 (1975), 429–64.

9. P.L. 21, p. 1129b.

10. *Cathem.* 11, 14.

11. *Sermo* 66.4.

12. Cf. A. Médebielle, "Annonciation," in *Supplément du Dictionnaire de la Bible* vol. 1, 275–78; cf. P. Bover, "Quod nascetur (ex te) Sanctum vocabitur Filius Dei Lc. 1.35," *Biblica* I (1920) 94 ff.; Brown et al., *Mary in the New Testament,* pp. 128–34; L. Legrand, "Fécondité virginale selon l'Esprit dans le Nouveau Testament," *Nouvelle Revue Théologique* 84 (1962) 685–805.

13. S. Lyonnet, "Le récit de l'annonciation et la maternité divine de la Sainte Vierge," *Ami du Clergé* 66 (1956) 45 ff.

14. Ibid.

15. Legrand, "Fécondité virginale selon l'Esprit dans le Nouveau Testament," pp. 785–800.

16. Ibid., p. 798.

17. H. M. Manteau-Bonamy, "Et la vierge conçut du Saint-Esprit," *Bulletin de la Société Français d'Etudes Mariales,* 7 (1970) 7–23.

18. Ibid., p. 11.

19. Ibid., p. 16.

20. Cf. F. J. Buytendink, *La Femme. Ses modes d'être, de paraître, d'exister* (Desclée de Brouwer, 1967), pp. 329–45: la vocation maternele.

21. Responsorial IX of the Office of the Immaculate Conception.

22. In *Jer. Hom.* 15.4.

23. In *Jn. Hom.* 2.6.

24. In Mich. 7.6; on Is. 40.12–13: Benoît and Boismard, *Synopse des Quatre Evangiles* (Paris: Cerf, 1965), p. 153.

25. In Is. 11.2; Benoît et Boismard, *Synopse*, p. 18.

9. Pray for Us Sinners

1. On this issue, see G. Greshke and G. Lohfink, *Bittgebet—Testfall des Glaubens* (Mainz, 1978); J. Sudbrack, *Beten ist menschlich* (Friburg, 1973); collective article "La preghiera del cristiano oggi," *Presenza Pastorale* 38 (1968) 971–1099; B. Barrofio, "Preghiera," in *Dizionario Teologico Interdisciplinare* 2 (Marietti, 1977), pp. 774–84; A. Verheul, "La sainte Vierge dans le culte de l'Eglise," in *Les questions liturgiques et paroissiales* (1969), pp. 235–51.

2. Cf. S. Cipriani, *La preghiera nel Nuevo Testatmento* (Milan, 1970).

3. Cf. E. Schillebeeckx, *Mary, Mother of the Redemption* (San Francisco, 1964), p. 163.

4. A. Müller, "Maria e a redenção," in *Mysterium Salutis* III/7 (Petropolis, 1976), pp. 176–81; R. Laurentin, *Breve Tratado de Theología Mariana* (Petropolis, 1965).

First in the Family!

Ken Viñales

ISBN-13: 978-0-9994018-2-8
ISBN-10: 0-9994018-2-3

Ken Viñales

Acknowledgments

Without my mother or big brother, I am not sure where I would be in life. As a young adolescent, they guided me in ways that I did not become aware of, until I began to look outside the box. Mom, everything that I do from this point on will be to provide for you and our family. Sometimes I sit back in amazement at the amount of things that you were able to accomplish, with such little support. Kyle, big bro, you showed me the way. When Dad left, you were the only male I could look up to. I've been watching you live your dreams. You have inspired me to grind relentlessly. Now, it's time for me. I will spread my wings and live out my purpose. I promise our lives will never be the same.

Author's Note

First, I would like to recognize you, the person on the other side of these words. You are witnessing an artist in the beginning of his purpose awakening. This is my journey to mastery. My desires will take years to manifest. Over time, I will be recognized as one of the greats. You were able to witness first.

Contents

Volume 2

"I recreated my future using my past."

-Ken Viñales

1

Testimony

Today is December 15th, 2018. It is also the day my life changes forever. Have you ever imagined an experience, but the actual one feels much different? Years ago, I envisioned this moment. Our encounter was preplanned. Never once could I have predicted that it would end like this.

I never imagined that a journey could lead to countless discoveries. I was once confused. Do you know what it is like to be unaware of where you will end up? As I end this journey, many signs point to a certain direction. That direction is leading me to achieve something legendary. That direction has led me to you.

Countless Possibilities

What if I told you that this was only the beginning? I am going to go back into my past, recreate my future, and show you why and how dreams come true. By the end, you will have done the exact same thing, but using the experiences from your own life. See, a lot of people, as they get older, begin to realize that life can take tragic turns.

Do you realize that tragedies occur at random moments? What a tragedy can create is a lack of faith. For example, this year, I witnessed shocking deaths. Deaths that caused me to question my appreciation. Have you ever experienced a death, which made you appreciate life from a different perspective?

A different traumatizing experience is family illness. Last year, on my 21st birthday, I received a sudden phone call. I was away at college, when I had to rush home. My mother called me in a panic, sighing that things may not be looking good. It was easy to tell from her tone of voice that she was in a lot of pain.

Pain from Tragedy

I rushed home only to find my mother in the middle of the floor. She was unable to walk. She did not have enough strength to get up. I spent my 21st birthday trying to process a wide range of emotions from anger to despair. It was not until months after that doctors informed us that my mom suffered a tear in her ACL, MCL, and was beginning to develop blood clots. She underwent surgery on January 4, 2018.

For a whole year, I had to witness my mother feel hopeless. For a whole year, I had to witness my mother work in pain. There are times where life can seem unfair, but there is a beauty in every struggle. Aside from my mother going through her medical condition, other members of my family began to get sick, opening my perspective on a more complex level.

The older I get, the more I begin to see that anything is possible. Whether the outcome is good or bad, anything is a possibility. As I end my journey, I go back into my past. By revisiting past emotions, memories, and feelings, more information reveals who you are, at a subconscious level.

Today's Past Reflection

Where you are today is a direct reflection of who you were previous years back. Think about where you were four years ago. How did you think? How did you act? Who did you want to be? Where did you want to go?

In the past, I was not able to answer those questions. I was confused. Do you know what it is like to live life, unsure of what your best abilities are? What is passion? How can you find passion, if you do not know how to guide the search? The most troubling aspect of living in the unknown is trying to figure out what is in store.

Collect and Transform

The experiences that we collect, incorporated with our encounters, display the magic of life, which is wisdom. Wisdom is applied knowledge that creates an experience, leading you to gain new information. I have spent many years reading. I have spent many years writing. For many years, I entered the minds of different business owners, influencers, and professional athletes.

My first reaction, when trying to find answers that I do not have, is to seek wisdom from individuals with more experience. That is how you broaden your perspective. Once you enhance your perspective, your reality will transform. As I look at myself, from outside of myself, I see things that could be changed.

Wisdom Transference

I possess much wisdom, wisdom that I will transfer onto you. In other words, I am going to recreate experiences that are beneficial to learn, relatable and valuable, through this story. You are receiving this message because it is the sign you need. I have answers to the questions that have left you curious for years.

I am here to unlock your mind. I have hope. I am the one who has inspiration and a message that can be transferred onto you. When I was young, growing up, I did

4

not understand repetition, timing, or dedication. Without knowledge of those three, success will be difficult.

I watched my mother go through many struggles. I watched her battle multiple divorces. I witnessed her overcome the fall of various business concepts, while finding a way to rise again. I analyzed her ability to raise two boys, myself and my brother, to be successful men in society.

Free from Illusion

I have a testimony. I have a story. I have something that you can relate too. When I was six years old, I woke up, and before I could go to sleep, my whole world was taken from me. I will explain more in chapter 6. I am teaching you the power of wisdom. The more wisdom you acquire, the higher you will rise.

Society has many blind followers. Humans are looking up to leaders who have never experienced what they are teaching. How can you teach something that you have never lived? College teachers teach business classes, but many have never operated their own business.

Social Media Influencers have found a way to create mass followings. Many are guiding millions of subscribers, followers, and fans on different activities that they have never engaged in. When you unlock your mind, something transpires, giving you an ability to see what is unseen.

Ahead of My Time

I am 22 years old, but at 19 years old, I was selling real estate. I am 22 years old, but at 20, I wrote my first book. I am 22 years old, but no one in my family has ever achieved this milestone. I am 22 years old, yet I found a way to reach you.

When I think about life, I think about the good things that can happen on any random occasion. Imagine the stories of those who go to sleep, only to wake up in their dream. What if I told you that happened to me? All it takes is for one situation, circumstance, or day for your life to elevate.

Time is Art

There is nothing that can explain random blessings other than perfect timing. When I began this vision, I did not know what would transpire, leading up to this moment. The only concept I understood was perfect timing. Perfect timing allows you to lock in. Knowing that you are going to be placed in the right position, at the right time, with the right people, gives you an ability to perfect your craft.

If you are curious, I am graduating college today. Not only that, I am the first person in my family to ever cross a

University's stage. Today, I acquire my B.A. in Psychology from Oakland University in Rochester Hills, Michigan.

When this journey first began, I was not aware that I was going to be the first to achieve this milestone. I was unaware of the connection you and I will form. Think about what you were doing four years ago. It's four years from that moment, and now you are here, reading my words. Words that will be here forever. The goal is to inspire multiple generations after me.

Failure Ignites Hopelessness

After high school, I had no hope. Everyone around me went away to college, but every college I applied to denied my access. My only option was to enroll at a local community college. I went into college confused, with no specific passion. I desired success, but lacked a concrete plan. It was hard to envision myself using school to get to where I wanted to be.

The second semester of my first year, I contemplated dropping out. Do you know what it is like to invest in something that you do not have faith in? I didn't have faith in school's ability to help me achieve success. I didn't know how to reach success. I did not know what experiences would lead to me achieving success.

Avoid Unnecessary Debts

I wanted to prevent debt. The more money you owe someone else, the less control you have. College students rush into school. Most of the time, it requires loans. Students are naïve. We enter college, believing that it is some magic formula. We believe it will automatically generate success, once the journey is over. The journey for college is over for me.

I am not worried. I am not pressured, only hopeful, for this next chapter of my life. College was some of the worst years of my life. I was handicapped, my body was free; my mind was restricted. School conditions students to be workers. Being a worker for my entire life is not an option.

Raised to Be Great

I was raised by an entrepreneur. My mother is a successful businesswoman. How could I spend my life, working for another man? All I know is independence. By any means necessary, I will find a way to provide for not only myself, but the people around me.

We all have something within us that we do better than anyone else. Some students feel as though school will help them achieve their dream. They have faith that college will translate into maximizing their potential. The problem with this belief is that school is merely a tool.

Expand Your Toolbox → Be strategic /analytical

Tools must be used accordingly. Have you ever seen a tool applied in the wrong way? This is what happens when people think a degree will result in things being handed to them. In other words, some people go to college and benefit. Some people go to college and fail. Some people go to college, but quit because the work load is excessive. The most common is dropping out because of cost.

At one point, I felt that a degree was more than a tool. I felt that a degree would provide me with a special power. I was unaware that it was just a fancy sheet of paper, stating that certain requirements were met in a concentrated field. It did not sink in until my junior year; it was September 1, 2016. That story will be shared in chapter 6.

Expect the Unexpected → Never expect/ be ready for anything

Now that my time has ended, nothing turned out to be what it once seemed. I did not expect my life to transpire this way. The older we become, the more we expose our mind to different levels of life, helping us understand complex scenarios. As an adolescent, the world *stimuli* ↖

is more theatrical. People, ideas, and experiences are perceived much grander than what they actually are.

When I realized that college was an illusion, other options appeared. Books made their way into my life at the perfect time. Books unlocked my mind. Over time, I was given an ability to see things that were once invisible. I began to approach life from numerous angles.

By my sophomore year, I changed my major over three times. The final decision was psychology. My choice was instinctual, meaning at the time I didn't fully understand why. As time went on, I began to see that things were happening in the way that they were supposed to.

Experiences Are Stories

Many people have questioned my decisions leading up to now, but as I am now here, living this actual moment, it is easy to see that everything happened exactly how it was supposed to happen, when it was supposed to happen. That is the art of time.

I have learned how to take experiences and turn them into a story. A story for you to interpret as knowledge. In my mind, I was not supposed to be here because of what I went through. The statistics and the odds were against me. The moment I came to life, the moment I was born, there were odds set in place for me to fail. → *overcoming the odds that were socially constructed.*

Although there were odds, I overcame them all. I am destined to prevail, not fail. It will shock the world, but this vision will manifest. Whatever you believe you can do, it is possible. When I was younger, I never knew the events that transpired in my life would lead up to this moment.

Beat the Odds

Today is not only the day I graduate, but also a day my life changes forever. As I mentioned, college is just a tool. I entered college, received a valuable tool and learned how to apply the knowledge to my daily life. I chose psychology because gives me power. This knowledge isn't available to everyone. My wisdom is sacred.

How many 22-year-olds have you met with the desire to inspire the next generations? This is my first book. This is the awakening of my purpose. I have found my life purpose. I have found my means to life.

The older we get, the more we begin to see that the world is not what we thought it was going to be. The only way to escape "reality" is to find out the purpose behind your existence. Why were you born? Have you taken the time to enter your past?

Artist Who Paints

It is easy to tell someone to go into the past, but there is a certain skill to the process that only humans like me possess. Psychology specialist are artful in their way of connecting the puzzle pieces of someone's life. There is a certain way to retrieve memories, piecing them together to create an answer.

First in the Family will help you unlock your mind, by going into your past and absorbing the information that is needed. I am going to recreate my past in a way that directly correlates with yours. Through this recreation experiences will expose the link between certain emotions, feelings and actions.

Many humans subconsciously desire things or act in certain ways, but are not aware of the reason. For example, throughout my childhood, I harbored much anger because of reasons that will be discussed later. Recreating past emotional experiences links subconscious actions to concealed emotions. Whenever I found myself feeling a certain way, I would act in ways, causing the very thing trying to be prevented. Much time is spent reflecting, helping pave this path.

; Psycho-analysis of oneself.

Searching for Answers

We are all looking for answers. Answers to why we are here, how to make our dreams come true, and what steps are required. You are in search of something just like me. You can relate to me, just like I can relate to you. *First in the Family* is a message that will go into the psyche of a young 19-year-old college student's mind.

What happens when you find your passion? <u>Can you recreate your world, with your thoughts?</u> *Yes* What if you could generate multiple streams of income. I was only 19 when life woke me up. All of a sudden I wanted more.

The next years of my life will be legendary. Everything that you see has already transpired, just in a different time period. In other words, I have already done many great things, expanded my network, traveled around the world, and imparted this message. When you are called to do something, <u>there is no reason to think. The only thing that you must do is act.</u> Take action, don't think!

Always Fail Forward

The problem with many people in society, myself at one point, is that we care about other people's feelings. We care about what other people think of us. We care about failing in front of others. I have learned that failure allows us to grow. Sometimes you must fail in order to get to the next level.

Today, I am receiving something that certifies the hours I invested. I have put in the time. As I complete this journey, I am debt-free. I am free from the years of interest. I am free from the years of phone calls. I am free from what holds many students back.

I have enough money to start my own business. I will invest into my passion. When you are called to do something, do not think, just act. I was called to write the most inspiring book of my generation. *First in the Family,* is the most inspiring book of 2019. It's a book of purpose. It's a story that will inspire you, the young and the old.

Manifest the Vision

Do you know what it is like to have a vision, but unsure of what direction to begin? It is impossible to reach a destination if there aren't directions. At a point in time, my goal was as simple as, wanting to get rich. I was like most people who wanted to make it to the "top", but did not have a specific plan to get there.

Recently, I have joined a small community. Very few people are able put their vision into precise words, planning a precise way to materialize what clenches to their mind. My testimony is something that you can relate to. I've come from where you come from.

Constructed Life Barriers

I come from struggles. I come from hurt. I come from pain. When I was six years old, I saw my father walk away from my mother, and in doing so, he walked away from my brother and myself as well. For many years, as we will speak about, I was confused, but today, I am doing something that was against the odds.

Minorities are expected to grow up without a father. I am a minority. I grew up without a father. Minorities are not expected to go to college. Not only did I graduate, I am walking across this stage debt-free, with a clear mind, vision, business, product and service.

How many people can say they launched their business while collecting their college diploma? I write, publish, and sell my own books. Everything I do is independent. The world that we live in today gives us an ability to create our own story through multiple platforms.

★ *The limits are only in your head*

I created my own story. I'm searching for new ways to prosper and grow. I'm only 22, starting a journey that many people would be afraid to take. I'm starting a journey knowing it will take years to result in rewards.

Sacrifice for Gains

I've sacrificed many hours just to make this moment happen. I've sacrificed many hours just to inspire someone. If you knew what I did the last four years trying to create this moment, you would understand why this moment is so monumental. Now that I have your attention, I have something that will change your life.

I'm 22 years old. I'm from Detroit, Michigan. This is my testimony. I have something, a story, a message that no one around me has ever thought of. When I think about the people around me, I've never met anyone with the desire to become an Independent Author and Entrepreneur.

I wrote, edited, published, and marketed *First in the Family* all alone. I even went as far as designing the cover and format. I want full control, meaning I can accept whatever the outcome is. If I fail, then it is on me, but on the flip side, if I succeed, then that too, is on me.

Crafting Powerful Message

On a daily basis, I am discovering new ways to create with the gifts provided. Life is defined by the level of peace you are able to reach. The best way to reach ultimate peace is to find a way to convert your passion, into a profit organically. We all have something within that we desire. No matter what it is, if you have envisioned that day, then it can be achieved.

When I look into my future, three years seem like a long time. The reason being is because every day I'm

*Marx → Freedom is labor

16

finding new ways to grow. Three years, I believe, will be enough time to share this message to millions of different people. In the first year, it will take time for the ball to begin rolling.

The path to greatness can be difficult in the beginning. Failures and mistakes play a big role in achieving success. Time after time, failure has found its way to me, but there is no turning back. That is the beauty of the process. That is the beauty of the struggle.

Undisclosed Hours

The beauty of the process is putting in the time. Put in the hours before anyone ever knows your name. Before anyone ever opened this book, I was putting in hours behind closed doors. Before anyone ever picked up this book, I was spending so many days constructing, editing, and recreating different messages. I wanted to find the one that would resonate, with the most impact.

It took thousands of hours, but I now know how to use my craft and passion, to reach people on a more cognitive level. I know what I need to do. I know that with time, perfect timing, will prove that I am ahead of my time.

Purpose behind Life

Life is about leaving your name behind. Life is about producing a rippling energy that travels. Why not create a

Choose & spend your time wisely

17

better life for the generations after you? People ask for goals, but don't take action. People ask for things, but never sacrifice. Everything that I am asking for, I sacrificed and prepared my mind.

If I was able to write a book this young, who's to say I can't inspire thousands with the same book? If I was able to be the first person in my family to graduate college, who's to say I can't be a first-generation millionaire? I want to provide jobs for the people around me. Life is special because mistakes can translate to amazing gains.

Our current moment is building our future. Our future is being determined today. Think about the habits you are forming. Your thoughts, day-to-day activities, and beliefs have a large influence on the next few years of your life.

First Failed Goal

We do not remember the normal day-to-day encounters, but everything that you think, do, and feel holds a subconscious impression on our mind. For example, as an adolescent, I spent many hours playing video games. When it came to judgment day, meaning when the time came to determine whether I passed or failed my goal, the result was failure.

It was the year I graduated high school. In that moment, I felt some of the worst pain to date. Have you ever had to look within yourself to realize that you're to blame? I did not understand hard work. I did not understand sacrifice. I did not understand what it would take to get to the next level. When you do not take your craft serious, the blessing is given to the person who does.

What is Success?

When I look at my present moment, I am happy. I see the past years are beginning to manifest. I go back and listen to old memos. I go back and read old journals. I go back and rewrite old books. Before a person reaches any level of success, a certain lifestyle is developed.

Success is revolved around certain habits. Everything that I do is tailored towards growth. I want to find a new way to grow into a better person. I want to work on my relationship with God, my family, and myself. I want to find a new way to reach my potential and hone in on my passion.

You have a passion. I have a passion. We all have a passion. You have a story. I have a story. We all have stories. What I have done is create something that differentiates me from the rest.

My story cannot be replicated. My story cannot be made up. Everything I am saying, I have encountered, I have done. I have the knowledge, I have the wisdom and the tools. Those three things allow me to open your mind to a different perspective, in a world, that was once not available to you.

Sometimes, all it takes is an achievement, an achievement such as being, the *First in the Family*. The more I think about my past, the easier it becomes to see that my path was already paved for me, many years before my coming to consciousness. Now that I am here, on this stage, seeing the joy on my mother's and father's face, I am so inspired to be great. Inspiration is sometimes all the fuel we need to launch that idea. Inspiration is what created this moment, by heightening this whole concept, leading me directly to you.

"Your past is the blueprint to your future."

-Ken Viñales

2

Raised to Be

The life we are living today is a result of our past actions. As I look out into the crowd, collecting this achievement, many past experiences, play in my mind. When I think about the path I am on, it amazes me. The moment you are now experiencing was planned long before it happened.

Many people think life is random. That belief is false. There are things happening behind the scenes that you are not able to see. The power comes when you gain awareness to the behind-the-scenes actions. That is how you take control.

Controlling your reality requires a strong understanding of your subconscious. Psychology taught me everything I need to know about our brain, the human brain. When I think about how I got to this point, on this stage, collecting this degree, talking to you, I think all the way back to the day I was four years old. I was four years old when I first found a pen.

First Person Ever

Fast forward 18 years later, I am collecting this degree in the process of doing something no one around me has ever done. Think about it. How many 22-year-olds do you know publishing their own book? Personally myself, I cannot name any. Now, I am sure there are people in the world who have, but how many of those people are you reading right now? You found your way to me for a reason. I found my way to you for a reason.

First in the Family is designed to change, the way you see the world, the way you see life. I will impart a message with as many people who need it. We all need some form of inspiration or hope. Hope or inspiration can act as fuel. What happens when you ignite gasoline? What happens when your reality becomes your dream?

Key to Growth

Do you look into your future and see great things? When I analyze my current, I cannot be anything more than thankful to God. Without God, I would not have been placed in this position, with this potential to change generations. The generations after you is what is most important.

What do you see, when you look into the mirror? When I look in the mirror, I see someone who has the potential to do great things. No one around me has my story. I know how life works. I know the magic of time. Growing up, people did not know who I would become. People did not know that I would find this passion and turn it into something that can travel through time, affecting multiple generations.

Manifest Your Vision

As my vision manifests, many people are going to come back. People will tell me how proud they are, insistent that they believed in me from the beginning. People do not follow, unless they physically see. Unless you physically do what you claim to be doing, it will be difficult for people to believe. They will not follow.

I have something physical. *First in the Family* is in your hands. *First in the Family* is in your ears. *First in the Family* is in your mind. I never knew the abilities that I had within, until I unlocked my mind, analyzing life from so many perspectives. Perspectives that many people are not aware of.

I began to go into my past. My past allowed me to see why I am, who I am, today. When is the last time that you went deep into your past, connecting the pieces of your life together? Life is a puzzle. Together, we will discover what experiences shaped you most. How can you take advantage of understanding that? I used past experiences, emotions, and associations to rewire my subconscious, drastically reconstructing my future.

Forming Positive Relationships

One of the most important aspects of life is forming relationships. Your ability to form healthy relationships truly begins in your early connections in life. How were you nurtured? What happens when you experience feelings of fear? In life, relationships play a big role in success and happiness.

We are required to build multiple relationships. We must understand people. You must understand yourself. Why are you the person you are today? I look into the mirror and see someone who is on their way to becoming great. I see someone who has potential to turn a simple craft into a generational business.

We live in an age of social media, where people can create any perception that they want. On social media, people can appear to have more money than they do. On social media, people look like they are happier than what they are. On social media, you can become whatever person you want to be. But when you go back into your real life, you still have to face those same problems haunting you.

→ SM → virtual arena

24

Envision before Manifesting

What social media has done is put less emphasis on the process. Social media has made people think that success comes overnight. One of my favorite quotes of all time is that it takes 20 years to blow up overnight.

I have been planning this for so many years. I have written many books. I have many ideas, but this was the only one that made its way to you. In life, you have to understand trial and error. You must try. You must keep going.

In life, you must never give up. That second that you stop going could have been the idea being searched for. That could have been the strike of gold. What I have done is take a simple craft and use it to become a better speaker, author, influencer, salesman, son and psychologist. I am showing my appreciation to God and the craft, by investing time every day.

10 Thousand Hours

To become a master at something, you must invest at least 10,000 hours. The legends invest much more than that. I stand on this stage today, looking into the crowd, collecting this degree, sharing this experience with you, and coming to the realization that I was raised to be everything that I am becoming, and so are you. You were raised to be something. If you are still looking for your passion, that means subconsciously, you are running away from the path that was already created for you.

If you are on a path that was paved for you, then you understand because your life travels in harmony. In harmony, meaning your thoughts, body, mind and spirit are in line. When we are in harmony, life unravels in a certain way. Everything that you want, everything that you desire, will find a way to gravitate towards you. You must become an object of desire.

Preplanned Destiny

I am on the path that was paved for me, but it took many years to discover. It took me until I was 19 to find out why I was on this earth. Once I found out why, I began to go in a certain direction. I began to search for wisdom. I began to search for new ways to hone in on this ability.

I wanted to find out why, how, and when. I wanted to find out the answer to these three questions. To know why you are gifted, helps you understand how you discovered the gift, leading you to the "when" the gift arose.

When was your passion discovered? Are you still searching for your passion? What if I provided you with the keys necessary to accomplish all of your dreams? The life you dream of seems far, but it is close. You are right there.

I go back into my past, realizing it was at age four when my gift emerged. My mother would tell me that writing was my calling, but I was too young to understand. Writing is not something that children usually enjoy, so my desire to write, at a young age, was amazing.

I began storytelling early in my life. As a young adolescent, it is hard to see the deeper aspects of life. When I analyze life from a more mature mind state, it is clear to see that I avoided the path that was already created for me, for a long time. It is hard to see what is important when you have not experienced much.

Retrace Your Steps

If I could go back, I would have taken my ability to write more serious. I would have written books at a younger age. The secret to life is not focusing on the past, in a negative way. The only thing that you can do is focus on the past, in a positive way.

Go into your past and figure out how you can recreate your future. I went into my past and discovered that when I was four, my gift to write came to life. I began writing stories. First, they started off as just one page, one paragraph. Then, they began to transform into two and three pages. By the time I was six, I had many notebooks filled, filled with multiple stories that I would show my family.

Everyone was impressed. As a kid, my confidence just was not there. I was unaware of the value of time. I was unaware that your path to the top can be different. For many years, I wanted to fit in. I wanted to do what everyone else was doing.

Unexpected Divergence

I stopped chasing my dream because I felt that a sport would make me more money. I did not care about the craft. I cared about what came with being an elite athlete. I wanted that great treatment. I wanted to be loved. I wanted to be cheered on.

At four years old, I did not understand the power of words. I did not like to read. I thought reading was boring, but writing always excited me. I associated reading with school. The only times reading was required was during school.

I had a unique ability at a young age. With the mind that I have now, if I could go back, then, yes, I would invest more time. The only thing that I can do is think about the situation like this. In my past, I neglected my gift. I strayed from my dream. That caused me to gravitate towards something that was not meant for me.

I met failure. We will discuss that in later chapters. But when I received the vision and the reemergence of this gift, the only thing that I could do was pray and thank God. Thank God because I was allowed another chance. Another chance, although I turned my back on the vision at a young age. Could you imagine finding a way to make God believe in you again?

The Minimal Requirement

All it requires is the vision. Once the vision is received, you know you have it! Could you imagine receiving the vision and being set free? Now that I have this vision, I am set free from all the pain, rain, and years of going insane. I think about all the years that my mother had to struggle. I think about all the years that my mother had to figure out a way to put food on our plate. She did her best to put us in a good place, to levitate and elevate above everyone else.

I could not do it by myself. So now, I am in a position for my whole family to win. I came up with a vision, and this is only the beginning. I stand on this stage, and I look into the crowd and I can see you, Ma. I look into the crowd and I can see you, Pops. I can just feel the emotion in the room between us. I am the first person in my family to graduate. I do not know how much more I can thank the man above for allowing me to live a story like this.

Elevate Your Mind

I am a creator with a powerful message, and when you receive this message, you will not be the same again. All you will desire after this book is success. Many humans are blind. Reading is power. Knowledge is power. Wisdom is power.

I have wisdom for the masses. My knowledge will transform minds. This power is not given mistakenly. I have experienced things that people my age have not. I went to another level just off being myself. I sold a house when I was 19. I wrote my first book when I was 20.

I was 21 when I got my personal trainer certification. I am 22, graduating from college today, December 15, 2018. I do not know what this next step is going to lead to, but I know that all I can do is just chase my dream. My dream is to figure out a way to provide for my family.

My passion will become a message. My message will become a story. This story will not only inspire you, but the generations after you. I just want to live this life doing what I love to do.

Employees are Slaves

When I look at jobs that provide salaries, jobs that pay you hourly, I cannot fathom trading my time for the amount of money those jobs offer. To me, it is disrespectful. Average people do not realize that they are raised to be employees. They do not realize that they are raised to go into debt. A lot of people are not aware that they were raised to fit in with society and operate like a robot.

Some people get up, go to work, go back home, and go to sleep. That is their life. When I look at life, I do not want to do that. I want to travel to different countries. I want to make sure my mother never has to work again. I want to make sure the woman that I spend my life with, never has to worry about anything.

I go back into my past. I invite you to do the same. Start to collect your experiences. Put pieces of the puzzle together. Where you are today was determined many years ago. Are you happy with who you are today?

Inner Improvements

What can be improved? What do you wish you would have done differently? I wake up in the morning, look in the mirror, and tell myself how great I can be, and I give thanks to God for blessing me. God blessed me with an ability to see things that are invisible to everyone, only those with secret knowledge. Now that I have this knowledge of psychology, it is like an art when dissecting experiences, emotions and thoughts.

To connect past experiences with emotions, associating them with one another is difficult. That is why many people must visit a psychologist or a therapist. A therapist can go into your mind. They go into your memories, helping you connect dots.

Through writing, studies, and my abilities, I was able to do that for myself. Now, I can teach you to do the same. There is something within you that you are meant to do. You have a calling! My calling was to find you through these words and wake you up! There are signs, don't live blind! Blind from the fact that you must act.

Activate Inner Power

There is something that can activate within you, taking you to another level. Will you take advantage if I teach you? I was not aware when I was four. The people that doubted me were not aware that one day, they would be reading my book. In life, when you're different, you stand out. People follow those who stand out. People want to follow individuals who are sure of themselves.

Become aware of our inner desire. Humans have a natural desire to believe in something or someone. How can people believe in you if you do not believe in yourself? How can people know you are taking them somewhere great if you do not have a direction in mind? You see, I know exactly where I am going.

I have a plan that is clear. You can see it too. I have a physical manifestation of my whole vision in front of you. All it takes is for one person to be changed by *First in the Family*, then the whole world will take wind. I know there are people that need inspiration, I am the voice, leading them to peace.

When I look around me, no one is doing this. I am finding a way to share my powerful knowledge, books, and wisdom independently. It is 2018. We are living in a different generation. We have the knowledge and the tools to create what we want. We do not need anyone to take action and begin running towards our dreams.

Separation is Elevation

I do not have a desire to fit in with society or work for another man. That is not my passion. I am willing to take whatever risk there is to achieve my goals. My goals are to live financially free, with an ability to see the world, and take care of my family. I will do this, while doing something I love to do.

Going into a nine-to-five every day is not something that I love to do. Now for some people, that is their passion. They excel at that. For me, it is constructing stories that resonate with you on a deep, cognitive level. I will resonate with millions.

As I go back to my past, unlocking memories and experiences, I begin to see the destiny in this moment. When I was young, my mother would always tell me that I would be a writer. She knew I would inspire millions of people through my stories. When you are young, you do not understand life, making it is easy for a child to take advantage, or take life for granted because they have not experienced enough. That was the case for me, at least. I did not know enough.

There is something about parents. They have a source of wisdom that is mystic. It is a mystic power that my mother has, and she has a way of seeing things long before they happen. As I look back into my past, as you look into your past, realize that this moment was predetermined.

For me, it began when I was young. My mother had an intuition. A feeling that was beyond my understanding. She would tell me, but I never wanted to listen. I never understood that I would be able to fall in love with something such as writing, speaking, and telling stories.

Story Imparts Desire

There is a special influence that great writers have on society. A great story can change your life. Think about all

34

the inspirational stories that has motivated you to rise. It was a story that changed me, influencing this entire moment. It was a story about a marketing guru who launched an ad. It was a Lamborghini ad in a garage.

This was a popular video in 2015 and 2016. In this ad, he described his rags to riches story. The moral of the story was that reading books can take you from sleeping on a couch, to making millions of dollars, and owning multiple businesses. We all know that stories are exaggerated. I know that success does not come overnight.

From his story, I understood that self-education is the key. When you motivate yourself to learn new information, you gain control. It was the way he explained stories. It was the way he explained the power of reading a book. I picked up my first book at 18.

After reading *Think and Grow Rich* by Napoleon Hill, my life changed in so many ways. I began to read multiple books per week. I began to write down thoughts. I began to document everything. Over time, idea after idea led to actions, creating new experiences.

The more knowledge that I gained, the more I wanted to act on the acquired knowledge. After four years, I have read hundreds of books, acquired a certification along with a license and degree. Now, I am in the process of publishing my own book and selling it through my own company. Essentially, I am building my business at 22 years old. You must look at life and realize that you were raised to be great! We were all raised to be great, but it is up to us to find out what it takes.

"Empty is the feeling that you sometimes need to feel in order to achieve great things."

-Ken Viñales

3

Fatherless Adolescent

Growing up as a fatherless adolescent, as a minority in society, and in America, I knew of the barriers against me, at a young age. My mother enlightened me. The best part is overcoming the barriers. When you achieve things people never expected from you, there is a change in their perception towards you.

I am technically a psychologist. I am an expert of the mind that controls you and me. I became a psychologist for two reasons. Not only did it unlock my mind, I am now here, unlocking your mind. *First in the Family* is a therapy session. My words will be impressed on your mind forever, guiding you to grow and become the best version of yourself.

The more times you read *First in the Family*, the more you will be able to perceive. You will notice flaws as well as strengths. As you begin to experience more, gaining information and acquiring wisdom, *First in the Family*, will create more of an impression.

Outside the Moment

As an adolescent, it was confusing not growing up with a father. At that young age, my perception of the world was still in the process of forming. In other words, my anger began to build. Anger blinded me. I was unable to see that life was preparing me to be great.

This moment that you are living in right now has already happened. In fact, it was prepared many years ago. What does this mean? Your future is a reflection of your current. Your current is a reflection of your past.

Many things remain hidden. It is impossible to see what cannot be seen. You have already read my book, it has not just happened yet. The moment I received this vision, your life began to travel in a certain way. You will one day cross paths with me, which means that it is time you listen.

Now that I have your attention, *First in the Family*, will serve as a turning point. Your life will travel in a positive direction after you digest the wisdom embedded in this book. Have you ever had a therapy session? I have used our experiences to create a relatable story.

You and I have much in common. There are two possibilities. We may have met before, but you have never seen this side of me. The second possibility is that we have never met, but now you are being inspired by my words. That demonstrates the power of belief. When you have faith, true faith, anything is possible.

Male Figure

I grew up without a father. The only male I could look up to was my older brother, Kyle. He is 4 ½ years older than me. It was hard to look up to my oldest brother, Derek. Derek is nearly 10 years older than me. He was a hustler, who was involved in the cold, Detroit streets.

His life was not something that I could relate too. I was not able to look up to him, but there was always an admiration there. He was making thousands of dollars per day. As a young adolescent, it was mesmerizing seeing the rewards of a fast life.

Both of my brother's instilled many great qualities. The work ethic that I have today originated from both, but Kyle especially. Kyle had a strong influence on the confidence within me. I looked up to my brother because he was everything that everyone wanted to be.

Kyle is still a star athlete to this day. Growing up, he had the girls, knew his destination, and generated attention. Over time, he accomplished every single goal that he set, except for one: making it to the NBA. That is the only goal that my brother has left.

Although my brother has not made it to the NBA, his story shows the power of aiming for the moon. You may aim for the moon and make it, but if you do miss, there is a possibility to land amongst the stars. Today, he travels the world as an international basketball player. He could very well play in the NBA, but there are politics to everything.

Independence Is Key

I took this approach for one reason. When you take an independent approach to something, no one can tell you what to do. I am an independent author, consultant, and online business owner. Everything I created was with my own knowledge, skills, and money.

It is amazing to live in a generation where you can make a name for yourself, by yourself. During the process of my first book, there were many trails, but in time I learned things that were once invisible to me. As a 22-year-old, I know that finding financial freedom will come if I create my own streams of income.

Books provide a way for me to do that. Books can be used as creative ways to tell stories, impart ideas, knowledge, and/or wisdom. I write my own books. I edit my own books. I publish my own books. I market and sell my own books.

The hard thing about independence is taking blame. You must take blame for everything. I have decided what I want to be, meaning I am responsible for everything, successes and failures. Would you rather have control of your life or leave it in the hands of another man?

When you grow up as a fatherless adolescent, people do not expect you to be successful. If you knew the statistics for minorities that grew up without a father, then you will understand my ambition. I am motivated because statistics say I would be behind bars just like the rest of my family. I was not supposed to be here, on this stage. I was not supposed to be this wise. Somehow, I am here, collecting this degree, communicating with you, and confident that these events are meant to be.

Blessing in Disguise

As a fatherless adolescent, it was hard to comprehend the meaning of life. When a parent abandons a child, it is hard for that child to see the deeper meaning. Everything in life happens the way it is supposed to happen, when it is supposed to happen. For many years, I was mad at my father. Angry at his decision to turn to drugs, leading him to get trapped in a system that would eventually trap my brother, Derek. The system almost trapped my brother Kyle. What if the system makes its way to me? With time, the invisible becomes visible. With time the stars align.

Have you ever looked outside the box, from inside of the box? In other words, think about a situation that was not your fault. Now, think of another situation that did not go your way. Hold both experiences in your mind, and take blame. Figure out a way to make that situation your fault. The moment I began to take ownership, my responsibilities increased, but my mind became free. Allow me to explain.

It is true that my father battled with drugs, demons and the prison system for many years. That situation was out of my control, but somehow I found a way to take blame, repainting the situation. Instead of blaming him for his wrong doings, I began to thank God for keeping my father away. Away until he became the man he needed to be.

You see, there are so many different perspectives that you can look at life from. Instead of looking from the perspective of being a fatherless adolescent or a motherless adolescent in a negative light, you can turn that negative energy into positive energy. I thank God for bringing my father back as a new man. My father is back in my life today, as a new man, with a different type of focus.

The crazy thing about life is that the future has already happened. We have already lived and died. Your death has already happened in another time period. Your dream is already a reality in another time period. The point is that my father had a dream to recreate himself and make up for lost time.

Throughout his years of drug use, it was hard to imagine us being in the same room. Today, we have been in the same room. We are building a relationship, which shows the power of faith. He envisioned something, and although it was difficult for me to see, it had already happened and now I am living in the time, creating a story that will inspire you.

I will go into more detail in chapter 6. In short, there was much anger within. My mind wanted to know why, but only time could reveal the answer. I questioned the order of events. What are you supposed to do when you search, but continue to come up short?

Blinded Desires

When you are unaware of who you are internally, subconsciously, you live a life, striving for things that are not meet for you. Without the proper guidance, it is easy for a young person to veer off on the wrong path. Minorities in America are a prime example. We lose our father to the system, leaving us with a struggling mother. Do you know what it is like to feel hopeless, watching your mother suffer in pain?

• know yourself

The cycle happens because nobody likes to sit back and watch their mother go insane. Crimes are oftentimes committed out of fear and hopelessness. Do you know what it's like to feel like you are not enough? All through life, I watched my mother go through so much pain and rain, just to create all these gains. I was given an opportunity to make a way, so how could I not have faith?

Right now, I am on a stage, collecting a degree, a degree that I am not supposed to have. I came to college confused. It was hard to envision making it out, yet now I am making it out. There were times where I was confused about my next step. Fears even began to grow.

Life is amazing. Time is magic. Put something out into the universe, pray on it, then act on it. I figured out a way to grow this vision, and over time, day-by-day, step-by-step, everything is now beginning to manifest. Do you know what is it like to live life blessed, knowing that you don't have to live with stress?

Meeting My Father

This story is an inspiration for anyone. Have you ever seen someone lose it all, just to get it all back? I talk to my father every day now, to make sure everything is going okay now. When I was younger, I never understood that a day like November 6, 2017, would happen. I met my father on my 21st birthday. For so many years, I lived with so much anger inside. My 21st birthday was a true testament to forgiveness.

It took much will-power to put my pride aside, but the end result was being wise inside. Pain creates wisdom. I have experienced pain. From my pain, you can gain invaluable information, experiences, and knowledge that will help you stay sane. *First in the Family* is designed to connect to your experiences, dissecting information you never considered.

Some people have an inability to look at themselves from outside of themselves. In fact, it was difficult for me at one point. The day I changed my perspective about my father's absence was the day my life started to change. Think about a heartbreaking situation, now shift all of the rain and pain into a gain. There is a way to turn every negative situation, in your life, into a positive awakening.

Incomplete Internally

The day my father stepped away from me, I felt incomplete. I was lost. I was hopeless. I was angry inside, but one day God sent me a message. That message was that people can evolve. People can become someone you have never met before, whether it is in a positive or negative light.

The day my father stepped away, he became someone my family had never known. The day he stepped back into our lives, he returned as a completely different, evolved man. What that showed me was that sometimes you have to go through a little rain and a little pain to achieve numerous gains.

As I stand on this stage, I look back at all the sacrifices that I have made to experience this moment. I sacrificed time, women, friends, money, sanity, all just to create a magical experience and inspiration throughout generations after generations. There are some people right now desiring to accomplish their dream, but confused on how it should be done.

For many years, I was confused about what my next move in life would be. I was not sure who I was, but as I go back and retract all my experiences, something begins to surface. I began to see that God knows what is best for me. Timing is everything. He places us in the right place at the right time.

Release Anger Within

When I was growing up, I was always mad at my father. I thought he was a deadbeat father. Who would teach me how to be a man if my father could not? If my father could not be a man himself, how could I? There are so many thoughts that clouded my judgment.

We are a reflection of our parents. Our perception is determined by our environment and the humans who nurture us. I was not nurtured properly because I was fatherless. The only male I could look up to was my brother, Kyle, and that is what I did. My mother and brother kept me on the right path. They kept my head straight.

In due time, I knew I could be great. What I was unable to see as a young adolescent, was the power of God. God removed my father because he was not right. He was on drugs. He was in and out of jail. He was doing things that he was not supposed to do.

Seasons of Reasons

If he was not removed, there was a possibility of a subconscious influence occurring. He was not in my life for a reason. In fact, he was gone for 60 seasons. 15 years later, he returned as a new man. What that showed me is that I can do anything I put my mind to. I'm inspired by my father's story because any man that can find motivation after losing everything, but their knowledge, is a man that can always inspire.

I was young when Derek, my oldest brother received his first prison sentence. My oldest brother and I have the same father. We have a different mother. He was heavily influenced by my father. My father taught him the ways of the streets. Derek took that, ran with the knowledge, and created his own destiny.

It was only a matter of time before my brother ended up in a situation behind bars. As an adolescent, if you witness your own blood and flesh enter prison, you begin to think that history may repeat itself. Do you know what it's like to grow up thinking that your life has a possibility to end up like your father's, who is a multiple count felon? And then your brother's, who is also a multiple count felon? → Subconsious fear, turns into reality.

Beat the Odds

I always had a cloud over my head, but somehow my mother, the way she raised me, made sure that my head was on straight. She raised me to believe in myself. She raised me to use my passion and gift to create something that nobody else could do. I took her knowledge. I am currently running with it.

I'm standing on this stage, collecting my degree, thinking about all the memories, all the times that I cried at night, all the times that I wished I could go back in time and fix my mistakes. I stand on this stage, looking into the crowd, seeing all the excited and nervous faces. I look within myself and see greatness.

Unaware of Me

The students on the stage don't know that I am the next great writer. No one right now can see that I have something manifesting right before their very eyes, and one day they may all read this book. You see, I came out of nowhere, just like a surprise, and going about life with a different sight, quite sure that no one understands why this is so right. If your vision does not scare you it is not large enough.

I'm 22 years old, around the same age as Derek, when he was arrested and entered prison. I'm the same age as my older brother, Kyle, who was arrested and later expelled from school when he was a senior in college. My family has been through some things. We haven't been through the most, we haven't been through the least, but what I can tell you is that our story is different.

Every day, I think about what happened in my life. I think about how my father returned as new man. I am inspired by his will-power. I am inspired because there are not many people who can rise through the ashes after hitting rock bottom. I am in the process of doing something no one has ever done. I stand on this stage, smiling because I know I am the one.

"Faith has a way of taking control of your mind, fueling you to continue, during times where doubt tries to enter."

-Ken Viñales

4

Faith

I stand on this stage, looking into my past, realizing that I was not supposed to be here. I come from a father who is a multiple count felon. My mother barely graduated high school, yet she birthed a genius. I look at the results of hard work, time, and patience, and that is when I begin to reflect on the things that are right here in front of me.

When you are living in the moment, it is difficult to detect certain things. One component is imperative. You must go into your past, reflecting on experiences with a different mindset. I go back into experiences, observing with a scientific mind, uncovering information from a more mature perspective.

Understanding the power of faith is vital to success. When you have faith, true faith and desire, there is nothing that can stop the force within you. I have witnessed faith take control many times in, not only my life, but those

· analytical perspective

around me. I witnessed my father take everything from my mother, from her savings to her dignity. One thing that she never lost was faith. One thing that she never lost was her experiences nor her wisdom. No matter what you lose in this life, you cannot lose what you have learned.

Expand Your Reality

When you take that into consideration, many things in the world begin to open up. As a young black man in America, the inner cities are not tailored for minorities to make it out. The creation of America's ghettos were designed to inhibit those raised there to have an equal chance. Sociology explains what happens when you remove resources, jobs, and education from a community. Have you studied sociology on a scientific level?

I was born in an inner city, Detroit, Michigan. My father and mother were raised in Detroit, Michigan. My oldest brother was raised in Detroit, Michigan. When you come from that type of environment, you see things that humans should not see.

You witness murder. You witness mothers abandoning their children. Drugs are in childrens possession. There are things that can cause you to become psychotic. The system designed communities in a certain way to trap men like me.

Once trapped inside of the system, it is hard to make it out; it is hard to see outside of that reality. When I look into my past, I see that my father came from prisons. My father was once trapped inside the system. The system trapped him and my oldest brother. What effect do you think this has on an adolescent's mind?

I stand on this stage, looking into the crowd, receiving the smiles from my mother, father and other family members. This is a monumental achievement. Have you ever sacrificed everything, just to see your family proud? As I stand on this stage, I cannot help but think about how far I have come.

Vital to Success

It was my freshman year when I thought about dropping out. The problem with dropping out is that you create a habit. My mom taught me that you must always finish what you start! It was my freshman year when I realized it may not be possible to make it out of my mother's house.

Worry began to build. I began to think about the future in a negative state of mind. However, one day, everything changed. I realized that my story was different. I realized that my story was going to provide me a way to take care of my family, in a way that no one in my family has ever done.

In society, people look at you strange when you choose a different way. College students eventually go off, get a job, living the rest of their life in debt. I did not want to do that. I wanted to live a life that was free. A life where I could travel, own real estate in multiple countries, while taking care of my parents.

Let Go, Let Life

I did not know how it would happen. I just had faith. I had faith that my experiences would lead me to this day, the day that I find you, connecting through the form of words, hooking your mind. Right now, I am imparting wisdom and experiences onto you that you will be able to benefit from. Think about a time where you have lost everything. A time where you hit rock bottom. Are you experiencing that now? Are you overcoming something today?

In a moment of pain, we experience a lot of emotions, which blind us from the truth. The truth is that no matter what you lose or sacrifice, every loss comes with an equivalent gain. The more you lose, the more you gain. Never lose sight of the long-term rewards that follow.

Witness the Unreal

Life is an equation. There are certain operations that work, and there are certain operations that fail. I do not want to work a job. I want to inspire people. I want to show you that it is possible to turn your dreams into a reality.

My dream is larger than life. My dream includes connecting me to millions. Millions of people. Millions of dollars. Millions of dreams. I have inspired people that I have not physically met. I have inspired people who are not alive.

This route is not common. Has anyone else ever considered this? Am I the only one that has taken action on this? That is the power of faith. I have faith because of my parents, especially my father.

My father has shared many stories with me since his return. Many of the conversations that my father and I have resulted in my perspective being expanded. When you witness someone lose everything, meaning they lose faith, hope, savings, sense of self, etc., only to evolve into a new person, it inspires you in a way that nothing else can. My father's return inspired me!

Prison's Power

I saw my father lose it all. When he went to prison, it changed him. He was not able to continue his life. In the prison cell, he realized many things about society. He was no longer able run away from his demons. It took him 22 years to get his life together, but when he came back, he was a new man.

The power of faith is something that everyone needs to understand. It is sad that not everyone can. Many people have false hope. They try to hide it, but on the inside it eats them up. They try being positive. They try acting happy. They try to seem like they have it all figured out, but deep down inside, they lack faith.

When a person lacks faith, their mind will not know when to keep going. Perseverance is fueled by faith. When things get tough, if you have faith, your mind will not allow you to walk away. When things get tough, if you do not have faith, your mind will stray.

↑ false consciousness

When I first entered college, I did not have faith. I did not have faith in myself. I did not have faith in my future. I did not have faith in my abilities. I have grown. Reaching this milestone has opened my mind even more.

Tell the Universe

I want to be the most powerful, influential writer of my generation. When I look around me, there are not many who have taken this path. My story resonates with you. No one around me has done what I am doing, so it is hard to look for guidance. I come from un-education. I come from the prison system.

I was affected by the prison system at a young age. That happened the day I saw my father in a cage. Do you know what it's like to live your life, knowing that history can repeat itself? There is still a possibility that history can somehow repeat itself. I am doing everything in my power to break the generational curse. That is why today is so powerful and can influence people through time. Generations after me have been affected by *First in the Family*.

A Strong Connection

When you read *First in the Family*, you feel a connection, you are drawn to the information. When you reach the end of these words, the way you see the world, yourself, and the people around you, will not be the same. I have primed your mind to see things in a different way.

I don't know why I was called to do something so grand. If you receive a vision, the last thing you can do is run. I will not run away from my calling or my purpose. I will embrace it. There will be mistakes along the way, but that is where faith comes into play.

Those before You

Study those who have come before you. There are always going to be roadblocks and detours, but that is the fun of any journey. As you rise, there will be forces trying

Know what not to do

56

to bring you down. Forces in place to turn you around. As long as you have faith and keep your mind on the prize, there is nothing that can stop you from enhancing your mind. Desires manifest when action is combined with time. By the time, I live out this journey, connecting with millions, I will have learned a lot about life. I can make you a better version of yourself.

Organic Growth

With this degree in psychology, I was able to go into my mind and unlock the way I see the world. I have this understanding of the world, myself, and society. There is nothing that can stop me from accomplishing my goal.

In life, what you must realize is that organic and natural is the best way to go. People try anything to achieve attention. "The more attention that I can get, the better I will feel about myself." Those are the thoughts of those who lack faith. When you lack faith, you are not sure of yourself. When you lack faith, you are not sure of your future. That is why you must reflect.

When you reflect on your life experiences with a more mature mind, you can pick things apart. You will discover things that were invisible during the moment. For instance, your life today created your future. What you are living today is a manifestation of the past.

Lack of Faith

You must understand that life works in a certain way. People who lack faith or confidence rarely succeed in life. How can other people believe in you if you do not believe in you? When people don't believe in themselves, they cast their perception of life onto other people. When ideas are shared with someone who lacks faith, they are likely to doubt, because they doubt their own abilities.

The more faith that you have, the more your mind will have to find a way, no matter what. When you experience trials and tribulations, your mind will not fold. Your mind will find creative solutions to overcome those problems and difficulties. Over the past four years, I have encountered many roadblocks in this journey.

Surpass the Obstacles

It years trying to figure out who I am, and what I wanted to become. When you decide who you want to become, and when you want to become it, your life will immediately get better. The problem that most people have is that they cannot choose. They cannot choose a major. They cannot choose a field to work in. They cannot choose who they want to be. They cannot choose who they want to be with.

People that lack faith are indecisive and indecisiveness is the number one inhibitor to success. When you are uncertain of yourself, you sway back and forth between judgments, trying to decide on which route to take. When you lock in and focus, with a definite goal in mind, there is nothing that can stop or deter you. There is no one that can inhibit you, except you.

As I stand on this stage, I realize that the day has come. I must dive into the ocean and dominate. Dominate my market. Dominate my field. Dominate my niche and become the best I can be. This is not something that most people dream to do, but for me, I'll be happy if I can write and travel the world. For me, I'll be happy if I can write and take care of my family. It is going to happen because I have words, I have wisdom that people need to hear.

I stand on this stage, looking into the crowd, knowing that no one knows. I am the next great writer of this generation, but as of now I am unknown. It will take time, but with time, everything I have in my mind will be mine.

"Unlock your mind to free yourself from society's illusion."

-Ken Viñales

5

Illusion

A false belief or an idea, in other words, an illusion, is something that the untrained eye has trouble seeing. Many humans have a hard time seeing through an illusion that they desperately want to believe in. At 18 years old, we enter something called emerging adulthood. I realized that I was no longer a child, but I was not quite yet an adult.

When you realize that your parents will no longer be able to provide for you, it creates dissonance in your mind. I was slowly entering the real world, where responsibilities were a reality. In this time of emerging adulthood, our mind begins to evolve. Our perceptions grow.

For me, it was realizing that life was not what I once thought it was going to be. This illusion of life makes it hard for people to see themselves from outside themselves. What this means is that many people have a hard time understanding what is really going on.

As you know, I did not achieve my dream of playing professional basketball. That hurt me. It made me very confused. For a long time, I did not know what my next step would be. Have you ever spent years building something, just to have it taken away in a day?

Break Free

When you are lost and searching for yourself, searching for your soul, searching for your purpose, it is easy to get caught up in illusions. People who are lost get caught up in what everyone else is doing. The reason is because they are so disconnected from their soul, their spirit!

My journey through college helped me turn my whole life around. As I reflect, I begin to see where illusions may have been created. With that information, I freed my mind from the illusion of society, the illusion of college, the illusion of following.

Humans are biologically designed to follow. I do not want to be a follower. I do not want to do what everyone else is doing. I do not want to walk the same path as another man. Who do you see, when you look into the mirror? I see myself being great. I see the people around me being great. I see the future as something magical.

Wake Up!

When you are trapped inside of an illusion, your mind is asleep. If the illusion seems to be tested, everything goes left. In an illusion, fake seems real, real seems fake. The danger is that nothing is real. You are in a walking dream. You are asleep. No matter how much you think you are awake, no matter how much you think you are doing the right things, when trapped inside of an illusion, you are falsely believing in something that is just not real.

The transition that I am going to make is about college. A lot of students, once we graduate high school, do what everyone around us does. Everyone around me was going to college. My mother influenced me to go to college. I had no choice. When I got to college, I was lost, I was confused. Was this where I wanted to be? Is this who I am becoming? How will college benefit my life?

Find the Answers

I began to ask myself questions like that. The more I questioned myself, the more questions started to appear. The more the hidden became the visible, the more I separated myself. As I elevated and separated, I was able to see things that I was previously blind to.

For instance, many people, today, are going into large sums of debt, just to acquire a sheet of paper. A sheet of paper that says hours were inside of an institution, certifying them in a certain field. The deeper I began to go into college, the more of a connection I made to the government, prisons, colleges, and the army. All of these programs were designed by the government. Allow me to explain.

These institutions all have a similar effect. They all brainwash you. They all reprogram your subconscious, causing you to unconsciously gravitate towards certain things. The army programs you to die for your country. The prison system programs you to commit more crimes, so they can make you work for pennies. School trains you to work for companies and organizations.

Before I made any wrong choices, I always questioned myself: "How much will it benefit you?" "Do you know the history?" "What will you do, once you accomplish what you envision?"

In the beginning, I was in the illusion that college would determine my success. I was in the illusion that college would benefit me more than it really could. As I cross the stage today, I realize that I broke myself away from the illusion, setting myself up for a successful future. I beat the odds and so can you!

Uncertainty of Life

Throughout my college journey, I have had a dialogue with many students. There are small subtle signs that I receive, dictating that they are still confused about their next move. The small signs are more powerful than spoken words.

Many college students and college graduates are angry. Angry at the amount of debt that they have acquired. Angry for the choices they made, desiring to go back to the past so they can reconstruct their future. I wanted to avoid that by any means.

I stand here today, on this stage, looking into the crowd and seeing the joy on my mother's and my father's face. It just makes me realize that they do not know. No one knows I am a legend in the making. This is only the beginning. They do not know the extent to their son's genius.

Their son broke free from the illusion. I no longer feel that college determines success. It is the individual. College is a tool that you must know how to use. For most people, college just brings on years of debt, which translates into depression.

We have choices in life. Sometimes we are put in certain predicaments and positions where the outside forces overpower our strength. But at the end of the day, a lot of what determines our outcome is the action backed behind our desires, prayers, and wishes.

Solitary Confinement

In the last four years, I have spent much time locked inside of a room, writing and reading books, studying those who have reached success many years before me. I am a student of knowledge. Through my years of research, there is some common denominator when it comes to successful people.

Success is a mindset. Success is a lifestyle. The mindset that you need for success cannot fall victim to illusions. It cannot fall victim to what everyone else in society is doing. I almost fell a victim to the illusion, but I created a way for myself. I created a way for my mother. I created a way that allowed me to be debt-free, with degrees, certifications, published books and licenses, all within four years.

Not only that, I was able to find my passion. I was once under the illusion that the more money you make in your life, the happier you will become. Do you value the craft or the money? When you remove money from the equation, are you still able to be happy? I found myself chasing a dream that was for someone else.

My brother's dream, since diapers, was to be an all-star. He wanted to be the best basketball player he could be. For that reason, his journey led him to his dream.

Youngest Sibling Advantage

As a younger sibling, you look up to your older siblings. You try to learn as much as you can. I looked up to Kyle, my older brother, trying my hardest to follow in his footsteps. Little did I know, his shoes were too big for me to fill.

Now, today, at 22 years old, as the first person in my family, to reach this type of milestone, I look back, seeing that I was under an illusion. I believed money equaled happiness. Are you aware of the illusion of money. Money does not equal happiness and peace. I once believed that if you strive for something that is not popular or sought out to do, then finding success will be much difficult. In actuality, that belief is false. When there is less competition you can dominate a certain market or niche.

After writing for thousands of hours, after constructing and manufacturing multiple books, I see that, for me, my dream is about finding a way to make the people around me better. I wanted to find a way to make the people around me smile. I wanted to find a way to help you grow.

What I learned about myself through these last four years is that you cannot get caught up in what everyone else is doing, or the timing in them, receiving their blessings. We all receive our blessings at different times, because we are all on a separate journey.

Trust Your Process

Someone may receive their purpose at 2 years old. And it may take another person until they are 25 years old. In short, just because someone else is receiving a blessing, that you may wish you had, does not mean it was meant for you to have. Timing is everything, trust your process.

For a long time, I was under the impression that I needed success immediately. I wanted to get rich overnight. I did not want to take the steps one by one. I did not want to take my days step by step. I wanted to receive everything at once.

Take a step back, studying those around you, who reached some success before you. Better your connection with your mother. Improve your relationship with your father. When I reconnected with my father, life took a positive shift. I began to see so many things differently. The illusion is so strong that when you are under one, you do not even know you're under it. That is what makes illusions dangerous.

Hierarchy of Power

In society, we are all under an illusion. Big corporations have us under an illusion. The media has us under an illusion. Our perceptions are manipulated at a young age. When we are babies, only our parents have an influence over us. As we enter society, our minds are quickly captured and become a part of a higher mind.

I went to college for computer science. I changed my major four times. After changing my majors four times, I discovered psychology, something that gives me meaning. My purpose was born. Psychology is something that not only benefits me, but also the people around me.

Reason for School

My knowledge and wisdom has improved who people are on the inside. Psychology has helped me unlock my mind. My mind is completely open. My mind is completely free. I know that what I see is going to happen. I know that what I see can manifest into something magical.

Have you ever closed your eyes and said those words? Before I could reach you, I had to free myself from the chains that society had wrapped around me. I had to break free from the chains that school wrapped around me.

School does not teach you how to be creative. School actually strays away from creativity. The higher you go, the more math and science classes you begin to take. Have you thought about that? Why do you think school is designed that way?

As you get older, the less art is incorporated into the systems. Schools do not want to exercise the right brain. The right brain is responsible for creativity. Math and science exercise the left brain. Corporations do not want people thinking outside the box, because when you begin to think outside the box, you create an organization and compete with them.

Refrain from Loans

I did not rush into school. I refused to go into debt. There are ways of getting an education that do not cost hundreds of thousands of dollars. Many students are so excited to get away from their parents after high school that they go out of state and take out loan after loan. With that comes partying and fun that are outside of getting an education.

I stayed at home and attended the local community college for my first two years. It cost no money. I was able to save up my money and come up with a plan that included you. When you are on the journey to somewhere great, doing things that people in society have never done, it is going to be difficult, at first, to understand the capacity of your actions. With time, you will see. That's why reflection is key. Reflection breaks the illusion. Reflection helps you become your true self.

Reincarnation

I like to think of myself as a phoenix. No matter how many times I die, fail, or fall, I am always going to get back up, recreate myself, and prevail. With an illusion, once you lose control, it's hard to get it back. Capitalize while you have control.

Out of high school, very few people have many responsibilities. Very few people have loads of bills. Very few people need hundreds of thousands of dollars out of high school. Life is more than the moment you are in. Plan for the generations after you. Make different decisions.

I spend hours writing. I spend hours documenting thoughts. Our thoughts are so important. Thoughts create our reality. If you aren't controlling your thoughts, someone else is. Do you want to fall even deeper into the illusion that big name companies and big name marketers are creating?

The people at the top have knowledge. They have an understanding of psychology that regular people like us do not have. I began to ask myself, "What can I do to find myself?" My only option was to soul-search. This led me to discovering who I am, which directed me right to you.

Use Your Past

Go back into your past. Reflect on all the old experiences. You will begin to pick up things that you could not see before. Once you start to see things that were once invisible, you break down the illusion. It is so amazing that I was able to go to college and graduate debt-free; go to college and acquire a real estate license; go to college and acquire a personal trainer certification; go to college and graduate with a degree in psychology; and go to college and have multiple unpublished books and one published book.

I did all of this without acquiring any debt. I did all this and wrote a book about how I did all of this. Time is a wonderful thing. Time has a way of revealing things that were hidden for a long time. I was hiding for a long time, but now it's time to show the world who I really am. What is done in the dark always comes to the light.

"Take all the blame, free your soul."

-Ken Viñales

6

2016

If one of your parents were absent, then you know the pain. If you have never experienced this, then I am sure you can imagine. The events after my father exited my family's life carved a deep wound. For many years, I contemplated in despair, unable to process many of my thoughts and emotions. Why would a man ever abandon his own flesh and blood? As much as I tried to ignore the fact, every day, anger continued to build.

One thing that always stayed on my mind was how we share a birthday. He was born November 6, 1962. I was born November 6, 1996. After 20 years, I still have yet to meet anyone who shares a birthday with one of their parents, which has always been fascinating. The seizing of a relationship can be difficult to cope with.

Unforgettable Wound

There were many times, at night, where I dreamed of having genuine father-son moments. There were times where I dreamed of my mother never having to struggle. As I type these words, we have yet to meet face to face. We have exchanged a dialogue, but the last time we were in the same room was nearly 15 or more years ago.

The way that he left, left a strong impression on my subconscious mind. After so many years, the situation is long behind me, but the wounds will never fade. At one point, there was much hatred. Today, there is no hate, only difficulty when I type these words. Can you imagine feeling empty for many years? Do you know what it is like to long for love that has no chance of returning?

Emotions have a way of determining our actions and influencing our mood. I tried to hide the hurt on the outside, but my emotions directed me to act, outwardly, in negative ways. As an adolescent, going through grade school, I would trouble would always find me. At the time my father left, I was six, today I am 20. At six years old, it was impossible for me to heal my mother's wound.

My mom divorced my father and through that divorce she lost everything. She lost her savings. She lost her happiness. She nearly lost her mind. Although my mother hit rock bottom, somehow, she managed to retain her ambition.

My mother is the strongest woman I have ever met. Could you imagine the love of your life turning into your worst nightmare? Have you ever witnessed someone reveal the mask they were hiding behind? Do you know what it is like when the person you thought you would spend your life with becomes someone you never knew? When my mother and father divorced, he stole everything from her. Her dignity, her savings, her life and all of her trust.

Behind the Mask

My mom found out my father was a heavy drug addict midway through their marriage. His addiction to drugs drove their marriage to the ground. When my parents went their separate ways, I was unable to cope with the feelings that I was experiencing. Emotions clouded my thoughts, which led to negative actions in social settings, especially school.

As I look back into my past, with a mature mind, there is something you can learn about your own life. I have an older brother, named Kyle Viñales. Today, he travels the world for a living, as an international basketball player. When people meet him today, all they see is the achievements and the skills that he possesses. What they do not see is the story that led him to the path he is on today.

I will tell you his story, how it affected mine and how all of this relates to you. The day my father stepped away, many seeds were planted. I began associating negative actions to situations that elicit feelings of abandonment, distrust and loneliness. School suspensions became common. I would fight. I would disrespect teachers. I began to lose my passion and gravitate towards things outside of my nature.

Transform Negative Emotions

Kyle was not the best student either. He also had a very bad temper. The only difference is that he learned how to channel his emotions, much better than me, at a younger age. Instead of acting outwardly, he used basketball to channel his emotions. As time went on, his emotions converted into a love for basketball. His love for basketball grew because it was the only thing that could ease his pain.

Today, he still puts his heart and soul into basketball. The reason is because it was the only thing there for him when he was down and out, other than family. My story and results were much opposite from my brother. Mentally, my mind was affected in a different way. My anger sent me on an out-of-control spiral.

Emotions have a way of turning us inward. At that age, how was I supposed to understand that anger was clouding my vision? How was I supposed to understand that harboring hate, only results in looking outwardly, through the lens of that emotion? In other words, I would cry easily, break easily, and lose my temper rapidly.

When people are under the spell of negative emotions, they are unable to see themselves from outside of themselves. Everything that is perceived, is perceived with the judgment of that emotion. For instance, I did not understand how to take ownership. Subconsciously, I saw the world through a skewed lens. If I did not have control over my father leaving, did I have control over any events in life?

Confusion Took Control

Another result of my father's absence was a weakness of mind. When things became difficult, it was easy to give up. The connection comes from not having meaning. As humans, we yearn for meaning, but after so many years without answers, it can be tempting to lose faith. Every day, I asked myself different questions, but it only caused my confusion to grow more and more.

Why did he have to take everything from us? Why did he leave the way he did? Is he going to return? Why did he have to ruin our family? These questions were a daily occurrence.

It created a roller-coaster of emotions. It was easy for me to lose control, which makes looking back into the past so intriguing. The only person I ever showed respect to was my mother. When it came to authorities, it was difficult for me to abide by any rules for an extended period of time.

The After Effect

Unlike my brother, my anger was not invested into something positive. I acted outwardly, in negative ways, towards other people. I was not seeing situations for what they were. I was seeing situations for what I wanted them to be. In other words, my pain caused me to seek outcomes that were negative. It was a tough transition for me. There was a struggle to handle the surge of emotions.

A few years after my parents divorced, my mother remarried and moved us out of the inner-city. There were immediate changes. My brother and I had to accept someone new into our life. We also moved to a nearby suburb, which resulted in transferring schools. Elementary was difficult because I attended three different schools in five years. Every time I would make new friends and get used to a system, everything would drop, we would move, and things would change.

When my mom finally remarried, we ended up in a nearby suburb nearly 15 minutes from Detroit. When we first moved to the new city, it was a shock for me. I was used to being around a certain demographic of people. The new city consisted of majority whites, with very few blacks. In fact, during the time we moved, there were less than 5 black families in the entire sub-division.

Sudden Culture Shock

My brother adjusted well. He instantly flourished, while I struggled. The school I transferred to was much different than I was used to. I was in a culture shock. Students talked different. Classmates acted and dressed much different. As soon as I made the transfer, many students were slow to warm-up. I was one of the four black people in the whole grade. There were less than 10 black students in the entire school. I hated it, everything about it. I did not feel like I could be myself.

When I would act as myself, many would talk about me. Around that time, I was trying to find myself. I tried playing an instrument. Experimented with rapping. The only other option that seemed viable was basketball. At the time, I knew I could write, but it was not something that many people dream to do, so it didn't cross my mind as a career dream.

Two Different Outcomes

For my brother, it was different. He was an instant basketball star. We transferred when I was in fourth grade. He was in the eighth grade. As soon as my brother's school basketball season started, he shined. Within a short period of time, he quickly became known by everyone in the school district. The amount of love he received for doing what he loved seemed unreal.

As a younger brother, I wanted to feel that same type of love. By the fifth grade, I decided to play basketball Initially, I did not take it as serious as my '

brother has a tremendous ·

adopted o‸‸

treatment, instead of looking at my own weaknesses and changing my habits, I blamed everyone around me.

In middle school, my attitude worsened. Trouble was finding its way to me more than ever. I had no control over my anger. There were so many things I was frustrated about, but I refused to talk about my problems. I did not understand that holding emotions in, only makes life more difficult. Little things made me mad. My mother would receive phone calls nearly every day from the school, then one day everything changed.

The First Message

One situation freed my soul from the chains of anger. From that moment until graduating high school, my 'de and outlook on life transformed. On July 4, 2010, d a message on Facebook. A message from was not expecting to hear from at all. It had s since the last time we had ever spoken or face.

day vividly. It was a normal Sunday in the family room spending time en Facebook notified me and formed me that I received a eone was my biological gan to pour. Not only that, it was finally my opportunity to speak my mind to the man that caused so much pain.

Before responding, I read the message aloud to my mother who was sitting right next to me.

He wrote,

"I know that your mama don't won't you to communicate with me. But I'm not a bad person. I hope one day we'll be able to communicate and you can get to know me for yourself. I found you/Kyle and Derek on Facebook. I'll continue to pray that we will one day have a relationship. Good luck in High School. I know that you'll succeed in all that you attempt because you have my blood. God Bless!!! Regards,"

It was hard reading that message the first time. Emotions took control of me like a hijacking. I was mad, yet happy. Happy because I could finally inflict pain in his life, like he caused in our life. Mad because he had stepped away and never showed any desire to heal the wounds that he created.

I then replied:

"i dont want a relationship with you u should have been in my life wen i was a baby now im 13 years old and u wanna get back in my life its too late now. wen i become succesful you'll regret the day that you left."

Writing this book has been the first time I looked at the messages since the day it happened and it is crazy to read. We messaged one another for two days. He tried justifying his actions, but they made no sense. I won't go into too much detail, but in that moment, things were said that needed to be. After our dialogue on Facebook, it seemed as though my anger slowly began to fade away.

The last message that I sent to him was on July 6, 2010, shortly before he was incarcerated.

The message reads:

"Well you aint dad to me cause you aint do nothin that a real dad is suppose to do. So you derek to me.. And wat makes you thinkk that not being in your son(s) life was the best idea you definitly are not a good father at all!. Your not my dad."

As I look back, the messages display a teenage boy hurting, yet trying to hide his pain, by creating pain in the person that walked away from him. Has someone ever hurt you, creating a desire for revenge?

Remove Shoulder Weight

When the last message sent, it was as if a weight had been lifted. That day, things began making a small shift. My temper was no longer out of control. Slowly, things were improving. My brother was doing well in basketball; he was on his way to college to play basketball. Our family was finally starting to come together. We were finally getting used to the guy that my mom married. My relationship with Kyle made a huge turn. The more I took basketball serious, the closer our bond became.

We began to connect on a deep level. The result was less arguments and more guidance. There is no way to predict what will take place next, no matter how hard you try. Right before high school, I was able to see the results of my brother's hard work. His journey inspired me to improve my skillset so I began investing more hours. Everything was beginning to fall into place, but overnight, life took a turn.

Result of Intuition

Before high school could start, there was a major change of course. A month before my brother was supposed to be going away to college, he had some sort of epiphany. The school that he had signed his national letter of intent for, he no longer wanted to attend. The school he had originally committed to was a division two school, but he wanted to play division one. The problem with this is that he was under contract and did not have any division one offers. With a sudden change of mind and limited options, there was not much time.

Since a young age, he always dominated higher ranked competition. His desire to succeed originated from being overlooked. He was not highly ranked due to lack of exposure. When you are not highly ranked, it does not allow for the same opportunities. It was sometime in the end of July 2010 when he changed his mind.

The day he told my mom, she instantly got active. Her first call was to the coaches of Grand Valley State University. After almost an hour of demanding, they refused to release my brother from his contract. My mother was furious, but more motivated to help my brother break free from the situation. For the rest of the summer, her time was dedicated to finding a different route.

Never Stop Believing

A week before time ran out, a random number suddenly called my mother. After making a few phone calls, she discovered the prep school route. Prep schools for athletes are private boarding schools that have different rules than public schools. A school from Pennsylvania, called The Phelps School offered my brother a scholarship. If he took the offer, he would become a fifth year senior, voiding his collegiate contract with Grand Valley State University.

As a younger brother, observing this process had a unique effect on my mindset. When my brother had his epiphany, he did not have a plan. All he knew is that he wanted more. As a younger brother, I was seeing life happen, years before it happened, through both of my older brothers. When he received another chance to obtain a division one offer, the power of faith emerged.

Trip to Pennsylvania

I remember the day we drove to Malvern, Pennsylvania to drop my brother off. It was my brother, my mom, my step dad and I. The drive took us about eight hours. We stayed there for the weekend, before leaving my brother to chase his dreams. He was beginning a new journey. That would be the last time the four of us would ever spend time together.

When we dropped my brother off, it was tough. Family always told me I would miss my brother, but my immature mind was not able to understand. It seemed as though, right when our relationship began to improve, life separated us. Separation was something that started to numb me within. First, life separated me from my father, then from my brother. The reasoning was different, but with trauma, all it takes is one experience to cause repressed emotions to remerge.

Another Failed Marriage

In the beginning, it was different. Instead of seeing Kyle on a daily basis, it turned into holidays to one a year.

When my mom, stepdad, and I returned back home, the toxicity of their relationship began to show. Arguments were more frequent. Love was non-existent. As the days went on, their breaking point arrived without warning or surprise.

Sometime in mid-October 2010, while my brother was back in town, a truck pulled up to the house. We were sitting in my room talking when suddenly a U-Haul truck appeared. Our stepdad, at the time, came inside and informed us that he would be leaving. At this point it was not difficult for me to handle the news.

I had become so used to people exiting my life that it was not difficult to digest. He hinted at the possibility of repair, but in my mind I knew that their relationship had reached a point of no return. It wasn't until four years later I saw him again.

Rollercoaster of Emotions

Life was starting to become positive, but the first year of high school was a difficult year to adjust to. Repressed emotions began to subtly influence my decisions. My repressed emotions did not come from my stepdad walking away, but seeing the struggles that my mom would have to encounter once again.

Imagine losing hope, regaining it all just to fail once again? Once high school began, everything was going downhill. It was hard for me, but it was even harder for my mom. The same thing practically happened to her twice. My mom was forced to work more hours because there was only one income instead of two. Between my brother moving, my step-father randomly leaving and my mother working consistently, I did not have anyone. The only thing I could do was turn to basketball.

I started to become serious about the craft. I wanted to find some sort of happiness and comfort. Although I began taking basketball serious, my results varied from my brother. Everything started off completely opposite.

Odd Basketball Journey

My first year, I barely made the freshman team. My ego took a strong hit, when my coaches revealed the news to me. My brother was the sixth man on varsity his freshman year. There were big shoes to fill. Those shoes did not get filled. Instead of turning inwardly, working harder, and increasing my focus, I blamed everyone else.

Over the summer of freshman year, my mindset began to change. Determined to change the outcome of what happened in my freshman year, I worked much harder that summer. I made the JV team my sophomore year, and averaged close to 20 points per game. I was the best player. In the middle of the season, my ego began to take control of me. I wanted the coaches to move me up to varsity.

Towards the end of the season, things began to heat up between the coaches and I. I did not get a chance to finish that whole season. I was kicked off the team because of my disrespectful and selfish attitude. When that happened, it was really a reality check for me. I only had two more years of high school. Time was ticking and the room for error was becoming smaller. During summer going into junior year, I took a risk, hoping that it would translate to great rewards.

First Trip to Connecticut

The summer going into my junior year, I decided to take a trip to Connecticut. I lived there for the entire summer. My brother played basketball at Central Connecticut State University. It was the perfect opportunity to improve my game. That trip really improved our relationship. I had only seen him about three times from the time that he left when I was in the 8th grade until the summer after 10th grade.

In July 2012, I talked to my mom and let her know that I wanted to spend the summer with my brother in Connecticut. At first, she was a little hesitant because she did not understand how well my brother and I would get along. Originally, I was only supposed to stay two weeks, but when I got there, it was the best experience of my life.

College Athlete Life

The reason I chose to go to Connecticut and spend the summer with my brother is that I wanted to get better at basketball. I would get the chance to compete with college players. I had the opportunity to use college facilities. It was the best decision that I felt I could make at the time. I had the opportunity to live like a division one athlete while in high school. That was enough motivation for me to start taking the craft serious.

I worked out with my brother twice a day for the entire summer. My game made a drastic leap. My brother was impressed by my growth. I had the support of my brother, so it was more motivation. I went back as a junior, a different person and player. I was out to prove something.

In my mind, I knew no one was working harder than me. I had just spent my summer working out with college athletes. No one had experienced what I did. I had an understanding of what it actually took and how to get there now. When the season started, half of what I wanted to happen, happened.

History Repeats Itself

I did make varsity my junior year, but I was far from a
starter or star player. In fact, my time with the team would
not last long enough for that to happen. After the second
game of the season, a heated argument with the coaches
ended with a separation. I wanted the coaches to play me
more. They wanted to make the best decision for the team.
I wanted the best decision for myself.

I remember the feeling after. Emotions have a way of
high jacking our mind. Have you ever lost control in the
moment? Do you know what it is like to lose everything
you built in the matter of seconds? My emotions were
blinding me from the truth. Have you ever retracted an
experience to find that it was your fault?

When you are under the influence of emotion, it has a
way of causing you to ignore things that are there. Instead
of taking accountability, I ran away. I pointed fingers.
Once you realize that a poor choice was made, everything
is spent trying to repair the broken pieces. I tried
everything to get back on that team. I apologized to the
coaches and players.

It became clear that the coaches were standing on
their decision. Eventually, the only person I could
apologize to was myself. All the hours of work, translated

to no results. It made me question the process. Most of all, it made me question myself.

Restoring Lost Hope

Have you ever questioned the process? Do you know what it's like to invest thousands of hours, but fail? I began to doubt the vision and hope began to fade, but one phone call changed everything. My mother has a way of finding light in dark situations. If it was not for her, many things would be different.

My mom made a phone call to one of my old coaches. He had become the head basketball coach at a school 15 minutes from our home. Hope was restored. I had one more opportunity to play at a college level.

I transferred schools in the 4th week of February 2013. I had to do that in order to be eligible to play my entire senior season. The transfer was originally hard because there would be adjustments. I did not mind because it is easy for me to adapt. At that point, I was willing to do whatever was required.

Second Trip to Connecticut

When the summer came back around, I went back to Connecticut with my brother. He had a great sophomore season. For an extended period of weeks, he led the nation in scoring. At the end of his sophomore season, he finished number seven in scoring leaders for the NCAA division 1. My brother was on track to breaking many records, which was a motivation for me to work harder.

The summer after junior year was better than the previous. My game had taken a big leap. I was determined to have a great senior season. When the season started, it was difficult to learn a new system. The coaches were different, which took time adjusting to. Midway through the season, I realized that it was not going to be like I expected. Nothing that I thought was going to happen, happened.

Final Wake-Up Call

One day at practice, the coach and I got into an intense argument. I had gotten angry with my coach. The argument was so heated that I just walked out of practice. I never returned. During the time, it was hard to take blame, but with growth came greater perspectives. As I look back, there're patterns in my behavior. My inability to observe myself from outside of myself, kept me repeating the same things, in different scenarios.

When I stopped playing basketball, life really hit me. The dream that took years to build took moments to shatter. What are you supposed to do when there aren't any more chances? I did not know what to do. Have you ever lost something, but could not accept it? Time and time again, fate did not seem to align with my beliefs. This time, who was there to be mad at?

When my father left, that was out of my control. No matter how much praying, wishing or hoping, there was nothing that could prevent my father's long absence. When it came time for me to face reality, there was no one to blame. The result of my actions led to failure. As I reflected on each situation, the pattern became apparent.

Take Accountability

Throughout my basketball journey, each situation was different. The problem was that one thing remained the same. I was the same. What can you say when you receive a second chance, but fail? The day you have to face reality is tough. My reality began to reveal a side of myself that could not hide behind any mask. My flaws and weaknesses began to appear, helping me discover something.

When time is invested, but failure is the result, it has a psychological effect. Do you know what it is like to invest years into something and the result translates into failure? On a daily basis, I began to question myself. Where did I go wrong? I began to think about different routes, but each one led to a dead end. *What if I invest years into something and history repeats itself?*

Recover From Failure

Are you willing to accept your role in the outcome? I played the biggest part in my failures. All my life, I had been in denial. Look into your past situations and see where things could have transitioned differently. History repeats itself, but in life it is hard to pinpoint. It may be a different situation, but the same outcome occurs. The root must be cured. If the root is ignored, outcomes will mirror one another.

The answers you need are in the past. You can learn from triumphs and apply that mindset to everything. As long as your mindset is stuck on winning, you will win in every situation. When you imagine things, only create one outcome.

I was entering different situations with an uncured root. This resulted in a damaged outcome every time. If a tree is not secure at the roots, how will it ever sprout? All I ever did was go into every situation with the same mindset. I changed everything, but did not change my mind.

Successful people succeed in everything that they do because success, first, begins in the mind! Everything about my skillset improved. I was around college athletes. My mind was exposed to the possibilities and responsibilities. What I did not do when I transferred schools was take responsibility for my actions and my mistakes. Sometimes a second chance makes us more ungrateful than before.

Love Inspired Me

When my brother started playing basketball, he never quit, he never gave up. He worked hard from the beginning. I could have been better than my brother, if I had started learning from him earlier. I would have had to develop the same habits, but at a younger age. When I failed, I started to take responsibility. That caused me to look at the situation in a completely different way.

There was much reflecting done after high school. The biggest change came when I fell in love during my freshman year of college. I remember the day she and I met. It was February 13, 2015. She created a desire in me that is still hard to explain. I knew she was "The One."

From the day I met her, I was inspired. I come from a strong, independent mother, so I was going to be great regardless, but she activated something in me. In my eyes, she was perfect. Her potential to be great outweighed any sacrifices. I have always felt that she would find love at a young age and marry someone successful. I did not think I was good enough for her.

The day she and I crossed paths, desire was born. My motivation was to become the best man she would ever meet. That is the only way I felt that she would never forget about me. The only way I saw was by fulfilling my purpose and making a generational impact on this earth.

There are not many people who understand me nor relate, but she understood me from the beginning. She played a role in rediscovering my gift to create with words. I never knew my talent could be awoken by love, but it was. When I experienced love, it made me rethink my future. Has that ever happened to you?

A Different Perspective

I went all the way back. I realized that it was not the coaches who were wrong. It was not the coaches who made the mistakes. It was me. I made mistakes. I changed because I did not want to continue with my life the way I took basketball. I did not begin to appreciate basketball until it was too late.

By me getting motivated in eleventh grade, I was already behind. Kids my age were years ahead of me because they made more sacrifices earlier. After high school, my goal was to get ahead. That is when I began reading. I knew I had to start taking responsibility. I knew I had to grow up, and I knew I had to do it mentally.

It took time for me to develop mentally. I was incapable of seeing certain situations from a mature perspective. I blamed everything on everyone else. I knew that in order for me to have a different outcome in life than I had in basketball, my mindset must evolve. That is why when I saw the video, by the person in the Lamborghini, it really inspired me to start reading.

Have you ever told somebody about your dreams and they questioned you? Did they ask how you will get there? People are going to say negative things about you, but you cannot listen to them. You just have to cancel all that negative noise out. Sometimes you cannot share your dreams with other people, because they are just going to shoot them down.

You see, I had already been shot down and doubted in high school. People compared me to my brother, saying how awful I was. I let all that doubt and ridicule affect my mindset. After high school is when I began looking at things differently. Then everything began to change even more when my father got released from prison.

Release from Prison

The last time I had spoken to my father, I was 13. The last time I had seen my father, I was six. Have you ever come to the conclusion that certain things occur for a reason? How much worst would it have been had my father been in my life with his strong addiction to drugs? There is a purpose for everything.

My father was not in my life because God did not want to place him there. You know those times when things get tough, but it is just God trying to test you? After much contemplation, the hate towards my father subsided.

The day my hate subsided, I wrote a letter. This letter was written exactly one year prior to sending it! When I wrote the letter, it was April 2014. My father was in prison when my mom received letters. There were multiple handwritten letters.

My mom read them first. I read them second. Has someone ever shared their story with you, and instantly, you were connected? His letter connected with me in a different way than the first time we communicated. You ever look at someone and see genuine change? After his release, I wanted to send the letter.

It reads:

"Dear Derek:

I know you are surprised to receive a letter from me especially after the last time we communicated, in fact I'm surprised to even be writing this letter. Before I start I want you to know that I don't have any intention of building a relationship with you in my future, for the simple fact that you've been gone for 13+ years and I'm doing well without you. The purpose of me writing this letter is not to criticize or knock you in any way, but just to express how I am feeling and to get things off of my chest. Moving on…..My mom let me read the letters you wrote her and After reading them I contemplated for weeks if I should write you or if you even deserved to hear from me after all the hurt you caused us, but I finally came to the conclusion that it would be a good gesture to write you because maybe you are really trying to change and get better and after all my past has shaped my future and we are doing well without you in our lives and I love where I'm at today in life. When I was younger I would always cry at night because I would just think what it would be like to have a father in my life and how things would have be different and why you weren't there. I used to act out when I was younger because I had to so much anger built up inside, but I did not know why until a few years ago. All of that change when I finally spoke to you on Facebook nearly 5 years ago. Speaking to you released a lot of the anger I had built up inside and I no longer acted out and I became very calm and laid back. After we spoke there wasn't much anger left because I said a lot of the things I wanted to say, but I also held back because my mom told me not to say some of the things I wanted to say because they were just too mean and hurtful. It was funny that you thought my mom influence me to say the things I said but in actuality, she didn't see none of our messages until we stopped communicating. You didn't know me back then and you really don't know me now, but I am a person that always speak my mind and never hold back. Looking back on it now I said mean things that weren't right to say but I was young and ignorant and by ignorant I mean the literal definition "not knowing". I didn't know how to handle the situation because it completely caught me off guard and that's how I felt about you at the time. Even though I didn't have much anger inside I still hated you, probably more than I did before we even spoke and it's sad because the only person I've ever hated in my 18 years happens to be my biological father. It also made me mad that you thought that my mom was having me say all of that stuff and that my mom told me bad stuff about you, but she didn't. All of that was me and how I felt at that time and THIS IS ME NOW, TODAY.. However, I've gotten over the fact that you were not in our lives and have come to accept it because I am who I am today because of what I have went through in life and I am content with the person I am, only god knows what my life would have been like if you were in our lives and he chose not to put you there for a reason and I trust in GOD and I believe that he has made the right decision. You missed out on your sons lives, that's your lost and YOU will have to live with that for the rest of your life. I realized that I still cared, not about you, but the fact that I really didn't know my biological father, but I've gotten over it, over time. I had a great life and my mom did an amazing job especially after all she's been through in her life, so if I could go back, I wouldn't change one thing, but that's just me. Alright last thing I'm going to say.... I read all of your letters and I hope that you do get better and that you do indeed change. I want you to know that I don't hate you anymore and I have forgave you for the pain you cause us, although I'll never forget. BUT that does not mean I want to form a relationship with you in the future. I told you that one day I would forgive you and that day has been come, I'm a man of my word. I also hope that you do not do to your younger son what you did to us! Also I'm currently in college pursuing a degree in computer science basically the same field you worked in many years ago... that's all I have to say, god bless....I actually wrote this letter last year April 6th 2014 but didn't know how to send it to you because I think you got a transfer but i updated it today. 3/30/15, From, Ken"

Relinquished Feelings

In high school, I wrote this letter to him, but I was unable to send it. He transferred to a different prison. I was unsure of how to contact him. When he was finally released, he became active on Facebook. I didn't want to change anything about the letter because it had emotion from the moment. I did not want any feeling from that letter to change. I fixed a few typos, but all in all I kept the letter the same.

Before you read these words, my father and I will speak again. The conversation will be much different because I believe that he has changed. When someone's actions match up with their words, with time, how can you not believe in them? In that moment, I forgave him. In that time, I could not see us building a relationship, but life goes on.

What does holding on to negative things do? When this letter was finally sent, another weight had been lifted. Has something occurred in your life that makes you get focused in every aspect? This happened to me in March of 2015. Have you ever gone from hating something to loving that same thing?

Impact of Reading

It was reading for me. I went from never reading a book to reading four to five books per month, sometimes more. When you are doing a lot of changing in your life, you usually do not have time to reflect. When you are trying to work a job, pay bills, and take care of responsibilities, you will not always have time to sit back and think about life. One day it will be required.

Sometimes you have to take a look at experiences from a completely different angle. Once that is done you will be able to understand hidden information that was not available in the present moment. How many different perspectives have you looked at your past from?

I believed reading books would make me rich overnight. I thought I would immediately become wise. I did not understand that it was more than just reading. In order to truly learn, you must engage in the actual task. You must act! That is why I chose to get a real estate license at 19 years old.

Transform Knowledge

Have you ever wanted to live out the experience, not just read about it. It was not until I began doing real estate that I saw it was not like the books depicted. Can you invest all your time into something when it is not out of love? Does the money matter if you are not happy? Could you imagine living out your dreams at 19? My goal is to grow with time, not get lost in time!

Today, my life direction changed. It is currently September 1st, 2016. "The two most important days in your life are the day you are born and the day you find out why." - Mark Twain. I believe that this day is the day I have figured out exactly why I was born. Today marks the day I have found my true purpose in life and I want to talk to you about it.

I have been searching for success, happiness, and wealth for the past two years, but I did not understand how I was supposed to get to those points. My mind was thinking money, but not purpose. I did not understand purpose leads to peace, prosperity, and freedom. Once I took my mind off trying to make the most money, searching deep within myself, I began to see true abilities buried within.

What did I find? How did I find it? It was not expected, but it was destined. First, I would like to tell you about this day. The strange thing about this day is that I've been looking forward to it for a few weeks now.

College Transition

I was excited because I was beginning my third year of college at a completely new college, a University. In my previous years, I attended a local community college. I knew transferring was going to be a completely different experience for me. I wanted to see what it was like to attend a university. That is why I was excited about this day, but I had no idea that this day was also going to be the day that I was going to find my purpose.

Before I tell you what exactly it was that I found out, I would like to start this story by telling you how my day went all the way up until this point. It is Thursday September 1, 2016. It is the first official day of classes at Oakland University for the 2016-2017 year. Well, it is the first day for everyone except me. My first class does not begin until tomorrow, September 2, 2016.

I woke up at 9 am, made breakfast while I listened to my favorite song, D.T.B interlude by A Boogie Wit da Hoodie. It was just a regular day, so I thought. I was trying to form the habit of waking up early and going to the gym. I made my breakfast, brushed my teeth, got dressed, left my apartment, and headed to the gym. Campus is about five minutes from my apartment.

I had been going to the recreation center before school actually started, so there was no one on campus. The reason being is that I moved into my apartment three weeks before the fall semester began. Since it is the first day of class, campus was packed. I had no clue that it was going to be that many people. As I pulled into campus, I could not believe my eyes. I said to myself, "This is what college is?"

I had a rush of so many positive emotions. I was finally at a University. I could finally be around people that were my age. I arrived on campus around 9:15 am, but my plans of working out were slightly delayed. Because of my excitement, I walked around campus for a whole hour, I was in complete shock. Going to a community college changed my life in so many ways.

I was at home while most people my age were away at college living the college life. I did not go work out until about 10:30 am. When I completed my workout, I left campus literally lost for words. "This is what I have been missing out on for the past 2 years?" was what I kept saying to myself.

After I left campus, I ran some errands, which took me a few hours. Around 4 pm, I arrived back to my apartment. I was very hungry, so I went in the fridge, grabbed a burger, and began seasoning it. I then grabbed my phone to turn on music, but that's when it started to hit me. It was like some weird intuition that I was having.

It had been a while since the last time I listened to J. Cole. Today, I had a strange urge to play some of his music. The first song I decided to play was from his very first mixtape, *The Come Up*. The strange urge I had felt like some sort of sign to me, so I had no choice, but to act on it. I went to my music library, clicked on albums, scrolled to *The Come up* and clicked shuffle.

Emergence of Past

The first song that came on was a song called *Dolla and a Dream*. As I walked into my bedroom to get my wireless speaker, the lyrics began to speak to me. It's like I began to get all these weird flashbacks. I saw everything so clearly; they were very vivid memories, but they were more than that. There were feelings attached to them.

It was as if I was in all these memories again, something that is hard to explain. The first flashback I had was about basketball. There was no longer any anger towards what occurred. Everything happened so fast, but my first reaction was to capture the moment. That is how I ended up in my iPhone notes talking to you.

As I began to receive these basketball flashbacks, it was like I saw something I hadn't seen previously. I saw something that had occurred when I was young that I never took the time to resolve. I quit the first team I had ever played on. It was four years later when I began again, but my mindset did not change.

It seemed as though every team I played on after led me to quitting. Previously, it was to my belief that it was everyone except me. It took until today to look at things from a completely different perspective. It helped me find the root of the problem. When you create habits early, it translates to other areas of life. You must always finish what you start!

Basketball was vital to my growth, but today, the reason has been revealed. The next thing that crossed my mind was the memories with my father. You already know what my feelings were about him up to this point. If you discovered a rare gift with an attached message, would you share it with the world? If this gift had the ability to change a life, would you listen to the doubts or would you take the chance?

What are you supposed to do when the fear of what could happen controls your mind? How am I supposed to believe in this new-found talent if I have failed in the past? There are so many thoughts going through my mind, but sometimes you have to unlock your mind.

Never Conform

Conforming to society is one way to end up unhappy. As I have taken a look back at my life, everything that has occurred has been for a reason. Many things were my fault because of my immature mind. It took much reflecting and experiencing to find out what is important. It was two years of serious search, but this is only the beginning. It is easy to be consistent for such a short period of time; however, it is about the long term. By looking into the past, I discovered a gift.

Something that I was unaware of for many years. Forgiveness is important because the longer you harbor negative emotions, the longer you will block your blessings. The day I forgave my father, a seed was planted. That seed sprouted into years of wisdom. With this wisdom, I was able to use a gift to rewire my mind, discover my purpose, and impart a message one by one, transforming lives.

"Sometimes you must die to come back to life."

-Ken Viñales

7

Death is Birth

Death and birth are one in the same. When you die, you come to life, and when you come to life, you die. Death and birth can be used as a metaphor in many situations and circumstances in life. When you think about death, it can be scary what happens next. Why did I die? Will I be missed when I'm gone? What type of impact did I leave on earth?

When you come to life, you have so many questions. What is this? Who am I? Why am I here? Why me? Do I have a purpose? But when you combine the two and you think about them together, you realize that these are just one in the same. For me, my death happened on September 1st, 2016. And my birth happened immediately after.

In order to get to where you want to go, you have to leave behind who you once were. In other words, when you die, you are leaving behind life, the life you once lived, the person you once were, to become a better and higher version of yourself. I will like to refer to my purpose awakening, and your purpose awakening, as a death and a birth.

Perspective Is Key

At 19 years old, I began thinking about the deeper things in life. What is your purpose? How can you achieve peace? What can you do to transform knowledge into wisdom? Every day, I asked myself these questions.

The only option left was to begin searching. I searched different ways that would lead me to prosperity. I wanted to know the route to success. When you die and come to life, you rise from the ashes. You rise from the ground. You rise from a place that you have grown out of.

When I found my purpose, I was in a very confused state. I did not know who I was. I did not know where I would be. Do you know what it is like to question future events? When would my dreams manifest into reality?

When you begin to look inside yourself from outside of yourself, the unseen becomes visible. When you begin to look from within yourself, outside of yourself, the impossible becomes possible. My invisible became visible. My impossible became possible.

Has your reality ever been enhanced? In fact, my purpose awakening led to my reality being expanded. My thirst for experiences grew. I wanted to see how much I could grow in four years. In four years, I was able to recreate myself into the person that I am today.

As I walk across this stage, I realize, this is yet another birth. I am dying to come to life. I am ending one journey to begin another, with no thought or hesitation. I created a plan; this plan was to go to college, find my purpose, make thousands, and come out debt-free. Today is December 15th, 2018, and I can say that as I walk across this stage, I exceeded my expectations.

Seeing It Before

After I realized that my plan to make it out of college debt-free was possible, I began to search for other routes. How can I acquire this degree, yet educate myself on different things outside of this degree? How can my degree be connected to other areas of life? Psychology is the foundation of life.

Psychology is the study of the human mind. The human mind is what controls you. The human mind is what controls me. The human mind is what controls everyone around you. Think about a situation where you were able to manipulate a situation and change the way someone was able to see an experience. Shifting perspectives can also have a positive effect as well.

I can tell you a story. Growing up, my mother would always preach to me, "You are going to be a writer. You are going teach people. As you get older, and begin to experience life, you will see that your true gift is, your power to use words, to create stories." That was her intuition. Growing up, I was unable to see things that my mother could. She was able to foresee my path long before I could.

Unknown Potential

As I got older, she placed me in certain situations to succeed. She gave me certain hints of knowledge that I could use to create new experiences. With my mother's wisdom, and her ability to influence my thinking, she was able to create the next great writer.

Now bringing you back to why I got my degree in psychology. When you understand psychology, you understand how to influence people. My mother has many great powers that she is not aware of. She does not have the scientific knowledge, from a specialized institution. She has a natural ability because she is a business woman.

When I began taking psychology classes, subconsciously, I began to study people. I conducted research. I experimented with experiences in my daily life. I began to write. I began to read. I began to take life from a completely different approach. The older I get, the more wisdom I acquire, and the better I am able to turn this wisdom into a story in order for you to interpret.

Multiple Achievements

I was able to go to school, acquire my degree in psychology, acquire a real estate license in the state of Michigan, and acquire a personal trainer certification from the National Academy of Sports Medicine, while remaining debt-free. Now I am connecting with people whom I never met, through words I wrote years before meeting you. When I think about all my achievements, something tells me that I need to set my goals higher.

Since I changed my daily habits and mindset, life has been traveling in a certain way. I study the human mind, meaning I have power. I have secrets and knowledge that were removed from the school system. The only obstacle now is reaching the masses.

Marketing is Vital

When you have a product, or when you want to be seen, marketing must be something you understand at a scientific level. Without marketing, all of the people at the top, without skill, would not be known. A lot of life is just marketing. 95% of marketing is psychology. I am a an expert in psychology. The purpose of a marketer is to hook the consumer.

As a marketer, what can you do to engage the viewer? How do you engage the observer, causing them to take action? The power of storytelling can unlock your potential. A great story creates a surge of emotion, which can transform into any action of your choice. What is your end goal?

Connection to Life

People are always confused when I tell them my choice of concentration. People's first reaction is that I want to be a therapist. My first reaction was to unlock my mind. Without the mind, we would not be who we are today. We have the largest brain amongst all species.

I have learned scientific methods through psychology. When I combine time with my experiences, I am able to create this inspiring story, which is changing you. *First in the Family* is the sign you have been waiting for. *First in the Family* was designed for you.

When I look back at life, as a high school freshman, I could not have predicted that you and I would be here, celebrating this moment. A moment that I am capturing in time. No matter how old I get, no matter when I die, no matter where I go, this message will always be here for you. I am your inspiration to elevation.

Unseen Prediction

When you read *First in the Family,* you are going to be connected. Memories are going to come to your mind. Characteristics are going to come to the surface. Ideas are going to sprout. I couldn't have predicted this moment years ago.

I am now a writer, but at one point in time, I did not believe. It wasn't something that I thought I could live my life doing. It wasn't something I thought I could find happiness in. Somehow over the past four years, I have also written five unpublished books, and one published book.

I died on September 1st, 2016, but I came to life immediately after. When I came to life, I received this vision. Within this vision came a purpose. With my purpose came a gift. With this gift, a strong desire awakened. A desire that I can't let go of until everything I envision manifest.

The Hidden Meaning

What I see in my head is more than just *First in the Family.* There are multiple meanings to the name. I came from the prison system. I came from drugs. I came from the streets. I came from a single mother. I came from un-education. I came from struggles. I came from trials and tribulations.

There are a lot of things I can do while I am here on this earth. I want to change the later generations. I have to take care of my mother, so she does not have to experience what she did 10 years ago, or what she had to experience 10 years before that.

My motivation and my desire are beyond self-rewards. I am the last concern, I want to help you. I want to help my family. I want to help the people around me. When I entered college, I was unaware of the power of knowledge.

Father Motivation

When I died, I came back to life. My vision included my father back in my family's life. As I walk across this stage, we have rekindled our relationship. He came back with an instant impact. The impact comes from endless wisdom.

One day, I asked him how he was able to stay motivated while locked in a prison cell; his response stunned me. What kept him from going crazy was knowing one fact. If someone takes everything from you, as long as you have life, then you still have what you know. When you have what you know, there are no limitations.

The power of knowledge is strong enough to help rise, if you fall. Someone can take everything you own, but when you have what you know, you can get back to where you once were, or even higher. I spent the years putting in the time. I spent the years perfecting this passion to write.

I've put in the time and now my time is here. I am not only graduating, but taking a leap of faith, to start in my career as an independent author, online business owner and consultant. I am an entrepreneur. I came into college, confused. I came into college and did not know what I wanted to do.

Looking Back

Now, as I leave college, I have a plan. I have a passion. I have a purpose. Writing is my passion. My purpose is to inspire and influence millions through my power to write great stories.

When you die, you come back to life. When you come to life, you die. Death and birth are just one in the same. As long as you do the same things over and over again, you will go insane. I went to college. I studied the mind. Now I am here, on this podium, thinking about how to further separate and elevate, demonstrating how anyone can go from average to great.

'There is no warning for the end of the beginning, you must take action and conquer your journey."

-Ken Viñales

8

First in the Family

When we come into this life, we do not have a choice. Our existence is predetermined, meaning our life is the result of someone else's actions. Once we make it to this life, over time, control is gained. You have a choice. You can choose what path you take. You can choose what decisions you make.

When I look into my future, the only thing that I see is massive success. I chose this path, subconsciously. This path was paved before my coming to consciousness. I was unaware of the meaning behind specific events, but time allowed me to identify the grander picture.

As an adolescent, I never understood the power of the mind. It was hard for me to understand the deeper aspects of life, reality, and the universe. It did not dawn on me what thoughts were, until I was 18. The fact, thoughts are things, is hard for some people to conceive.

Thought Power

Thoughts are not detectable by the human eye. Thoughts cannot be grasped. Although thoughts are undetectable by our six senses, they are more real than any physical entity. Since I began this journey, my goal has been to discover and utilize my purpose.

Before achieving this milestone, I was confused. I was unsure what my journey through college would lead to. Would I come out successful? Would I come out a failure? Would I even make it out?

I was unsure of my purpose in life. I was soul-searching, trying to find a way to peace. Today, as I walk across this stage, there are many emotions. Could you imagine being the first person in your immediate family to receive a college degree? Aside from being the first person in my family, I am the first man in my extended family to walk a university's stage.

Overcome the Odds

The feeling is surreal. Knowing what my family has endured, reassures that this was not supposed to happen, according to statistics. Statistics are not favorable for minorities that come from households of single "uneducated" mothers. Statistics are not favorable for mothers who have little support. Statistics are not favorable for black men who are born to felons.

When I look at the uphill battles that, not only my mother, but also my father has faced over the years, I become more motivated. Both of my parents have seen hell on earth, so I want to be the reason they experience heaven on this same earth. Before beginning this journey, I was not aware of how much wisdom would be collected. As I end this journey, I possess endless wisdom. In other words, I spent years studying those before me and now I am acting on what I have received.

Storytelling Animal

Once the knowledge is acquired, action is the only ingredient that can manifest any results. In the past four years, many experiences and ideas have been collected. The beauty of life is turning our experiences into stories that deliver a powerful message.

First in the Family is a powerful message that has resonated with individuals who have not made it to earth yet. My words are going to live forever, meaning even after I am gone, millions will find my story, fall in love with it, and be transformed by it. By nature, we humans are storytellers. Our minds gravitate towards great stories that evoke emotion.

Whether we are aware of it or not, we live in a world of stories. Stories that we tell our family, friends, coworkers, and clients. Stories we share over the phone and in person. Then there are the stories that constantly play themselves out in our heads. What about the stories of whom we love, despise, and that inspire our spirit?

Step by Step

As you read *First in the Family,* you have recalled different stories, experiences and people, which suggest that life is merely a story. You have a story just like me and we have a story just like the person you last spoke with. *First in the Family* is my first book, but this is only one chapter.

Today is just one step, the bottom step. My family is proud. People have congratulated me, but I have not yet started. If people are this proud at this achievement, then they will be speechless, within two years. *First in the Family*, is larger than a self-published book by a 22-year-old independent author.

First in the Family is more than being the first person to receive a bachelor's degree. *First in the Family* is a story that represents overcoming unforeseen obstacles and rising to unimaginable heights. Achievements are great because they are a physical manifestation of the hours invested. I invested many hours in unlocking my mind, by seeking knowledge, and transforming it into wisdom.

First in the Family symbolize that anything is possible. I was blessed with the opportunity to change the generations after me, by breaking the trend of the generations before me. *First in the Family* symbolize that it is possible to be a first-generation millionaire.

Leap of Faith

With psychology, my understanding of the mind and the power of social media, any outcome is possible. When I look around me, there are not many with the same level of passion as me. When I was 19 years old, I acquired a real estate license. I was tired of reading books. I was tired of experiencing through the lens of someone else. I wanted to experience it for myself.

Through my experiences, I was able to convert my knowledge into wisdom. After real estate, I wanted to expand my skillset, so I began to study exercise science. My motivation behind learning the human anatomy derived from my interest in helping form elite athletes.

Achieving in Life

My expertise in both areas would allow me to harmonize my mind, body, and spirit, teaching other people to do the same. In four years, I went from being confused to creating my own future. In four years, along with a B.A. in Psychology, I am also a licensed real estate agent, certified personal trainer through National Academy of Sports Medicine, and now an independent author with a goal to change generations.

When you have a direction of where you are going, it does not matter the steps it takes to get there. My direction was always independence, finding a way to provide for myself and family. In the beginning, people were confused with my choice to pursue a degree in psychology. The vision I constructed was far beyond seeing myself working for another man.

Magic of Psychology

With psychology, I am a specialist. I understand the mind. I understand what creates desire within you and me. I understand the connection between mind and body. I understand social interaction. Instead of pursuing a field that would land me a job right out of college, I took a unique approach.

Psychology has played a role in enhancing my perspective, giving me the ability to see what is invisible to the normal eye. With that, I am able to influence and create powerful stories that resonate in an individuals' mind, your mind. What I want to do for you is help you see the world from a different perspective. I want you to go into your past and recreate your future. In your past, are all the answers you need.

Past of Answers

In your past are many answers. In your past, there will be vital information causing changes internally. For example, love has been a difficult concept for me to accept. As time progresses, I find myself in many complicated situations.

Situations involving lovers and situations involving friends. Friends that betrayed me. Lovers who are left in confusion because of my suddenness to withdraw. For many years, I blamed everyone but the person in the mirror. Now, I take ownership because of my ability to see what was once hidden from me.

My expertise gives me supreme abilities. For instance, I used my past to unlock the confined perspectives needed for me to evolve into a higher level of thought. From that, I was able to detect the problem with many different aspects in my life.

Poor Nurturing

In this case, I detected a problem in my nurturing and altered my thought process when forming new connections. Our relationships, friendships, and connections to people are vastly influenced by things beyond our field of vision. The power of going into your past, collecting pieces, then recreating your future is much greater than you realize.

When you uncover the truth about your psyche, invisible things begin to unveil. My problem with love began at a young age. The bond that I formed with my father affects me in ways that I'm still unable to see. What I learned is that my early formation of love, elicited a feeling of abandonment.

Do you know what it is like to feel alone, empty, desiring love that is not available? Growing up without a parent creates a feeling that can never be forgotten. What that translates to is a ripple effect in other areas of life. Have you ever found yourself in the same situation twice? Different scenarios, but very similar outcomes?

Cure the Roots

For many years, I went blind to the root cause of my problems. Although scenarios were different, the common denominator was me. You do not know what you are not consciously aware of, meaning the outcomes of my situations were being determined by my past. Through constant retrieval and reflection, studying my life in many ways, something came to my level of awareness.

The best way to grow is to begin taking blame for situations that you feel may not be your fault. For example, when I began to look outside the box, I discovered what my mind had been avoiding for so many years. Whenever I find myself in a situation that elicits the feeling of abandonment, my immediate reaction is to withdraw. It is an unconscious action that I developed at a young age.

By withdrawing, I cause the exact thing that I am trying to prevent. My instinctual nature retreats back to my first impression of love. I'm thinking that I'm preventing the situation, but subconsciously, I'm recreating my childhood relationship all over again.

Life is about perspective. Life changed when I opened my mind. By seeing how much my past affected my current, it motivated me to do more soul-searching. I began to look at all areas of life differently. By detecting the problems within my relationships and friendships, I was able to discover important details about myself.

Hidden Gift

There is something special within you. Something that no one else can do, but you. The way that my mind now processes information reveals many things about my life, which can also reveal things about your life. At this point in life, it is obvious. After many trials, many errors and countless hours, there is a gift within, waiting to come to life.

My gift is to write. Not many people can write a book, although there is a book inside of everyone. There is a book inside of you, waiting to come to life. For the past four years, I have been perfecting this craft, building this vision, trying to connect with you. The journey that it took to manifest this moment came with many sacrifices.

Sacrificing time to write a book, while attending college, enrolled in programs, and working a full-time job originated from my desire to succeed. My mind has been focused to reach another level, a level higher than the one I was previously on.

Follow Your Instincts

Over the years, I have tried to find any way to increase my thought vibration. Allow me to explain. I began writing off of instinct. I shared the story earlier. I didn't know what writing would lead to, but day by day, the ideas kept building, one by one. As the ideas built, I began to search.

I began to search within my past, discovering when my gift was originally born. The gift was born at a young age. I always had the passion. I never knew that I would be able to take a passion, such as writing, and turn it into a way of life, generating a stream of profit in other people's life.

What I am creating, is not something that many people can say they have done. A lot of people try to give advice on things that they have not lived. When you are in the process of becoming great, when you're in the process of becoming a legend, your success is a way of life. What seems unexplainable to someone else will to seem normal to you. Normal to you because it is what you breathe, eat, and sleep.

When I have conversations with people, at this stage in my life, their first reaction is amazement. As much as we try to see ourselves, outside of ourselves, seeing ourselves through the mind of someone else is impossible. From my perspective, my actions, my path is normal. It was determined long before my existence, so by going against it will just cause pain.

Directing the Vision

It is unnecessary to create suffering, by ignoring the signs that are directly in front of you. The signs in front of me are telling me to go a different route. Take a route that no one has ever thought of but comes natural to you. How can you expect to reach a destination, without a direction in mind?

What makes my vision special is that there is a precise direction. There is a plan, backed by action. In the past, failure was the result because my plan was not clear. Aside from not having a concrete plan, my action was not backed by faith, making it easy for me to walk away. Today, when I explain my vision, it is clear, precise, and easy to believe in.

When I think about this stage of life, people around me are searching for ways to find that great job, sign that big salary, or enter graduate school. For me, I want to find ways to generate income on my own. I want to learn how to take my knowledge, wisdom, and gift, and generate more money that any job can provide for me. I want to help you reach your potential!

Our Generation's Advantage

The generation that we live in today is growing up on social media. What this means is that it becomes easier to sell products and or services to a mass amount of people. The key to finding peace and financial freedom is using your own gifts and passion to make a living.

Allow me to shift your attention. Shift your mind back to my passion to write, by relating it to something in your life. I have an older brother. We've already talked about him; his passion is basketball. As I observe my brother's life and study him subconsciously I take in information and process it below my awareness. We all study the people around us, whether it's consciously or subconsciously. Have you considered that?

As I've studied my brother's life, I have noticed something particular about the way time works. No matter what you do, as long as you immerse your mind in that task, for a number of hours, that task will slow down mentally. This will result in detecting more information that was previously below your awareness.

The Required Process

What are you great at naturally? Think about that, now hold it in your mind. I stumbled upon my ability to write one day off of instinct. My only thought became to figure out how to capitalize off this new desire, so I began to write every single day. Within a month, I was done with my first book. I read it, and edited it, over and over again.

For three months, I created, crafted, and constructed a book that I will forever keep in a lock box. What I began to do was, instead of edit, recreate. In other words, I wrote new books from scratch for three years before ever releasing *First in the Family*. Life is about trying things, until you find the right one that works.

The first book that I wrote was impressive because it birthed something that was not appreciated originally. Over three years, so many things have happened, which is how *First in the Family* came to life.

After I wrote the first book, I wrote another book from the perspective of my brother. After his book, I wrote a love story. After the love story, I began journaling every day. Before writing *First in the Family*, I helped my mother write, edit, and publish her book, *Damn I Should of Saved*.

Now, all of this took months, years, thousands of hours. Aside from writing books, I began to document in different ways. For example, I have hours of footage and voice recordings. Everything I do is timed. Everything I do is dated. Everything I do is signed. The reason for that is, I want to track and study my hours.

Focus on Craft

Now, let's shift this back to you. There is something that you do in your life better than you do anything else. There's one thing that you do best. I don't know what it is. Only you know that. Whether it's play an instrument, whether it's make art, sing, or play a sport, there is something that you do that you are better than everything else at. So now, let's magnify that ability. Is there a way that you can invest more time?

If your first instinct was yes, then you are not working hard enough. You may be working tirelessly, day in and day out, but there is someone investing more time than you. They are investing the maximum amount of effort, time, and energy day in and day out. When I ask myself that same question, my instinctual response is yes.

Although I have accomplished some extraordinary goals, there is much more in store for me. The achievements that I have now are small to me because I want more. I'm not where I want to be. Is there room for improvement? How many times do you ask yourself that question? What inspires me to continue going is knowing that there is more room to grow.

Magic of Time

When I first began writing, there were many aspects that were not available to me. It required much thought, making it hard create harmony. Over time, deeper aspects, such as influencing the reader's emotions, using different storytelling techniques, became available to me. The more hours I invest, the better I become at crafting perfect stories.

The magic to life is that time may be the only key necessary for making the impossible possible. Can you recall a right time, right place situation? There is nothing more unexplainable than perfect timing, it just the way of the universe. When time is incorporated into any equation, the possibility of outcomes broadens.

Begin First Step

Now, when I first started writing, there were a lot of flaws. There were a lot of grammatical errors, there were a lot of different problems with the way that I wrote. I knew that investing more time would slow down the task, allowing my mind to focus on deeper aspects. Whatever it is that you are endeavoring to achieve, just invest the time, with faith and passion. Your mind will manifest everything else, by any means.

When I first began this journey, I wasn't sure what my journey would consist of. I wasn't aware some instinct to write would transform into a book, multiple books. I wasn't aware that I would begin selling real estate at 19, writing books at 20, and launching my own business at 22. I am motivated to break this generational cycle and elevate the generations after me. It is easy for someone to talk, but the person that takes action is the one who achieves their dream. I took action. Action has led me directly to you!

Word Power

I received a vision that I was going to be a once-in-a-generation writer, a writer that is rare, a writer that society does not get often. I have a special power with the pen. With the pen, I can paint an image, any image, in your mind. With a pen, I can reconstruct my own mind and cause growth, rapid growth. Words are more powerful than people consider.

The day these words reach you, because they will reach you, there will be a certain change of course in your life. What I mean by that is, the way you see people, yourself, the past and future, will all be enhanced. *First in the Family* provides you with many keys. I'm priming your mind in a certain way that you aren't conscious of. That's the power of psychology, that's the power of a powerful writer.

Who Am I?

I, myself, am only 22 years old, but for a 22-year-old, I have a lot of wisdom. I have more wisdom than I can use, so my first reaction is to give, give you knowledge, give you power, give you wisdom, that you can take and apply to your own life. I am a walking testament of, it doesn't matter where you come from, where you are raised, or what your family has been through. My whole life has been a mental war, battling between emotion and logic. The betrayal of my father affected me in many ways, but it did not handicap me. I am a walking testament of, you can accomplish anything you want in life.

Growing up, I never imagined being the first man in my entire family, extended and immediate, to achieve such a milestone. I didn't have any knowledge of this. I didn't have any knowledge of my true power or potential. None of this began to happen until I unlocked my mind with the key.

I have a key, and with this key, I can make anything I believe manifest. I can make anything you believe manifest. I have exactly what you need. The mind is very powerful because there are two parts. You have a subconscious mind and you have a conscious mind.

Blind Puppets

Many people believe that they have control over their desires. They believe they have a control over what's happening around them. Do you think you have control over your future? Many people are living blind, believing they are in control. Our conscious, the mind that we use to focus, is not the decision maker. You aren't making your decisions. I am not making my decisions.

The sudden birth of this skill was planned, it was primed, it was subconsciously planted in my mind at a young age. My gift came to fruition at the perfect time. Your collection of desires is predetermined. The things that you like, buy, and gravitate towards aren't things that you're consciously choosing. You may feel like you are making the choice, but there is much more going on behind the scenes, unavailable to your knowledge.

What influences many of your choices are things that you are unconsciously feeling. The unconscious emotion, feelings, and desires have most of the control. This means that our mind takes in information we may not have awareness of and influences us greatly. The moment we entered the world, our minds began scanning the environment.

Leaders vs. Followers

There is a power that comes from understanding what is truly controlling you. Our conscious is the director and observer. What this means is that, as you grow older, you must take control of what you allow into your world. You must feed your subconscious mind with powerful affirmations, precise plans, and positive thoughts.

The difference between leaders, the successful, and the mentally free, is the understanding of the two minds. Have you taken the time to study how to harmonize both? What about aligning your mind, body, and soul? Since a freshman in college, which was four years ago, June 1st, 2014, I have used my conscious mind to reprogram my subconscious.

Many people living today are blind. Blind to the fact that more things are taking place behind the scenes, than in front of the scenes. What do I mean? Well, before I began this journey, I had no idea what my future would hold. I stayed up, late nights, unable to process, trying to figure out what the next steps would consist of.

In between my confusing moments, were small revelations; signs guiding me to what appeared to be my destiny. As I grow older, my mind desires wisdom. My mind desires knowledge. In other words, new experiences and education are what drive me.

Rewire the Subconscious

After realizing that I am blind to many things, I began searching. That is when I discovered emotions such as passion, desire, and things like the subconscious. When the student is ready, the teacher will appear. When the voyager is ready, paved will be the path.

What I mean by that is, the things that you are reading, listening to, and watching, have a large impact on the events transpiring in your reality. Environment also plays a large role because the things that you don't see are influencing the part of your mind that you aren't aware of. The part of your mind that you aren't aware of is what is directing and causing you to make certain choices. How are we supposed to see what is invisible to us?

Before the rewards and manifestations, many unanswered questions elicit pressure. After four years of searching, the answers for all the unknown questions are now here. I was the first in my family to graduate, but that won't be all the first I am.

First in the Family

I want to be the first person in my family to make a million dollars and provide jobs for the other people in my family, my cousins, my nieces, my kids and grandkids. I'm providing a path for them to succeed. When I think about *First in the Family,* I get goosebumps because people who are not alive are already reading my story in a different time period, finding enough inspiration to manifest their vision.

What you can take from my story is inspiration. What you can take from my story is a hard work ethic. What you can take from my story is passion. When you are truly passionate, it shows. You do not have to talk.

Passion shows in the way you carry yourself. It will show in the way you create. It will show through your interactions with people. When you learn how to produce a vision, first built in the mind; with your own hands, there is no limit to your capabilities.

Passion Promotes Peace

You gravitate towards passion. I gravitate towards passion. We all love to see people passionate about their dream and craft. I wrote this book out of passion. I created my business, The Rare Few, out of passion. I am living my life through passion.

You were able to witness a Master on his journey to Mastery. Mastery is a topic that people have fear of learning. They fear understanding mastery because it requires a different method of thinking. There are some people who wake up every day unaware that they are not in control. The human mind is complex.

To perform a single action causes a process in the brain that we are not able to see. We are only aware of the outside action, making us blind to what is going on at the nucleus. When an individual becomes aware of mastery, their perspective and way of thinking evolves. It requires them to take control, but how can you take control of something that has been controlled for so long? How can you see something that is invisible to you?

Concept of Mastery

The first step to understanding Mastery is understanding the process, behind the scenes. The main reason I became interested in psychology is because it would give me the blueprint to understanding you. It gave me the blueprint to crafting a message powerful enough to resonate with your soul.

The only key needed in a world filled with humans is understanding humans. The goal of anyone aspiring greatness should be to implant their desires, crafts, and beliefs into their subconscious mind. Once the subconscious mind has been influenced, time will do the rest. That is the power of the subconscious mind. That is the secret to becoming naturally gifted.

Find your passion, then implant it in your subconscious mind by investing countless hours of energy. The only way to take control of your life is to take control of your subconscious mind, controlling what it is exposed to. You must constantly expose yourself to things that revolve around your dream. When you control your thoughts, you control your life.

Ending to Begin

It has been a long journey for me. There have been countless failures, and there will continue to be obstacles to overcome. As I stand on this stage, looking in the crowd, the only thing that I am able to do is thank God. Without God, I would not have been able to achieve anything up to this day. Without God, I would not have had a mother who was willing to sacrifice in order to provide a way for her children.

As I look into my future, all I can see are great things. When is the last time you met an independent author, whose story inspired generations, long after his existence? This is only the beginning. My name, words, and wisdom will travel through time and space. You have joined a journey to prosperity!

ABOUT KEN VIÑALES

Ken Viñales changed the generations after him, by chasing his dream. When time catches up to his vision, people will see that he was a genius all along. The thing about life is that before the moment, you are unable to fully see the moment. Before his books ever began selling, he was destined to be a powerful writer in his generation. You were able to witness the beginning.

Dedication

to

"The One"

One day, you are going to read these words. On that same day, you will realize how special you are. On that same day, you will recount all of our experiences, dating up to this moment, that we meet once again, but through these words. How could I not thank God for introducing me to someone powerful enough to inspire a legendary writer in our generation? We were brought together by love! Real love never fails. Time is showing the power of faith, now it is time to prevail. I am on a journey that you have played a role in from the beginning. This is my dedication, this is my sincere appreciation!

35337033R00090

Made in the USA
Middletown, DE
06 February 2019

Margaret
and Me

ALSO BY WILLIAM J. THOMAS

THE TABLOID ZONE: DANCING WITH THE FOUR-ARMED MAN

MALCOLM AND ME: LIFE IN THE LITTERBOX

HEY! IS THAT GUY DEAD — OR IS HE THE SKIP?

GUYS: NOT REAL BRIGHT — AND DAMN PROUD OF IT!

Margaret
and Me

William J. Thomas

Stoddart

Published in 1998 by Stoddart Publishing Co. Limited
34 Lesmill Road, Toronto, Canada M3B 2T6
180 Varick Street, 9th Floor, New York, New York 10014

Distributed in Canada by:
General Distribution Services Ltd.
325 Humber College Blvd., Toronto, Canada M9W 7C3
Tel. (416) 213-1919   Fax (416) 213-1917
Email customer.service@ccmailgw.genpub.com

Distributed in United States by:
General Distribution Services Ltd.
85 River Rock Drive, Suite 202, Buffalo, New York 14207
Toll-free Tel. 1-800-805-1083   Toll-free Fax 1-800-481-6207
Email gdsinc@genpub.com

02 01 00 99 98 1 2 3 4 5

Canadian Cataloguing in Publication Data

Thomas, William J., 1946–
Margaret and me: all humour needs a victim and
Mom's #1 in my book!

ISBN 0-7737-3051-6

1. Mothers and sons – Humor.
2. Canadian wit and humor (English).* I. Title.
PS8589.H471Z53 1998   C818.5402   C98-931481-2
PR9199.3.T465Z462 1998

Jacket Design: Bill Douglas @ The Bang
Text Design: Tannice Goddard

Printed and bound in Canada

*We gratefully acknowledge the Canada Council for the Arts and
the Ontario Arts Council for their support of our publishing program.*

I dedicate this book to my mother, Margaret Mary McLean Thomas, the source of whatever goodness and humour I possess.

Margaret is and always has been the kindest, sweetest, gentlest soul on the face of the earth. A saint, really. So much so that I've often offered to send a letter off to the Vatican to get her name on that list for beatification.

And every time I mention this, she says the same thing: "That's nice, dear, but they charge so dang much. I'll just get your sister to give me a perm."

Okay. So this woman is not quite grasping the concept of beatification. This doesn't make her a bad person, does it?

Contents

Warning

This is not *The English Patient*.

This isn't even the patient of Dr. Dave Hurst, the Chief of General Surgery at the Welland County General Hospital who lives a twenty-minute walk from me on Camelot Bay. Dave lets me move into his bunkhouse on the beach to write my books. (He promised that if I mentioned him in this book, he'd give me a key to the main house so I could use the john. Which brings me back to my point.)

This is not a book to be read right through. This is a collection of stories about my mother, Margaret, and is best read sporadically, as it was written, over a period of time.

As Bill Kelly of CHML Radio in Hamilton once said in an interview: "Your books belong in the john. I read one story every time I go there. I hope you're not offended."

No offence taken, Bill, as long as you're a regular guy.

And to all readers, including Bill Kelly — the book comes out of the john with the same number of pages as when it went in. That's the deal. Okay?

Don't aim to be
an earthly Saint,
With eyes fixed
on a star,
Just try to be
the fellow that
Your Mother thinks
you are.

— WILL S. ADDIN

JUST TRY TO BE THE FELLOW

Margaret
and Me

A Woman of Ominous Origins

My mother, Margaret, named after the famous ship *Santa Margarita*, was born the same year Christopher Columbus discovered Ohio. Fortuitously, the *Santa Margarita* was wrecked when it went aground on Interstate 71 at the last exit for Cincinnati, an incident later celebrated in the Jimmy Buffet song "Santa Margaritaville" and the tequila-based drink of the same name.

Okay, so the details of my mother's beginnings are, at best, a little sketchy.

Margaret was born in 1906 in Victor, Colorado, a town that is much the same today as it was then: deceased. I like to refer to my American-born mother as the Mighty Mick from County Cork because it makes as much sense as everything else in her early years.

Margaret was the second daughter of southern Irish immigrants, an itinerant extended family of miners who knew neither what mineral they wanted to mine nor where they would find it. From the treacherous holes drilled through Colorado mountains, to the lightless coal shafts of Sydney, Nova Scotia, to the dull yellow-veined gold tunnels that ran for miles beneath Timmins, Ontario, her family moved like a band of Celtic gypsies with a grudge against the sun.

My mother often said the McLean family would follow her father anywhere — just out of sheer curiosity.

When Colorado's mining industry collapsed after World War I, the family travelled east by automobile, halfway across America, then up to Nova Scotia, and a few years later west, halfway across Canada to toil in the Hollinger and McIntyre mines of Timmins and Schumacher, Ontario.

My father came from the opposite direction, but on the same career coal car. Born in Pontardulais, northwest of Swansea, Wales, he was a young, strong-backed coal miner hammering out a living with a pickaxe in the hard-scrabble, soot-stained countryside that Richard Llewellyn gave life to in *How Green Was My Valley* and Dylan Thomas drank to in *A Child's Christmas in Wales*.

There have always been and always will be generations of adventurous and naive young bucks willing to risk life and limb doing perilous work to help make millionaires out of wily prospectors and cunning insiders. My father was one such man. If you've ever been to the clapboard cubby hole of Schumacher and tried to imagine this town as the "promised land," you'll understand the depth of the problem. Dreamers never let reality into their world for fear it'll wake them up.

Another such man, with matinee-idol features and forearms of iron, was my mother's brother Johnny. He died young, working in the McIntyre mine underage as a matter of fact, the only male breadwinner left in the family when their dad died of TB, the miner's "black lung." Struck down in a minor cave-in, Johnny McLean didn't report his injuries so as to keep his job. Instead he took two weeks' vacation and returned to family in Nova Scotia to recover in secret.

Eventually somebody discovered a hole in the ice of Giant's Lake, Johnny's dog and hunting rifle beside it. Never more than that. Prior to this discovery, he was the target of one of the largest searches in Canadian history and the first, I'm told, that involved military aircraft.

My mother never really recovered from or truly believed in his death. For most of her life, she scanned newspapers looking for a face or a missing-person report hoping beyond hope that he'd developed amnesia and would some day come back into her life.

So my mother came from the south and west and my father came from the north and east and the two-person collision happened on September 27, 1930. As far as my mother can remember, it wasn't much of a ceremony followed by a poor reception, particularly by those who'd already met my father. It was one of the few times, the minister admitted later, that he felt obligated to caution the family and friends of the bride: "No booing!"

I have two older sisters, Joan and Gail, and if we had ever experienced one of those *Back to the Future* kind of events, we would surely have hobbled my mother to keep her home that day. If phrases could be copyrighted, today as surviving offspring of that marriage, we'd all be living high off the royalties of "shit happens."

Eventually all mining families from Northern Ontario move to southern Ontario. Either you get out early with your health intact and seek a better job than that of a human mole or you stay too long and have to go south to be close to the province's best TB sanatoriums.

Both my sisters were born in Timmins. I was born in Welland, Ontario, and when I was two we moved six miles south to the tiny town of Dain City. I have at best a sporadic recollection of Dain City, a village where 120 people sustained a post office, a general store, a Sunoco station, two variety stores, one school, a tavern, two bookmaking operations, one fertilizer factory, one bootlegger, a railroad station, and two lift bridges, both straddling the Welland ship canal that cuts through the village from north to south.

Many of my memories revolve around either the Welland Canal or the Welland Drive-In, and rare are the moments when my mother wasn't right there beside me.

From hockey practice to baseball games to nervously pacing on the banks of the canal watching me learn to dog paddle — though she couldn't swim a stroke herself — my mother seemed to fit and flourish in the role of both parents. In Dain City, in the '50s, this was not that unusual. Mothers did everything except actually earn a wage. Fathers worked and drank. For most husbands in my immediate neighbourhood, home was where they nursed their hangover.

In Welland we lived in one of those clapboard matchboxes known as a wartime house at 124 Dunkirk Street. If you were over six feet tall, you couldn't live in one of these houses because your feet stuck out the bedroom door and you tripped people walking down the hall.

Although it never made much sense at the time, it turns out my mother had been a war bride, sort of. I found this out only recently over idle conversation and a couple of cold beer.

I can't remember what prompted my questions. I was sitting by the fireplace in my cottage looking out over a brooding, grey Lake Erie swell. Perhaps it was just the cold, dull days of November, a moribund month that brings with it Remembrance Day, plastic poppies, and very, very old men marching with military berets and rows of precious medals.

"So what did Dad do in the war, Mom?" Actually, I didn't say "Mom," though I should have. I said "Marg." At some point in my late teens we struck a deal: she wouldn't call me Son of William and I wouldn't call her Mom or Mother and we wouldn't buy birthday cards that rhymed the word "love" with "dove." "Bill" and "Marg" would suffice as lovable labels in most cases of communication. We'd been through a lot together and decided we were close enough friends to work on a first-name basis.

"So what did Dad do in the war, Marg?"

Actually, I didn't say "Dad." I said "Glyn." Glyn would be my father. He would be if he were still alive, which he is not and has not been for twenty years. As I mentioned, my father was a quintessential Welshman, coal miner, gold digger, and finally a security guard at a steel mill in Welland known as Page-Hersey. My father's fatal flaw in life, like so many other Welshmen, was that he mistook singing and drinking for a profession. He died in Hamilton, Ontario, alone and a stranger to all who knew him.

To be precise, I put this question to my mother: "So what did Glyn do in the war, Marg?"

I may have taken a long time coming to the question but the answer was instant.

"He played the piano in Dunnville!"

Now, I've read enough to know that the Canadian forces distinguished themselves by storming the beach-heads of Normandy and by blowing up the bridges at Arnhem, but apparently history has largely overlooked the heroic piano playing that went on in the tiny town of Dunnville, Ontario, a thirty-minute drive from our wartime house in Welland.

"He played the piano in Dunnville?"

The No. 6 Service Flying Training School was located in

Dunnville during World War II. It was one of 132 such bases in Canada that produced fighter pilots and crews for the Allied war effort. This particular squadron drew air force personnel from all over the Western world, and especially from Australia and New Zealand.

Ah, yes, they were all coming back to me now — the war stories from Dunnville. The Aussies then and now have a strong inclination towards ale and wild pranks. Australians think mischief is a rite of passage.

There was a large pond just outside the base. It was a freshwater reservoir that in no way resembled the churning surf of the Great Barrier Reef. Yet it was not uncommon after an all-night pub crawl near Dunnville to see the Aussies at daybreak leading a force of enlisted men into the reservoir on ironing boards screaming, "The surf's up!"

Whenever they missed the last bus back to camp from downtown Dunnville, they just hopped on bicycles, anybody's bicycles, and rode back to the barracks. This practice ended abruptly when the Dunnville chief of police showed up on the base one morning to retrieve *his* bicycle.

There were a few women living on the base, and the Australians sometimes drew attention to this fact by hoisting a pair of borrowed bloomers in place of the Union Jack. To them, it was just as inspiring as a rousing rendition of "Waltzing Matilda."

By far their most daring escapades were sort of job-related, in airplanes that appeared suddenly out of the sun with identification numbers well taped over. Anybody could fly over the Peace Bridge between Fort Erie and Buffalo, they reckoned. It was only logical, then, that the Australians began flying semi-regular flights *under* it. More than one family out for a Sunday drive and craning to look over the bridge's railing were treated to the sight of an oncoming Harvard fighter that dropped down at the last second and disappeared under their car. The deafening roar of the engines stopped traffic, but by the time the passengers ran to the rail, the planes were long gone.

And through it all — the war adventures on the Dunnville front — my father, a corporal, tagged along for the ride and played the piano back at the base. I can see the scene, the piano surrounded by Australians and New Zealanders, its top festooned with pints of draft and everyone belting out "We'll hang our washing on the Siegfried Line — if the Siegfried Line's still there." I can see him giving "In Flanders Fields" a little Hoagy Carmichael spin.

My father never got shipped out to Europe. But he did get to come home on weekends. And it's not as if he saw no action whatsoever — I was born shortly after the war.

Perhaps his piano playing was so good it was felt his talents were better served in Dunnville than Dieppe. My mother prefers to believe his playing was so bad that the RCAF felt even the Germans didn't deserve that kind of punishment.

In an incredible ironic twist it turns out my mother, who worked at the Grand Valley Canning Factory in Dunnville, stuffing pears and peaches into bell jars, spilled more blood during the war than my father did. And they called *her* job piecework!

Needless to say, my father who played the piano for the duration of World War II never received a Victoria Cross, but I believe there was some talk of a Grammy nomination. "And after the war," said Marg, "he bought himself a ticket and went to Europe to have a look at the damage." So it's not as though he was totally uninterested in the global fight against fascism.

Today, Dunnville No. 6 Service Flying Training School of the Royal Canadian Air Force is a turkey farm, no doubt in honour of my father's war record.

A little travelling music, please.

Boy, How Things Have Changed!

What a difference nine decades make.

According to my encyclopedia, in 1906, the year my mother, Margaret, was born:

- Canada was beset by labour problems.
- In a time of restraint, Canadian MPs voted to keep their high salaries.
- Native Indians were threatening to take their land disputes to the King of England.
- Millions of people around the world were starving because of flooding and crop failure.
- A major earthquake struck San Francisco.
- Muslims and Hindus were fighting in India.
- China and Britain were fighting over Tibet.
- There was political unrest in Central America.
- There was political unrest in Cuba.
- There was racial tension in America — "Negroes were on the march."
- The president of the United States blamed his problems on the media.
- And the National Meteorological Office of the United States boasted: "The ability to forecast weather is within our grasp!" We're still waiting!

My Mother's Two-Word Turkey Recipe

My mother was never a woman of many words, mainly because my sisters never gave her a chance. But when my mother spoke, particularly in a crisis situation, the message was clear and concise while the meaning carried weight well beyond its words.

I will never forget the Thanksgiving Day in Dain City when, for no apparent reason, my father decided he would take an axe and slaughter the turkey himself, as the Pilgrims used to do. Since he was not a history buff, I could only assume the Pilgrims were a Welsh rugby team that killed and cooked their mascot after home games.

As someone who verily hates professional mascots like B. J. Bird and the San Diego Chicken, I believe my father might have been onto something back then.

Like all my father's best ideas, this one was bad, conceived with a bottle of Hudson's Bay Rye Whiskey and nurtured with a chaser of Labatt's India Pale Ale. Yet somehow this particular brain-fart survived the hangover and managed to surface the next afternoon.

My mother was dead against this plan, but it happened before she could stop it. Given some warning my mother could almost always derail my father's bad ideas by subtly planting other bad ideas in his mind — ones that did not involve an axe.

I was six, standing with my mother and my dog, Penny, on the side porch of the house on Forkes Road as my father removed this squawking fowl from the trunk of his car and walked past us to a spot behind the garage where he had strategically placed an axe and a chopping block stump topped with kernels of corn. From where we stood, we could not see the sacrifice. For this my mother added: "Thank God!" Then she crossed herself.

That's when the seriousness of the situation dawned on me. My mother was no idle genuflector. When my mother crossed herself it was either a respectful salute of gratitude or a sober signal to God that if He wasn't too busy He ought tohave a look here.

Penny was a friendly, midsized, reddish blond mutt, a male with a female name, which is why young boys should never entrust their older sisters to name the family dog.

We stood still, the three of us, listening intently for a very long time. I was holding Penny by the collar; he was agitated and whining. When the turkey let loose a partic-ularly piercing screech, the dog bolted free. I moved to follow him, but my mother's grip was unrelenting on my shoulders.

Growling, Penny ran full-tilt towards the back of the garage and then all at once we heard a thud, a scream, a yelp, and a man yell: "Goddammit!" My mother's hands flinched and tightened around my neck and I had to pull at them in order to breathe. Still she never said a word. We waited, stiffened by tension and silenced by fear.

Suddenly Penny appeared around the far corner of the garage. He fell to his knees, his face and chest soaked with blood.

"Good God, he's killed the dog!" my mother wailed, shoving me into the kitchen through a door that wasn't quite open. That was a mouthful for my mother. By this point both of us believed there were very few irrational acts my father was incapable of committing — but murdering the family pet with an axe broke new ground.

I climbed up onto the kitchen sink, and was able to watch the drama unfold through the window.

My father came to the porch proudly holding a headless, limp turkey in his right hand, blood splattered up both sleeves and the front of his white shirt. Never an easy thing to do, my mother ignored my father and walked towards Penny, bloody and hunkered down on the lawn. As she got closer to the dog, he barked and growled, his way of protecting the prize head of a turkey he held between his teeth.

My mother's shoulders fell in relief. Nobody who wasn't supposed to die did.

"Clean it!" my father said, smiling as he offered her the turkey. Standing there dripping with blood and grinning, he looked like a butcher with a learner's permit doing an ad for Butterball turkeys.

My mother walked by my father and the turkey, passing with an icy stare that froze them both in place. She walked slowly up the porch and on the top step she turned and offered up her recipe for fresh-killed turkey.

"Stuff it!" she said. Then she entered the house and locked all the grief and gore outside with the flick of a deadbolt.

Ah, yes, brevity, the soul of wit, and nobody comes by it more honestly than the Irish.

I didn't get a beating, which is how I know my father did not hear me laughing on the other side of the door.

He never killed a Thanksgiving turkey again, of course. Like the rest of us, he was dumbfounded that he had managed to do it even once without incurring heavy neighbourhood casualties.

Add to that experience the incident in Carey, North Carolina, a few years ago in which a woman artificially inseminated her sister with a turkey baster and, well, I'm pretty much a glazed-ham guy when it comes to major holiday dinners.

Like her mother, my mother surrounded herself with handsome, hardworking, big strapping men. Men — not real bright and damn proud of it!

In the tiny town of Dain City, my mother had plenty of company. "Dain City," as they used to say, "where men are men and women just find that so damn funny."

The Shelter Lady

I was born on October 18, 1946, at the Welland County General Hospital, in Welland, Ontario.

My mother, Margaret, was forty years old, which is why we were turned away at the maternity ward and sent down to the Minor Accidents. Even today when I pass a billboard for Planned Parenthood, I think to myself, that could be my smiling photo up there, over the words "Dire Consequences."

I was delivered just a few hours after Nadine Jowett. Two scrubbed-red, screaming, twitching, naked babies in adjoining beds. I fell madly in love with Nadine Jowett, even though at one point that day, she was at least ten times my age.

A little later in life, after Nadine and I spent Grades 7 and 8 at S.S. No. 4 in Dain City locked in googly-eyed stares across the classroom, we became so much in love that the principal, Mr. Hodgkins, had to bring in the Jaws of Life to separate us.

Love dies an agonizing death when you're twelve, and losing her plunged me into a well of depression so black, so deep, so desolate, only Kim Campbell's political strategist has been there since.

I had nothing to live for and even less to look forward

to. There was, for me, but one way out — death. So I tried to kill my best friend, Malcolm Hilton, with a railroad spike. Really, it was an accident. He still has the scar. This was the worst thing I'd ever done in my life . . . until a couple of years later when Alan Creighton took me duck hunting at Mud Lake and I shot him. Really, it was an accident. He still has the scar. Fortunately he had a shotgun and I had a pellet gun.

Rather perturbed, Malcolm later broke my arm in three places with a wheelbarrow and on another occasion buried a garden hoe in my hand. Much later in life I would name my cat after Malcolm and dedicate a book to him. They both walked funny. (I'm certain he never read the book. But I am not the least bit hurt by this. Apparently cats would rather sleep than read.)

We decided, as kids do, but generals don't, that the score had been evenly settled and called a truce that has lasted to this day. I see Malcolm socially and we're still good friends provided nobody shows up at the party with a railroad spike, a wheelbarrow, or a garden hoe. When that happens, all bets are off and it's every man for himself.

My mother refereed these battles as well as the romances. As I said, my mother was always there for me.

Almost always. Three exceptions come immediately to mind.

At fourteen days of age, family tradition dictated that my mother turn the frail and frothing baby boy over to his older sister to hold in preparation of a decade of babysitting to come. And they say my sister Gail was a very good holder of newborn baby boys, but she had the attention span of an Asian fruit fly.

"Oh, Joan," Gail yelled to my other sister, rushing to the living-room window, "there goes Roger Carbonneau, that cute guy you like so much!"

Gail forgot one thing. Me. Eyewitnesses, my mother being one, would later marvel: "He bounced . . . He hit the hardwood floor head first and he actually bounced right up in the air."

Although there is no record of this incident in the sports pages of the *Welland Tribune*, I believe I was the first kid in Canada ever to be spiked. It was a shame that Gail, by this time, was trying to pry the window open to call out to Roger, otherwise she might have made a gem of a recovery, catching me on the first bounce. Which by the way counts for five points when you're playing Babyball 21 Up.

Despite the early efforts of my older sisters, I lived to the age of two, whereupon Gail was generous enough to include me in her daily neighbourhood bicycle rides. Had my mother known that Gail had a two-year-old balanced on the back fender with his feet on the wheel nuts and his fingernails embedded in the leather seat, she'd have beaten her severely about the neck and ears with Plymouth Cordage Grade B hemp rope.

What Gail lacked in mental sharpness, she more than made up for in friendliness. "Follow me," she said to a man in a car who'd asked directions to a neighbour's house. And off we sped with me hanging on for dear, sweet, young, precious life.

When a car backed out of a driveway ahead of us on the right, Gail cut left, causing the man in the car following us to ram us from behind. I was thrown into a ditch and a coma. Gail, as was the case in all our early death-defying calamities, came away without a scratch. When I was released from the hospital several days later my mother diligently followed the doctor's orders and woke me up every hour on the hour so I would not lapse back into unconsciousness. My mother followed the instructions religiously but the doctor did not do a follow-up call. So, she did that, bless her heart, until I moved away to Kitchener to attend university. Even today I sleep in 59-minute intervals.

I would live to see both Joan and Gail reach the apex of their misspent youth — the Shelter Lady game. In this game, the origin of which is largely accredited to a South American dictator's torture techniques, two grown-up girls taunt, torment, and terrorize a three-year-old boy with the story that he was adopted, that he was abandoned on the doorstep of the Children's Aid Shelter by a band of migrant tobacco pickers, and today — if he's not good while the parents are away — today is the day the Shelter Lady comes to take him away.

They got a good year of cruel and unusual punishment out of the Shelter Lady game, but by age four I began to believe the reassurances of my mother, backed up by a certificate of birth and an unpaid invoice verifying the event. Like it or not, I was hers.

Then one day while my parents and Gail were out of the house and after I'd mixed all my sisters' perfume together in the bathroom sink, Joan called the Shelter Lady.

I'd heard this all before, of course, so I laughed and continued to aggravate my oldest sister to the best of my ability. I laughed right up until I heard the rap of the cane on the back door.

When I saw the old black hat, the black veil, and black gloves, I knew I was in serious trouble. The dark, damp stain forming at the front of my shorts confirmed it.

In the eerie recesses of a young mind, where terror goes to hide, I saw myself back in the Shelter Lady's slammer with a bunch of tobacco-picking orphans. Suddenly, proper behaviour, sibling obedience, and Dain City looked pretty good to me.

She was so absolutely scary that even Joan ran to some remote corner of the house and crouched in silence as the Shelter Lady snarled and banged her way around the kitchen and living room. I hid under my bed and held my breath until my parents came home. For a month I locked myself in the bathroom whenever anybody knocked at our door and shook uncontrollably at the sight of anything black. I was a model child for at least nine years after the incident. Later, when I was a marketing representative with the 3M company, my manager used to get record sales out of me by threatening to bring the Shelter Lady to the next motivational meeting.

It would be years until I learned that Gail and the Shelter Lady were one and the same witch.

So if you're thinking to yourself as you read this book, "Boy, is this guy screwed up or what," please have some compassion. You're right, of course, but I had a real rough childhood. They say the hazards that are most likely to kill you are located right in your own house. It's true. I know. I'm still related to most of mine.

But my point is, my mother was always there for me. Contrary to the allegations of two sadistic sisters, my mother was there when I was born. My mother was there for me when I was bounced on my head, nearby when I was hit by a car, and ready to drive me to the hospital when Malcolm Hilton pushed me out of a wheelbarrow and broke my arm. That's right, my mother is a jinx!

But she's all I got. Be kind to yours . . . because if you're not, one of these days my sister Gail, dressed as the Shelter Lady, will come out and pay you a visit. Trust me, being kissed on the lips by *The Godfather*'s Luca Brasi is a better way to go.

I've Been Reared in Small Towns

And as David Letterman would say, we all know how painful that can be.

Having been born in Welland, Ontario, I lived in nearby Dain City for the first seventeen years of my life and now just down the road in Wainfleet for the last seventeen years of my life. So whatever else they say about me, one thing's for sure — I'm no social climber.

There's no city in the world smaller than the one I grew up in, Dain City, Ontario, Canada. Back then Dain City was a friendly backwoods village, midway between Mud Lake and Bethel, bordered by Crowland and John's Creek on the north, Ramey's Bend to the south. Today Mud Lake is a bird sanctuary and the rest of those places wished they were.

Dain City, however, has survived in spirit and in name, albeit unofficially. It's now a comfortable bedroom community, south of Welland, north of Port Colborne, not too far from Niagara Falls, and on the same line of latitude as Puke, Albania. Honest. I got a detention for mentioning this in geography class once, but you could look it up.

The other day I was trying to describe my remote little hamlet to a friend from Toronto and I said, "You know, half the town voted for Trudeau."

"A lot of people voted for Trudeau," he replied.

"Yes," I agreed, "but in the last election?"

A few years ago, down at the red-brick Dain City school house, they brushed clean the blackboards, rang the last recess bell, and locked the doors up forever. It's gone. Gone condo, as a matter of fact. My mother was furious. Somehow she remembered there was a plaque of some sort with my name on it inside that school and she was determined to rescue it from the wrecking ball. And she did too! Today on my office wall hangs a heart-shaped wooden and brass tablet: The Sunnyside Dairy Award — Bridgeview Public School — Awarded Annually To The Pupil Showing Most Skill In Basic Arithmetic. Arithmetic! I get a brain cramp whenever I read about the three Dionne Quintuplets. Unless they've now expanded to include Celine and Marcel, sorry, I don't get it. Yet I will cherish this plaque always, because across the top on the fancy brass plate on which they usually etch a school's motto in Latin — something like "Emeritus, Veritas, Utilitas, Acne" — this one is blank.

I love that. Either Bridgeview Public School couldn't think of a clever motto to live by or they did have one but nobody could translate it into Latin. Maybe they intentionally left it blank in an effort to stimulate participatory jingoism. "So you think you're so smart — fill in your own Latin logo!" And someday I will: "Me mater victorio le Wrecking Ball."

(It's also true that after I graduated from Welland High and Vocational School, they closed that institution down too. And after I graduated from Waterloo Lutheran University, they quickly changed its name to Wilfrid Laurier University. But as my mother said, if they didn't want me to return, why didn't they just ask for some sort of donation and they'd have never heard from either one of us again.)

The village of Dain City and our school deserved a better fate. In the beginning, the place had a perfectly good name. Since it was not a city (if more than six people left town at one time, it lost its legal classification as a village) and the word "Dain" had no apparent meaning to anyone who lived there, I therefore thought it a good name. At least as fitting as Airline Junction, its previous meaningless moniker.

Dain City was once the envy of . . . oh, I don't know. This world is so weird I'm sure somebody, somewhere envied us, but they were too embarrassed to admit it.

Dain City was once a humming little hamlet known throughout the region for its drive-in theatre. The Welland Drive-In was the social hot spot of Welland County and the place that conceived — sorry, the place that coined the famous line that now graces the bumpers of trailer-park vehicles from here to Holland: *Ulop niet wanneor je deze auto rochin ziet!* — If This Baby's a-Rockin', Don't Come a-Knockin'!

Okay, so we never invented the modern romance novel. So sue us!

In the mid-'50s, Dain City went the way of White Pigeon, Netherby, and Perry Station, towns that simply ceased to exist. The land grabbers on Welland's city council amalgamated the Village of Dain City and changed its name to — are you sitting down? — Welland Junction.

Profound originality aside, you can imagine the cross the sons and daughters of Dain City had to bear, explaining to perfect strangers that they came from a place that was the lesser part of Welland.

I got around it by saying I was from Salt Lake City, Utah.

In the beginning, our public school had a perfectly good name — S.S. No. 4. The number gave us validity, balance, rank, and order. We weren't No. 1, but then on a scale of 10 we were doing better than most.

Nobody knew what S.S. meant. It didn't matter. What mattered was you could chisel "S.S. No. 4" into your desk top in less than one minute and never get caught. Just as quickly, you could tattoo "S.S. No. 4" on Jimmy Nelson's butt with a sharp fountain pen, provided four guys were holding him down at the time.

No matter what sport we played, the whole student body would fill the bleachers and scream, "We're No. 4! We're No. 4!" And we usually were. And there was no anxiety or disappointment. We were by our number destined not to win, place, or show. But we were always close enough to be in the photo finish.

I suspect the school board thought S.S. No. 4 sounded too much like a secret training base for the Luftwaffe and they changed the name to Bridgeview Public School. Why? Because you could see the Dain City Bridge, or rather the Welland Junction Bridge, from the school house.

Clever creativity notwithstanding, you could also see Doris Evans's General Store and Post Office, but nobody suggested Evansview School, something that this dear lady deserved. You could see our stalwart crossing guard, Ida Griffiths, standing at the corner by the bridge for twenty-five accident-free years, but they didn't name the school Griffiths Public. You could see — and smell — Paul Pietz's farm from the school, but they didn't call the place Paul Pietz Public after the reeve of Humberstone Township and grand gentleman of Dain City.

Instead they chose to honour a bridge, one that was rendered useless after the canal was rerouted. Thank goodness you couldn't see old man Michener's outhouse from the school. Our school mascot would have been a giant roll of two-ply tissue.

And poor Doris Evans. Not only did they change the names of the village and the school but one day they moved the highway from the front of her store to the rear, and she's had to do her business out the back door ever since.

And finally they closed down the Welland Drive-In. One day carloads of teenagers with hormonal imbalances showed up and there it was — gone. When the new Welland ship canal was rerouted, engineers first drew a line straight through the drive-in theatre and then carved it out with bulldozers. Not that it really mattered. I understand that during the first season it was closed, attendance actually increased. It was quieter without the speakers.

Every kid should be so lucky as to have a drive-in at his back door. Talk all you want about sex education for today's children. They use books. Me and Malcolm Hilton had binoculars and the Welland Drive-In Theatre. We were watching X-rated movies long before they were invented.

Industrial planners never see the human side of progress. Sure, we've now got one of the greatest waterways in the world, but where have all the horny people gone? Gone to graveyards, every one. And dead-end dirt roads too.

You learned things at S.S. No. 4.

You learned that lying could get you into trouble, as it did Clare Piper the day he told the teacher he was late for class because he followed a man's footsteps in the snow to a hole in the ice in the middle of the canal. A half day, two fire trucks, a police cruiser, and an ambulance later, Clare admitted he had overslept again.

I learned the sweet thrill of victory when I laid a

beating on Frankie Smith at the 2:15 afternoon recess on the last day of school before summer holidays. At the 3:30 bell, I learned how fleeting fame can be when Frankie's friend Larry Sonnenberg got hold of me and hit me so hard, so often, they had to use Penny, the family dog, to identify me when I got home.

I learned about word association. I still can't hear the words "cloak room" without some strange primeval feeling for Denise Gagnon. Mrs. Leach, our Grade 4 teacher, could make us write "the cloak room is for coats and footwear" 100 times, but after I kissed Denise, 100 lashes were not going to convince me that a cloak room was only good for jackets and galoshes.

You learned to cope quite well without modern media. We didn't need newspapers or radio to find out what was happening. We had Mrs. Hilton, my mother's best friend, and she had a party line. Even back then she was known as Internet Alex.

I have fond memories of my mother and me, the times we spent together when I was a kid growing up in Dain City.

My mother pulling me all the way up Forkes Road, by the ear, to Doris Evans's store to return the tin of shoe polish I'd stolen. (Yes, once I was a thief, but a spiffy thief nonetheless.)

Catching the biggest black bass ever caught off Ort's dock and rushing home to show my mother, only to total my bike turning into our driveway and jamming a fish hook through my thumb that required surgery to remove it. It was the only case ever recorded of a fish dying in a bicycle accident.

And the time she let me lick all the icing off the egg beaters on my birthday and my sister Gail had to dash in from outside to turn the Mixmaster off. Sometimes my mother was distracted.

A few years ago I took Margaret back to Dain City, to the church basement where they were having a tea social to commemorate the closing of Bridgeview Public School.

I spotted Mr. Gregory, one of my favourite teachers from public school, and I crossed the room to shake his hand. I introduced myself and told him how much I appreciated the special attention he'd given me during the two years I had attended his classes. He gave me a friendly reply, but I knew he did not remember me.

I mentioned the times he had come to our house for dinner and again he was polite but perplexed.

At my mother's request, Mr. Gregory had helped me with my valedictorian address upon graduating Grade 8. (I believe I was the school's second choice after Hubert Rynberk turned it down.) I now thanked Mr. Gregory for it. He nodded vigorously, but I was still a missing person in his mind.

At that, he pulled out a picture of our hockey team, the

champions of Humberstone Township in 1957.

"I was wondering if you could help me identify some of these boys," he said.

"Sure," I said, gripping one side of the photo he was holding. "That's Earl Nugent and Ray Arnott and Wes Boyd and Ricky Koabel, and you see this kid, Mr. Gregory? The one with the big ears, down in front with the 'C' on his sweater, holding the trophy? That's me, Mr. Gregory!"

He looked at the photo, up at me, down at the photo, and then he said: "No, no, I don't think so."

I was just about to strangle the son-of-a-bitch when Sharon Marr walked through the front door . . . Sharon Marr who had, in the vernacular of the day, a body built like a brick shithouse.

"Sharon Marr!" exclaimed Mr. Gregory, leaving me holding the photo of the hockey team as he rushed across the room to greet her. "It's been ages!"

Well, he can have Sharon Marr, but he's not getting the photo back.

My mother and I left shortly after.

Today, as we wallow in the images of hooded hijackers, high-profile murderers, and people who wear diaper pins in their noses, my mind wanders back to a peaceful place that was as overlooked by the outside world as it was unappreciated by those who lived there. But now that they've renamed it and reclaimed it, moved but not improved it, closed and disposed of its landmarks — you know, I just can't get to Dain City from here anymore. But there are many days when my mother still lives there in her mind.

Growing Up, Out of Order

Every month, it seems, a new pop psychology publication bursts onto the book scene, giving daytime talk show hosts yet another social theory with which to scramble the brains of their studio audience. Which, if you've ever taken a good look at these audiences, is not what I'd call a tough assignment.

Most of these bestsellers deal with the question of why we humans are such repulsive beings that even dogs wouldn't live with us were it not for smoked pig's ear treats and regular recreational rides in the car.

Not too long ago the flavour of the month was *Birth Order*, a book by Edmonton psychologist Paul Koziey that claims our personality traits are developed according to our birth placement in the family — be that first, last, or middle born. Dr. Koziey's theory: we are what we are according to our estimated time of arrival on earth.

Accordingly, first-born children are controlling, dominating dictators. Middle-born are sandwiched siblings, ever the mediators, but ordinary and overlooked. "They have the fewest pictures in the family photo album," says the doctor. Last-borns are the babies, the cute and special ones, charming "because people always like to have a baby around." Not to be confused with puppies, who, as a rule, don't wear diapers but should.

Well, let's see how Dr. Koziey's theory applies to children growing up in a place called Dain City where small animals outnumbered people and often outpointed them at the local obedience school.

In Dain City, the prevailing pattern of child development adhered to the pummelling principle — the bigger, older kids thumped the smaller, younger kids, who in turn waited until they were bigger and older to thump those kids coming up behind them who were, not coincidentally, smaller and younger.

You did this because you could. And you did it until your mother caught you and invoked her own personal pummelling principle. (For the record, my mother never once hit me. Nor did she ever assign my father to do the job. She never needed to. My mother had a look, a look of hell fire and damnation that could have burned a hole right through Johnnie Cochran and sent O. J. Simpson screaming from the courtroom: "I did it! I did it! Just make that woman stop lookin' at me!")

True to Dr. Koziey's theory, several first-born from our neighbourhood went on to become dominant and imposing figures excelling in many areas of education and industry, even while they were still on parole.

I'm sure many of our middle-born did great things with their lives, but of course nobody noticed and there's no record of their existence. Some last-borns proceeded to become cuter and cuter as they got older and older until a few became so downright pretty and perky they turned into television weather forecasters and had to be humanely put down.

As if to intentionally defy these psychologists, my mother gave birth out of order. Beginning in 1934, my mother brought three kids into this world, all six years apart.

Being the youngest of three, with two older sisters, I am definitely not Dr. Koziey's typical last-born child. (Wait, wait, wait . . . this does not in any way imply that I am Dr. Koziey's son or rather that he was or even is my father. What I meant was . . . just a second . . . Okay, my mother has just confirmed that she's never met the man in her life and that's good enough for me. So let's just drop it, all right?)

Anyway, due to the age disparity I was more like the sandwiched sibling, always ordinary and overlooked, although my photo does appear frequently in the family album. You just can't tell it's me because, thanks to Gail and Joan, my babysitters and protectors, I'm usually wrapped in bandages or wearing a body cast.

On the other hand, my sisters would remember me not so much as cute and special but more as Kid Torment, a terrorist tot on training wheels, the baby brother from beyond hell. (Hey, I say if you can't use live snakes and dead mice to your advantage in wars of sibling rivalry, then you probably *are* the little twerp they say you are.)

True to *Birth Order* form, my older sister, Gail, the middle-born, appeared in very few family photos — mainly because my sister Joan took scissors and cut Gail's head out of every snapshot. (Puppies may not wear diapers, but sisters should definitely be declawed.)

A bit of an entrepreneur, I would scoop up the shots of Gail's head and paste them to the bodies of naked African tribal women recently ripped from the pages of our school's *National Geographic*.

I admit charging Malcolm Hilton and Frankie Sokoloski a nickel a look might have been a pretty tacky thing to do, but believe me, before kids in Dain City set up their lemonade stands, they came to me for venture capital.

Dr. Koziey's book may explain why each of us was born six years apart. (Lord knows, my mother's unwilling to do so.) It must have taken twelve years for my mother to recover from having brought a dictator and then a mediator into the world, and after "cute and special" me arrived, she gave up altogether.

My mother, sweet and sensitive person that she is, has never actually discussed this unusually long gap between children, but I once found a magazine quiz form she had filled out, and beside the line "If I could be anything in the world, I would be . . ." she had written "spinster."

Yes, the three of us have made dear Margaret's life a

living nightmare, but apparently it's not our fault, we just grew up out of order.

According to Dr. Koziey's rationale, any child born more than five years after the previous one comes under the category of first-born. In other words, a child of five would re-enter the system as a new first-born child. And this of course is where his theory falls apart. If not entirely impossible, then this is at least unusually painful, and I think any woman who has ever delivered a five-year-old child will back me up on this one.

But seriously, according to the five-year-equals-first-born rule, my mother, not unlike the country of Haiti, gave birth to three dictators in a row. Hence, what my mother needed more than a psychologist was a Canadian peacekeeping force. That or the business card of a reputable adoption agency.

Suffice to say we love you, Margaret, but thanks to modern psychology, we have no idea why.

I Took My Mother on My Honeymoon

It's true. My mother came along on my honeymoon.

I feel like I just made that statement while nervously standing in front of a support group for men suffering from the latest pop psychology aberration, the apron strings syndrome.

Yes, I was married once, and anyone who's ever spent a couple of days with me agrees, once was more than enough.

I was married on September 15, 1973, and a week later me, my new wife, Nancy, and my long-time mother, Margaret, took off for Europe together. No one was more surprised than Nancy. She found out when my mother read her a revised edition of the prenuptial agreement at the check-in line at Pearson International.

Actually I think the whole thing was Nancy's idea. Margaret's a lot like a good-luck charm: once you spend time with her you're reluctant to let her get out of reach. And since she'd never been to Europe or the British Isles, bringing Margaret on the honeymoon seemed a logical thing to do. She takes up very little room. Besides, she'd be with us on a three-week holiday through England, Scotland, Wales, and Ireland and then on to Paris with my sister Joan while Nancy and I set off backpacking for a year.

It wasn't long before three became a crowd. Oh, Nancy

and Marg had a helluva time — I was not this crowd's pleaser.

Checking into a bed-and-breakfast hotel on Russell Square in London was fun.

"Number of beds required?"

"Just one," I said, to see how high up an Englishman's eyebrows will go.

"Shall we knock you up in the morning, then?"

"We have no plans to start a family, and when we do, it's the kind of thing we'd like to do ourselves. Canadians are old-fashioned that way."

England then and now is not the most modern of countries, which is why, I suppose, it is the most charming. In the '70s, central heating was unheard of, and the hot water flowing from the bathtub taps was coin operated. Even in private homes.

Not to get into details, but I don't think you've lived until you find yourself running back and forth across a busy hallway with hands full of shillings trying to keep two women from freezing their bums off. I felt like the change-maker in a badly run bordello.

The first night I suggested we all stay in, rest up, and read up on all the museums we'd be visiting. The next thing I knew I was standing in the hallway in my pyjamas saying goodnight to Margaret and Nancy as they took off for "one of those pubs where everybody sings dirty limericks."

I remember studying Frommer's *Europe on Ten Dollars a Day* and making calculated notes in the margin as we sped across the top of Wales on British Rail with Margaret and Nancy drinking beer and telling jokes to Belgian tourists in the bar car. Innocents abroad they were not.

I remember the ferry crossing from Holyhead, Wales, to Dun Laoghaire, Ireland, the women enjoying a picnic supper on their bunks below while I blew my lunch off the stern into the swells of the Irish Sea. Travel tip: Downwind is a bad place to be when you're with me at sea.

I remember arriving in Dublin and seeing my mother's dream of a St. Patrick–green Erin dashed by some of the filthiest graffiti to ever deface public monuments and city walls. People who say politics and sex don't mix have not seen what a devious Irishman can do with a can of spray paint and a flat surface.

And the cabbie, trying unsuccessfully to steer us away from the bed-and-breakfast I'd selected from the Frommer guide. Thinking he was just going to stiff us for a longer ride or take us to his family's hotel, I was having none of it. Until finally we entered the slum he warned us about and he stopped in the middle of the road. Turning to me in the back seat, he said: "Son, this is the place where if anybody ever paid the rent, the police would be called to find out where they got the money."

We stayed at a nice quiet Irish hotel, owned by the cabdriver's family.

I remember we stayed with Nancy's aunt and uncle in Scotland, on a farm near Peterhead. We toured the local scotch distillery, and I was fascinated by the fact that scotch whisky, before it's aged or caramelized, is clear as tap water. How powerful could that be, eh? While Nancy and Margaret shared shandies I went with "the water" — theirs and mine. I don't know if you've ever seen rural Scotland spinning around you like you're the ball on a whirring roulette wheel, but it's not something you soon remember.

Back in England, I remember climbing halfway up the Tower of London before Margaret's claustrophobia kicked in and we had to turn around and ease our way back down the narrow, winding stone staircase. Nancy and I had no problem with this. It was the busload of American tourists coming up behind us who requested Margaret be beheaded alongside Anne Boleyn.

I suppose the last straw was the dart game in the Trafalgar Pub near the Wimbledon tube station in London. Nancy and Margaret were having a great time clinking pints of ale and winging darts that sometimes actually hit the board. I felt it was a little dangerous and suggested they abandon the game.

It was at that moment I learned never to kill the joy of women who have been drinking and are holding three darts each.

It was also at that moment Nancy made a formal request to switch return airline tickets to Canada. No, not her and Marg. Nancy wasn't going home. She wanted me to switch tickets with Marg so I'd go home and she and my mother could backpack across Europe.

In the nick of time Joan arrived in London and we got her and Marg organized and on their way to Paris. You've never seen such crying. The thought that Marg was leaving us and I wasn't — well, Nancy was a mess.

Before we set out hitchhiking to Dover, Nancy asked if it would be okay if we dropped in to the Canadian Consulate in London to pick up some mail we were expecting and to ask someone in an official capacity to divorce us.

Hey, I'm kidding. It would be seven years before Nancy got that smart.

I must say, however, that it was during this year abroad, tramping across Europe and North Africa, that Nancy persuaded me to become a writer.

Years later she was quite disappointed that I became a writer of books, movies, and humour columns. From the very beginning, it was Nancy's dream that I become a travel writer . . . and spend long periods of time away from home. That way she and Marg could have the place to themselves.

How Mom Came to Visit but Stayed

At eighteen I graduated from Welland High and Vocational School, then left home and never went back.

I went to first-year university at Brock in St. Catharines, worked a year on the swing grinders at Atlas Steels in Welland, and finished up university with two years at Waterloo Lutheran in Kitchener.

I sold books to universities and colleges across Canada for Merrill Publishing of Columbus, Ohio, got married, backpacked across Europe, sold audio-visual equipment for 3M, backpacked across Europe, wrote for and then became editor of Niagara's *Alive and Well Magazine*, got unmarried, created and ran Niagara's *What's Up Niagara* magazine for four years, set up housekeeping on Sunset Bay in Wainfleet, Ontario, to write full time and, until today, lived independently and alone.

With me off to university and her last excuse to stay in the house gone, Marg left too. For a time she rambled around a bit herself — a nursemaid for an invalid Hamilton lawyer, a sandwich maker for the Hamilton Tiger Cats, a long-distance babysitter — anything to keep her head above water and me in school books. However, for nearly thirty years my mother has lived with my sister Gail and her family through three Ontario cities. She has helped raise Gail's two children, Whitney and David, who, to everyone's amazement, are now adults. As "Chief" of the household who rightfully earned that nickname, she somehow managed to survive a chicken that started out as a science project, a duck that started out as a chicken egg, and two Irish setters who started out but never did manage to grow up. When Harry, a gorgeous but astoundingly stupid dog, ate my mother's false teeth and she did not move out . . . the true depth of her love for this family was finally understood.

We kept close and always in touch, Margaret and me, but it was usually by phone and special-occasion visits.

All of a sudden, with my sister Gail now in the middle of moving and starting a new business to boot, my mother, Margaret, the Mighty Mick from County Cork, is my new roomie.

Exactly how in hell did this happen? When she mentioned she needed another place to live, I said, "Great!" I thought she meant Florida. When she asked if it would be all right if she moved in here with me, I took one of those laughing fits where the tears stream down your face and you can't quite catch your breath.

End thirteen years living alone in a house where music is a must but clothes are merely optional? Give up a life of weird hours, strange friends, good wine, and bad diet? What a sense of humour this woman has.

Seeing my mother standing on my doorstep with all

her belongings, all I could do was cry, then laugh, then lunge for the lock on the door. But it was too late, she was in. She's fast for eighty-six!

I was dead set against her moving in until my mother produced a document, which a lawyer declared legal and binding when I described it to him on the phone — a document that listed me as the mortgagee and her the mortgagor.

Damn. It was good to see her again. Not since the renewal at $9\frac{1}{2}$ percent had I realized how much I'd missed this woman. (Mortgage — noun, from the word "mort" meaning till death do you pay and then only on the interest.)

I live in a summer cottage that I've turned into a winterized home. It's on the north shore of Lake Erie, up fifty feet from the beach and well within flood damage distance from the nasty November storms nobody told me about when I bought the place.

I have "summer people" on either side of me, so fall and winter are the quiet and private times, whereas in late spring and summer it's like living at a resort up in Muskoka.

The cottage is solid but old, small but practical. Except for used automobiles, it's the first major purchase I've ever made. I bought the place when I became single after a seven-year marriage and my mother took back the mortgage. As she said at the time, it was cheaper than taking me back.

With no thought of ever owning anything I couldn't drive or carry, this elaborate cabin with its working fireplace and cathedral-ceiling living room just felt right the moment I stepped through the door. The basement with the beer fridge cinched the deal.

Now, in a flash my single life passed before my eyes because before my eyes stood Mom. But I'll tell you, I couldn't be happier, because at this point in our lives, my mother and I, we're able to share . . . What the —? Excuse me for a second . . .

"No, Mom, I told you! The catnip. I said the *catnip* goes in the top drawer. The cat goes outside . . . whenever he begins breathing again."

So now there are three of us. Malcolm is 125 in human years and Marg is 86, also in human years. Not to dwell on my mother's age, but to put it in historical context, the year my mother was born, Sir Wilfrid Laurier was a prime minister, not a university, the Kenora Thistles won the Stanley Cup, Jack Minor was trying to domesticate geese, my favourite Renaissance man, Paul Cézanne, died, and for some unexplained reason, Enrico Caruso was fined $10 for harassing Miss Hannah Graham in the New York Zoo's monkey house. It may have been the first sexual harassment case involving a primate. Honest, you can look all this stuff up.

Now don't get me wrong, she looks like she's in her low seventies, but the fact remains she's closing in on ninety at about that speed, in miles per hour.

It's been several months now, and don't misunderstand me, we are all getting along. Like three goldfish in a shot glass.

Essentially, I have two roommates whose combined age is a robust 211 years. And this poses no problem whatsoever unless of course you want to do something a little on the adventurous side — like communicate.

Me: "Get off the couch."

Mom: "What?"

Me: "I told him to get off the couch."

Mom: "Why, I'm not hurting anything!"

Me: "Not you — him."

Malcolm contributes one wheeze and two sighs to this conversation and shifts so that all four paws are now straight up in the air.

The phrases "Huh?" and "Whadyasay?" seem to dominate all household conversations these days, and Malcolm has his head cocked in that inquisitive pose so often we're not sure whether his cervical vertebrae have fused or he's impersonating the RCA Victor dog.

Of course there are a lot of advantages to having Mom living with me.

For instance, it's a real big time saver to sit down at the end of each day with the crossword puzzle and find it's already done.

I've significantly reduced my electricity bill since my

mother moved in. There's no need to leave a light on while I'm out, now that there's somebody standing at the door, looking at her watch, and tapping her foot every night when I come home.

I've lost weight. Who can eat real food when it's teatime twenty-four hours a day?

And of course I spend more quality time with Malcolm now that he's chosen to hide out in the same place as I do. The tool shed.

We have moments, the three of us, of which memories are made.

Me: "I gotta go to the store and get some litter so I can clean out Malcolm's box. Do we need milk?"

Mom: "I just cleaned out the fridge yesterday, dear."

Me: "I said the litterbox, not the fridge!"

Mom: "Well that's a stupid place to keep the milk!"

When they film my mother's life story, it will star the ghost of Gracie Allen. "Say goodnight, Margaret." "Goodnight, Margaret," says Margaret.

Confused by all of this, Malcolm paces back and forth between the litterbox and the fridge not knowing what he should do if an opportunity arises at either location. His mind races back and forth between a bowl of milk and a bowel movement until finally he works himself into a great big nap.

It's an eerie feeling to be sitting in a party of three and you're the only one who hears the phone ringing. And when you get up to answer it, both of them look at you like you're a psychic.

Sometimes I'll answer the phone when it hasn't been ringing and I'll proceed to have a loud, animated conversation with an editor or a producer and I'll use coarse language and tell him as a writer I have my artistic integrity and I'm just not going to take it anymore. When I return, they both seem pleased I stuck up for myself, and Lord knows I feel a lot better.

My mother never cared for cats, but she absolutely loves Malcolm. She'll talk to him and play with him and then she'll rough him up a little too much and Malcolm will rake her hand with his claws. That's usually when I walk in.

They both look guilty — one's bleeding, the other's cowering. I want to send them both to bed without their dinners. Or better yet, sit them down at the dining-room table and switch their dinners.

I don't know who to trust anymore. I'm sure she's sneaking him treats when I'm not home and I'd bet money it was Malcolm who tipped my mother off to the beer fridge in the basement. (Just because I'm not naturally a paranoid person, it doesn't mean at least one of them isn't out to get me.)

More than once I've thought of taking out one of those "Free to a Good Home" notices, and frankly I'd just as soon flip a coin to choose which of their names appears in the ad.

Call me crazy, but I don't think a man of forty-five should have to hide the *Playboy* magazine under the sofa every time his mother walks in the room. Yesterday, I found the swimsuit issue of *Fab Felines* under Malcolm's litterbox, so he's obviously feeling the pressure as well.

On the bright side, both Malcolm and I are looking forward to growing up tall and strong now that we're eating all our greens, and we're equally astonished at how much dirt had accumulated behind our ears during the time we were living as bachelors.

The situation, however, is not without humour. The first day I watched Malcolm brushing his teeth after every meal, I damn near hurt myself laughing. Mothers, at any age, never really stop mothering.

It was in the midst of all this mayhem that I read about an interesting phenomenon evolving in Japan, as if anything that develops in a country where they feed beer to beef cattle and raw fish to people is not, at the very least, interesting.

It seems that the Japanese are burned out and succumbing to stress-related diseases because they work fourteen-hour days producing expensive electronic gadgets that we Canadians buy in one minute with a credit card and then work overtime and part-time for the rest of our lives paying them off. It's murder living in a material world — thank God for the escapism of VCRs.

The article revealed that the Japanese population is

rapidly ageing and with their children off chasing the almighty yen, the older folks are lonely. That's why a personal service company in Tokyo is offering to rent — I'm not making this up — a "stand-in" family to lonesome Japanese couples to fill the void left by their real family. The fee for these "entertainers" is $1,300 for half a day of companionship and communication.

I tried to imagine what kind of people would rent family members out to strangers for monetary gain. Has the devaluation of human life finally come to this? Did that company in Tokyo think for one minute they could just run an ad in a newspaper and find "spare" family members who would just pick up and . . .? Did they even once consider the feelings of . . .? Did anybody not notice the . . .?

I had the woman in the classified section of the local newspaper on the phone within minutes and reading my ad back to me.

Are you a little lonesome these days? Do you have a yen to stop yawning? Just the two of you in that big old pagoda with nobody to talk to? Could you use a little company and light entertainment? Do you have cash? For less than $300 a day, you could rent MARGARET AND MALCOLM — a congenial couple of cut-ups known professionally as THE LADY AND THE TRAMP. She does magic tricks! He sleeps through them! They both love ice cream! Call now. Operators are standing by.

The ad wasn't what you'd call successful, but the offer still stands. And if you're interested in renting my family and you phone and get my answering machine, I've worked out a system to handle my calls and those calls that are for my mom. If the message is for me, just say it's for William Thomas, and if it's for Marg, you could just say it's for William Thomas because *she listens in on the extension!*

It's a shame the print ad didn't work because I was going to follow it up with a promotional video on the MuchMusic station featuring Annie Lennox of the Eurythmics. I envisioned a fast-paced, action-packed little music movie starring Margaret and Malcolm and entitled *The Arthritics.* "Coming soon to a sofa near you!"

Of course I'm just kidding. Hey, it's great living with Mom again. As a matter of fact, I think I've become much more accommodating and flexible as a direct result of our communal living arrangement. For instance, just to ease the tension around here, I've planned a family outing for next week. Friday, I'll be taking Marg and Malcolm to the Toronto Zoo. And if everything goes as planned, I'll pick them up on the following Thursday.

The Senior Citizen Fitness Workout

Did I mention my mother is living with me? Temporarily?

Did you read about it in my newspaper column or are you the one who refuses to pay the taxi driver and instead sends Margaret and her luggage back to me with a nasty note every couple of days? Have you no compassion whatsoever?

Hey, I'm kidding. Yes, my mother is living with me now, but we're getting along like a couple of kids at camp . . . that would be Yasser Arafat and Benjamin Netanyahu at Camp David.

Every time I write about her, all her friends call her up and say, "Margaret, let's sue the little S.O.B.!" But she never does. And in the '90s I think that's a true testimonial to love, when a mother and son can always settle out of court.

My mother is surprisingly fit for her age and on most days a cane-twirling dynamo of energy and enthusiasm. For instance, she can wash and dry the dinner dishes in less than twenty minutes, and that includes the time it takes me to fish the pieces of my favourite wine glass out of the bottom of the sink. She can put away the cutlery and china in a fraction of the time it takes me to find them and put them back where they're supposed to be.

And she can sort and put away the laundry in the same amount of time it takes me to realize I'm struggling to put on *her* track suit, not mine.

Recently, I've figured out why she's so fit. She's on the same workout program as all other Canadian seniors. It's called the Walk, Run, and Jog from Doctor to Dentist to Druggist to Chiropractor to Test Lab to Grocery Store and Home Again in Under Four Hours Three Times a Week Workout.

Yeah, who has time to get sick when you spend all your time on the treadmill of preventive maintenance?

I know the procedure — I'm the driver, the doorman, the escort, the bag boy, the valet, and the personal secretary.

After a couple weeks of this, I'm convinced there's no medicinal value in any of the prescription pills given to the elderly — they're all placebos. The labs give out the same blurry x-ray results to all Canadian seniors. There's nothing wrong with their upper plates or their lower lumbar regions. There's nothing whatsoever wrong with these people. They're healthy as race horses, thanks to clever government social programs that keep them in constant motion and confusion. It's the '90s Aerobics Appointment Program. Miss one and you'll never see 90.

It's a proven fact, senior citizens never die. The adult children who take care of them do.

Doctor/dentist/druggist/chiropractor/lab/A & P — my mother, with an artificial hip, can outrun and outlast the

Energizer Bunny. Me? I keep begging her doctor to give me something for chronic fatigue syndrome.

I keep having this recurring nightmare that begins when we burn out my Honda Civic with all this running around and I have to ride my ten-speed bike with Margaret sitting on the handlebars. I always wake up when Marg yells: "Watch the puddles, you'll ruin my dress!"

I feel so lousy, last week I went to her chiropractor. I don't know how it happened; one day, there I was sprawled out on Dr. Bosilac's massage table, looking up at him. He asked me where it hurt. I said it didn't, I just wanted to get some rest.

Pretty soon I'll be asking her doctor for pep pills and gulping down cans of her strawberry Ensure.

I don't know how much more I can take.

One day in the not-too-distant future, we'll be making our daily cross-country dash for good health, but now she'll be driving the car and I'll be mumbling in a fetal position from the back seat. "Don't hit the pot holes," I say so meekly. "It makes my teeth hurt!"

In my weakened state, I age rapidly and hallucinate to the point where my mother begins to look younger and younger. Before you know it, we'll pass each other at fifty going in opposite directions.

She starts to date one of my high school fraternity brothers and I move to Florida and live in a trailer park with one of the ladies from her bowling team. (We win the Peachtree Trailer Park Shuffleboard Tournament, but really, it's no consolation.)

I send her postcards, writing mostly about the weather and the high cost of health insurance; she sends me Polaroids from the last beer blast and asks if she can borrow my backpack for her trek across Europe.

I know I deserve this — the coming full circle of the mother/son relationship. She spent some of her best years hauling me from hockey games to baseball practice, from swimming in the canal to Sunday picnics at Cedar Bay.

The whole thing reached the depth of daftness yesterday, when, while driving her to some clinic, just pick one, I turned to her and said: "If you don't turn that music down, you're going to go deaf one of these days."

And my mother, with that coy attitude that teenagers have, turns to me and says: "Huh?" Then she turns away and stares out the window, like how could anybody my age ever understand her.

My mother is living with me temporarily. Temporarily — of a brief period, a short duration of time, soon to conclude. If she's not out by May 15 — I mean it — I'm running away from home.

Things I'd Rather Not Explain to My Mother

- The big surprise in *The Crying Game*.
- How much her MP will collect in pension if he sits in the House for two terms.
- The Heaven's Gate, Nike shoes, vodka shooters, Hale-Bopp rendezvous.
- Why I had to quit university and work for a year after Rick Sernasie and I devised a sure-fire system to break the bank at the Fort Erie Racetrack.
- Why Nancy Murphy and I didn't realize the power went out that time we were studying together in the basement.
- How I sometimes somehow manage to run out of ice cream while she's visiting.
- That when I knew Mike Harris in university, he had the same number of toes as me.
- Why Pepsi won't send her a free case even though she tells everybody it's ten times better than Coke.
- What I did with my tap dancing shoes the day the guys from the ball team spotted me coming from lessons across the Dain City Bridge.
- That all the nice ladies who visit her every Tuesday and Thursday get paid.

- That Meals on Wheels is not a beer and a sandwich on a casino shuttle bus.
- The link between Grey Power Insurance and the blue rinse set.
- How these days June Allyson makes a pretty good living peeing in public.
- That Queer Nation has nothing to do with Luxembourg.

"Don't Think *to Me in That Tone of Voice!"*

Just a second, I'll go see.

Yes, as a matter of fact, my mother is still living with me.

Sorry, I must be a little punchy from running back and forth to the neighbours to see if *their* washroom might be unoccupied.

So, did you read about my mom living with me or did I stop you on the street and ask if you'd consider taking her off my hands in exchange for my entire life's savings, a 1991 limited-edition Miata convertible, and my Nolan Ryan rookie card? I just forget.

Not that we're not getting along, mind you. Sharing the same roots and the same heritage, we're getting along just as well as any two people thrown together in tough times and asked to share common ground. Like the Bosnians and the Serbs.

The big problems we work out — like what to eat, when to run errands, and whether or not Geraldo looks younger now that he's had flesh taken from his ass and injected into his face. (Mom says she'd have to see a before-and-after of both before she'd make a decision. I say if you've seen either, how could you tell the difference?)

The big things you deal with, but it's the little things that push you over the edge when you're co-existing at close quarters.

For instance, my mother, who is . . . I'll say elderly because ancient makes her sound like she once dated William the Conqueror when in fact it was never a serious relationship although I am named after him . . . has this cute little habit . . . no, it's not really cute, it's more of a peculiar little thing . . . no, peculiar is not the word . . . it's more of a vexing sort of thing . . . actually annoying comes more to mind . . . but wait a minute . . .

Okay, I'm back now. I just went into the kitchen and put three dashes of Tabasco sauce in her strawberry-flavoured liquid nutrition supplement because: THE WOMAN TALKS TO HERSELF AND IT'S DRIVING ME OUT OF MY FREAKIN' MIND!

The first time I broached the subject by explaining there really should be a minimum of two people in a room during a conversation, she flatly denied talking to herself and walked away in a huff.

Rather than argue, I've decided to agree, whole-heartedly — my mother does not talk to herself. She just *thinks* out loud. Okay?

It goes something like this. I'll be sitting at my desk in my home office when I'll hear my mother *thinking* in her room: "Gee, I wonder what Gail is doing . . . maybe I should call."

And then I'll go into her room, pretending to look for something, and I'll say: "Gee, Mom, I wonder what Gail's up to. Maybe you ought to give her a dingle."

To which my mother gets this incredibly astonished look on her face and says: "You know, dear, I was just thinking about calling her. You must be physic or something!" (She means psychic, which I am, which helps in translating Margaretspeak.)

A little while later after reflecting on some bad news from my sister Gail, I'll hear my mom *think*: "Poor Alex, I should send her a card."

Then I'll happen to go by and say: "Here's one of those Group of Seven stationery cards I just got in the mail. You should send one of these to your friend Alex. It might cheer her up."

And my mother will get this amazed look on her face like she's just seen the Virgin Mary come out from behind the wine rack and she says: "You won't believe this, dear. I was thinking that very same thing!" Then she takes the card and goes off to some other part of the house, shaking her head, reluctant to let me out of her sight.

So in a very short span of time, my mother has gone from presuming her son is not bright enough to hold down a real job to believing that at some point in her life she has given birth to the Amazing Kreskin. And the best part is, I'm not even holding personal objects to my temple when I come up with all this stuff!

It's gotten to the point I don't even let her finish her thoughts anymore.

Mom *thinking* aloud: "Maybe I'll just make a pot —"

Me from the other room: "Marg, if you're making tea, I'll have a cup." Silence. Deep suspicious silence.

I don't even have to be there. I can feel *the look* — a mix of wonder and paranoia like somebody's successfully tapping her telephone before she even picks up the receiver.

Yesterday, the game got a little ugly. The cat was circling and searching for food when I heard my mother in another room *think*: "Maybe I'll just give him a treat, to tide him over until —"

"Why don't you feed him from one of your doggy-bags!" I yelled.

My mother would sooner part with her artificial hip than a doggy-bag of leftovers.

Mom, not thinking but actually speaking quite clearly: "Why, you stupid article!"

That's when I flew into a rage. I really, really lost it on that remark and we broached the brink of the worst confrontation we've had since she moved in.

I mean, it's my house, I pay the mortgage, I buy the groceries, and nobody, but nobody, calls my cat a stupid article. Except me.

Margaretspeak

- *Stupid article* — a term of endearment for her son that she began using forty years ago, long before she knew he would make a career out of writing stupid articles
- *Snazzy* — I'm standing before her, wearing a tie and a jacket
- *Grand* — an enchanting, rather elegant version of *great*
- *Don't count your chickens before they hatch!* — a private joke between her and Colonel Sanders
- *Just because you own a rosary, that doesn't make you a nun* — a moral warning
- *Go to blazes!* — annoyed
- *Take a long walk off a short pier* — very annoyed
- *Go to grass!* — angry
- *Go to grass and eat clover. And what you don't eat, roll over!* — ballistic
- *Buzz off* — I just played the "intercom pizza delivery guy" trick on her three times in a row
- *I'll crown you* — time for me to chill out in the royal penalty box
- *Nothing at all* — we've just had a bit of a row and she's still staring at me and I say: "What are you staring at?"

- How are you doing, Marg? *Anybody I can!* (For the record, I'm not so sure my mother understands the implications of this response and I have no idea where she picked it up. Either she's been sneaking out to the Rex Hotel while the other seniors are carpet bowling or Sunset Haven's "quiet hour" ought to be investigated.)

The Worst Day of My Life

You know how I've been whining about the *Three's Company* living arrangements at my house? Well, I take it all back. There's only two of us now.

Malcolm, my cat of eighteen years, up and died today. He got old in a hurry and his organs shut down. All except his heart, which was twice the size of Wainfleet, so Port Colborne's Dr. David Thorne, the pet world's Marcus Welby, came out to the house on a mission of mercy and helped the little guy into the deepest, sweetest sleep of his full and wonderful life.

Death expected is no less painful than a sudden surprise. It's just not as startling as that awful, sudden kick in the gut. But when you never pass up an opportunity to pet him, tease him, talk to him, or rough him up every time you walk by him, there are at least no regrets.

I did, however, have one nagging thought as I drove towards Toronto later the same day, to a meeting that could not be postponed. My mother didn't know about Malcolm. I mean, she knew that he was gone but she didn't know that Malcolm's resting place — at least (here comes that word again) temporarily, in the first stage of his journey to that grand, glittering litterbox in the great beyond — was in fact my beer fridge in the basement.

I'm sorry, but you don't take a dearly departed friend of two decades and dump him in a hole in a field. Not unless you're a mobster and that friend is Jimmy Hoffa.

After Dr. Thorne explained to me the cremation procedure — the freezer, the pickup, the communal firing, the drop off — I decided to go this one alone. Malcolm would get a private cremation and I would get only *his* ashes back. All I needed was a place to keep him cool for four days.

Choked and missing him already, I willed myself to get to Toronto, get through the meeting with my publisher, sign the contracts, and get home to deal with the fallout. Ahead of me lay a career opportunity of a lifetime. Behind me, the sadness and silence of the sweetest little soul that . . . Oh-oh. I'd forgotten about that other sweet little soul that now resides on the wrong side of the welcome mat.

Good Lord! What if my mother goes downstairs to filch a midday drink! I'll lose both my best friends all on the same day!

Oh, sure, Malcolm was all bundled up in his favourite blanket and enveloped into a clear plastic bag, then neatly secured with a bungee cord, but even so, my mother's curiosity would take over and the surprise, after a long unwrapping procedure, would be too much.

As I had not had the time to explain his imminent cremation to her, my mother would wonder long and hard why I'd kept him in the fridge.

"What if something happens to me?" she'd say to herself, out loud. "Would he put me in the beer fridge too?" she'd ask. "And why? For what purpose?" she'd ask and then she'd snap a beer, more now out of necessity than thirst.

More irrational thoughts would follow a second beer, maybe even a third, and by the time I got home the place would be crawling with cops and sealed off with yellow crime tape. I'd be the guy they caught with the cat in the fridge.

All my neighbours would step forward and one by one convict me with that damning line, the line you hear said about every sick serial killer ever arrested: "He seemed like a nice guy . . . Quiet . . . Kept to himself a lot."

By now they would have searched the fridge in the kitchen, opened the freezer and found my real secret: club soda ice cubes for scotch.

Under pressure Dr. Thorne would rat me out. He'd be handcuffed and spilling his guts: "It was him! *He* called *me*! I didn't want to do it but he said it would be best for everybody! 'Humane' is the word he used!"

I could see as clear as if it were Tuesday night at ten: a big guy in plainclothes, with a hooked nose and sweat beading upon his bald head, steps under the yellow tape, flashes a badge in my face, and says, "Detective Andy Sipowicz, NYPD Blue."

Then he grabs me by the neck, slams me against the side of my house, and a geranium planter falls on my head, covering me in black loam, red petals, and the spare key to the front door. "So you and the Doc here," says Sipowicz, "youse two get your jollies from stickin' needles in animals just to watch 'em die?"

"No!" I yell. "I'm innocent! I swear!"

"Yeah, sure," he says with disgust. "They're all innocent where you're goin'."

"You hit him again," yells my mother, "and I'll lawyer him up."

He slaps me across the face anyway, more as an afterthought, and tells a uniformed cop: "Get him outta here."

"No," shrieks my mother. "He's my only son!" She hugs me and says she's sorry, says she was looking for baking soda in the fridge, but I can smell Sleeman's Lager on her breath. Two, maybe three of them, just as I suspected.

"I did it!" she screams. "I killed the cat!"

"What the hell you talkin' about?" says Sipowicz, coming towards her.

"Last week I killed the dog!" she screams. "I put him in the freezer!"

"What dog! What freezer!" bellows Sipowicz, incredulous.

"That's your job, you're the detective," says my mother as she slams the door in his face, locks it, and returns to her knitting as if nothing happened.

Just then a truck tire came bounding down the QEW towards my car, narrowly missing me and giving the guy in a Volkswagen convertible behind me a really cool haircut. And that's how my daydream ended.

"Nothing happened," I said to myself, out loud.

And nothing bad did happen.

I signed the contracts for my next book, Margaret had a pot of tea instead of two or three beers, and Malcolm's ashes now rest on a mantle over my fireplace in a custom-made mahogany urn.

And if you watched the last episode of *NYPD Blue*, you might have noticed Andy Sipowicz has been demoted for conduct unbecoming a police officer. Even in a dream sequence, you don't cross Margaret and me without paying the price.

*B*reast Implants at Eighty? Mom! Say It Ain't So!

I'm not a very good listener. I am particularly not good at listening to my sister Gail, who can turn a chance meeting in the supermarket into something akin to *The Winds of War* miniseries without the benefit of commercial interruptions.

It was several years ago when Gail called from Fonthill to update me on family business. At family headquarters, the E. F. Hutton reverse rule is always in play: "When Gail talks — everybody walks." My nephew David's lacrosse team advancing to the Minto Cup got us through the lunch hour and my niece Whitney's upcoming marriage took us into early afternoon.

A phone call from Gail is actually a blessing because in person she insists on bringing photographs to support the narrative. You know how in typical suburbia somebody is constantly dashing off to a meeting and backing the car over a bicycle in the driveway? We have the same rotten luck with slide projectors in front of my sister's place.

So when Gail talks, I tend to tune out. I bailed out of her phone call during a vivid description of the Red Dog Saloon in Juneau, visited on her latest cruise to Alaska.

I cut the lawn, cleaned the gutters, and gave the tool shed one coat of primer and got back just as Gail wrapped up by telling me my mother was going into the hospital to have breast implants.

Breast implants!?!

I hung up in silence, but continued to stare at the phone.

Good gawd, I thought to myself, bouncing off the walls and fighting back the tears, the 1980s — the decadent decade of me, more, and mammary glands — have caught up and consumed my own mother. The carnival called cosmetic enhancement had swept up the lovely and Irish Margaret McLean, the cuddly Mick from Colorado.

Where would she get such an inflated idea? Hell, she isn't even dating. Is this what it takes to turn the balding heads of elderly senior citizens? My mother, the Pamela Lee Anderson of the carpet-bowling corps!

She had to be stopped. I phoned back to family headquarters, truthfully telling the operator it was an emergency, and cut into a conversation of my sister telling my other sister, Joan, in Toronto about the Red Dog Saloon and how they throw the peanut shells on the floor where they blend with the sawdust . . .

"I gotta talk to Mom," I said curtly. "It's a matter of life and breadth."

When my mother came on the line, I was irrational. My brain buzzed with the image at the other end of the line of the smiling face of my dear mother over the ghostlike, gigantic chest of Jayne Mansfield.

"Marg, listen to me," I begged. "Do not have that surgery! It's wrong! It's not you! You'll be eighty-one years old next month. For gawd sakes, you don't need a pair of artificial fun bags to be happy in your golden years!"

There was silence on my sister's phone, maybe for the first time since its installation. I wasn't sure whether I was winning or losing this one. I closed my eyes to compose myself and I saw my mother sitting at the reception desk at radio station WKRP, in Loni Anderson's body.

My mother's words came down like a final judgement, as if inspired by Judge Wapner himself: "I am having the surgery. I am only having one done. I am not eighty-one years old." She hung up.

One! Only one? Oh, no! My mother, of sound mind and strong heart, was having a single breast implant. As well as being seduced by this scalpel-happy society, she had developed a serious kink.

I called right back. I got a different operator to break in on Gail's conversation in which she was telling the first operator about the handsome piano player and the large steins of Yukon beer at the Red Dog Saloon.

The first operator recognized my voice. "You must be very proud of your nephew getting that lacrosse scholarship to Ithaca," she said.

"Please, this is urgent!" I said abruptly. Gail went up

and got my mother. I imagined her walking towards the phone, half mother, half Dolly Parton, swishing, swinging, singing "Nine to Five."

"Marg, listen to me. Please. You're not even seeing anybody right now. What good would it do? What good would one do? And what about bras? Do you have any idea what a 42D/36C would cost to have made?"

"I'm going to have the surgery," she said as resolutely as before, "and if you tell anybody I'm eighty-one, I'll tell everybody you used to wet the bed."

No idle threat this, when you consider I didn't kick the habit until my second year of university.

My sister picked the receiver up off the floor.

"I don't know why you're coming unravelled like this," she said, like this was a regular thing for the Thomas women, having their bosoms bolstered one at a time. "It's a simple operation. Dr. Robert says she's fit and strong and the hip area allows easy access —"

"The hip?" I blurted. "She's going to have a breast implanted on her hip? Gail — I know we all admire her sense of humour, but this . . . this is crazy . . ."

"She's having a hip implant, you dolt! A hip implant! You never listen, do you?"

Blood returned to my ashen face, oxygen to my brain.

"No . . .," I said faintly. I closed my eyes and saw Jayne Mansfield, Loni Anderson, and Dolly Parton — all six of them intact and none of them attached to my mother.

Honest, I'm really going to start to listen. Yes, even to my sister Gail. Okay, okay, I'll glance at the photos and flip charts too.

My Mother's Not Playing with a Full Deck

So how are things at home now that my mother has made it her home too? Well, a lot better, now that I've started drinking heavier, earlier.

The fact of the matter is, my mother, Margaret — sweet wisp of an Irish-American leprechaun lady — is not playing with a full deck. Granted, she's not as young as she used to be. Technically, she's not even as young as some fossils used to be, but she's a helluva lot more fun.

I wasn't sure if she wanted to celebrate her birthday last week. I'm no longer at liberty to divulge her age; she made me promise to keep it out of print. Boy, some women sure are sensitive about their birthdate, especially when it's chronologically connected to the Ice Age.

So it was, at best, a last-minute affair, hastily arranged at my place. I had some Christmas gifts I really hated, so I wrapped those up. I made a nice card out of the hydro bill. As for a cake . . . where would I find a birthday cake on a Sunday?

I dashed into town to the No Frills store and managed to find the perfect cake. As soon as we carved "GET WELL HARVEY" off the top and smothered it with whipped cream, I was off and running for home.

After making a wish and blowing out the candles with some assistance from one of those hand-held Black & Decker Vac 'n' Mulch leaf blowers, Margaret cut the cake.

Then came the question I did not want to hear.

"Where did you get such a lovely cake, dear?" she asked. You know as well as I do that you can't lie to your mother. At least I've never been able to in more than four decades of trying.

"No Frills," I mumbled, sheepishly.

"Where?" she asked.

"No Frills!" I shouted.

"Where?" she asked, this time with a hand cupped behind her ear.

"NO FRILLS!" I screamed.

And she verily beamed with pride as she said: "Oakville?"

My face fell into my hands.

"You know, dear," she continued, "a lot of sons wouldn't drive all the way to Oakville to get their mother a birthday cake."

"I do what I can," I said and then quickly changed the subject. Modesty, after all, is something my mother taught me.

Truthfully, the woman is a saint and I worship the — Excuse me . . .

"Mom, that's the Blue Box you just set fire to. The gas stove is over here and it has an automatic electric starter."

One problem creating a little tension around the house is that Margaret doesn't always remember what's in the bags she keeps in the closet in her room.

Like the other day, after we got back from shopping, the two of us were having a quiet moment when we heard scratching and gnawing noises coming from her room. It sounded like somebody was trying to break out.

I knew it wasn't a mouse because I have a new mouser. I now have Weggie, the mother of all mousers, except he's a cocky young male tabby with the balls of a burglar and the cutest face this side of Caledonia. (Let's just say the line "I'll never get another one!" is the big lie all true pet lovers love to tell.) No, I knew it wasn't a mouse. Since I got young Weggie, mice have not been spotted east of Manitoba. Since I got Weggie, moles have shown signs of genetically developing eyes.

We went into the room to discover my cat had gone through all her bags until he retrieved "my surprise," a hard stick of pepperoni sausage. He had already eaten both ends of it.

This escalates into a three-way argument when Weggie's glare reminds both of us that, technically, we've territorially infringed on his exclusive marketplace, i.e., the floor.

I distinctly remember asking Mom if she put all the food in the fridge. It was not the first time this kind of thing had happened.

My mother's memory is not as sharp as it once was. Which is great when I'm late with a mortgage cheque but bad when it comes to food forgotten in one of her many bags. I say this warrants a search, Marg flatly refuses, and Weggie says finders keepers, give me back that damn stick of spicy sausage.

Between the forgotten food, and the hidden linen, my mother has become a prime smuggling suspect at my house. Weggie and I are seriously considering being fitted for blue customs uniforms and wearing badges.

Me: "The facts, Ma'am, just the facts. The kitchen kettle, which I keep on the stove, has been missing for several days now. I'm getting tired of cold coffee and my partner here misses the gravy warmed over his meaty mixed grill of minced intestines from animals larger and more domesticated than himself."

Suspect: (Reaching down into a cupboard) "It's right here where it's supposed to be, dear — in the cupboard where you hide your scotch."

Weggie: "Are you concealing any contraband perishable goods, ma'am, like hardened and compressed pork parts?"

Suspect: "Dear, you're so talented. I didn't even see your lips move that time."

My mother loves the simple things in life and she's ever so appreciative. She thanked me several times last week for buying a new deck of cards for her afternoon solitaire games. (She used to play strip poker with the guys at the seniors' hall until they caught her hiding really bad cards up her sleeve.)

Yesterday Weggie and I were making a routine search of some yummy-smelling bags in her closet when we came across a five of clubs.

And that's why I say she's not always playing with a full deck. It never stops her, however, from playing the game and enjoying it more than most people who do have all their cards.

Ripe fruit does not possess the sweetness of this woman. Which reminds me of what Weggie found in her suitcase this morning: the bananas that look like they've been in her bag since the day she moved in.

Helpful Hints for Seniors

As a keen observer of senior citizens and the proud son of one ("No, it's Bill, Mom. Bob is the guy on *The Price Is Right*"), I believe this group of people could benefit from a few helpful tips.

Drawing up a short list of helpful hints for seniors came to me recently when I spent two days behind a very sweet elderly lady at the Eight Items or Less checkout counter at my local A & P. I remember once seeing a tabloid newspaper headline: "Sisters Reunited After 18 Years in Supermarket Checkout Line." At the time I thought this was a funny foul-up; now I understand how this could happen.

First of all, when you're checking out, it's not absolutely necessary to read every headline on the tabloid rack out loud and follow up with a personal commentary of your own. Everybody agrees these Hollywood stars are all a bunch of freaks, so really, one "tch, tch, tch" for each headline is sufficient.

And if I've learned one thing in all the years I've been doing my own grocery shopping, it's that when you show up at the checkout counter with items you have removed from their shelves, they're going to expect payment. Oh, yeah, you can count on it. That's why being presented with an itemized receipt should come as no surprise to you. That's why you may want to start breaking into that portable vault women affectionately refer to as a purse well in advance.

So the first tip is: grocery shopping requires payment and lettuce can wilt and die in the time it sometimes takes to produce legal tender at the cash register.

This brings me to another curious habit older women practise: spending hours rummaging through their purses and never actually finding anything. You must remember that purses with multiple compartments, snaps, zippers, and button-down leather latches were designed by a sick individual who hated his mother. In the time it takes you to open the purse and dump three pounds of loonies onto the counter, you could have paid with the $20 bill that fell on the floor when you first took your gloves off. You thanked me for picking the $20 bill up and handing it to you, but really my motives were purely selfish. *I was hoping to get home for Easter!* Sorry, I know that was a cheap shot, but really, would it kill supermarkets to have aisles for people in a hurry and a couple of other aisles for seniors who have time to take a line-dancing lesson while they're going through the checkout?

And while we're on the subject of purses, not unlike garages, it's always good to clean them out at least once a year. The last time my mother went to the hospital for a test, she produced so many health cards, she was suspected of being the ringleader in an elaborate scheme to sell gallstone operations to illegal immigrants.

Please, trust me, the quality of health care in this country does not improve just because you can produce enough expired cards to make up a euchre deck. Tip: any card bearing only your maiden name comes out of the wallet and goes into the family album.

Meanwhile, back at the express checkout line — which now looks like a bogus job application call at a General Motors plant — you have paid, you have received your change, and you're cramming those coins into that elusive little change purse when a really bad idea comes to mind. No, no, please. No matter how close your money compartment is to the photos of your grandchildren do not, I repeat, do not take them out to show the cashier.

I know you think of the cashier as your friend. But if you'd look behind you at the sea of faces flushed with anger, you'd realize that to the rest of us, she's a potentially dangerous witness and the last thing standing between you and the mob. Sure, she's still smiling pleasantly at you. That's because she's matured a lot as a person since you first arrived! We're all smiling at you because you're cuddly and cute as a button, but please, not the family photos!

Okay, if you've already got the photos out, then you gotta promise: just names, ages, grades, recent accomplishments, and brief testimonials from teachers and coaches. And that's it. If you get into what they did last summer, I'm tossing a large bill down on the counter and I'm going over you with my groceries like an airborne Buffalo Bill on third down and goal to go. (And I promise I won't knock anybody down, just like the Buffalo Bills!)

And please don't make the same mistake I did and ask to see the accountant under the counter. It's called a price scanner and nobody, including the cashier, knows how it works. Think of it as an electronic Jeanne Dixon and everything will work out fine. It's magic. Leave it at that.

And finally, let's remember: old age is that stage of life when your conversations get longer but your body gets shorter.

When you senior men are driving out there on the roads, or almost on the roads, it's just not enough for us to see knuckles on the steering wheel to confirm the presence of a person in that car.

Wave every so often, so we know for sure you're in there. Okay? It's a safety thing.

P.S. And that ain't the worst thing about being an old man. No, the worst thing is I'm gonna be one soon. Sooner than you can say "Regularity Rules!" So many cheap shots — so little time left!

A *Few Supermarket Tips for Seniors*

- Yes, that is the actual price of cheese and no, they don't offer mortgages.
- Don't even try to remember where everything is. As soon as you do, the store will change it all around. It's policy.
- Jostled by other shoppers at peak shopping periods? For anyone over sixty-five, the grocery cart can be used as a defensive mobile weapon.
- Annoyed at screaming kids in grocery carts? When the mother's not looking, give them things that are really sweet and gooey.
- No, as a rule the major chain stores will not haggle on price.
- You're okay, impulse buying does not apply to sweets.
- No, they can't put the plastic bags and the twist ties in the same place. That would be too easy.
- To save money, when you go to the store always wear plastic poppies, daffodils, Scout tags, Girl Guide tags, and ribbons of every colour.
- Warning to seniors: Some products may not contain bran!
- Staff will become suspicious when you slap "Day Old $1.00 Off" stickers on canned goods.

- "Extra Old" and "Well Aged" refer to cheese and certain cuts of beef. Don't take it personally.
- When caught exceeding the Eight Items or Less rule, loudly accuse the person behind you of trying to slip stuff through on your tab.
- No, the carry-out boy doesn't go as far as Elm Street.
- When in doubt, remember my mother's rule: "I'd sooner go without than pay that price. That's ransom!"
- No socializing in checkout lines. That's why so many of our park benches sit vacant.

Questions I Used to Ask My Mother That My Mother Now Uses on Me

- What's for dinner?
- Why? I'm not hurting anything, am I?
- Can I clean it up later? I'm busy right now.
- Why not? All the other seniors have one.
- How come there's nothing good on TV?
- Don't look at me. You're the one who put it away!
- Can we go out and eat instead?
- Just one beer from the downstairs fridge. Who's gonna notice?
- Right. I suppose it just flew out the window?
- What makes you think I want to be strong and healthy?
- I'm not cleaning it up. He's not my pet, is he?
- You don't have to stay up. Can't you just leave the door unlocked?
- Who died and made you the boss?
- I never said it was fair, did I?

I Am Not Having an Affair with Wally Crouter

Did I mention my mother is living with me temporarily? Okay, but did I also mention I've applied for membership in the Hemlock Society, but they won't let me join without references, and Dr. Kevorkian says he doesn't know me well enough to kill me himself?

Hey, I'm kidding. We're getting along as if we were . . . well, family. Need I say more?

Seriously, most days are fine — breakfast with Marg on the lakeside patio, a beer on the breakwall before supper, and real good bitch sessions about the government, health care, and why pills that cost four cents to make cost $40 to buy.

But not today. Today I'm having a real bad sexual identity day.

You have to understand that Margaret is now almost — Whoops! I almost broke that promise that forbids me to publicly reveal her age.

Oh, sure, go ahead and smirk. You've had some pretty cheap little chuckles over the years at Margaret's expense. But no more. I'm through doing old-age jokes about my mother, and this time I mean it.

And I'll tell you another thing. I don't know what good

deeds your mother has done lately, but I'm damn sure when they found that perfectly preserved four-thousand-year-old man in a glacier in the Swiss Alps a few years back, *your* mother didn't offer to go over and identify the body.

So my mother wakes up this morning, which at her age takes care of the number-one item on her list of things she hopes to accomplish today. And I asked her if she'd slept well.

"Oh, yes," she said. "I had a great sleep." Then she pauses, raises her eyebrows, and adds, "Until I heard that other man's voice."

"What other man's voice?" seemed like a logical question to ask, since there were only two of us in the house, Margaret and me. Weggie had missed curfew again.

"You had a man in your room this morning," she said. "I heard him talking."

Oops! There went my life-long secret of being an early-morning closet gay guy! A man in my room? "Oh, it must have been Wally Crouter," I said.

Marg thought about it for a few seconds and then said: "He's married, isn't he?"

I tried to explain that my clock radio is set to Toronto's CFRB and it comes on automatically with the "Wally Crouter Show," but my mother wasn't listening. No, by this time my mother was tearing apart my kitchen in her quest to rid the world of its diminishing supply of bran muffins.

That's how my day started, with my dear sweet mother suspecting I might be a little light in my loafers and a radio personality groupie to boot. I'm just glad she didn't hear Wally and Bill Stephenson doing "Sports Talk," otherwise my mother would have thought I was involved in some kind of weird threesome.

Now, we're having tea and muffins with the sun streaming through the bay window and as I open up the morning paper, Marg puts a stack of old newspapers on her lap and pulls out — I swear I'm not making this up — the new Fabio calendar.

Please let me explain. Last week, I wrote a column about Fabio being women's first choice as the perfect man. (He's so nurturing, trust me, someday that guy will accidentally lactate.) Then an anonymous and somewhat deranged female reader from Hamilton sent me this oversized, full-colour calendar with twelve semi-nude photographs of the Italian Tarzan. Then she taped my column photo on top of Fabio's body on the cover. Truthfully, I'd rather be stalked.

"Mom, I didn't buy that calendar," I said matter-of-factly.

"I didn't say you did, dear," she said without looking up.

"And I didn't stick my face on that guy's body either," I assured her.

"No, of course not, dear," she said, stopping to shake her head at the photo of Fabio, naked and writhing on a bearskin rug in front of a roaring fire. "He looks very strong," she said, innuendo dripping off the adjective.

I tried to move her off the topic of Fabio, bringing up our long-running argument over who's cuter on *Married with Children* — Al Bundy or his son, Bud — but she wouldn't be budged today.

As long as I can remember, my mother hardly ever called one of her children correctly on the first try. It's usually "Joan — er, Gail — dangit — Bill!" I may be over-reacting, but today, when she called me Joan, she was very slow in correcting herself.

Just after lunch, I heard her talking on the phone in my office. I couldn't hear what she was saying, but I prayed she wasn't talking to Wally Crouter's wife. Now whole families would be destroyed.

Any way you look at it, this can do nothing for my image as spokesman and chief apologist of the Middle-Aged Stupid Straight Guys Association of North America. I'm afraid by the time my mother gets off the phone with her friends, I'll be lucky if I can get punched out in a bar fight over a lap dancer. I'll probably have to join the Reform Party, just so I can get called a redneck, macho, gun-lovin' ladies' man.

But humour being my life, I couldn't resist getting in the last word on this one. I had to sit in my office with the receiver to my ear pretending to make a phone call for nearly fifteen minutes before my mother walked by the door. That's when I spoke into the receiver, loud enough for her to hear: "I can't meet you tomorrow morning, Wally. My mother is getting suspicious!"

And that did it. There was no more discussion. We had a silent supper and agreed on an early-to-bed evening.

I'm just thankful my mother's memory isn't what it used to be. Now that I've turned the radio wake-up off, we should be able to sleep in tomorrow and start the day with a clean slate and all will be forgotten.

Maybe tomorrow I'll pull out my wedding album at breakfast just to re-establish things a bit.

"Goodnight, Marg," I said.

"Goodnight, Joan," came the reply. And then nothing.

"Well, I Never!"

Of course I have — I get nasty letters all the time, but after my "Helpful Hints for Seniors" piece appeared in print, the letters just kept on coming.

Suffice to say, in order to be any more unpopular these days, I'd have to be the illegitimate son of Sheila Copps *and* Mike Harris. (Get that smile off your face, Sheila, it's just a metaphor.)

I haven't received so much hate mail in one week since I wrote a piece about breastfeeding in public, and that I'm against it. (For the record, it was in a restaurant and I was jealous that the kid was getting his food immediately while I'd been waiting twenty minutes for my bowl of soup. That and the fact the kid was eighteen years of age. But it was in Nova Scotia, eh?)

Seniors, as I pointed out in that story, may be a bit slow in the checkout line at the grocery store, but they're certainly quick off the mark when it comes to penning hate mail. Here are but a few letters picked randomly off the top of the pile.

"Why, you stupid article!" Sorry, that wasn't a letter. It was a Post-it note left on my fridge by my mother, held there by a dagger magnet.

Dennis, a senior in Stoney Creek, Ontario, wrote to

say: "I would think you are ashamed of yourself, saying all those nasty things about that elderly lady at the checkout. It could have been your mother. She still loved you, even if you may have been the ugliest baby in the ward. Don't forget, you gave her pain when you were born . . . There were times when you filled your diapers with caca and your mom was glad to clean you up."

First of all, I had a little trouble with your handwriting, Dennis, and I'm hoping that you referred to me as the ugliest baby in the "ward," not the "world." It's a very big world out there, Dennis, and the last time I checked, Roman Polanski was still in it.

Secondly, I'm sure I caused some pain for my mother at birth, but remember, Dennis, I wasn't always the size I am today.

And finally, Dennis, "caca"? I believe the correct terminology, sir, is "baby poop."

Collin from Carnduff, Saskatchewan, wrote to say: ". . ." Well, never mind what he said. Let me just say there's no need for that whatsoever, Collin. I have no immediate plans to become a father anyway. And nobody puts those things in glass jars except veterinarians. So there.

From Fredericton, New Brunswick, Victor, eighty-four and still exceeding the speed limit, was kind enough to send along a little safety tip. Victor warned me not to walk alongside any road he's driving on, otherwise he'll run me over. Chances are, Victor, without a stack of pillows under that bony butt of yours, someday this was probably going to happen anyway.

And Betty, seventy-five years of age, from Egmondville, Ontario, challenged me to a 7:30 a.m. foot race to see which one of us arrives at the Tasty Nu first. I have no idea where Egmondville is, but I'm not stupid. Betty, even if I leave Wainfleet at 6:30 a.m., you'll be in your downtown Egmondville before me. (I'm guessing the name of the town used to be Edmonton, until the local paper, the *Expositor*, got a new computer with a spell check.)

Anyway, if the seniors would please stop referring to me as that part of the horse you most clearly see from the hay wagon, I will gladly explain my behaviour because —

We interrupt this story to bring you a late-breaking, really bad joke from a field in southern England!

First Cow: "So, Irv, are you worried about this mad cow disease?"

Second Cow: "Me? Worried? I'm not worried. Why should I be worried? I'm a penguin!"

The truth is, I ate beef in England several months ago. I had a steak on New Year's Eve on the Isle of Wight and a beef curry in London several days later.

I thought nothing of it until a few weeks ago, when, feeling a bit bloated, I asked the guy who checks my gas meter if he wouldn't mind milking me. I would have loved to have seen the look on his face, but unfortunately

I had my head down and I was eating the grass around the well cap at the time.

Just yesterday, I skidded into a ditch while chasing a turnip truck down Lakeshore Road. I'd have caught it too, except that, as I rounded the Camelot Bay curve, my right front hoof went clean through my Reebok and I spun out of control.

Thank goodness I live in Wainfleet, where people with hooves don't attract any attention.

I know you find this utterly preposterous, but that's my story and I'm sticking to it — I have mad cow disease. I'm sorry. Please, be patient with me — I'm up half the night regurgitating.

Things That Margaret Would Consider "Just Grand"

- Something in writing to prove that a beer a day is good for you and two a day defies mortality.
- A pamphlet outlining the joys of inactivity.
- All the words to "When Irish Eyes Are Smiling."
- A hijacked truck full of fine tea and English biscuits.
- A cure for gravity.
- Eyeglasses that beep when lost.
- A special-needs program that includes cuddling.
- Medication encased in M&M's.
- A little black book that lists the names of men who aren't just doctors and pharmacists.
- A really, really big eye chart in the doctor's office.

Dinner with Marg — Adventures in Doggy-Bag Land

Let's see, they call it the empty-nest syndrome when your children mature and move away. And when the parent moves in with the adult child? Oh yeah, that's the one-flew-over-the-cuckoo's-nest syndrome.

Yeah, it's great because I . . . Excuse me . . .

"What? No, no, not there . . . I said food scraps go down the garbage disposal, my old sweatshirt goes in the hamper.

"No, it's okay. Nobody's blaming you, Marg. Sure, I can always buy another sweatshirt with 'Waterloo Lutheran University — 1970' across the front and my name embroidered on the back by a hippie girl named MaryJo who's a missionary in Guatemala today."

There's always a bright side to everything. The hamper is no longer just for dirty clothes. Now it's a planter box too.

Not many guys are fortunate enough to share these kinds of memories of living in a very small house day in, day out with their mom. Oh, sure, there are some innocent people incarcerated in the Canadian prison system whose every move is watched by a guard — but not that many, really.

But age is of no consequence. What's important is that we're doing things together, all day, and getting along just fine. Like Neil Armstrong and Buzz Aldrin in the same astronaut suit.

That's why we both jumped at the chance to go out to dinner. It'll give Weggie the cat some peace and quiet. I mean, we could stay home and I could cook a nice meal for my mother according to her diet — a salt-free, cholesterol-free, sugar-free, fat-free meal.

At this rate, I think the next major scientific breakthrough for senior citizens will be the food-free meal: all their pills and medicines attractively arranged on a bed of tofu garnished with plastic parsley.

Rather than eat at home, I think it's more fun to go out to a restaurant where, if my mom has a bad reaction to something, she can always sue the chef. So the other evening we went to Porta Romana, a classy Italian bistro in nearby Port Colborne where, as usual, we had a great meal.

The problem is, my mother doesn't eat very much. (Who can eat when you're waving at all the longshoremen walking by on the street?) But Margaret, bless her heart, likes to order the full-course meal and then transport everything home in several Styrofoam boxes. In any restaurant, when they ask "Eat in or take out?" my mother's answer is "Yes, please." She's the only person I know with a Diners Club card that stipulates "Shipping and Handling Free." The doggy-bags do provide a week's worth of lunches for my mom, but no matter where we go to eat, when we leave we always look like staff making home deliveries.

So I went up to the bar, first of all to compliment the chef on his fine fare, and then to ask the waitress if she would explain to my mother the new ANTI-DOGGY-BAG LAW now in effect in this restaurant (wink, wink, nudge, I'll leave a tip this time, I promise).

Subsequently, this sweet young lady, who apparently aspires to being an actress, launched into this table-side lecture about bacteria in warmed-over food and the illegality of reselling restaurant food, all of which convincingly led to this anti-doggy-bag legislation.

The waitress was so good, I leapt to my feet and screamed, "We'll get a lawyer and fight this thing all the way to the Supreme Court!"

"Well, I never," said my mom after the waitress had left. At this point, she seemed to find her second appetite and began eating what was a moment ago leftover lasagna. "That's the dumbest thing I ever heard," she continued, taking a vindictive stab at her Florentine chicken, which, I can assure you, was in no way involved in this doggy-bag debacle.

"I think it's probably Bob Rae's idea," I said.

(I've never been able to tell my mother that Bob Rae was voted out of office because he serves as such a great clearing house for all major screw-ups.)

"Of course it's Bob Rae's idea," she said. "It's the dumbest thing I ever heard." At that, she polished off her salad and broke off another piece of crusty bread.

"Pass me your purse," I said.

"I thought you said you were going to pay," she replied very quickly.

"I am paying," I said. "Give me your purse and we'll fill it with food."

"Well, I never," she repeated.

"Well, you never had to until now," I said. "Now give me the purse and you can smuggle all the food out."

"Me?" she asked. "I thought *you* were going to carry it out."

"Me, with a purse? How would that look?"

She gave me a semi-sarcastic look like she still wasn't sure about that alleged affair I'd had with Wally Crouter.

"I don't want to get charged," I said.

"Charged!" she yelled. "This is the stupidest thing . . . That dang Bob Rae."

At this point, the waitress, fearing a food fight was about to break out, came over and spilled the beans. (In this restaurant, they're actually fava beans sautéed in a lovely picante sauce.)

My mother's reaction was quick — she smiled at the waitress and kicked me hard under the table.

"You little scamp," she said, after the waitress had gone.

As we walked out of the restaurant, Mom, leaning on me for support, explained to the entire staff why she hobbles a bit these days: "Because this stupid article's always pulling my leg, now it's longer than the other one."

Is this the sweetest lady on earth, or what? As soon as we were out the door and on the street, she gave me another shot in the shins. And this physical dexterity from a woman who next month will celebrate her — Oops! I can't tell you how old she'll be, but at her age, I believe the appropriate gift is something from the Mayan ruins.

Once we're home, the cat doesn't even make a fuss over the boxes of food. He knows that when it comes to Marg and doggy-bags, pets don't stand a chance.

Never Argue with Your Mother

Did I mention that my mother was living with me these days? Well, she's not. She moved out. Honest.

A quick check of my life lately: my mother moved out; I wrecked my knee running last week and it feels like it requires surgery, again; Weggie cries to get out at three o'clock every morning; and today's paper shows that Canada Trust, the company holding my life savings, had a bit of a year-end shortfall of $571 million. (Thank goodness, as the manager explained to me, I had my savings in Canadian dollars. That way I've already cut my losses by almost 40 percent.) I wouldn't say I'm going through a rough patch, but if I had a pick-up truck and it broke down, my life could be a country-and-western song.

As a matter of fact, my mother moved out after we had what could only be called a difference of opinion. She wanted desperately to keep on living in my house, and I had a different opinion.

We're no different from any other close-knit, loving family in which strong-willed individuals speak their minds and sometimes suffer the consequences later. But it wasn't what you would call an amicable parting of the ways. It took nearly two pounds of Polyfilla just to cover up the gouges she made in the door jamb with her nails as I dragged her out to the taxi. I'm kidding, of course. I drove her to the Thorold bus station and dropped her off myself.

Seriously, our cohabiting was always a temporary arrangement, and Margaret has now settled into her own place, with my sister Gail, in nearby Welland. (The sound you hear is me, a largely non-religious guy, crossing himself.)

And gee whiz, how time flies when you're enjoying the quiet and serenity of living alone again — it's time for Marg to visit already! The truth is, I miss her, so we've worked out a schedule for weekend visits. She'll come out to my place for long weekends while Weggie takes his toys and checks into the nearby Rathfon Inn.

Yes, my mother is coming out for the first of many extended visits, and let's see — I got the ten-gallon pail of Tums and a trunk full of crossword puzzles, and the bran muffins are stacked on pallets in the basement.

Just for the record, when my mother said she was "coming out," she meant to my place. I know I may be over-reacting here, but I'm very nervous about all this stuff and I believe it's CTV's Lloyd Robertson's fault. If you watched that *Ellen* "coming out of the closet" episode on CTV, you'll remember Ellen cozying up to the other woman and blurting into an open airport microphone that she loved her when all of a sudden CTV goes into their "Stories We're Working On" mode. They cut to a clip of rescue volunteers throwing sandbags at the overflowing Red River south of Winnipeg, and then back to anchor Lloyd Robertson, who looks straight into the camera and says: "Will the dykes hold?"

I thought, They probably did, Lloyd, and I missed the whole thing.

Anyway, when my mother left a message on my machine that she was "coming out," I found myself asking her to be a little more specific. When the word "lesbian" came up in our conversation, she assured me that she's never even been to Lebanon. "Okay, Mom," I said, "I'll pick you up in twenty minutes . . . No, Mom, not plenty of minutes. Let's be a little more exact. Twenty. Twenty minutes." Lord, I forgot how much I missed her.

This time my mother, Margaret, is coming to my place for a ten-day visit because my sister Gail, who has only begun to share an apartment with her, was last seen heading for the United States, lips quivering and mumbling about hollow-points, clips, and getting even with some people in a post office down there. Yes, Marg can be a handful at times.

So I pick Mom up at her apartment and the first thing I have to do is assure all her friends in the lobby that, no, she's not moving out. It's just that she prefers to bring *all* her clothes to my place and wear *all* of them, *all* at once, as a kind of subtle hint for me to turn up the heat in this, the hottest July since forest fires raged through downtown Toronto.

As we crawl out of the parking lot, with the frame of my Honda Civic scraping the pavement, the kinfolk yell: "Jed, move away from here! Californy is the place you oughta be."

A minute from the apartment, we pass the Tim Hortons Donuts, and my mother tells me the same story she tells me every time we pass a Tim Hortons Donut shop. It's become a family parable illustrating the pride we Thomases have in our young, particularly Amanda, Marg's great-granddaughter, and the last time I looked, our only young.

"Can you believe how smart that child is, Bill?" Marg begins. "We went by here the other day, and when she saw the sign she said, 'Do-no! Nan, do-no!'"

I never say I've heard the story before. It could lead to an argument I will lose.

Instead, I agree immediately that this kid is a genius, not letting on that she's in second-year journalism at Carleton; it would take the sheen off the sweetness of the story. (Okay, the kid's five years old, and just for the record, when she passes a Mac's Milk she also goes, "Mooo!")

On the outskirts of Welland, we pass a business that always catches Margaret's eye for the sheer number of vehicles parked in front, and she always gives me the elbow and says: "Boy, they're doing well there. Must be some sale, dear."

I never argue. I nod and say, "Some sale, all right." But what I really want to do is ask her if she thinks it's just a coincidence that the first three rows of vehicles in that lot are '95 Ram Chargers with dealer sticker prices on the windshields.

What I really want to do is scream, "It's a freakin' Dodge dealership, Marg!" But I don't, because it's only the first fifteen minutes of a ten-day sleepover, and I know my sister Gail has left false names and phone numbers all over the island of Nassau so she can never be reached.

When we get to my place, the first thing my mother does is greet Weggie by calling him Tiger, the name of her cat. He cocks his head, waiting for the correction, which comes immediately: "Oh, sorry, Malcolm."

That's it for Weggie. He disappears into the basement, vowing not to come up until he hears the sound of luggage leaving.

Actually we had a great time together, Marg and I: tea and toast for breakfast, and an evening field trip to the Belmont Hotel for draft beer and chicken-in-the-basket, where, by phoning ahead and making a special request in honour of my mother's visit, nobody mooned us.

We love you, Marg, but I have a bit of bad news. You know how Gail and Joan and I have always vowed you would never go to a . . . ho . . . ho . . . ho . . . (I can barely bring myself to say the word) home?

Well, Mom, I'm afraid you should start preparing yourself now to spend some time in a . . . a . . . you know what. Because once Gail and I are permanently settled in Lunacy Manor, we'd sure like it if you came to visit us once in a while.

Things I Wished My Mother Would Stop Doing

- Trying to pay off Philip, the paper boy, with Mexican pesos.
- Blaming the cat for hiding her shoes.
- Filing important documents and financial information in places where an archaeologist would never think to look.
- Locking the door behind me when I go around back, to my office.
- Calling Beth, her friend of five years, Bev.
- Slamming her foot down on her imaginary brake pedal when she thinks I'm driving too fast.
- Slamming her foot down on my non-imaginary foot when I *am* driving too fast.
- Putting on the most expensive coat in the closet every time we leave the hairdresser's.
- Using her cane as a baton.
- Denying she loses her keys and accusing the home care nurse of "borrowing" them.
- Trying to pick up the bartender in the lounge at the Pillar and Post. Oh, sorry, that comes under Things I Wished My Sister Gail Would Stop Doing.

- Admiring all the Christmas lights along Lakeshore Road and then as we pass the cemetery saying: "Gee, it's kinda dead around here, eh, Bill?" (Margaret: cheap humour is my job and I work alone. Okay?)

Partying — We're Just Not Very Good at It

My sister Gail and I are planning my mother's upcoming birthday party and we're trying very hard not to make the same mistakes we made the last time the Thomas family congregated to celebrate her birthday.

My mother turned eighty-nine on September 24, and I can now divulge her age because she is no longer living with me and therefore not in a position to hurt me while I'm sleeping. "I'll crown you," was the way she put it. I will pass on putting eighty-nine years in some sort of perspective, except to say the year my mother was born, wood was also discovered in a remote area north of Winnipeg.

My sister Gail, the supreme organizer, hosted a small, informal get-together for Margaret at their apartment. The party got off to a rousing start when an old family friend, Scott Misener, showed up with his cute little schnauzer, and Tiger, the family cat, took this opportunity to beat the hell out of the dog. To herald a landmark anniversary, a lot of people would opt for bagpipes, but I don't think you can do any better than hissing, howling, a bit of bloodletting, and a lot of skidding on linoleum.

Once the dog was bandaged and dispatched to the car,

Richard, Scott's teenaged son and a boy Margaret used to babysit, had an attack of asthma in the kitchen. This emergency served to showcase the true talents of the Thomas clan as my nephew, David, helped the young man out of the apartment and down to the parking lot.

To the wild cheering of every member of our family, David was the recent recipient of something he had been denied in five straight years since graduating university — a real job. Apparently I stood alone in thinking that five years as a bartender was a wonderful way to serve his fellow man. (Yes, he would slip me the odd free one, as a matter of fact.) As luck would have it, David is now gainfully employed by a pharmaceutical company and he happened to have a brand-new puffer in the trunk of his company car.

For those of us who used to believe David was just too nice a kid to make it in today's tough world of business, it was a sight to behold. In less than two minutes, Richard was on his knees with both hands wrapped around his own neck while my nephew had him up to $39.95 for the puffer and offered to throw in a free spacer, if he chose to pay in cash, on the spot. At least that's the way it looked from the sixth-floor window.

Like all our family reunions, we spent most of the rest of the afternoon trying unsuccessfully to avoid Amanda, my five-year-old niece, who was selling magazine sub-scriptions to work her way through kindergarten. This kid, who only learned to talk last Tuesday, is the Grand Champion Salesperson at Prince Philip Public School in St. Catharines. Honest.

This program was ostensibly created to supplement the cost of field trips, but when I asked Amanda where the money was going, she quickly touched her chest with her index finger three times. (This silent gesture eliminates any possibility of incriminating taped audio evidence ever being presented in a court of law.)

You wouldn't think a five-year-old would spend an entire Sunday afternoon pestering relatives to buy magazine subscriptions, especially after she spent all week pestering her neighbours to buy chocolate bars to support her daycare centre. I'm not kidding, in one month this kid has already tripled the gross monthly sales of David, the legal drug dealer we're all so very proud of.

At one point I had to intercede and diplomatically avoid an ugly incident by patiently explaining to Amanda her uncle David's new-found interest in dermatology, after he had inquired about the availability of skin magazines.

Oh, did I mention we were gathered here to celebrate my mother's eighty-ninth birthday?

Yes, my mother had a grand day admiring all her brood and wondering why at least half of them haven't yet been fitted with electronic ankle bracelets.

My mother sat on the couch enjoying the company of

my uncle Ralph. Ralph, a gentle man who likes to talk, was once a dynamiter in the gold mines of Timmins, so we had bull horns placed at convenient locations around the room so we could answer any of his questions.

At one point Ralph's hearing aid went haywire, causing the schnauzer to howl so loud he set off the automatic theft alarm down in the car where he was recuperating.

Anyway, everything worked out just fine. We sent Amanda down to deal with the police, the asthma patient lived, the dog healed, Tiger the cat wants his name changed to Iron Mike, and I'm on page 35 of my first issue of *Crochet Digest Monthly*.

Some people hire jugglers or magicians for their parties, but in the Thomas family we just make our own fun. And we wouldn't change a thing, unless it's a security guard at the door and an ambulance parked near the lobby.

Once again my sister Gail, who actually used to be in the party catering business, had chosen the perfect theme for our family celebration: Calamities "R" Us. In anticipation of just such an event, I had a large banner printed up and hung across the room: "Happy Birthday, Margaret — Nobody's Blaming You!"

How I Helped My Mother Flunk Her Short-Term Memory Test

My mother, Margaret, is nearly ninety years old. I'm nearly fifty years old. I've spent a lot of time with her over the last while, and everybody comments on how I really don't look my age anymore. I now look her age, they say.

I love this woman, but Lord knows, it ain't easy.

Recently, I got a message from my sister Gail to pick Margaret up at their apartment and get to a doctor's office for a test at 1:00 p.m. The hurried instruction I got on my answering machine gave me only the address of the Welland clinic, the time, and the caveat: "Urgent!"

Gail and I are trying to get approval for a government home care program in which a trained health care technician will come to the apartment several times a week, spend time with my mother, and then leave with an incredibly bad headache.

So at 1:05, my mother and I sit down with the local geriatrics specialist. It's the first time I've ever not spent an hour waiting to see a doctor, so I'm already a little suspicious. The doctor has no idea what kind of test he's supposed to administer because, of course, the family doctor who did the referral hasn't yet forwarded the paperwork.

"So what's wrong with her?" the specialist asks in a matter-of-fact manner, and then he begins scribbling in an open file. The doctor is middle-aged, meticulous, and humourless.

"Well," I begin, "my mother will be ninety years old in a couple of months. She has arthritis in both hands, and one knee gives out now and then. She's been in two car accidents, which have left a bump on her head, a lump on her throat, and pain across her shoulders. She has an artificial hip and cataracts on both eyes, completely covering one eye."

I swear to God he looked directly at me and in a very professional voice said: "Has this caused her any problems?"

I instinctively turned around to look behind me to make sure he wasn't talking to someone else, perhaps the evil phantom son who would whisper, "C'mon, Doc, it's only a hangnail. She's a chronic complainer!"

So I said, I swear I said this: "Well, she's thinking of quitting playing hockey in the Welland Industrial League."

He did not smile, smirk, or sneer. He looked down at the file, shuffled some papers, made a notation on one of them, looked over at my mother and said: "You know, at your age, Mrs. Thomas, you shouldn't be on the ice." I swear he said this. A cold chill went up my spine at the thought that in another place at another time, our medical system might put a scalpel in this man's hand.

At this point what I should have said, had I been thinking quickly, was: "Oh, no, Doc, it's okay. She's a goaltender. She hardly ever leaves her crease!"

Of course, my mother is oblivious to all this, because like most seniors, she still prefers to keep her $400 hearing aid in a secret compartment of her purse, for safety's sake.

"I'm just going to ask your mother a few questions to test her short-term memory," says the doctor.

This is not good news. Believe me, if my mother ever went on *Jeopardy*, the last thing you'd ever hear her say would be: "I'll take Short-Term Memory for 100, Alex."

"Mrs. Thomas," he begins, "what's the date today? What day of the month is it today?" Then he has to repeat the question so loudly I expect the receptionist to yell back the answer.

My mother looks up at the ceiling, then down at her shoes, then realizes he's preoccupied with reading and making notes on his papers, so she looks over at me, shrugs, and mouths, "Eight?"

I give her a blank stare. She gives me another inquisitive nod and silently says, "Eight?"

It dawns on me that my mother is asking me to help her cheat on her short-term memory test. I'm stunned. My biggest fear is that if I help her, she'll finally figure out how I managed to get through university.

It occurs to me that I've known the doctor all of six

minutes, while I've known my mother, well, all my life. I owe this guy absolutely nothing.

"Six," I mouth back.

My mother looks again to the heavens, pretending the answer came from that general direction, hesitates, and finally says: "It's the sixth today."

"Sorry, it's the fifth," says the doctor, and makes a big check mark on one of his pages. My mother puts a hand to her forehead, looks at me, shakes her head, and gives me that "I can't believe you got through university" look.

My mother is just now learning what I knew as early as Grade 5 — never cheat on a test from a person who also hasn't cracked a book the night before.

"What month is it?" asks the doctor.

My mother shoots a quick look in my direction and I point over my right shoulder to a calendar on the wall.

"May," says Margaret.

"Very good," says the doctor, and my mother gives me a wink.

It was a proud and touching moment, the kind Alvin "Creepy" Karpis and his mother must have shared.

"What year were you born, Mrs. Thomas?" asks the doctor and he returns to studying the file.

Technically we've moved from the category of short-term memory to ancient history, so as far as I'm concerned, we're playing this game under protest.

My mother looks at me and nods inquisitively. With

the doctor preoccupied with his paperwork and badly needing to redeem myself, I hold up five fingers and a thumb.

My mother shakes her head. Again I show six digits and again she rebuffs me with the quick shake of her head. I can't believe it. It's like she's a fastball pitcher and I'm the catcher, and I just gave her the curve ball sign. Good Lord — *my mother is shaking me off!*

"Six," I say, almost out loud, and stab the air with six fingers.

My mother hesitates, thinking I'm still working on that "day of the month" question, the one she's already been burned on.

The doctor looks up.

"It was about 1906," says my mother.

The doctor looks at me because, of course, he doesn't know the answer.

For one fleeting moment of fantasy, I consider saying: "Sorry, it was 1908." But my mother has a cane and I'm well within striking distance. For that matter, so is the doctor.

"Close enough," I say.

The doctor nods at my mother and says, "Okay."

As he looks down at his notes, Margaret smiles and gives me the thumbs-up sign.

An alarm goes off in the back of my brain telling me to get out of here. I read about this test somewhere. When the doctor gets to the "name the seven dwarfs" question I can just see myself doing an impersonation of Richard Nixon in order to get Marg to say "Grumpy."

No, I can't take any more of this. It's too ridiculous. If I start laughing uncontrollably, I just know he's going to ask me to take the test next. Besides, if she gets one more answer correct, I'm sure she's going to bound out of her chair and high-five me. Then the doctor will really be suspicious.

"Look, I have to pick up some groceries, I'll be back in a half hour," I say as my mother shoots me a look of betrayal, like I'm baling out on the team.

But before I can close the office door, she says: "Don't forget the bananas."

Right. If the short-term memory test involved bananas, bran muffins, and Sleeman's Lager, my mother would have aced it by now.

About a week later, we got word that Margaret's home care application had been approved.

When I picked her up to bring her out to my place at the lake for a few days, the first thing she said to me was, "I guess I did pretty good on that test, eh, Bill?"

And what did I say? And immediately? "Yeah," I replied, "you did just great, Marg." As I've said many times, never argue with your mother. It's one of those direct ratio things: the older she gets, the slimmer your chances of winning.

There was absolutely no way in the world I was going to try to explain to my mother that you have to fail the short-term memory test in order to successfully qualify for the home care program.

Frankly, I just couldn't take the sigh, the shaking of the head, and the look that says: "That's why this country's in trouble, Bill — university graduates!"

Merry Christmas, Marg. Wake Up, We're Home

It would seem my mother is a bit bored with life these days, spending too much time alone in the apartment.

True story — she telephoned me recently and described, in graphic detail, how this country is in the midst of the dreaded flu season.

"Bill," she said, "you have to have a word with your sister Tiger — uh, Joan — uh, Gail. Gail was supposed to take me for my flu shot two weeks ago and didn't. She was supposed to take me for my shot last week and cancelled. And today, I'm all dressed and ready to go, when she telephoned to say she's too busy.

"Bill," she said, in a low voice of concern, "if I don't get that flu shot pretty soon, I'm going to miss the whole season!"

The flu to my mother is like baseball and hockey to guys. She doesn't care whether she gets the shot or the flu, we don't care if they strike or get locked out — but none of us wants to miss the whole season.

(Hard to believe she'd be concerned about the flu after surviving the Black Death, which halved the population of Europe in the mid-fourteenth century. By now, her immune system might more accurately be called infrastructure.)

Anyway, just to set her mind at ease, I went out and found a guy on the street who looked weak and nauseated and brought him up to my mother's apartment. They had tea, I switched the cups, and now my mother's sick in bed with the flu and happier than she's been in years.

No, I did not do that.

What I did was take my mother on a senior citizens' excursion. It was about time my mother had a little adventure, because as she readily admits, the most exciting thing in her life these days occurs when she stands up too fast.

The only regular exercise she gets is punching out her purse trying to find her key ring or stickhandling the cat's bowl around the kitchen with her cane until it flips on its side and she's able to pick it up.

So my mother and I joined an outing organized by the Niagara Credit Union and made a three-hour bus trip to see the Cullen Gardens Christmas Lights Exhibit. Cullen Gardens and its miniature village are located four miles north of Whitby, Ontario. On a Tuesday, Seniors' Day, the lineup for the washroom begins in nearby Markham. (Boy, if they ever want to eliminate senior citizens loitering, just ban coffee!)

The bus ride up was a lot of fun, and I finally figured out how seniors have so much free time. They've developed a unique system that allows them to cut their interpersonal conversation time in half: they all talk at the same time. There's no waiting for the proverbial lull, never any need for an answer. Silence happens on a seniors' bus trip only when everybody's asleep.

On the bus, there was quite a discussion over what temperature should be maintained for the duration of the trip. Some said 73 degrees Fahrenheit; others wanted 78 degrees Fahrenheit. My mother wasn't happy with either suggestion. In any room or moving vehicle, my mother insists on, first, wearing a zipped-up parka and, second, setting a nice "cozy" temperature — the temperature at which food cooks. I know that when she stays at my place, once I feel the beads of sweat running down my back, it's just "toasty" for Marg.

Cullen Gardens is a wonderful Yuletide experience — acres of Christmas lights, intricate animated outdoor exhibits, and covered bridges passing over the rush of icy streams. Inside the emporium, they have a variety of souvenir and craft shops. This worked out well because my mother, who had not to this point bought a single Christmas gift, found at least six items that interested her so much she brought me over to look at them and said: "Can you believe the price of that?" Ever since her World War II rationing coupons ran out, my mother has refused to pay full price on any retail item except Tums.

We were treated to a traditional Christmas play in the tea room that ended with a sing-along by half a dozen small children, who were tricked into leaving their seats in the audience to perform on stage. First, mothers and grandmothers lured their kids onto the stage with bright shiny trinkets from the "jingle bell basket." Then the actors, all on bended-knees, led them in a robust rendition of "Jingle Bells" while the children stood there in silence, looking at their cheap prizes, as the mothers and grandmothers, cameras flashing, warned them to sing or else.

Truthfully, it looked like more of an unauthorized work stoppage than a Yuletide sing-along. The children performed so little, by the time it was over, civil-service-job recruiters were standing by to interview them.

We had a very nice chicken supper in the solarium overlooking all the outdoor Christmas scenes. We were joined by a delightful gentleman who was well read and well travelled. The three of us had a great conversation.

His name was Hildebrand and he was seventy-three years old. My mother's most frequent contribution to this conversation was, "Gee, are you still single?" I wouldn't say my mother is somewhat older than this man, but I did feel compelled at one point to take her aside and explain the term "jail bait."

On the bus home, I was feeling a little mischievous, so, in the spirit of the season, I passed a couple of bottles of hard liquor around and we mooned all the competing credit unions and trust companies we passed.

Not true. Actually we sang Christmas carols on the bus

ride home, thanks to Pete, a terrific bus driver, but a man who would not be allowed in the same building as the Robert Woods Singers.

Merry Christmas, Margaret. Let's make this an annual. Wake up. We're home.

Things Senior Citizens Really Ought Not Do

- Play any game that requires protective cup or elbow pads.
- Go into outer space for the sole purpose of having weightless sex with John Glenn.
- Equate the good old days with "when I used to have my own teeth."
- Take any job that involves wild animals and a whip.
- Participate in any activity in which the instructor says: "Try not to look down!"
- Say you feel like a twenty-year-old then go out and hit on one.
- Expect a fair trial by a jury of your peers after you turn one hundred.
- Register with a dating service but submit a photo of one of your children.
- Stand on a walker to change a light bulb.
- Stand and raise your right hand whenever you hear the word "history."
- Enter any competition that includes "the clean and jerk."
- Agree to be a passenger on any excursion that has the word "Iditarod" in the title.

- Play Ex-Lax-and-chocolate practical jokes on each other. Funny, but real wrong.

Ma Bell Has Nothing on Ma

Advanced age and modern technology are widely divergent forks in the inevitable path of evolution. (I know, I'm firmly planted on the wrong shoulder of both those roads.)

Now, take my mother, Margaret. (For a weekend or just a long walk around the block.) The last couple of years Margaret's memory has been fading. Before, whenever she'd call me, she'd usually blurt out the names of both my sisters, my niece, and my nephew before she hit on mine. Now she reams off all those family names plus those of the cast of *Friends* before she finally gets to "Bill."

I don't mind the low billing. It's the wait that's hard to take.

My mother has never had much use for modern technology because she had a bad experience with one of the mechanical wonders of her day. The Precambrian stone axe fell on her foot and broke her baby toe. (Hey, I'm kidding, of course. My mother lived in Pompeii, not Precambria.)

My mother has never quite grasped the concept of the answering machine. She is never sure if it's a recorded voice she's hearing at the other end of the line or a rude person of very few words.

I used to get messages on my machine in which Margaret would carry on a conversation with the machine, ask it a question, curse mildly, and hang up believing I was on the line but saying nothing just to aggravate her. (Okay, maybe once or twice I was, but mostly it was just her and the machine.) Often her message was, "You think you're so smart. Well, one day you'll call me for something important and I'll just stand here and say nothing like a dope and see how you like it! Good-bye."

When I'd call her back, she'd be as cheerful as ever. My mother simply cannot hold grudges. Her memory will not permit it.

Lately Margaret has developed a new policy on communication as it applies to the phenomenon of the answering machine: who needs to talk when you can get your message across by hanging up? As beautiful in its simplicity as the telegraph system invented by Samuel Morse, Margaret Code has even eliminated the essential dots and dashes. Margaret Code, which I believe will soon be as popular with senior citizens as cooking sherry, involves only a click.

On my machine, the sound of the click preceded by the crashing of her phone to the floor and then the rattling around of the receiver until she finally rams it into the cradle and then the words "Dang phone" or "Go to blazes." That's it right there, the signal that my mother has contacted me and requested a return phone call, at my convenience. Oh, it's her all right — nobody loses more fist fights to the modern telephone than my mother.

At the end of the day, a single click on my machine represents a casual conversation to come and no cause for alarm.

Two clicks in one day include casual conversation, a weather warning, and something she left behind at my place on her last visit, which could be anything from her solitaire deck to her pills.

If she's forgotten her box of chocolate Slow Pokes, that warrants three clicks.

Four clicks are serious. Four clicks are all of the above plus a late pension cheque or a listless cat with a tummy ache. (Occasionally Tiger's hairball will both relieve the upset stomach and produce the lost cheque.)

Five clicks are equivalent to a 7.5 on the Richter scale. On the fifth click in one day on my answering system, Bell Canada has instructions to send Niagara Regional Police officers to seal off her apartment and order everybody out with their hands up.

Six clicks would be like an untested nuclear weapon off course and headed for Wainfleet. Click! Click! Click! Click! Click! Click! "Vacate the township immediately! We do not expect survivors!"

Now, a lot of people might be annoyed to come home and find that someone has called and hung up on them up to half a dozen times. Not me. I can translate Margaret Code and it spells love and real concern.

And when I call her back and ask her why she hung up so many times, she has absolutely no recollection of such events. And given my mother's memory — unlike our justice minister, our prime minister, the head of the RCMP, most generals in the Canadian army, and many more famous "can't recallers" — my mother's quite likely telling the truth.

Margaret Joins the Club

In Welland, my mother has lived for several years now with my sister Gail on Denistoun Street, a thoroughfare that stands apart from others in that city for its obvious poor spelling.

Unfortunately, you cannot stick your head out my mother's bedroom window because the design of new apartment buildings forbids it. Way back, when my mother lived in wooden tenements and rickety boarding houses from Antigonish, Nova Scotia, to Timmins, Ontario, not sticking your head out the window meant your communications link to the outside world had been severed at the source.

But if you could stick your head out my mother's Denistoun apartment and look to the right you'd see the spanking-new single-storey, red-brick Rose City Seniors Activity Centre, where every day hundreds of the city's pensioners and retirees gather to play cards and a variety of games, watch television, do crafts, or exercise. It's bright, vibrant, and inexpensive and for Margaret, about ten cane tosses from her front lobby. (If cane tossing is approved as an Olympic sport, there's every chance Margaret and her walking stick will someday represent Canada abroad.)

My mother will not go to the Rose City Seniors Activity Centre, although I've taken her twice for a tour of the facility. Why? Because according to Margaret, who has more miles on her than the speedometer of a Ransom Eli Olds Speedwagon, (the auto and the band) — "the place is full of old people!"

Oddly enough, I understand this and agree with her entirely. It's the same logic that will not permit me to go to a hospital — it's full of sick people. I could catch something. My mother, by coming in contact with active senior citizens, most of whom are twenty years younger than she is, could conceivably contract the dreaded disease: oldness.

Oh, sure, go ahead and laugh. But last year in the retirement community of Elliot Lake, Ontario, a town wholly sponsored by Polygrip, an epidemic of doddering raged through elderly residents, and forensic scientists later discovered it had been spread by a virus in bingo dabbers. (Okay, so I made that up.)

So my mother avoids places frequented by senior citizens because for the last two decades her three children have neglected to tell her that she *is* one.

This did not make my job any easier when I sat her down to explain that we had enrolled her in a supervised daycare program over at Sunset Haven, a nursing home that is no such thing, if you know what I mean.

"They have their own limo service," I lied.

"A limo!" replied Margaret, impressed.

"Well, yeah, but it's bigger and more comfortable. They call it a Handy Trans," I said.

"Oh," said Margaret, wondering if everybody was naming vehicles these days, like they do pick-up trucks and summer cottages out here in Wainfleet.

"And it's got card tables and a big-screen TV, a cafeteria, and a craft shop," I said.

"So it's a recreational centre?" she offered.

"Not exactly," I said. "It's like a . . . a . . . what's the word I'm looking for . . . it's a . . ."

"Club?" she asked.

"Exactly!" I said, like she'd just answered a skill-testing question and won a trip to Mexico.

"So it's a club," she said, rolling the idea around in her mind.

"You know that hoity-toity women's club at Lookout Point in Fonthill where those rich women play golf and put way too many drinks on their husbands' tabs?" I asked.

"I'm not playing golf!" she cut in.

I took notice that although she ruled out the game, excessive drinking at someone else's expense was still very much on the negotiating table.

"That's why this club is perfect for you. No golf," I said.

"Well, one of these days maybe I'll give it a try," she said.

"Monday, 9:30, in the lobby," I replied.

"Monday?!" she shot back.

"Monday, Wednesday, and Friday, Marg. It's a regular club."

My mother never said another word but she definitely got the feeling I wasn't just making this up as I went along. There was most certainly a plan in place that she wasn't party to. Yet, Monday, there she was, down in the lobby at 9:30 sharp, suspicious as a fugitive felon about to board a bus with bars on the windows.

But all went surprisingly well. Margaret liked her "club." In a span of just two weeks Margaret won a carpet-bowling contest, won a jar of jelly beans by guessing the correct number inside, and resumed her hobby of weaving wool baskets. Somehow she was able to overlook the fact that the people at Sunset Haven were old. That, or this group of devious seniors played a big practical joke on my mother by masquerading as young people every Monday, Wednesday, and Friday.

She took day trips around Niagara, celebrated a lot of birthdays, had a hot lunch each day, and generally returned home around three o'clock in the afternoon to complain about all the men who were paying way too much attention to her. Theresa and the other daycare workers told a slightly different story. My mother, they said, didn't interact all that well with women, or so they thought. They weren't sure, because from the moment she arrived she was seldom out of the company of men.

"Well, we all know what they're after," she confided to

her friend Beth back at the apartment, over Pepsis.

Good Lord. My mother, at eighty-nine, still breaking hearts, and even those with pace-makers attached!

One morning while they were all gathered round the big-screen television set in the lounge, I appeared on the screen, a guest spot on CTV's *The Dini Petty Show*. Apparently my mother did everything except pass around business cards that listed her as my agent. As a humorist, it's a great advantage to have your mother in the viewing audience. Those around her respond with laughter and applause or pay dearly for their disinterest.

I told a story about Margaret at the top of the show, which through the miracle of selective hearing, my mother ignored entirely.

Later that day back at the apartment, she told me how proud she was to see me on television and told me I did real good. "And after everybody saw you on television," she added, "they let me go to the front of line for lunch in the cafeteria."

Good Lord. I've created a monster, an advanced-age stage mom throwing her weight around at Sunset Haven.

Hell, she probably could be an agent. I've had two so far in my career, and neither one of them has gotten me anything close to a preferential spot in a food line.

What Worries My Mother Most Is . . .

- Strangers in the laundry room.
- The people at pharmaceutical companies who set pill prices.
- That Revenue Canada will find out about that little babysitting gig she had back in the '80s.
- That terrorists will occupy and burn all the land where bran is produced.
- That the Catholic Church lied and she's going to hell anyway.
- That there will be peace in Ireland, but she won't be around to see it.
- Salt.
- That Frank Sinatra in his memoirs blabbed about that night in Buffalo at the Town Casino.
- That they'll discover a cure for ageing and she'll have to put up with me for another fifty years.
- Anyone in the driver's seat.
- Scatter rugs and extension cords.
- That all the people whose names she forgets will soon start forgetting hers.
- Long periods of time without anything to worry about.

Happy Birthday, Margaret

We celebrated Margaret's birthday on a Saturday, September 28, 1996, although she was born four days and ninety years before.

It was a day fit for a queen, and my mother suited that regal role perfectly. She wore her favourite forest green dress, the one with the three gold chains across the front, the one that she tells total strangers her son bought for her. She wore gold earrings and the gold locket that contains words of love from her three children and she wore a day-long smile that lit up the room and warmed the hearts of everyone in it.

And her hair was perfect, thanks to the girls at Jean Michee's in Port Colborne. I know, because I took her to the appointment and returned to pick her up just in time to tip.

You see, my mother's sense of pricing was established in the days of the depression of the '30s, when two sandwiches were payment in full for a hungry man to cut a cord of wood. So to her, $42 ought to cover return airfare to Vancouver, not a haircut.

"But they're so nice and did such a beautiful job," she'll say, bouncing her right hand off the wave of hair in the back, "I left them a $2 tip."

I commented that it was a little on the extravagant side, but then she reminded me they'd all be sharing it equally.

That's my cue. In any payment for services rendered, I'm like Margaret's personal clown: I follow her around handing loonies and toonies out to the staff as if produced from behind my right ear. Throwing money in all directions, I've often been confused with a Liberal in a close election.

So there she sat, proud and elegant on a loveseat in the living room of her apartment, holding court with each and every of the fifty people who dropped by to wish her well.

Ninety red roses in a gold vase graced the footstool in front of her.

Normally, my mother takes a lousy photograph. At the sight of a camera, she juts her jaw out like a bulldog, beads up her eyes, and scowls. Then when the prints come back, she walks around showing everybody and saying, "See, I told you. The camera hates me. I can't figure it out!"

On this day, however, Margaret is radiant and relaxed and happy. We have the photos to prove it.

There's a shot of her and her longtime friend Duncan MacFarlane. To see these two together makes my palms sweat. Duncan is a lawyer. Duncan does libel.

There's a great photo of the Hon. Richard Reuter, the mayor of the City of Welland, presenting Margaret with a sealed certificate to commemorate her achievement. Only I saw her shake the envelope the certificate came in to see if by some chance a cheque might fall to the floor. (C'mon, Dick, would a buck a year for this outstanding citizen have busted the city budget?)

Bona, the mayor's wife, was impressed not only by the certification ceremony but by the fact that my mother kissed her handsome husband approximately four times more than this civil ceremony calls for.

I suppose at ninety you'd be kind of proud to be gossiped about in a scandalous love triangle involving the mayor.

Like bookends to a life lived long and well, her friends lined the room. On the one side, there was Mrs. Ziraldo from the mining days in Timmins, Mrs. Tougas from the wartime houses, and Mrs. Acaster from her Dain City bowling team. Across the room, dying to rip into the cake, was her best friend, Amanda, her six-year-old great-granddaughter.

And Uncle Ralph, her dear and gentle brother-in-law, was there laughing and chatting and enjoying the family for what would so sadly be his last time.

The day went on like that — warm laughter, sincere handshakes, a lot of long-overdue kisses — Margaret's mutual admiration society with the turn-of-the-century birthday girl presiding. It was a glorious occasion for a splendid lady, a milestone to which time will no doubt deny us all such a marvellous encore.

At the appointed moment, Amanda offered to help her Nan open the gifts and blow out the candles on the cake.

To Amanda, "helping" constitutes ownership on certain gifts she deems to be cool, so it was just as well we had Duncan the lawyer present.

When the time came to blow out the candles, there they stood, the old and the new, Marg and Amanda, one foot and eighty-four years apart, with their lungs full of air, mouths puckered, ready on the count of three to blow out ninety candles. (Or as I like to call it, "Run for your lives, the wax factory's on fire!")

Then suddenly Margaret, to the amazement of all and particularly Amanda — I'm not making this up — Margaret ran around the table like a bad kid and blew out all the candles in the holders Gail had set out for the buffet.

The family is never sure, when Margaret does these kinds of things, whether it's serious slip-up or well-timed slapstick.

After somebody told her to exhale and she began breathing again, nobody laughed harder than Amanda. There's no doubt in her mind, her Nan is that crazy lady in those *I Love Lucy* reruns.

Happy ninetieth birthday, Margaret. There'll be a brass band playing for your hundredth birthday, plus I'll arrange it so the mayor's wife is out of town.

(Although my mother was none too thrilled about

having her age revealed in print, I must admit she has never once lied about it. No, what she does is, she brags about how old she was when she gave birth to me, and then she lies about *my* age!)

What Most Seniors Really Want

These days you cannot thumb through any magazine or newspaper without full-colour advertisements jumping off the pages selling senior citizens on the concepts of waterfront condominiums, golf course freehold homes, reverse mortgages, and green belt bungalows with tennis courts and archery.

These ads should be slugged: "For rich, young seniors only!"

Most real senior citizens would settle for a lot less than a bayfront condo that includes a slip for the sailboat. Most seniors, like my mother, Margaret, are older, fixed-income pensioners who live in apartment buildings and would gladly settle for:

- a few wooden lawn chairs or a park bench by the flower garden out back
- an off-duty cop to catch the cretins who are stealing clothes from the laundry room
- an off-duty cop to catch the cretins who are stealing the holiday wreaths off the apartment doors
- a vending machine in the lobby that dispenses hard candy, nylons, unsalted peanuts, and cans of cold beer
- windows that actually open

- regular weekly meetings with neighbours to discuss things of no importance
- a nice polite kid who'll run an errand for a buck
- the names of everybody in the building embroidered in large letters on their clothes at eye level
- a door lock that opens with a fingerprint instead of a key
- a janitor who sings like Al Jolson
- the phone numbers of all those rich, young, single senior citizens who live in waterfront condominiums

Mother's Day

Sunday is Mother's Day. And I sincerely hope this is one holiday on which the politicians don't hog all the attention and monopolize the photo ops. All I hear is people talking about that mother Mike Harris and that mother Lucien Bouchard. Gee whiz, I think, these are the last people we should be sending flowers and candy.

But boy, do I have a special day planned for Sunday. First of all, breakfast in bed — coffee, eggs over easy, toast with crunchy peanut butter, more coffee, and a glass of cold milk. Then a long leisurely read through the *Sunday Star*, followed by a late-morning tennis match at the Port Colborne Club and I hope to be at Fort Erie Racetrack in plenty of time to bet the double.

Yes, nothing's too good for — Who? My mother? Oh, I don't know. I think she's going shopping with my sister or something.

No, that's my special day and it's just unfortunate that it falls on Sunday, which, if the rumour is true, is Mother's Day.

Hey, I'm kidding, of course. We all make a big fuss over Margaret on Mother's Day, even if it isn't a legal holiday. (Really, shouldn't we work on Labour Day and get a holiday to celebrate motherhood?) Simple and so easy to please, all Margaret wants is her children around her, grand and great included, healthy, happy, and not hand-cuffed to correctional officers.

Gifts of jewellery, fine clothes, or a trip? Not Marg. One rose delights her and a box of Turtles, a book of puzzles, a six-pack of lager spell bliss on any special occasion. Oh, yeah, and enough Tums to make the Jolly Green Giant belch and kill every damn one of those little Keebler elves.

It's not that she didn't enjoy what I gave her last year — a baseball mitt in my size and tickets to a Buffalo Bisons double-header — she'd rather not try to repeat perfection, or so she says.

I think I might take her bowling. I know, I know, she's ninety, but think about it. My mother used to be quite a bowler in her day, back when they used boulders for balls and headstones for pins.

Seriously, she was the ace of the Dain City Ladies Bowling Team, and in the late '50s she recorded more strikes than Canada Post.

It's still my mother's favourite sport, and now that she has a touch of arthritis in her throwing arm, I think I can finally manage to beat her.

Even now that she uses a cane, it's kind of neat to watch her bowl. She lets the ball go really early, like from the bench where she's sitting, and if it's headed for the gutter, she chases after it and stickhandles it back to the centre of the lane.

As a matter of fact, her scores are a lot higher these days because nobody dares correct her arithmetic as long as she's wielding that cane.

Afterwards, we'll probably go to the Belmont Hotel for chicken-in-the-basket and a couple of glasses of beer. My mother was relieved to learn recently that the Belmont finally got the spelling of karaoke straightened out on the signboard out front. For the first couple of weeks they made so many spelling mistakes, it looked to all the locals that they were presenting "Karrot Kake" every Thursday and Saturday night.

My mother likes the Belmont because it's such an entertaining place. She won't do karaoke, that would be humiliating. She makes me get up and do it. Actually, what she does is, she makes me get up on the stage, go down on one knee, and sing "Danny Boy" to her.

Sure, all the guys make fun of me, but it's still cheaper than buying a gift.

*T*hings *Margaret Still Believes*

- That ginger ale and a threat can still cure a sick kid within one school day.
- That having a temper is a very good thing, which is why you should never lose it.
- That she could still stretch $20 a week to include groceries and a movie.
- That sons are less trouble than daughters.
- That you must have money to spend money, plastic cards be damned.
- That professional wrestling is fixed, but so is televangelism.
- That she might still live forever, and as she says: "So far, so good."
- That stumbling through life is no fun but it does postpone the big fall.
- That where men are concerned, twenty-four hours a day and twenty-four beers in a case was no coincidence.
- That the Protestants and Catholics of Ireland will eventually settle their differences once they're down to one of each.
- That money can buy a lot of books, but you still need brains to read them.

- That Julius LaRosa's voice came from God.
- That it's important to be our own best friends to keep us safe from our own worst enemies.

You Know You've Become Exactly Like Your Mother When . . .

So I'm at this reception for the Roselawn Centre in Port Colborne, mingling with the locals and looking into the eyes of this woman whom I should know, I mean I do know but the name is not coming up on my mental screen even though the fingernail gnashing on my right hand is my secret signal to activate Recall.

It was about a year ago that my brain, swept away by this conservative cost-cutting craze, fired two people in Recall and merged Memory with Lost and Occasionally Found.

"So how's . . .," I say, as my brain runs through the categories of "your husband/your job/your car/your recent breast augmentation surgery?"

"So how's things out your way?" I ask, assuming she's not a neighbour.

"Same old same old," she says, and now I'm not so sure she's not a neighbour.

I'm spinning my wheels of fortune here and this woman is not revealing so much as a measly vowel.

"Excuse me," I say, "but I have to, uh, go do something." Walking away, I think, Gee, what a clever line. Apparently "Pardon me, but Billy's gotta do a tinkle" was temporarily out of stock when I called upstairs to Response.

As I move to another room, I steal a quick glance in a mirror and there she is! No, not the woman I don't know, the one I know only too well! My mother! Margaret!

That's exactly what my mother does: she plays who's-in-my-face? with everybody she meets. But she does it so much better than I do.

"It's been ages," my mother will say to someone she doesn't recognize. "The last time I saw you must have been . . ." and then she'll stare off in space until a clue is forthcoming. And she'll wait whole minutes if that's what it takes to elicit a response.

And then no matter what the mystery person says, you know what my mother's answer is? "No, no, that wasn't it," which is followed by another long silence and yet another clue or two.

Yes, every day is a *Front Page Challenge* for Marg. For me, it's about every other day.

Damn! I've become exactly like my mother, only taller.

At some point, it'll happen to you too. You'll be whistling your way down the street and without even thinking, you'll bend down and pick up a tarnished old penny. And as you're standing there, stunned by your own behaviour, you'll let loose an ungodly shriek because staring back at you on that coin is not Queen Elizabeth but your mother. Okay, so the crown has slipped down over her forehead, but the facial expression is unmistakable — "and you thought you were so smart!"

Although you can't avoid it, you can prepare yourself. Here then are a dozen sure-fire signs that you've become exactly like your mother.

- You send her one of those gushy lovey personal cards . . . and mean it.
- You ask her what she had for lunch at the seniors' centre, to make sure she's eating right.
- You find yourself saying "Eat it. There are senior citizens starving in the former Yugoslavia."
- You've come to realize the Beatles really were a noisy bunch!
- You ask her to take her shoes off at the door because you just washed the floor.
- You won't let her in the bathtub for an hour after she eats.
- You persuade her to use a cane by telling her all the really cool seniors like Lauren Bacall use them.
- You find yourself saying to her: "Why, why, always why — just do it, okay?"
- You buy her clothes a size too small so she'll shrink into them.
- You check the cushions of the couch to see if she hid the pill she promised to take.

- You interrogate the old guy in the elevator who just left your mother's apartment.
- You hold her hand, tell her everything'll be all right, and hope like hell it will be.

Argue with Your Mother at Ninety and You'll Never See Sixty Yourself

Have you ever noticed that as people get older they tend to become very set in their ways? Headstrong, if you will? Pig-headed, if you want.

The other day, a beautifully warm, fresh Indian summer day, I was walking my mother out to the lawn behind her apartment building where she holds the position of official greeter. Naturally friendly and outgoing, my mother exchanges pleasantries with each and every tenant we encounter on our walk, and the fact that she never manages to address them by their correct name does not diminish her enthusiasm. Nor theirs, for that matter. I'm not sure Ernie relishes being called Doris, but he takes it in stride.

Exiting the building, I get into a brief skirmish with the double doors, trying to help Margaret through first and dragging her lawn chair along behind. I turn for a moment to untangle the chair and Marg bolts down the sidewalk, off the curb, and onto the parking lot, her cane never once touching the ground. It's the penny-pinch routine.

Although my mother's eyes are covered with cataracts and her glasses are always so smudged Windex weeps on contact, she can spot a tarnished coin in a crack of a sidewalk at thirty paces plus. And despite the arthritis and artificial parts, she can retrieve that penny in one fell swoop, like her waist is made of rubber and her fingertips are magnets. "It's good luck," she says, but the recovered coins never seem to last long as souvenirs.

Margaret will deny she does this a lot, but I can tell you, if Revenue Canada had a category for street change, I'd have to declare this as part of her annual income.

So we finally get settled, her in her lawn chair, me on the grass, and we're having one of those long, languid mother-and-son moments when Margaret, gazing somewhere off behind me, says, "That's what I want, Bill, an apartment with a balcony."

I look over at the other apartment building with severely limited expectations because we've been through all this before — none of the apartments in this complex have balconies. There's no apartment in the city of Welland with a balcony that suited my mother's needs and income. This has not stopped her, however, from bringing up the balcony issue every chance she gets.

I turn around to see nothing resembling a balcony. As I mentioned, except when spotting other people's money, my mother's eyesight is not what you'd call sharp.

"There, at the top," she said. "I'd love to have a balcony just like that."

Shifting my gaze and shading my eyes from the sun, I was able to make out two guys cleaning the outside windows of the penthouse apartment. They were standing on one of those portable platforms lowered on cables from the roof.

This conversation is headed for trouble, but in the early stages I can't resist.

"Marg," I said, "there's two guys up there washing the windows of that apartment."

Just then I felt a chill, a cool headstrong wind blowing up the back of my shorts. I had dared to bring reality into the conversation.

"You see, Bill," she said smiling, "when you got a balcony, it's a lot easier to get at the windows."

It's always at this point I'm never sure whether my mother is being serious or pitching for her own sitcom on network television, *The Platinum Girls*, starring her, Phyllis Diller, and the ghost of Mother Teresa as the frail but flying nun.

I put both my hands on my forehead and began rubbing the area over my eyes, the spot where the headache would touch down first. I bit my lip, took a deep breath, and decided on silence as the best and only course of action. I have learned that after your mother is a certain age, say eighty-five, any debates that require logic will almost always win you the consolation trophy. I dropped this conversation like a steaming little spud from P.E.I. I know my mother.

Had I pursued this argument and insisted it was not a

balcony but a gondola, the proper term for this cleaning crate, I know exactly what would have happened. First she would have stared blankly into my eyes. Then she would have shaken her head slowly, as if to say, "I can't believe you ever got through university." And finally she would have gently patted me on the knee and said, with great sympathy, "Really, dear, what would two Italian men be doing in a boat on the side of that building?"

Trust me, I know these things.

So I said it was probably some rich people who had the balcony built illegally. I'd talk to Heather, the super-intendent, and I promised her it would be gone in a couple of days.

She bought the explanation, and sure enough, a few days later, the "balcony" was gone. I had successfully dodged another octogenarian bullet.

One week later we were out sitting on my breakwall at the lake, at sunset, a windless fall evening with waves rip-pling playfully along the shore. I poured Margaret's one-a-day treat into a tall chilled lager glass. I truly believe she likes the clinking of glasses and the accompanying "Cheers!" more than she savours the beer.

I had already poured myself three fingers of Laphroaig and carefully placed one ice cube into the glass. To spill even a drop of this smoky single malt Islay scotch annoys me to no end.

To eat or drink with my mother means a consistent

string of refusals because she's always trying to give you some of this, or half of that.

Something off Morgan's Point, a sailor or a windsurfer, distracted me momentarily. When I turned my attention back to my mother, there she was smiling, raising her glass and saying "Cheers!"

As I raised my glass, I noticed it was full, overflowing in fact, with a foamy head of beer. Single malts are usually gold, but I saw nothing but red.

"I gave you some of mine, dear," she said. "You only had a little in your glass."

"Cheers!" I said through teeth clenched so tight I think I may have sprained a jaw muscle. And then I took a reluctant sip of what might be the most expensive boilermaker in the history of bartending.

Did I even mention this little mistake? Not on your life. No, never, not a chance. As I've said before, argue with your mother after she's ninety and there's every chance you'll never see sixty yourself.

Margaret and Amanda —
Two Kids on the Carpet of Life

The female lineage of the Thomas family goes like this: Margaret at the top, then her daughter Gail, *her* daughter, Whitney, and *her* daughter, Amanda. (All husbands are exes — it's a rule.)

My mother, Margaret, is now ninety years old, her great-granddaughter, Amanda, is six years old, and suddenly they've arrived at the same place in time — an innocent world of play and pretend thanks to a combination of irrepressible youth and the beginnings of mild senility. You could leave the two of them in a room for an entire day and the only thing you'd hear would be laughs and giggles gently, slowly, subsiding into the sweet, soft wisps of sleep. And then the odd snore as well. (People contemplating marriage take note: the difference in age of eighty-four years seems to be just about right for any two people to achieve complete compatibility.)

Margaret's room in the apartment is transformed into the romper room during Amanda's visits. Into the closet goes the knitting bag, out comes the toy bag.

"You wear this, Nan," orders Amanda, and never one to disobey an officer, my mother dons a blue navy gob hat. Without question, Amanda is the boss. Seniority is a word she can neither pronounce nor abide by.

Amanda selects a black top hat with a red bow, a souvenir of a rowdy New Year's Eve party in Ellicottville, New York. It's as big on her as Marg's gob hat is small. Perfect!

Without a word, both of them are on the floor in stitches as the door of the Fisher-Price Family Barn opens with a "Moooo!"

My mother has milked cows, Amanda drinks milk, and apparently that's the only connection necessary. "Moooo!" The cow backs into the barn, understandably nervous at the sight of these two. It's barnyard bedlam as teeth flash and bony knees are slapped again all around.

To a smattering of laughter and applause the other farm animals come to the door to quack, squawk, snort, crow, and bark, but Bessy seems to be the headliner of this show. One smooth, unrehearsed "Moooo!" is the comic grenade that levels this particular room.

Alas, boredom is also the enemy of cows on the comedy circuit, and Bessy is soon replaced by the Big Game Book. It's huge, it's electronic, it lights up and tells stories. This is silent, riveting stuff. My mother can't believe a book can talk and she can't take her eyes off it. My niece can't believe my mother's never seen a talking book and she can't take her eyes off her.

Amanda at six is an electronic whiz-kid. As far as computers go, my mother at ninety has only heard a rumour that they're coming. She doesn't believe it, of course, but that's the rumour.

At the self-entertainment centre the spotlight moves from the electronic big book to a small book that doesn't talk. From this her Nan reads her the story of the three little pigs and Amanda verifies the math by counting off the characters with her own little pinkies.

In this version of the fable, updated for the '90s, the three little pigs go to the market as paid lobbyists for the Meat Stinks movement. Unfortunately, they show up at the wrong market, the commodities market, and like many others in that day are killed by falling stock prices. (Okay, that's my adaptation of the story, which is why they won't let me play.)

There follows a rousing rendition of "Row, Row, Row Your Boat" by two people who should sing only if they're trying to alert police.

It's an appropriate song that aptly describes the lost art of wailing. From within the room and between refrains come the sounds of two people banging against furniture in roughly the same rhythm required to actually row a boat.

Somehow the illusion does not travel well outside the magic room because at the juice break, walking past the adults in the living room, Amanda was asked if it was a big boat or a little boat they were rowing.

"It was a stool, silly," she replied, with the rolly-eyed look of "duh!"

Meanwhile, back in the chamber of fantasy, Margaret is drawing stick people and Amanda is colouring them hideously, something she knows she will be questioned about by her mother or grandmother. But Nan the great-grandmother thinks it's just grand.

When the Fisher-Price Circus comes out, Amanda is of course the ringmaster, putting her Nan, Baby Jumbo in this sequence, through her paces. Elephants never forget, and these days Margaret seldom remembers. Perfect!

Engineered by Amanda, the magnetically linked train — engine, cars, and caboose — is sharply derailed by a John Deere tractor with Margaret at the wheel.

The crash site cleaned up, Amanda reaches into an empty toy bag . . . "Eeeoooow!"

The screams are followed by Tiger, the family tabby, strolling nonchalantly out of the toy bag.

Concerned, Nan asks the child if she was scared.

"No," confirms Amanda with a halting giggle that means she didn't quite wet her pants, and then they both collapse in laughter and before they're through at least one of them probably will.

And it doesn't matter because the common denominator that reduces it all to the level of nervous joy is surprise. For the young child, the whole world is one big surprise, and she copes by pretending to know and often feigning boredom. For the aged woman, that she can still be surprised is the key to carrying on in her often anxious world. This she doesn't know, nor needs to.

It's the meeting of these innocent minds, the sudden, spontaneous union of the unexpected, that bonds both and amazes an outside observer caught somewhere else in the system of senescence.

It's a thing of beauty, the capricious collision of two children separated by almost a century in time, joined as one in moments of mirth that will live on in the telling for another hundred years.

Life's little moments make the big bad stuff tolerable, and nobody knows this better than children. Children of all ages.

Mama's Got a Brand-New Club

On this day Amanda, Margaret's great-granddaughter, was utterly unhappy, a matter made worse every time she stepped on and tripped over that pouting lower lip. Normally Amanda's a pretty even-keeled kid, but once in a while she snaps. Like a couple of years ago when she called from school to give her grandmother Gail proper hell.

During long telephone conversations Gail would often tell Amanda she was going to bring Tiger, the family tabby, to the phone and then she'd begin speaking in a high-pitched silly voice. Not only did Amanda fall for the gag, but while she was going through a tough family situation, she actually told the cat things that were troubling her, things she was withholding from the adults in her life.

This worked well until Grade 2, when one day she made a frantic phone call to Gail and said: "Grandma, I've been telling the kids in my class about Tiger talking on the phone. And they all think I'm nuts! You gotta tell me right now — does that cat talk or what?"

Gail, borrowing from the Santa Claus "believers only" defence, wangled her way out of it. (I suggested she go down to Amanda's school and do her act for the whole class with the cat drinking from a glass of milk on her lap. Gail called me "unhelpful.")

This day's dictate was not quite as desperate but no less unequivocal.

"You gotta talk to Nan about this 'Pam' thing," she told my sister Gail. My mother used to babysit for the Misener kids, Pam and Richard, and they adored her. However, lately, Margaret had been having memory lapses and calling Amanda Pam during their romper room adventures.

So Gail sat down with my mother in another room and patiently explained that Amanda was the only child of her granddaughter, Whitney, and that Pam and Richard Misener, on the other hand, were family friends and now all grown up. However, because Pam, when she used to look after her, was the same age as Amanda is now, my mother was getting their names mixed up.

My mother immediately understood and apologized for her obvious error. When Gail suggested she straighten things out with Amanda, Margaret went directly into the living room, sat down beside a brooding Amanda, and said: "So, Amanda, how's your brother, Richard?"

This sent Amanda fleeing the room in tears. This also sent a signal to me, the last one I really needed, that there was more going on here than just some mild memory loss.

With Gail at work during the day and out most nights, Margaret was spending way too much time alone in the apartment. Margaret's entourage of doctors, home care workers, and sitters was getting longer and costlier, and still her isolation was disturbing and potentially dangerous.

I'd visit, her friend Ernie would come up, Heather the super was exactly that, and her young friend Beth would spend hours splitting Pepsis with her. And Monica Rose was so much like a daughter, Marg often mistook her for just that. But there were still long periods of loneliness interspersed by moments of — this is going to hurt me a lot more than it's going to hurt you, Marg — oncoming dementia.

There was that wad of cash she hid in the garbage, a flooded kitchen from a tap she could not turn off, and many more illogical events that culminated in a fall when nobody was there to help. She had also been choking on food occasionally, but so far always with one of us present.

All this and the "How's your brother, Richard?" line, delivered less than a minute after apparent comprehension of the situation, sent me into the realm of second sober thoughts.

About to breach a promise I'd made her, I began a tour of nursing facilities on Margaret's behalf. It was, to say the least, a real eye-opener. From what I saw, with limited resources and an overflow of applicants, the people who manage this network of government-operated residences for the elderly are doing a terrific job. They're upbeat, optimistic, with the patience of Job. The residences are clean, busy, and as cheery as is humanly possible.

But a tour of these homes breaks your heart. A lot of the residents, at least one quarter of them — contorted, incoherent, and drooling in their laps all day — are crying out for something better, something merciful. Please, they're saying, and my generation will say even louder, give us a swift and dignified alternative to such misery.

And if this is a pressing problem right now, wait twenty years. At the rate my baby boom generation is ageing, by 2020 there'll be more Kevorkian Walk-In Clinics down at the mall than photo-development drops. (And, of course, with the Baby Boomers, the most annoying "want it all and want it now" generation, there won't be a lot of objections.)

I couldn't help but plead in silence: Please, Mr. Chrétien, call a meeting. A meeting of the elderly, the children of the elderly, the doctors, a minister, a priest, and the Hemlock Society — and come to some humane accommodation.

From all this comes a phrase I have coined: the benevolent betrayal. It's a euphemism for something that's still wrong, like a necessary lie. May you never be guilty of this terrible transgression, but at the rate we're all getting grey and our grey matter's just not getting it, you'll likely find yourself one day on one of the edges of this two-sided sword.

For the record, "Ho-ho-ho" is not only the sound Santa makes down at the mall. "Ho-ho-ho" is the stammer an adult child of an ailing, elderly parent makes trying to say the word "home" when it's preceded by the word "nursing."

My mother used to go pale when she heard those words, remembering vividly when she had to put her own mother in one. Nanny was eighty-five and the picture of good health when she started running away from the family home. But that was back when nursing homes were institutions with locked doors and barred windows.

You could hardly categorize today's nursing home, with its craft centre, recreational facility, gardens, pub, and big-screen television sets, as an institution. Such a place is Northland Manor in Port Colborne, where my mother now resides.

It was neither an easy nor a kind thing to do and the jury is still out on whether I did the right thing. But I did it. And quickly too. According to the people at the place-ment services, today's available room in the home of your choice may not come up again for another year or two.

And so it was that I settled on Northland Manor, just seven minutes down the road from my house, as the residence in which my mother would have round-the-clock medical attention and supervision and the company of eighty other senior citizens and three meals a day with bingo and bus trips on the side and her own private room with a Pepsi machine just down the hall and . . . and if I've convinced you it was a good and fair decision, that's great. It's Margaret and me that still aren't buying it.

Gail and I took her there on a spur-of-the-moment tour. I took the "Mama's got a brand-new club" approach — bigger, better, no stairs, no commuting, with a variety store, a hairdressing salon, and a beer pub on the premises. It's like one-stop senioring, I enthused. And the best is: "You can stay overnight!" I described it as Club Med for brittle hipsters. Palms sweaty, I made an impressive presentation, using everything but a support video and set of coloured flip charts.

My mother asked but one question: "How's it heated?"

I had a lot of answers and alibis ready but nothing that dealt specifically with the plumbing and heating.

"A furnace," I replied. "In fact, it's kind of one big furnace with windows and hallways. Some days it gets so hot here they tell you not to touch the hand rails.

"In fact, it's so hot, Margaret, I thought I spotted Glyn shovelling coal in the basement."

"That's good," said my mother, who likes to be in a room where the temperature makes metal pliable. Or maybe she was pleased that her late husband had found work in hell. "Okay," she said, to my great surprise and even greater relief, "I'll give it a try." And like the trouper that she is, she took off her coat and sat on her new bed and looked around a bleak room that would soon be decorated up as her home.

But there was that moment, an instant of awful, undeniable truth where her accusing eyes filled with tears of distrust, saw right through me, and said: "But you promised never to put me in a home." And though no words were spoken, my eyes, also watery with tears but these of lingering guilt, shot back: "But I believe I'm doing the right thing, Marg, honest to Christ I do."

That moment passed quickly by us both, except it's never far below the surface of our thoughts as long as Margaret's living at her "new club."

Benevolent betrayal — necessary, wise, practical, logical — dress it up any way you want and it's still just a double-cross in care-giving clothes.

Things You Hate to Hear at a Nursing Home

- The words "old folks' home."
- "They're plastic, they don't need water."
- "They're charging for extra desserts! We demand to see the warden!"
- The phrase: "Getting down to the short strokes."
- "Wrestling matches may be arranged for interested parties in the rec hall, *not* in the TV room, during *The Jerry Springer Show*."
- "That 'kid' on the organ is actually a new resident."
- "They shut down the Kleenex factory! Are you sure?"
- "Would the person who walked off with balls B-8 and G-52 please come back to the Bingo room immediately."
- "Lost and found is now officially filled up."
- "All excursions are hereby cancelled until the women learn to keep their hands off the bus driver."
- "Remember, Wednesday your families will bring potluck supper. Medication to follow."
- "This Sunday's service will close with 'Little Drops of Water.' One of the ladies will start quietly and the rest of the congregation will join in."
- "Attention, please. A pet snake went missing during

yesterday's magic show. Please look closely at all lumps in your bed."

- "Successful therapy sessions are their own rewards. Please, no more champagne showers."

- "No, Marg, he didn't say Niagara, he said Viagra. Now go back and tell him you don't want to go for that ride."

Seniors Not Going Gently into That Night

With the planet well within a pitch shot of the millennium, it seems our elders are not just defying old age but tearing up the senior citizen code of conduct and throwing the bits of paper in the faces of the young.

In Arles, France, Jeanne Calment died in August of '97 and until then she was the oldest human being in the world at age 122 and still riding a bicycle around town in her last year. (She may well have succumbed to the pressure of my mother closing in on her.)

Jeanne Calment actually knew Vincent Van Gogh, who lived in Arles and painted many of the locals. Asked on her 121st birthday what Van Gogh was like, she said, "He was an ugly little man with alcohol on his breath." Beautiful! The older you get, the less BS you tolerate or advocate. (Van Gogh's ear must be turning in its envelope!)

When asked by journalists who descended on her home each birthday how she saw her future, she stared at the dumb questioner and said: "Short!"

On Jeanne Calment's 120th birthday she recorded a rap song. A rap song at 120 years of age! A lot of L.A. gangster rappers are not making it to twenty-five and here's a bike-ridin' mama born sixteen years before the invention of the Duryea gasoline automobile and four years before the light bulb, belting out: "I'm old, I'm bold, I been rocked and I been rolled!"

I actually have no idea what lyrics Jeanne sang on her rap song, I just know that if the recording company were target-marketing her age group, that CD's not going platinum any time soon.

I just can't imagine my mother, Margaret, dueting with Snoop Doggy Dogg on his *Doggfather* CD. I could see her singing "How Much Is That Doggie in the Window" with Arthur Godfrey on the ukulele or "Hang On, Snoopy" with Gilbert Godfrey, but a rap song for a senior! I don't think so.

In Redwood, California, there's an eighty-three-year-old man by the name of Foxy still playing ice hockey in a league with a bunch of geezers that includes Charles Schulz, the creator of *Peanuts*.

I know what you're thinking — an eighty-three-year-old hockey player who is somehow not currently playing defence for the Toronto Maple Leafs! How'd they miss that guy in the draft? But it's true and it's scary and I'm hoping the league would immediately outlaw hip checks. Ice hockey after eighty is something my generation can't comprehend.

Of course hockey's out of the question for my mother, but I can see her sending Foxy a somewhat provocative fan letter.

In Walnut, California, eighty-five-year-old Carol Johnston is defying gravity and his years by regularly pole vaulting 7' 6", a world record for his age.

In Loyalton, California, ninety-three-year-old Hal Wright — the reporter, copywriter, editor, and ad salesman for his newspaper, the *Sierra Booster* — delivers copies to rural subscribers by dropping them out the window of the airplane he pilots.

You see the problem with amazing seniors like Carol and Hal, don't you? One of these days they're going to be involved in a midair collision! No, this stuff really worries me.

In Howard, Kansas, 103-year-old Rose Nix Leo still writes a weekly column for the *Elk County Citizen-Advance* and a monthly column for *Tallgrass Country* magazine. And no, she's not a sex advice columnist.

However, in Rome, eighty-three-year-old Nilo Silva, who keeps fit with daily workouts using an exercise bike and weights, is Italy's newest porn star. It's true. Spotted by a talent scout in a disco with his grandson, Nilo made international headlines when he said he'd be delighted at the opportunity to make "a film with beautiful young girls." Really? I think when you find an old man who *doesn't* want to get naked with young women — *then* you've got a story.

And Rosanna Della Corte, the oldest woman on record to give birth, at age sixty-two, was also from Rome.

Coincidence? Boy, I hope so. Because if little Ricardo is the son of sixty-two-year-old Rosanna and eighty-three-year-old Nilo, you've got a baby with more wrinkles than one of those Chinese shar-pei dogs.

Okay, so maybe Nilo didn't spend all of his time riding the bike. It still makes me a little squeamish to hear about seniors cavorting on camera and having babies who become great-great aunts at birth.

I won't even tell my mother about these two for fear she'll put the grab on Joe, the Italian guy two rooms down from her, and I'll wind up pushing a pram around the nursing home.

No, I'm sorry, but there are some things seniors just ought not do. Recording hip hop music and fornicating on film are pretty good places to start. I mean, do I have to draw up a list of senior citizen activities that are officially banned?

Seniors' Activities That Are Hereby Officially Banned

- Hitchhiking.
- Having babies while collecting Canada Pension.
- Posing for lingerie ads in the Victoria's Secret catalogue.
- Comparing varicose veins for prizes on a television game show.
- Dating any man whose business card is printed on a condom.
- Smoking marijuana for medicinal purposes and pretending not to enjoy it.
- Giving each other the tongue because the director says "it's integral to the story line."
- Appearing in any rap music video filmed during a real drive-by shooting.
- Streaking the Oscars ceremony in memory of Jessica Tandy.
- Entering the Paris–Dakar Rally in motorized wheel-chairs.
- Paying a psychic to read their liver spots.
- Driving heavy equipment after purposely mixing up their medication.

- Spiking their nutritional supplements with Absolut Vodka.
- Engaging in any activity that could result in a high-risk takedown by men in camouflage outfits.

Margaret and Me on the Grand Walk for Memories

As of the last census, taken in 1997, there are 30,286,596 people in Canada, and 3,725,833 are over the age of sixty-five. Of these, 3,353,250 are living in private households and 372,583 are now living in facilities commonly called nursing homes.

This particular nursing home in Port Colborne, Ontario, is called Northland Manor Home for the Aged. It has forty-one rooms for eighty-seven residents. The average age of the twenty-one men and sixty-six women who live here is eighty-three and I'm rapping gently on the door of Northland's newest resident, a woman who in her ninety-second year is way above average. (Northland also has a staff of eighty-two — seven of them operate the facility and seventy-five of them try to keep an eye on my mother.)

I know I'm standing in front of the right room because there's a name plate next to the door that reads "Margaret Thomas" and above that a very large hand-printed bristol-board sign that reads "MARGARET THOMAS." If the staff could afford a town crier to stand at the door ringing a bell and yelling, "Yes, this is your room, Margaret Thomas!" they would. Marg doesn't always find her way back to her room. She also doesn't believe she's been living in this room for the past ten months. She wants to go home, although she's not sure where that is. Nova Scotia? Schumacher? Dain City? She never goes back as far as Victor, Colorado, but everywhere else from Antigonish to Fonthill can be her home on any given day. I don't fight it anymore. My new policy is: "Oh, give Marg a home where the mind's free to roam and the dear will be happy all day."

It's a good room overlooking the backyard and gardens, with a large window where the morning sun streams through to light up her calendar and two family photo collages, a bulletin board with birthday and Christmas cards, an antique highback chair, and an old floor lamp she loves. "My son bought me that chair and that lamp," she'll say, gushing. "You're welcome," I'll say directly. She'll hesitate, look from the chair to the lamp to me, and say: "Oh, Bill, I'm sorry."

The room has its own thermostat, which Margaret throttles like an automobile accelerator to push that furnace into overdrive. On days when the sun shines hot and the thermostat is at its max, Finnish guys show up at her door with towels and loofahs.

On this afternoon, the last of the March snow melting in the dead flowerbeds out back, I enter her room quietly and she's stretched out on the bed, dressed but lightly dozing.

Gently, I tap the end of the bed. She wakes up, frowns, squints, and then bursts into a big smile when she recognizes me: "Oh, Bill."

I love to hear those words and I fear the day they will stop coming.

She's tangled in a couple of afghans, and as I straighten them out she explains that she's got a bit of a cold and she needed to rest a little. Concerned, she lowers her voice and asks me if I've seen her mother, who, she says, is also under the weather and went to have a nap in her room.

I no longer have the heart to tell her that Nanny went for her nap in 1967 and for the past thirty-one years she's been under more than just the weather.

It was only a few years ago that Margaret was living in an apartment and cooking her own meals. It was only a couple of years ago she was living at my place on the lake — temporarily, mind you — and doing her Wonderword puzzle in the recliner, later walking the beach with her cane and a glass of beer.

Today she's waiting for David to come home from school, except he's thirty-two years old and owns his own home in Oakville.

"Don't ever get old," Margaret still warns me, but she has, almost overnight.

I have a lot of regrets about how she ended up in this room, and the one that keeps making its way to the top of the lament list is that she didn't come here sooner when she could still make friends, settle in with a clear mind, adjust, and enjoy this place.

Margaret's not grasping the nursing home situation, and I fear that if she keeps going into the rooms of the other residents looking for the kids, or her mother or me, her next room will be in the secure wing.

About a month ago I was sitting in a tiny office down the hall with the counsellor from the Alzheimer Society. This lady could not have been kinder.

"Your mother's just the sweetest thing. Everybody here adores her. She's so proud of you and she told me all about the family." (The family tale not only included Joan and Gail but also Esther, the sister none of us has had the pleasure of meeting.)

Then the counsellor threw the word "elopement" into the assessment and honestly, I've not had that great a surprise since my last prostate examination.

"Elopement!" Hell, she flirts a lot but I had no idea there was some serious dating going on here.

"Elopement!" I tried to imagine a scene involving my mother, a man, two walkers, and a ladder.

For the record, "elopement" is the official word in nursing homes for wandering off. On at least two occasions Marg had eluded staff and walked through the automatic front doors towards Northland Avenue. The four-lane highway is one block away.

It's quite possible she knows exactly what she's doing:

searching for the other rich and handsome half of that elopement deal.

The choice for me was made clear: agree to move Margaret into the secure wing, where I've seen residents at the locked door pleading with me to open it, thereby denying her what little freedom she still maintains, or risk having her wander off some night.

I notice the decisions regarding an ageing parent are just like the questions on *Jeopardy* — they get harder as the game goes on.

Normally, I'd have left Marg to her afternoon nap and returned later, but today is kind of special. Today is the Alzheimer Society's Walk-for-Memories and the band is already playing in the rec room near the lobby. So it's up, on with a sweater, hide the purse where she's sure nobody, including her, will ever find it, and we're off to the Alzheimer walkathon. Then back to the room because we both forgot the walker.

The lobby is a cash bazaar with volunteers selling half 'n' half draw tickets and lunch coupons and filling out pledge sheets for the walkers. There must be a hundred or more people in the Hardy Room as the Olde Tyme Fiddlers bend their bows and stomp their feet in the far corner. There's a festive mood as residents, family, and staff pack the room, some having lunch, a few doing little dance steps as they return to their tables, everybody chatting and laughing. Marg no sooner ditches the walker and takes a seat before her hands and feet are doing double time to the music.

The Olde Tyme Fiddlers are a country band of three who wear shamrock green cowboy outfits. Their western/Irish message is clear: Yes, we do play sad, torchy songs but we can drink Guinness and fight if we get a request.

A few women residents link arms and start a chorus line beside the band. They're enthusiastic but badly in need of rehearsal time. If I had to come up with a name for this group it would be the Olde Spice Girls.

The band plays "Danny Boy," and tears well up in my mother's eyes. For anybody with Irish blood, this is the obligatory action/reaction response.

Marg passes on the bowl of chili, saying she's not hungry. This, however, does not stop her from doing some serious damage to the tray of chocolate cookies and fudge squares somebody unwisely placed in front of us.

"Just to go with my tea, dear," she says.

A couple women on staff come by, and although Marg doesn't recognize or hear them, they use words like "precious" and "darling" when referring to her. Marg's a huge hit here at Northland Manor, and since she seldom hears and never remembers the expressions of praise being heaped upon her, her ego has remained intact.

After lunch the band wraps up, the hearing aids are turned down, coats are brought from nearby closets, and everybody lines up in the lobby for the walk.

In the beginning, the event is in such disarray and so slow in starting somehow I think the government's involved. But eventually the front doors of the manor fly open and out into a windy but sunny winter's afternoon the ageing troops in their war against time begin their long march to . . . to . . . the end of the driveway and back.

It may not be a marathon — down the circular driveway to the road and back up the driveway to the lobby — but it's a valiant struggle all the same. An amputee being pushed in a wheelchair, others with walkers being carefully supported, some with canes, one with crutches, everybody holding hands or clutching arms — we look like an army returning from a war in which we got the living hell beat out of us. It's like we went up against a division of Gurkhas and they had two guns for every one of our garden hoes.

But that's the scene from afar. In the midst of this parade, hearing the laughter and loud breathing, the joy of the moment and the pain of the next step, it's really a portrait in courage. They're troupers, these residents, every one. Many of those on this Alzheimer Society stroll won't remember it once they're back in the building. I don't think I'll ever forget it.

The struggling, the shuffling, the soft sound of stutter steps — all headed in the direction with a single purpose at heart — to keep moving and moving ahead. Today is fun, most days are not. Still, it's all about the struggle to keep moving ahead. It's slow, it's awkward, to passersby it's laughable. But for these residents who never wanted to be here, never wanted to ask for help, it's a small victory on the long, scary, uneven road of living when there's no other choice.

They're alive and on a mission, and once or twice around the driveway proves it to those who doubt. On most days the doubters are themselves. Today is validation day.

The ones inside, the ones who opted for TV instead of the walk, they're the ones who need help the most, not this ragged band of misstepping marchers being supported by family and friends. Oh, sure, the residents in the TV room are more comfortable and smarter and okay, wiser, but . . . Where was I? Oh, yeah, we were Mr. Hope and Mrs. Great-heart pounding the asphalt pathway of *Pilgrim's Progress* and yes, actually making a little. But we don't have to make it all the way to the Gates of Heaven, just back to the room with Margaret's name plate next to the door.

Bracing against the March chill, my mother gets this feisty look on her face like she's not going to quit if it rains, hails, or blows gale-force winds. "No more Mrs. Knitting Needles" say the watering eyes and the clenched jaw.

As we skirt the end of the driveway onto the shoulder of Northland Avenue, we turn into a stiff, cold wind and Marg clutches at the collar of her thin jacket. This, however, leaves nobody's hands on her walker. As I grab the walker that's about to tip over, I step in a puddle of water.

So on the last lap of the Walk-for-Memories, Marg has one hand at her collar, one hand on her walker, and I now have one hand on the walker to make it go in a straight line, with the other hand supporting her arm. Plus I have a soaker. Boy, this symbolic walk for the very essence of life and the spirit of survival is a lot tougher than I thought.

We do finish, the sweet victory of all marathoners, but in the final portrait of courage, Marg is shivering with her arms folded in front of her and I have one foot off the ground. But we're smiling.

I'm smiling because at the worst point of the walk, with Marg freezing and stumbling into her walker, I tell her that she's doing it wrong and she responds by saying: "I'm trying, Bill. I'm trying." And that's it right there. My very reason for being there is fulfilled. The most precious words in Marg's dwindling vocabulary. "I'm trying."

Those are the words I most want to hear when I visit her except, of course, for her very first words — "Oh, Bill!" — followed by the beam of a smile, the blush of love, the hug, the kiss, the last bit of recognition we both cling to.

All women become like their mothers. That is their tragedy. No man does. That is his.

— Oscar Wilde
The Importance of Being Earnest